Indebted Societies

MW01089942

In many rich democracies, access to financial markets is now a prerequisite for fully participating in labor and housing markets and pursuing educational opportunities. *Indebted Societies* introduces a new social policy theory of everyday borrowing to examine how the rise of credit as a private alternative to the welfare state creates a new kind of social and economic citizenship. This book provides a rich study of income volatility and rising household indebtedness across OECD countries. Weaker social policies and a flexible knowledge economy have increased costs for housing, education, and raising a family – forcing many people into debt. By highlighting how credit markets interact with welfare states, the book helps explain why similar groups of people are more indebted in some countries than others. Moreover, it addresses the fundamental question of whether individuals, states, or markets should be responsible for addressing socio-economic risks and providing social opportunities.

Andreas Wiedemann is Assistant Professor of Political Science and International Affairs at Princeton University and the School for Public and International Affairs. He is also a faculty affiliate with the Niehaus Center for Globalization and Governance and the Center for the Study of Democratic Politics at Princeton. He studies the comparative political economy of advanced democracies, focusing on economic inequality, redistribution and social policies, and electoral politics. His most recent work has been published in the *American Journal of Political Science* and the *British Journal of Political Science*. Wiedemann's research has been supported by the Social Science Research Council, the Andrew W. Mellon Foundation, the Horowitz Foundation for Social Policy, and the Krupp Foundation, among others. He received the Gabriel A. Almond Award for the Best Dissertation in Comparative Politics and the Ernst B. Haas Award for the best dissertation on European Politics and Societies from the American Political Science Association.

Cambridge Studies in Comparative Politics

General Editor

Kathleen Thelen   *Massachusetts Institute of Technology*

Associate Editors

Catherine Boone   *London School of Economics*
Thad Dunning   *University of California, Berkeley*
Anna Grzymala-Busse   *Stanford University*
Torben Iversen   *Harvard University*
Stathis Kalyvas   *University of Oxford*
Margaret Levi   *Stanford University*
Melanie Manion   *Duke University*
Helen Milner   *Princeton University*
Frances Rosenbluth   *Yale University*
Susan Stokes   *Yale University*
Tariq Thachil   *University of Pennsylvania*
Erik Wibbels   *Duke University*

Series Founder

Peter Lange   *Duke University*

Other Books in the Series

Christopher Adolph, *Bankers, Bureaucrats, and Central Bank Politics: The Myth of Neutrality*

Michael Albertus, *Autocracy and Redistribution: The Politics of Land Reform*

Michael Albertus, *Property Without Rights: Origins and Consequences of the Property Rights Gap*

Santiago Anria, *When Movements Become Parties: The Bolivian MAS in Comparative Perspective*

Ben W. Ansell, *From the Ballot to the Blackboard: The Redistributive Political Economy of Education*

Ben W. Ansell and Johannes Lindvall, *Inward Conquest: The Political Origins of Modern Public Services*

Ben W. Ansell and David J. Samuels, *Inequality and Democratization: An Elite-Competition Approach*

Adam Michael Auerbach, *Demanding Development: The Politics of Public Goods Provision in India's Urban Slums*

Ana Arjona, *Rebelocracy: Social Order in the Colombian Civil War*

Leonardo R. Arriola, *Multi-Ethnic Coalitions in Africa: Business Financing of Opposition Election Campaigns*

David Austen-Smith, Jeffry A. Frieden, Miriam A. Golden, Karl Ove Moene, and Adam Przeworski, eds., *Selected Works of Michael Wallerstein: The Political Economy of Inequality, Unions, and Social Democracy*

S. Erdem Aytaç and Susan C. Stokes *Why Bother? Rethinking Participation in Elections and Protests*

Andy Baker, *The Market and the Masses in Latin America: Policy Reform and Consumption in Liberalizing Economies*

Continued after the index

Indebted Societies

Credit and Welfare in Rich Democracies

ANDREAS WIEDEMANN
Princeton University

CAMBRIDGE
UNIVERSITY PRESS

CAMBRIDGE
UNIVERSITY PRESS

University Printing House, Cambridge CB2 8BS, United Kingdom

One Liberty Plaza, 20th Floor, New York, NY 10006, USA

477 Williamstown Road, Port Melbourne, VIC 3207, Australia

314–321, 3rd Floor, Plot 3, Splendor Forum, Jasola District Centre, New Delhi – 110025, India

79 Anson Road, #06–04/06, Singapore 079906

Cambridge University Press is part of the University of Cambridge.

It furthers the University's mission by disseminating knowledge in the pursuit of education, learning, and research at the highest international levels of excellence.

www.cambridge.org
Information on this title: www.cambridge.org/9781108838542
DOI: 10.1017/9781108975209

© Andreas Wiedemann 2021

First published 2021

A catalogue record for this publication is available from the British Library.

ISBN 978-1-108-83854-2 Hardback
ISBN 978-1-108-97158-4 Paperback

Contents

Figures

Tables

Acknowledgments

I started thinking about the ideas in this book as a graduate student at the Massachusetts Institute of Technology. I have long been fascinated by the role of financial markets in modern societies and their relationships with governments, societies, and people. As I saw how deeply credit and debt had become embedded into the social fabric of our communities, and how destructive financial crises can be to people's livelihoods, I wanted to understand what the growing availability of credit meant for the provision of public goods and services and the structure of social rights and responsibilities across rich democracies. This book examines how the rise of credit as a private alternative to the welfare state shapes the ways in which individuals and their families cope with social risks and seize social opportunities.

True to the title of the book, I have developed my own "indebted society" that provided me with the intellectual guidance, support, and comfort to tackle and unpack these relationships with conceptual rigor and the empirical tools of modern social science. First and foremost, I owe immense debts of gratitude to my dissertation committee. Kathy Thelen has been a tremendously helpful and encouraging source of guidance, inspiration, advice, and support at every step leading to this book. She taught me not to shy away from asking big questions and inspired me to incorporate the American political economy into a comparative perspective. David Singer continuously helped me sharpen the argument and think about the empirical implications of my theoretical framework. He deepened my knowledge of the role of finance and pushed me to integrate international and comparative political economy. Torben Iversen had a lasting influence on my thinking about the welfare state, social insurance, and popular support for redistributive policies. His careful guidance toward conceptual clarity undoubtedly improved the manuscript. Danny Hidalgo provided invaluable support and advice about empirical methods and research design and offered a fresh eye and sharp questions on issues of indebtedness in advanced economies. I could not have wished for a better group of scholars and colleagues and am deeply thankful for many hours of support and advice that made this book possible. They also showed me what it means to be a dedicated mentor and caring teacher, and I can only hope to repay this debt to others.

My gratitude extends to many more colleagues and friends in the Cambridge area – some of whom have moved on to other places – who took the time to read and discuss parts of this project and helped me improve it. I would like to thank especially Suzanne Berger, Adam Berinsky, Andrea Campbell, Devin Caughey, Peter Hall, In Song Kim, Rich Nielsen, Ben Ross Schneider, Lucas Stanczyk, Lily Tsai, and Teppei Yamamoto for their guidance and mentorship. This book would not exist without my graduate school friends. I owe so much to Elissa Berwick, James Conran, Fiona Cunningham, James Dunham, Jeremy Ferwerda, Tom O'Grady, Susana Cordeiro Guerra, Yue Hou, Nicholas Intscher, Marika Landau-Wells, Philip Martin, Nina McMurry, Ben Morse, Tesalia Rizzo, Leah Rosenzweig, Guillermo Toral, Martin Liby Troein, Weihuang Wong, Yiqing Xu, and Ketian Zhang. Their personal friendship, intellectual support, and critical feedback often led me to rethink my arguments and made me a better scholar and, hopefully, writer.

Earlier stages of this research project benefited from comments and feedback at the Social Science Research Council SSRC Dissertation Proposal Development workshops, particularly from Isaac Martin and Abhit Bhandari. David Brady hosted me at the Wissenschaftszentrum in Berlin, which allowed me to develop the book's core argument further. Ben Ansell was kind enough to invite me to a brief stay at Nuffield College, Oxford University, and has been a tremendously helpful and inspiring mentor since. The manuscript came fully together years later, again at Nuffield College. The Prize Postdoctoral Research Fellowship made the completion of this book possible by providing a unique place to write, think, and engage with a remarkable intellectual community. I was fortunate to hold a book workshop at Nuffield with Ben Ansell, Charlotte Cavaillé, Pepper Culpepper, Jane Gingrich, David Rueda, and Tim Vlandas. They all were more generous with their time than I could have hoped, read the manuscript in incredible detail, and offered invaluable feedback, suggestions, and advice that greatly improved the manuscript. I owe all of them a deep debt of gratitude as well.

I am tremendously grateful to Desmond King, Chloe Thurston, and Tess Wise, who have read parts of the book, provided feedback at many stages, and have crucially shaped the ways I think about finance and credit. I thank David Dreyer Lassen, Jacob Gerner Hariri, and especially Amalie Jensen for many conversations about my own work and for letting me use part of our survey data we had collected for a larger project. Christian Lyhne Ibsen generously facilitated access to the Danish register data and supported the project along the way. Finally, Mark Manger and Andrew Walter deserve a special thank-you note. Their guidance and advice during my time at the London School of Economics ultimately convinced me to embark on an academic route.

I would like to thank many colleagues at various institutions for helpful conversations about and critical feedback on parts of this project, especially Søren Kaj Andersen, Jens Arnholtz, Lucy Barnes, Rachel Bernhard, David Brady, Aslı Cansunar, Michael Donnelly, Andy Eggers, Jacob Hacker, Tim Hicks, Larry Jacobs, Patricia Kirkland, Martin Vinæs Larsen, Maxime Lepoutre, Jonas Markgraf, Lucas Müller, Darius Ornston, Barbara Piotrowska, Patricia Posey, Soledad Prillaman, Alexander Reisenbichler, Kilian Rieder, Nelson Ruiz, Leonard Seabrooke, and James Wood. I also am grateful to countless participants and discussants at conferences and at seminars at Harvard, Oxford, the University of Copenhagen, the University of Toronto, University College London, and the Wissenschaftszentrum Berlin. I would also like to thank Iver Kjar and Anders Ellesgaard at Finanstilsynet Denmark and David Michaelson at Statistics Denmark.

I finished the manuscript after joining Princeton's Politics Department and the School for Public and International Affairs. My colleagues and graduate students are exemplary in their devotion to ideas and rigorous social science scholarship and a true source of inspiration. I thank all my colleagues for their advice and continuous support, and I am especially grateful to Rafaela Dancygier and Deborah Yashar for their valuable comments, feedback, and encouragement along the way.

This research would not have been possible without the generous financial support from many sources. I am thankful for funding and grants I received from MIT, in particular the Department of Political Science and the Center of International Studies. The Social Science Research Council and the Horowitz Foundation for Social Policy generously supported data collection and analyses. The Krupp Foundation and the Center for European Studies at Harvard University enabled an extended research trip to Germany, Denmark, and the United Kingdom. The survey data I draw on in Chapter 7 was generously funded by David Dreyer Lassen's European Research Council Grant No. 313673. The Mamdouha S. Bobst Center for Peace and Justice at Princeton helped with research support. I thank all of them for their financial support. Yutian An and Owen Engel provided excellent research assistance for the credit regime permissiveness measures. Amanda Pearson and Sergey Lobachev helped with thorough and swift editorial and indexing support in the final stages of the manuscript.

Robert Dreesen and Sara Doskow at Cambridge University Press are fantastic editors who enthusiastically supported the book. I am grateful to both for patiently guiding me through the publishing process as well as to two anonymous manuscript reviewers who provided excellent and thoughtful comments and suggestions. The manuscript has undoubtedly improved as a result and hopefully lives up to their expectations.

Finally, I owe the deepest gratitude to my family. Alisa, who sailed with me through this journey, helped me put things into perspective, and provided refuge in a world beyond academia. With her wit and humor, she always kept my mood and spirit high. And to my mother, who inspired me to ask questions about social justice and supported my academic journey into the United States. I am more than grateful for everything she has done for me and I will keep trying to make her proud. I dedicate this book to her, for always being there.

1

Credit and Welfare in Rich Democracies

Many people these days are no strangers to debt. People borrow money to pay for childcare, to get training, or to take out student loans to attend college and university.[1] They take out mortgages to buy homes, perceived by many as the cornerstone of a middle-class life because homeownership helps build wealth and unlocks access to vibrant labor markets and neighborhoods with good schools. But people also go into debt to address financial gaps that emerge because of volatile incomes, rising expenditures, and limited support from the welfare state. In short, financial markets are now woven deeply into the social fabric of our communities, societies, and economies. They provide opportunities that mitigate how social status, parental wealth, or skills affect socioeconomic outcomes. But as more and more people rely on financial products to borrow, save, and invest, the downside risks become more visible. When the Swiss central bank in January 2015 unexpectedly lifted the peg off the Swiss franc against the euro, which had kept the value of the franc stable by fixing the exchange rate, the repercussions were felt way beyond Switzerland. Homeowners in Eastern Europe who had taken out mortgages denominated in Swiss francs rather than in their local currencies suddenly saw their monthly debt repayments increase by more than 20 percent as the value of the Swiss franc soared.[2] Market volatility affects not only homeowners but also workers and retirees. Many pension systems have moved away from defined-benefit plans – which guaranteed fixed monthly pensions throughout retirement – to

---

[1] See Maureen Pao, "U.S. Parents Are Sweating and Hustling to Pay for Child Care," *NPR*, October 22, 2016, and Kara Baskin, "A Mortgage for the Future," *Boston Globe*, September 15, 2013.

[2] See, for example, Danny Hakim, "Homeowners in Poland Borrowed in Swiss Francs, and Now Pay Dearly," *New York Times*, January 28, 2019. Patryk Wasilewski, Sean Carney, and Veronika Gulyas, "Poland and Romania Face Strain on Mortgages over Climbing Swiss Franc," *Wall Street Journal*, January 19, 2015.

defined-contribution plans in which monthly investments in capitalized pension funds yield variable pension payouts based on market returns. In the United States, the Great Recession of 2007–08 wiped out about $9.8 trillion of wealth as many Americans saw the values of their homes and retirement accounts collapse. Meanwhile, rising levels of student debt in the United States and the United Kingdom prompted Occupy's Strike Debt! group in 2013 to buy off $15 million worth of American student loans from banks with the goal to free student borrowers by "abolishing" their debt.[3] But this relief proved short-lived as the amount of outstanding US student debt alone has reached a new record of $1.51 trillion in 2019 (Federal Reserve Bank of New York 2020).

These examples show that small ripples in one corner of the financial market can create tsunamis in households' own financial lives. As debt piles up, borrowers become more and more dependent on stable incomes to make debt payments on time. But despite the global reach of financial markets, household debt levels vary considerably across and within countries. Panel (a) of Figure 1.1 shows that between 1995 and 2015, household debt, measured relative to the size of the economy, has grown in nearly all rich OECD countries, with the notable exception of Germany and Japan. Denmark, Australia, and the Netherlands stand out as the countries with the highest debt-to-GDP ratio in 2015, even higher than other liberal market economies and almost three times as high as Germany's or France's. Panel (b) focuses on debt as a share of households' disposable incomes, thus capturing households' debt burdens, and reveals similarly strong increases over time but large differences across countries. From 1995 to 2015, the debt burdens of Danish households have grown by over 50 percent, while those of Dutch households have nearly doubled, leaving households in both countries with about three times more debt relative to their incomes than German households and over two-and-a-half times more debt than American households.

These cross-national patterns of indebtedness are puzzling because they do not align with country clusters frequently used in the dominant political economy frameworks such as *Varieties of Capitalism* (Hall and Soskice 2001) or typologies of welfare regimes (e.g., Esping-Andersen 1990, 1999). Countries such as Germany and the Netherlands that are typically classified as conservative coordinated market economies have very different levels of household indebtedness. Some Nordic countries share similarly high debt levels with liberal market economies even though this literature typically locates them on polar opposites of the spectrum of welfare states. So why do we see such strong variations in debt levels across countries? Why do some households borrow more than others? And what are the political consequences of rising indebtedness?

---

[3] See StrikeDebt! (https://strikedebt.org) and Adam Gabbatt, "Occupy Wall Street Activists Buy $15m of Americans' Personal Debt," *Guardian*, November 12, 2013.

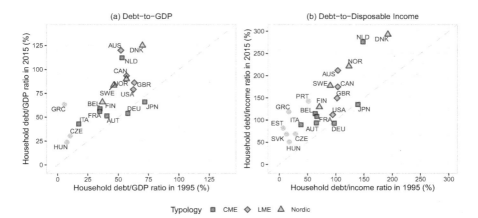

FIGURE 1.1 Household debt ratios in OECD countries, 1995 and 2015

Notes: The markers show country-year observations. Total debt includes the debt of households and nonprofit institutions. Countries located above the 45-degree line have increased their debt ratios from 1995 to 2015, while those below have decreased their debt ratios. Countries on the 45-degree line saw no change. Markers indicate common political economy typologies of Liberal market economies, Conservative coordinated market economies, and Nordic Social-Democratic economies, which are grouped as follows: Liberal market economies (LME): Australia, Canada, Ireland, New Zealand, Switzerland, United Kingdom, and United States; Conservative coordinated economies (CME): Austria, Belgium, France, Germany, Italy, Japan, Netherlands; Social-Democratic (Nordic) economies: Denmark, Finland, Norway, and Sweden. *Sources:* Panel (a): BIS Total Credit Statistics (2018). Panel (b): OECD National Accounts (2019).

This book addresses the political causes and consequences of the growing reliance on credit and the expansion of household indebtedness in rich democracies. It sheds light on the fundamental transformation of social rights, responsibilities, and resource allocations that has occurred over the last two decades, as financial markets have emerged as private alternatives to the provision of public goods and services. One important but understudied reason why people borrow money is the gap between the financial costs of fragmented employment patterns and life course trajectories on the one hand and welfare states' financial protections against social risks and support for social investments on the other.[4] Individuals change jobs more frequently, either voluntarily or because of short, temporary employment contracts. Individuals take time off work to take care for children or elderly family members and to get more education and training. These absences from work lead to income losses and higher expenditures that in many countries are insufficiently or inadequately

---

[4] The concept of "life course trajectories" captures individuals' movements between different life stages, from raising children to pursing education and training to employment and retirement (e.g., Mayer 2009).

addressed by social policies, as I show in Chapter 3. Weak unemployment benefits or unpaid sick leaves, for example, expose Americans to much greater social risks and financial burdens than Danes, who receive more generous unemployment and sickness benefits. Publicly subsidized childcare and paid parental leave reduce the financial costs of having children while helping parents reconcile family life and career choices. In sum, when social policies are insufficient or lacking, individuals must increasingly address social risks and finance social investments themselves by drawing on savings or family support, or by borrowing money and going into debt. The book's main focus lies on the provision of financial liquidity by credit markets, in particular through unsecured, non-mortgage debt.[5]

Consider the case of Frank Walsh, for example, a forty-nine-year-old electrician from Annapolis, Maryland.[6] When Walsh lost his job in 2011, he and his family supported themselves through a combination of various odd jobs and unemployment benefits, but during this time, Walsh also ran up about $20,000 in credit card debt to make ends meet. The financial shortfall between his prior income and the social policy support he received is sizable, since at the time unemployment benefits in Maryland were about half of the weekly average wage up to a maximum of around $380, and paid out for a maximum of twenty-six weeks. Or take Raquell Heredia from Fontana, California. She quit her jobs as waitress and bartender because she suffered from severe pregnancy-related morning sickness and her employers did not provide her with paid sick leave. Her new job at a pharmacy offered inadequate maternity leave benefits, so when her first child was born, she decided to leave that job, too.[7] Both examples reflect a grim reality that many Americans face. Unemployment, sickness, and raising a family can pose considerable financial challenges. Many individuals in situations similar to Frank Walsh's turn to credit markets and borrow money to smooth income losses. Raquell Heredia's circumstances, too, are not uncommon for many Americans who would like to take time off work to care for their children but have to take unpaid leave – often risking their jobs because this type of leave is usually not job-protected. Women like her often have little choice but to go into debt.

In other countries, however, fragmented employment patterns and life course trajectories pose much smaller, if any, financial risks to people like Frank Walsh and Raquell Heredia, limiting the need to borrow money. Compared with the United States, Denmark provides low-income Danes with better financial protections against social risks such as unemployment or sickness and

---

[5] Informal fringe lending markets such as payday lenders and pawnshops are alternative coping strategies but beyond the scope of this book's analysis.

[6] See Binyamin Appelbaum, "The Vanishing Male Worker: How America Fell Behind," *New York Times*, December 11, 2014.

[7] See Claire Cain Miller and Liz Alderman, "Why U.S. Women Are Leaving Jobs Behind," *New York Times*, December 12, 2014.

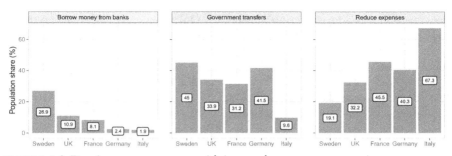

FIGURE 1.2 Dominant ways to cope with income losses across countries
Notes: Question: "In the past two years [2008, 2009], have you or anyone else in your household had to take any of the following measures as the result of a decline in income or other economic difficulty?" Respondents could select multiple coping strategies. *Source:* Own calculations based on LITS Wave II (2010).

social investments through education and family policies. The life of Mette and Christian Miller-Harris, a Danish dual-earner couple from Copenhagen, with a thirteen-month-old daughter, is considerably easier – financially speaking – because the government offers subsidized childcare, paid parental leave, and flexible work hours, which allow Danish parents to both take time off work after childbirth and enroll their children in childcare.[8]

The extent to which welfare states insulate similar individuals from social risks and provide social investments differs considerably across OECD countries. The results are large financial gaps in some countries and much smaller gaps in others. How do individuals cope with these financial shortfalls? Survey data from the Life in Transition Survey (LITS II), conducted in 2010, reveal considerable differences in private means to address financial gaps such as credit markets or expenditure cuts. In the wake of the financial crisis of 2007–2008, respondents across a range of countries, including five Western European ones, were asked how they dealt with declining incomes and economic difficulties. Respondents could choose from several options, including reducing expenses, relying on government transfers, and borrowing money from banks. Figure 1.2 shows the share of individuals in each country that selected any of these options. Government transfers such as unemployment benefits are the most important coping strategy for all households in each of the five countries, even though their use varies from nearly half of all Swedish households to about a third of all British households. With regard to *private* coping strategies, however, the country differences become more pronounced. In Germany, about 40 percent of households reduce expenses (nearly the same share of households that would draw on public benefits) but only 2 percent would borrow from a bank. Sweden displays almost the opposite pattern of

---

[8] See Lucy Rock, "What Britain Could Learn from Denmark's Childcare Model," *Guardian*, February 18, 2012.

how households address economic shocks. Only 19 percent of households cut expenditures, while 27 percent borrow money from a bank. The United Kingdom occupies a middle ground between both countries with regard to private and public coping strategies.

An obvious candidate that would explain the cross-nation variation in households' coping strategies in Figure 1.2 is the structure of the welfare state. In some countries, social policies protect individuals much better from social risks than in others. But there is also considerable variation *within* countries. Around 45 percent of Swedes rely on government transfers while another 27 percent go into debt, suggesting that the welfare state insulates some groups more than others. This insight implies that only considering the structure of the welfare state is not enough to fully understand why and under what circumstances individuals go into debt. The structure of credit markets is equally important. Countries like Sweden, Denmark, and the United States have what I call "permissive credit regimes" that make borrowing money relatively easy for households. Danes and Americans can easily access a broad array of financial products, including mortgages, home equity loans, and interest-only loans, for which borrowers at first pay only the interest but not the principal amount. Credit cards and other bank-based unsecured loans are widely available and used in both countries. Marketing-intense web-based loans and so-called SMS loans, especially popular among young adults, have grown considerably in Denmark during the past decade. Other countries, however, have more restrictive credit regimes that make borrowing fairly difficult for households. In Germany, for example, home equity loans and interest-only loans do not exist. Credit cards are used much less frequently than in other countries and function more like charge cards that have to be repaid in full by the end of the billing cycle. Instead, savings rates among German households are considerably higher.

These differences in welfare state support and credit access shape patterns of indebtedness across and within countries. Figure 1.3 shows that in 1989, a Danish household in the middle income tertile had on average about 20% of unsecured debt relative to their income. That number climbed to 37% in 1998 and 50% in 2012. Among American households in the same income tertile, unsecured debt leverage increased from 20% in 1989 to 27% in 1998 and 31% in 2013. For similar households in Germany, unsecured debt leverage remained at about 11% between 2002 and 2012. Even more revealing, however, is the variation in indebtedness across the income distribution. Unsecured debt leverage is positively correlated with income in Denmark, negatively correlated with income in the United States, and virtually uncorrelated with income in Germany. Put differently: debt leverage is concentrated among higher-income groups in Denmark and among lower-income groups in the United States.

To shed light on the questions I posed earlier and to solve the macro-level puzzles sketched out in Figures 1.1, 1.2, and 1.3, we have to look closer at micro-level data to understand which households go into debt for what reasons

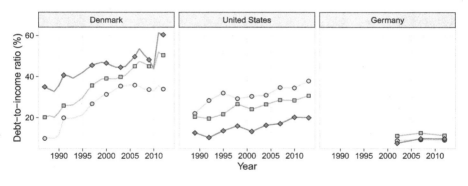

FIGURE 1.3 Unsecured debt leverage in Denmark, the United States, and Germany by income tertile

Notes: Unsecured household debt as a share of disposable income by income tertile. Weighted survey responses. *Sources:* Own calculations based on Danish full population administrative records, the US Survey of Consumer Finances, and the German Socio-Economic Panel.

and how the particular macro-level constellation of the structure of welfare states and credit markets shapes such borrowing behavior.

THE ARGUMENT: A SOCIAL POLICY THEORY OF EVERYDAY BORROWING

In this book, I offer a new perspective on how financial markets shape political economies, affect the social fabric of our societies, and reach into people's daily lives. I develop what I call a *social policy theory of everyday borrowing*, arguing that the constellation of welfare institutions and credit regimes shapes patterns of indebtedness across and, perhaps more importantly, within countries. The ways in which welfare states insulate groups from social risks and provide social investments determine individuals' demands for private means to both address social risks and seize social opportunities. Moreover, the ways in which credit markets shape people's access to credit determines whether households use credit to bridge financial gaps or finance social investments.

Welfare states distribute resources across individuals, typically from high-income to low-income groups, through poverty relief, social assistance, and redistributive policies to reduce income inequalities. They also provide insurance against social risks and allow individuals to smooth income losses during unemployment, sickness, and retirement. And, finally, welfare states promote social opportunities and mobility and support people throughout the life course by providing social investments in education, childcare, or paid parental leave programs. The transition of Fordist manufacturing economies into flexible knowledge economies has created economic, social, and political disruptions (Boix 2019; Iversen and Soskice 2019) with profound impacts on individuals' employment patterns and life course trajectories. Some countries have shifted away from social consumption toward social investment policies, most notably in the form of the "embedded flexibilization" approach of the Scandinavian countries (Thelen 2014). Yet welfare institutions in other countries are increasingly at odds with individuals' financial circumstances. More frequent employment disruptions, growing income volatility, and higher expenditures have placed new financial burdens onto individuals' shoulders (Morduch and Schneider 2017; Weil 2014). At the same time, welfare state retrenchment and policy drift have weakened social policy support and created financial gaps in individuals' daily lives. Both trends have shifted the costs from governments onto the shoulders of individuals for not only social risks, as Jacob Hacker (2019) documents, but also social opportunities. These trends have also increased reliance on private coping strategies such as savings and credit. As I show in this book, borrowing is not only a response to welfare state retrenchment. It also helps individuals address the financial burdens of interrupted employment trajectories, educational choices, and raising families.

It may seem surprising to argue that credit markets can fulfill functions that resemble social policies, not least because welfare states were in part designed to respond to market failures and cushion against adverse market outcomes. Yet credit markets mirror welfare states' tasks in three crucial ways. First, they too redistribute resources – although not across individuals but through time, moving resources from the borrower's future self into the present. Credit markets also provide financial liquidity through credit cards, bank loans, payday loans, and home equity loans, helping people address financial shortfalls or meet expenditures. And credit markets allow people to invest in both human capital (e.g., using student loans to finance their education) and financial assets (e.g., taking out mortgages to buy homes).

Whether households go into debt and borrow money to address income losses or finance social opportunities, instead of relying on other private means, depends on the structure of what I call a country's *credit regime*. This concept describes the institutional and policy environment that shapes the breadth and depth of financial markets, the allocation of credit between businesses and households, and regulatory and fiscal policy incentives to borrow money. These factors jointly influence who gets credit in the economy and how easily individuals can borrow money during periods of financial distress. I introduce the concept of credit regimes because it helps explain, in conjunction with the structure of the welfare state, why households in some countries have much easier access to credit than in others. Permissive credit regimes support open financial markets and have larger pools of capital and credit. Close institutional ties between banks and households, combined with political incentives to borrow money, make credit more easily accessible for households. Restrictive credit regimes, by contrast, are less open to global financial markets and have smaller pools of capital. Strong institutional links between banks and businesses tend to channel credit flows more toward the business sector. In a policy environment that incentivizes saving instead of borrowing, households find it much harder to access credit.

Credit Markets and Welfare States: Complements or Substitutes?

The particular constellation of welfare state and credit regime structures shapes how individuals cope with social risks and harness social opportunities. When welfare states address social risks such as unemployment or sickness and provide social investments in education, childcare, or family policies, individuals have little need to go into debt. In these cases, the structure of the credit regime matters little. However, when welfare states are limited and leave people financially exposed, the structure of a country's credit regime determines whether households go into debt to fill financial shortfalls. In restrictive credit regimes, people have limited access to credit and are rarely able to borrow money to address income losses. Instead, they internalize costs and income losses, for example by using their savings, making expenditure cuts, and/or relying on family support. Credit only emerges as a private alternative to welfare states in permissive credit regimes that make it easy for households to borrow money.

The macro-level interaction of credit market and welfare state structures results in three unique constellations, each with a different set of distributive consequences for individuals' abilities to address social risks and finance social investments. A *complementary relationship* between credit markets and welfare states arises when social policies protect economically disadvantaged groups against social risks and provide social opportunities, which obviate their need to go into debt. Instead, borrowing is concentrated among more affluent and economically secure groups that receive less support from the welfare state. Here I use the term "complement" to describe a context where credit markets coexist with comprehensive (but stratified) welfare states and complement each other in the provision of financial support, either privately through access to credit or publicly through government transfers.[9] In other words, credit markets and welfare states co-exist as complements to one another, allowing better-off groups to use credit markets to "supplement" their less generous welfare benefits. Denmark illustrates this case. By contrast, a *substitutive relationship* between credit markets and welfare states arises when weak welfare states push the financial cost of addressing social risks and financing social investments to a much broader range of people, including economically vulnerable ones, who compensate for insufficient or absent social policies by borrowing money. This is the case in the United States. Permissive credit regimes enable complementary and substitutive functions depending on

---

[9] To be clear, I do not use the term "complement" in the sense that an increase in the use of good A increases the use of good B.

which groups are protected and covered by social policies. And, finally, restrictive credit regimes suppress credit markets, which precludes households from borrowing. Instead, they rely on a combination of welfare state support and private savings, family support, or expenditure cuts. An example of this case is Germany.

Risk Buffers and Social Investments

These different coping strategies suggest that credit has different functions for different types of individuals. On the one hand, individuals use *credit to address social risks*, for example to smooth income losses during unemployment as Frank Walsh did. Similar to welfare states' social consumption policies (e.g., unemployment and sickness benefits), credit markets provide financial liquidity. But the key difference is that credit markets privatize risks, requiring borrowers to repay their loans with interest. On the other hand, individuals use *credit as bounded social investment*, enabling them to invest in human capital and financial assets with the expectation of economic gains and upward mobility. People invest in human capital by taking out loans for education and other training programs or by compensating for temporary pay cuts when they switch from one job to another, perhaps assuming or hoping that the new job is a temporary step toward a more rewarding career. People invest in financial assets such as their own homes – typically the largest financial asset individuals acquire during their lifetimes – by taking out mortgages. Much like social investment policies (e.g., education, active labor market policies, and family policies) seek to improve individuals' well-being, skills, and family lives, credit can fulfill similar functions by privately providing individuals with the financial means to do so. Credit helps individuals address expenditures for childcare, education, and housing as well as the opportunity costs of forgone income while outside the labor force.

But whether people engage in credit-financed social investments, and whether expectations of upward gains are realized, depends crucially on the structure of opportunity costs. This is why I call this type of borrowing "bounded" social investment. The returns to credit-financed social investments are bounded and constrained by how leveled the social policy playing field is, and what types of opportunity costs are associated with it. Weak social policy support increases the opportunity costs of borrowing money to invest in education or childcare, or to take time off work. Consider the case of childcare: Only households with adequate savings or sufficiently high incomes can afford childcare that is prohibitively expensive – for example if it is not publicly subsidized. In Denmark, government-subsidized parental leave and childcare allow parents to continue to work while their children are in daycare. Although the financial costs of these policies vary across income groups – high-income groups pay more than low-income groups – this is in stark contrast to the United States, where having children and raising a family has become increasingly expensive, in large part because childcare costs have risen dramatically and paid parental leaves are limited or lacking altogether.[10] For example, in 2019 the average cost for center-based childcare for one child ranged from $6,890 in Arkansas to $20,913 in Massachusetts, where infant care costs $8,134 more per year than in-state tuition for a four-year public college (EPI 2020). Or take the example of education: When education and training programs are prohibitively expensive, students from economically disadvantaged backgrounds may be less likely to consider attending college or taking time off work to get training.

Social policies level the playing field by reducing entry costs and enabling more individuals to reach social opportunities. Some groups will realize upside gains from credit-funded social investments in childcare, education and training, and career changes that lead to higher incomes and upward mobility in the future. But others will not. When public support is insufficient or nonexistent, it forces parents to take unpaid time off work or pay for increasingly expensive childcare and to borrow money to smooth income losses and stem expenditures without realizing any upside gains. Taking time off work or paying for childcare becomes an economic necessity. In these cases, going into debt to cope with financial shortfalls is not an investment but another form of consumption smoothing.

Economic Insecurity, Social Stratification, and the Future of the Welfare State

Some individuals borrow money to address social risks, while others use credit markets to seize social opportunities. Credit markets, in other words, privatize opportunities, allowing borrowers to take full ownership over the fruits of their investments, but also privatize risks, which pushes the burden of debt repayment onto borrowers and increases their downstream economic insecurity. In Chapter 7, I show that relying on credit markets as a private alternative to welfare states shapes peoples' social policy preferences. Easier access to credit markets allows individuals to self-insure against risks. Knowing that they can borrow money to smooth income fluctuations, buffer shocks, or meet higher expenditures, individuals' sense of economic security and perceived wealth increases, which lowers their demand for social insurance. I call this the *insurance effect of credit access*. I demonstrate that easier access to credit makes people less likely to support social insurance even when their self-reported risk of unemployment increases. By contrast, respondents who report having a hard time accessing credit markets to borrow money demand more social insurance as the risk of unemployment grows. But as credit and debt privatize opportunities as well as risks, the type of credit use drives social policy preferences apart. I call this the *privatization effect of credit markets*. On the one hand, credit markets allow individuals to opt out of the welfare

---

[10] As of 2020, the United States has no federal paid maternity leave policy.

state and instead rely on private, credit-funded options, effectively privatizing opportunities and upside gains. Student loans might pave the way to higher-paying jobs. The ability to pay for childcare might help individuals reconcile family life with career aspirations. There are two reasons why this type of borrowing might lower people's support for social insurance. Debtors want to either limit their tax burdens in light of having to pay debt and interest payments or opt out of publicly provided services that would benefit others, because they expect positive economic gains from their social investments in human capital (e.g., student loans) and financial assets (e.g., housing) in the form of better jobs, higher and stable incomes, and upward economic mobility.[11]

On the other hand, credit markets concentrate economic risks on borrowers, thus increasing their financial insecurity (Porter 2012*a*; Warren and Tyagi 2003). Debts need to be repaid, regardless of individuals' circumstances. This becomes painfully obvious during economic recessions, and, most recently, during the coronavirus pandemic, which began in early 2020 and is still raging as I finish this book, when millions of people were suddenly out of work but still had to make their debt payments. Indebtedness increases borrowers' vulnerability to earning losses and income volatility, which could force debtors into arrears – or worse – bankruptcy. In these circumstances, indebtedness might strengthen demand for social insurance for two reasons. Borrowers want to avoid going into debt to address inadequately covered social risks in the first place, or they seek protection against future income losses that would make debt repayments more difficult and, therefore, increase the probability that they either fall behind on debt payments or fail to make scheduled payments at all. As debt privatizes risks, demand for social insurance increases.

Political ideology emerges as an important force that drives a wedge through the social policy preferences space as indebtedness grows. Political conservatives, who tend to believe in market efficiency and free-market conservatism and that people should be personally responsible for their own socioeconomic fates rather than relying on welfare states, are more likely to favor (credit) markets over government intervention. Liberals, by contrast, are more willing to let governments provide some goods and services, more skeptical about market efficiency, and more supportive of social responsibility. As debt levels increase, liberals demand more social insurance, whereas conservatives either keep their social policy preferences stable or become less supportive. These effects are much stronger in the United States than in Denmark, suggesting that the complementary relationship between credit and welfare institutions rests on (and requires) a broader political support coalition than the substitutive relationship.

The emerging social cleavages and distributional fights between debtors and creditors on the one hand and between debtors who borrow for consumption and those who borrow for investment on the other hand are less about

---

[11] For a similar logic in tertiary education, see Busemeyer and Iversen (2014).

the degree of welfare spending than about how social goods and services are funded (publicly or privately), who is responsible for people's socioeconomic fates (the individual or society), and who can opt out of the public system.

CONTRIBUTIONS AND IMPLICATIONS

This book's argument and empirical evidence reveal a more complex relationship between financial markets and welfare states and shed new light on research in comparative political economy on social policies, financialization, and economic risks and inequality.

First, the book offers a comparative theoretical framework that integrates credit regimes and social policies in the study of comparative political economy. Rarely are credit markets seen as part of the welfare regime, nor does research on financial markets systematically incorporate social policies into their comparative analyses. The dominant comparative political economy frameworks such as *Varieties of Capitalism* (Hall and Soskice 2001) or typologies of welfare regimes and social policies (Esping-Andersen 1990, 1999) remain largely silent about household indebtedness. Despite the magnitude and importance of household debt, we know little about the ways in which credit markets interact with welfare states and how this relationship shapes variation in patterns of household indebtedness both across and within countries, often because we lack comparative micro-level data to study these questions. This book attempts to fill these gaps. I argue that the structures of welfare states and credit regimes are key to help us understand how individuals and their families cope with social risks and seize social opportunities by drawing on credit markets. This framework yields two important contributions to the comparative political economy literature. First, it reveals that credit can not only substitute for social policies but also complement welfare states in the provision of financial liquidity. This mutually constitutive relationship between social policies and financial markets, however, only emerges once we focus on individuals' behaviors within their particular institutional contexts. Second, this framework forces us to consider the specific ways in which individuals use credit. Not all debt is the same. Some people borrow money to address social risks, while others use credit as a social investment to harness gains and opportunities, which influences socioeconomic welfare and shapes social policy preferences.

This theoretical framework and the dynamics between financial markets and welfare states have implications for two domains that are not in the immediate spotlight of the book but are critical to the distribution of risks and opportunities between individuals and societies in the modern knowledge economy: housing, which provides spatial access to vibrant labor markets, high-quality schools, and desirable neighborhoods increasingly located in expensive urban areas; and education, which helps pave the way to reap these benefits by obtaining high-paying or high-status jobs (e.g., Grusky, Hall, and

Markus 2019; Le Galès and Pierson 2019). If housing markets and educational opportunities are privatized or accessible only with the help of credit markets, distributional outcomes and life chances are further skewed and will benefit what Charles Tilly (1998) has called "opportunity hoarders."

By documenting how the institutional constellation of credit regimes and welfare states affects similar "types" of individuals across countries in very different ways, this book shows that the focus on culture and language as the root causes of a country's aversion to borrowing and penchant for saving, for example in the case of Germany, might be misplaced. Culture, conceptualized as shared understandings of available strategies (Swidler 1986), is reflected in and shapes outcomes through a country's institutional environment. But, as Garon (2012) argues, to characterize the proclivity to either borrow or save as the result of a country's culture heavily discounts the role of institutions and deliberate policy choices that create, sustain, and promote savings institutions. Neither saving and cutting expenditures nor borrowing money are normatively or economically preferable private coping strategies. Each has different implications and ramifications depending on individuals' economic circumstances and the institutional contexts in which they live.

Second, this book contributes to political economy research on states and markets, in particular on the links between welfare states and financial markets. The current scholarship conceptualizes the relationship between debt and the welfare state predominantly as a trade-off. Spearheaded by Kemeny (1981), a large body of research documents that welfare states are less comprehensive in countries with larger mortgage markets and higher homeownership rates because homeownership and housing wealth act as a "nest egg" or a form of private insurance during retirement, reducing the need for social policies.[12] This equilibrium is supported by political parties' ideological and electoral concerns (e.g., Kohl 2018) as much as by voters who are willing to forgo social insurance as long as they can privately insure themselves through homeownership and housing wealth (e.g., Ansell 2014). More recent work has shifted the focus beyond housing markets, connecting indebtedness with people's desires to maintain their living standards in light of growing levels of inequality (Kumhof, Rancière, and Winant 2015), wage stagnation (Rajan 2010; Stiglitz 2015), luxury consumption and the aspiration to "keep up with the Joneses" (Frank 2010; Frank, Levine, and Dijk 2014), and limited fiscal redistribution (Montgomerie 2013; Prasad 2012; Trumbull 2014).[13] Ahlquist and Ansell (2017) introduce a partisan link between inequality and the demand for credit, arguing that left-wing governments resort to fiscal redistribution,

---

[12] See, among others, Conley and Gifford (2006); Prasad (2012); Reisenbichler (2021); Schelkle (2012); Schwartz (2008); Schwartz and Seabrooke (2008).

[13] The empirical evidence for the link between inequality and borrowing, however, is mixed (see, for example, Bordo and Meissner 2012; Coibion et al. 2020).

whereas right-wing governments replace welfare spending with policies that improve credit availability.

In this book, however, I argue that the focus on a substitutive relationship between financial markets and welfare states in much of the political economy literature is oversimplified, incomplete, and ultimately misleading. These arguments are more likely to apply to the Anglo-Saxon world, while their emphasis on income inequality as a driving force of household indebtedness cannot explain why Denmark and the Netherlands, for example, have higher levels of household debt than the United States and the United Kingdom – despite having lower levels of income inequality and more comprehensive welfare states. Germany experienced stagnating and even declining wages in the 2000s, but debt levels remained flat (DIW 2009).

Recent work has begun to provide answers to these puzzles and questions by adopting a more nuanced comparative perspective beyond the focus on inequality and credit markets' substitutive relationship with social policies. Johnston, Fuller, and Regan (2020), for example, draw on aggregate cross-national data to show that strong trade unions and collective bargaining institutions are conducive to more household borrowing when housing finance institutions encourage mortgage lending. But if we want to systematically understand why some countries have much higher levels of household debt than others despite similarities in labor markets or welfare regimes, we need to adopt a comparative micro-level perspective, studying how *individuals* within particular institutional constraints cope with social risks and seize social opportunities.

Doing so is challenging, not least because it requires a comprehensive set of comparative micro-level panel data. Many studies instead focus on the macro-level, comparing aggregate measures of welfare state spending and indebtedness, which masks crucial variation in how societies distribute social benefits and what types of debt different groups hold. Single-country case studies, by contrast, rarely link household indebtedness explicitly to the social policy context, nor do they establish a causal link between welfare state generosity and levels and types of debt.[14] The conceptual and empirical focus on the macro level neglects how the constellation of credit regimes and welfare states shapes households' behaviors and, therefore, obscures and misses an important additional dimension: Credit does not always substitute for the welfare state. It also complements social policies depending on the ways in which welfare institutions insulate individuals from risks, or fail to do so. Nor is the use of credit limited to income-smoothing functions in lieu of social insurance policies. Credit also functions as a social investment in human capital such as childcare and education, allowing individuals to reconcile family and work obligations. But in countries where regulatory and fiscal policies systematically restrict access to credit markets, credit neither substitutes for nor complements

---

[14] For a study on the link between sub-national variation in social policy benefits and household debt across US states, see Wiedemann (2021).

the welfare state. This book is one of the first to draw on a broad array of comparative micro-level data to demonstrate how the constellation of welfare institutions and credit markets shapes patterns of indebtedness across and within countries.

Third, the concept of credit regimes speaks to research in international political economy on capital flows and the allocation of credit in the economy. It demonstrates how the structure of credit regimes filters and channels macro-level credit flows to the micro-level, shaping the sectoral allocation of credit between households and businesses and influencing households' incentives to borrow money. Global capital flows, facilitated by deregulated capital markets and fomented by an abundance of savings, have raised global asset prices, fueled credit growth, and often precede financial crises (e.g., Ansell, Broz, and Flaherty 2018; Chinn and Frieden 2011; Schularick and Taylor 2012; Tooze 2018). While such capital flows are largely exogenous sources of credit, a country's credit regime structure mitigates or amplifies these effects. In restrictive credit regimes, close institutional ties between banks and business, stringent lending regulations, and little, if any, fiscal incentives to borrow money make lending to and borrowing by households less attractive. This complements recent work by Copelovitch and Singer (2020), who argue that in domestic financial systems in which banks compete with securities markets to provide business finance, capital inflows amplify banks' appetites for risk, increasing the likelihood of banking crises. However, when banks predominantly lend to firms because securities markets are underdeveloped, capital inflows are less likely to trigger banking crises.

Even though global financial markets can constrain national governments' ability to make policy choices across various domains (e.g., Garrett 1998; Jensen and Schmith 2005; Mosley 2003; Streeck 2014), focusing on the structure of credit regimes indicates that governments preserve some regulatory and fiscal policy leeway to shape the allocation of credit in the economy. The permissiveness of a country's credit regime is the result of deliberate attempts by governments to engineer economic growth as well as interest groups' influence who either favor legislation that expands access to credit, such as the financial and real estate sectors in the United States and the United Kingdom, or seek to suppress it like the export industry in Germany (Baccaro and Pontusson 2016; McCarty et al. 2010; Mian, Sufi, and Trebbi 2013).

Fourth, this book shows that the emergence of credit markets as private alternatives to welfare states reflects a more fundamental transformation of social rights, responsibilities, and resource allocations, revealing new forms of inequality. While credit markets and welfare states *appear* to fulfill similar functions, they both allocate and distribute resources in opposite ways and follow different underlying logics: welfare states are governed by politically determined and legally enshrined entitlements that are based on past insurance contributions or universal social rights. They typically tax the rich more heavily and redistribute resources to the non-rich, often in a progressive fashion. By contrast, financial markets create credit flows "from the future," so to speak, expecting that debtors repay not only the original amount borrowed (i.e., the principal) but also any interest charges in the interim. As a result, financial markets have become gatekeepers, without any democratic accountability, in regulating social inclusion and exclusion.

Rising income and wealth inequality compound the structural differences in how financial markets and welfare states allocate resources across individuals. Ample evidence shows that the share of income and wealth held by people in the top percentiles of a countries' income and wealth distribution has grown enormously in many OECD countries since the 1980s, albeit to varying degrees (e.g., Jordà, Schularick, and Taylor 2015; Piketty 2014; Piketty and Zucman 2014). As the rich become richer, they also save more (Fagereng et al. 2019; Mian, Straub, and Sufi 2020) and accumulate further wealth by lending money to the non-rich through the financial system (Kumhof, Rancière, and Winant 2015; Mian and Sufi 2014; Rannenberg 2019). While social policies provide government transfers to buffer economic shocks such as unemployment, credit markets amplify market dependence and increase inequalities because debtors have to repay their loans even during economic downturns, generating stable returns for lenders. As more individuals rely on credit to address social risks and seize social opportunities, the financial sector's reach and structural power expands (Braun 2020; Culpepper and Reinke 2014; Jacobs and King 2016; Reisenbichler 2020; Woll 2016), while social policies and their visibility recede, deepening what Suzanne Mettler (2011) calls the "submerged state." This book shows that instead of reducing inequalities through taxation and redistribution, the financial system increases inequalities by lending money to the non-rich as a private alternative to the welfare state.

It would therefore be a mistake to think that credit markets are truly equivalent substitutes for welfare states. They are not. The sociologist Gøsta Esping-Andersen famously argued that welfare states "de-commodify" individuals, by which he meant that income transfers and other forms of public support allow "individuals, or families, [to] uphold a socially acceptable standard of living independently of market participation" (Esping-Andersen 1990, p. 37). Borrowing money as a private alternative to welfare states reverses this relationship. Instead of de-commodifying individuals by making them independent of market participation, credit markets *re-commodify* individuals because borrowers receive money from financial markets and, more consequential, their debt repayments depend on stable, long-term future income streams.

The ability to fully participate in credit markets and reap their benefits further assumes that everyone has equal and fair access. This has not always been the case. In the United States, discrimination against minority borrowers, especially Black Americans, was most pervasive through "redlining" practices (Freund 2007; Massey and Denton 1993) but also occurred in other credit markets such as basing differential access to credit cards and insurances on neighborhood characteristics (Cohen-Cole 2011; Squires 2003). There is evidence for race-based discrimination in mortgage markets through credit scoring systems in the Netherlands (e.g., Aalbers 2007) and in rental housing markets in Germany (e.g., Auspurg, Hinz, and Schmid 2017). In many countries, social movements had to fight for equal participation in financial markets for minority groups, women, and economically disadvantaged individuals. Chloe Thurston (2018) highlights the contested nature of credit access by documenting deep political struggles between privileged groups and excluded groups (e.g., Black Americans, women, and low-income individuals) over the fair participation in financial markets. American activists challenged discriminatory credit regulations by emphasizing that private credit markets provide public goods that help individuals both cope with uncertainty and invest in their futures, for example through homeownership (see also Hyman 2012).

Even today, equal access and participation are still not guaranteed (Dwyer 2018). Modern credit scoring technologies, combined with "big data" and predictive algorithms, introduce new forms of bias, discrimination, and inequality. Credit histories shape access to loans, rental housing, insurance, and even jobs (Dobbie et al. 2020; Kiviat 2019; Traub 2013). Low-income people already pay higher interest rates than high-income people because of a higher (perceived) probability of default. And ethnic minorities in the United Kingdom are only half as likely as White customers to receive refunds from banks in cases of fraud.[15]

The structure of the welfare state further intensifies these inequalities and introduces new types of risks. When social policies fail to provide a level playing field to equalize opportunities, credit markets allow some groups to accumulate wealth and "move upward," while others borrow money simply to maintain their standard of living and "move onward." This book shows that the emergence of credit markets as private alternatives to welfare states reflects a new "winner-take-all" politics (Hacker and Pierson 2010; Hopkin and Lynch 2016) that can amplify and solidify the positions of opportunity hoarders. For some people, credit enhances their socioeconomic opportunities by providing access to education and housing or by helping defray the costs of raising a family. For others, however, credit is less an opportunity but rather a financial necessity. Access to credit can ease families' financial gaps in the short run, but the resulting debt load can increase their financial burdens and amplify their economic insecurity, particularly for those who are already economically disadvantaged (Porter 2012a). Credit markets privatize not only social risks, which have shifted from governments and societies to individuals (Hacker 2019), but also social investments in education, training, and families. Credit's privatization effects further widen income and wealth disparities and create opportunity hoarders in countries where credit markets substitute for welfare states. This is less likely to be the case when credit complements welfare states because social policies protect against risks and provide social investments for economically vulnerable groups, while middle- and in particular high-income groups contribute to the welfare state through taxes and complement more limited welfare benefits through credit markets.

Finally, the book offers a new theoretical framework and empirical evidence about how access to credit and indebtedness shape perceptions of economic insecurity and social policy preferences. We know very little about the role of credit markets and indebtedness as potential drivers behind welfare state support. This is partly because our micro-level theories of social policy preferences focus largely on income (e.g., Meltzer and Richard 1981; Moffitt, Ribar, and Wilhelm 1998; Romer 1975), labor markets risks and skill specificity (e.g., Estevez-Abe, Iversen, and Soskice 2001; Iversen and Soskice 2001; Margalit 2013; Moene and Wallerstein 2001; Rehm 2016; Thewissen and Rueda 2019), and, more recently, financial assets (e.g., Ansell 2014; Hariri, Jensen, and Lassen 2020; Margalit and Shayo 2020), but they fail to systematically incorporate the role of credit markets and indebtedness. We also lack comparative micro-level data that combine information on households' balance sheets with political preferences. This book fills these gaps with new theoretical insights based on original cross-national survey data. I show that credit markets influence social policy preferences by affecting debtors' sense of economic security and relationships with the welfare state. On the one hand, access to credit markets allows individuals to self-insure and opt out of publicly provided goods and services, effectively reaping the benefits of private alternatives. These insurance and privatization effects reduce individuals' demands for social insurance. But credit markets privatize both opportunities and risks. Debt can strengthen support for social insurance when borrowing to smooth income losses increases risks, or it can lower support for social insurance when borrowing yields positive economic gains, either expected or realized.

These findings can help explain why in some countries rising income volatility and inequality have not led to a welfare state expansion or stronger electoral demands for more redistributive policies. For voters, credit markets offer a private alternative to the welfare state, undermining people's perceived need for social insurance. For policymakers, expanding the reach of and access to credit markets is not only fiscally convenient but also politically viable. It allows policymakers to address growing societal demands and fiscal constraints by circumventing politically contested issues around taxation and redistribution (Krippner 2011; McCarty, Poole, and Rosenthal 2013; Rajan 2010). Deficit spending has been replaced by a model of "privatized Keynesianism" that rests on the expansion of private rather than public debt (Crouch 2009).

EMPIRICAL STRATEGY

This book explains the causes and consequences of rising household indebtedness by adopting a comparative approach. In particular, I compare how the institutional context affects similar "types" of individuals across countries in very different ways. By placing individuals and their families at the center of the comparative analysis, this approach allows me to study how individuals cope with similar economic experiences (e.g., unemployment or taking time off work to care for children) in light of different institutional constraints (e.g., a limited welfare state or a permissive credit regime). It also sheds light on individuals' responses to exogenous changes in institutional settings, for example when access to credit becomes easier or when social policies become less generous.

I substantiate the book's argument with three complementary empirical approaches. First, to understand variation in patterns of indebtedness across countries, I develop a novel continuous measure of credit regime permissiveness in Chapter 4 for seventeen OECD countries spanning the period from 2000 to 2017. This measure serves two purposes. It allows me to empirically demonstrate that the substitutive relationship between credit and welfare states only emerges when credit regimes are permissive. And it serves as a principled approach to select country cases that vary along the spectrum of credit regime permissiveness.

Second, to understand variation in patterns of indebtedness across households within countries (and, therefore, within particular institutional contexts), I draw on longitudinal micro-level panel data from Denmark, the United States, and Germany. The choice of these three countries is motivated by the empirical implications of my theory. The countries vary with regard to the structure of not only their labor markets and welfare regimes but also their credit regimes, and they display considerable variation in levels of household indebtedness, as I show in Chapter 4. This allows for paired comparisons of these cases, holding constant either the structure of the credit regime or leveraging variation in welfare state generosity. Denmark and the United States share flexible labor markets and permissive credit regimes that easily channel credit to households. However, both countries have very different social policy regimes, as I document in Chapter 3. The more limited American welfare state exposes larger segments of society to considerable financial shortfalls and economic risks compared with the more comprehensive Danish welfare state. This allows me to compare how groups with different levels of welfare state protection cope with similar economic shocks such as unemployment. Low-income Danes are much better protected by the welfare state and receive relatively high unemployment insurance benefits. By contrast, low-income Americans are more heavily exposed to social risks by a limited welfare state and cope with income losses by going into debt. High-income groups receive less social policy support in both countries and, as a result, borrow money to address social risks and seize social opportunities as credit is easily accessible. Germany provides an important comparative case to highlight the role of credit regimes in structuring individuals' coping strategies and shaping patterns of indebtedness. Germany's labor market is segmented into a protected core with stable, long-term employment and generous social benefits and an exposed periphery with precarious and unstable employment and more limited social benefits. However, Germany's restrictive credit regime makes it much more difficult for households to borrow money, especially during unemployment.

The empirical evidence to support my argument comes from a comparison of households within each of the three countries. Conceptually, the household is the appropriate unit of analysis because we can expect resource sharing within the household if one member of the household loses their job, falls ill, or takes time off work to take care of children or get training. Empirically, focusing on households facilitates cross-national comparisons because many surveys report household-level socioeconomic data for the head of the household. I draw heavily on micro-level panel data to follow households over time, studying their responses to economic shocks and life course choices within a particular institutional environment. For Denmark, I use administrative register data that cover the entire population since the late-1980s.[16] Since full population administrative data for my variables of interest are not available for Germany and the United States, I rely on several panel data sets that contain information on labor market status as well as on income, assets, and liabilities. I use the Survey of Income and Program Participation (SIPP), the Survey of Consumer Finances (SCF), and the Panel Survey of Income Dynamics (PSID) for the United States, and the SAVE Panel Study and the German Socio-Economic Panel (SOEP) for Germany.[17]

This book is designed to carefully balance internal and external validity by identifying causal relationships and demonstrating broader applicability beyond a single case study on the one hand and by highlighting the importance of institutional change and policy choices on the other. To that end, I draw on two policy reforms as quasi-natural experiments in Denmark and Germany that allow me to identify the causal effect of exogenous changes in credit access and social policy support on households' borrowing behaviors. First, I use the introduction of home equity loans in Denmark in 1992 to show that borrowing in light of income losses increases when credit constraints are alleviated. Second, I use the German Hartz labor market reform of 2005 (Hartz IV) to demonstrate that in the context of a restrictive credit regime, cuts in welfare benefits do *not* increase borrowing as we would expect in more permissive regimes. Instead, debt leverage declines as people start to repay their loans, cut expenditures, and draw on savings to address income losses. Other parts of the book rely on subnational variation in social policies – such as variation in levels of unemployment insurance generosity across US states and over time – to demonstrate that individuals who lose their jobs borrow more in states with less generous unemployment insurance benefits.

---

[16] Access to the Danish full population administrative records was approved by the Danish Data Authority and granted by Statistics Denmark.

[17] More details on data sources and how I constructed variables appear in Section A in the Appendix for Chapter 7.

Finally, to understand the political and socioeconomic consequences of the rise of credit and debt as private alternatives to the welfare state, I draw on original cross-national survey data to show how access to credit and indebtedness influence individuals' economic insecurity and social policy preferences across welfare regimes.[18] One reason we know very little about the political consequences of credit markets and indebtedness, particularly for individuals' social policy preferences, is the lack of data. Most surveys contain either the standard batteries of socioeconomic and political variables or, alternatively, information on assets and liabilities. But they rarely combine both, which has made it very difficult to study the political and economic consequences of the links between household debt and social policies across countries. This survey fills these gaps by collecting data from over 20,000 individuals across nine OECD countries on their socioeconomic background, income, and wealth as well as measures of economic security and financial well-being, public opinion, and political behavior.[19]

By comparing individuals across institutional contexts, this book combines macro- and micro-level data to study the causes and consequences of rising indebtedness and use of credit markets as alternatives to welfare states.

LOOKING AHEAD

The remainder of this book is organized as follows. Chapter 2 lays out the social policy theory of everyday borrowing. I first discuss the extent to which welfare states protect against social risks and provide social investments. In many countries such services have become insufficient or inadequate in light of individuals' fragmented employment patterns and life course trajectories, resulting in increased reliance on private means to address financial gaps due to volatile incomes, earnings losses, and rising expenditures. I then introduce the concept of credit regimes, arguing that the institutional structures and regulatory and policy environments shape credit regimes' permissiveness and households' access to credit. I explain how the constellation of welfare state and credit regime structures shapes the role of credit as a coping mechanism. When credit regimes are permissive, households borrow to address social risks and use credit as social investments. This means that credit either substitutes for or complements welfare states, depending on which groups social policies protect and support. By contrast, when credit regimes are restrictive, households draw on savings, utilize family support, or cut expenditures because

[18] The survey was designed together with Jacob Gerner Hariri, Amalie Jensen, and David Dreyer Lassen, implemented by Epinion, and generously funded by David Dreyer Lassen's European Research Council Grant No. 313673.

[19] The countries include Canada, Denmark, England, France, Germany, the Netherlands, Spain, Sweden, and the United States. More details on sample sizes and response rates appear in the Appendix.

the borrowing option is precluded. The chapter concludes by arguing that the reliance on credit markets instead of social policies reflects a much more fundamental transformation of social rights, social responsibilities, and the allocation of resources and risks.

Chapter 3 documents how structural changes in labor markets, life course trajectories, and welfare states have increased income volatility and financial shortfalls over time and across countries. I develop a new measure of financial shortfalls, comparing households' annual gross and net income volatility based on panel data from Denmark, the United States, and Germany, revealing considerable variation in income volatility across and within countries. I show that the Danish welfare state absorbs much larger amounts of gross income volatility that the flexible labor market produces compared with the United States. In Germany, the welfare state also addresses a sizable share of gross income volatility. But unlike in Denmark, gross income volatility has declined slightly since the mid-2000s, while net income volatility increased during the Hartz reforms period in the early 2000s. This chapter also shows that in Denmark and the United States, income volatility due to life course events such as taking time off work to raise families or to get training and education is much more prevalent than income volatility due to unemployment or sickness. In Germany, by contrast, employment disruptions still drive more income volatility than life course choices.

Chapter 4 builds on the analytical framework of credit regimes developed in Chapter 2 and introduces a new measure of credit regime permissiveness for seventeen OECD countries spanning the period from 2000 to 2017. I estimate country-specific credit regime permissiveness scores on the basis of six empirical indicators that capture the breadth and scope of financial markets, the allocation of credit between households and businesses, and supporting regulatory and fiscal policy choices using principal component analysis. The Anglo-Saxon economies, the Netherlands, as well as Denmark and Sweden have the most permissive credit regimes, providing households with easy access to credit. By contrast, Southern Europe, Germany, and Austria have the most restrictive credit regimes, making it more difficult for people to take out loans. I then show that credit regimes determine how easily households can borrow money and shape – from a supply-side perspective – the distribution of debt across and within countries. I complement the empirical measures with an in-depth discussion of the institutional and policy features of the Danish, American, and German credit regimes. I conclude this chapter with two pieces of macro-level evidence, documenting considerable variation in how households in different countries cope with social risks. First, I rely on data from LITS II to show that in Sweden and the UK (countries with permissive credit regimes), households are more likely to go into debt to address unexpected income losses than in restrictive regimes such as Germany or Italy. Second, I use my credit permissiveness scores to demonstrate that households only go into debt to compensate for weak unemployment insurance generosity when credit regimes are permissive.

Chapters 5 and 6 are the main empirical chapters that draw on a range of micro-level data from Denmark, the United States, and Germany to document the extent to which different types of households go into debt to address social risks and seize social opportunities. Chapter 5 focuses on borrowing to address social risks that arise from disrupted employment patterns such as unemployment, sickness, or fluctuating work hours. I show that within permissive credit regimes, households that are least protected by the welfare state borrow the most. In Denmark, upper-middle- and high-income groups who experience more substantive income losses during unemployment borrow more than low-income groups who are well protected by the welfare state. The limited and shrinking welfare state in the United States, by contrast, greatly affects low- and middle-income households that increasingly tap into credit markets to bridge income losses due to fluctuating work hours, temporary employment, and job losses. The situation is quite different in Germany, where individuals who experience unemployment rarely borrow money to address financial shortfalls because Germany's restrictive credit regime makes it very difficult for them to access loans. This chapter also demonstrates how political choices affect the relationship between social policies and household debt. First, I use exogenous variation in the generosity of unemployment (UI) benefits across US states and over time to document that individuals who become unemployed borrow more in US states where benefits are less generous. Second, I show that although the German Hartz labor market reforms of 2005 significantly cut social benefits to the long-term unemployed, they did *not* increase debt levels for affected households because access to credit remained restrictive.

Chapter 6 turns the focus on credit as a form of bounded social investment in light of financial shortfalls that arise during the life course. I show that the Danish welfare state provides strong financial support, particularly for low-income households, through comprehensive family and educational policies such as childcare services and other in-kind benefits that limit families' financial exposures and lower households' opportunity costs for taking time off work, sending children to childcare, and pursuing education and training programs. Middle- and high-income households are the ones that draw on credit to smooth income losses when a spouse temporarily leaves work, for example to take care of children or to get training. This "investment borrowing" is more prevalent than "consumption borrowing" to cope with labor market–related risks, which I document in Chapter 5. By contrast, many more American households, including low- and middle-income ones, borrow money to cope with the financial consequence that arise throughout the life course, including income losses due to parental leave or expenses for childcare, education, and training which would be covered or subsidized by most European welfare states. As life course trajectories have become more fluid and flexible, and as the traditional single-breadwinner model has declined, Germany's restrictive credit regime continues to make it hard for households to borrow money.

Chapter 7 introduces a new theoretical framework that helps explain how access to credit and indebtedness shape social policy preferences. Credit markets privatize both risks and opportunities. They enable individuals to self-insure against social risks and to opt out of publicly provided social services, reaping the benefits of private, credit-funded alternatives in human capital (e.g., education) and financial assets (e.g., housing) with the expectation of economic gains and upward mobility. But indebtedness can also increase economic risks by making borrowers vulnerable to downstream income volatility and income losses that threaten debt repayments. Using original cross-national survey data, this chapter documents considerable divergence of social policy preferences across countries (depending on the structure of the welfare state and credit regime), across households (depending on whether they borrow for consumption or investment), and across the political ideology spectrum (depending on people's relative belief in personal responsibility and market efficacy).

Chapter 8 concludes the book by discussing its broader political and socioeconomic implications. I first delineate the politics behind credit regimes and reflect on the underlying political coalitions and dynamics behind credit markets' complementary and substitutive relationships with welfare states. I then examine how credit markets amplify old and create new forms of social exclusion and inequality through discrimination, credit scoring, or differential credit access. As credit markets have grown more influential and increasingly determine life chances, equal and fair access to credit is now a prerequisite for full participation and inclusion in labor markets, housing markets, as well as educational opportunities and wealth-building trajectories. I end this chapter by discussing potential ways in which credit markets and welfare states can work together, not against each other, to ensure a fairer and more equal distribution of social risks and opportunities.

Considered together, these chapters show how the structure of both welfare states and credit regimes influence and shape patterns of indebtedness across and within countries, shedding light on the political causes and consequences of relying on credit as a private alternative to social policies and revealing a profound transformation of social responsibilities, social rights, and allocation of risks and opportunities that shape people's abilities to fully participate in society and the economy.

2

A Social Policy Theory of Everyday Borrowing

"Life Takes Visa" was the slogan of America's largest credit card issuer up until 2009, when the Great Recession had already begun to affect the economic and financial lives of millions of people in the United States and elsewhere.[1] But credit cards are no longer only a means to easily purchase goods and services. Many individuals cannot live without some form of credit such as mortgages, personal and educational loans, and credit cards. Borrowing money has become an essential part of many people's daily lives, and it increasingly determines life chances and full participation as economic citizens (Krippner 2017). This is reflected in the tremendous growth in household debt over the past decades in Anglo-Saxon economies such as the United States and the United Kingdom, but also in European countries such as the Netherlands and Denmark. American households, for example, carry a total debt load of $14.3 trillion (Federal Reserve Bank of New York 2020), while in the United Kingdom household debt reached a record of £1.28 trillion in 2018 (ONS 2019). Across the OECD, the total sum of debt, measured as a share of households' disposable income, has grown from an average of 78 percent in 1995 to 126 percent in 2019 (OECD 2020b). In other countries, however, most notably Germany and Japan, household debt as a share of income has remained stagnant.

This chapter presents an overview of the book's argument and develops what I call a *social policy theory of everyday borrowing.* I begin by laying out how welfare states' social consumption and social investment policies support individuals as employment patterns and life course trajectories have become fragmented, and the extent to which financial gaps arise between households' financial needs and welfare states' financial support. I then introduce the concept of credit regimes, showing how institutional structures and regulatory

---

[1] See Suzanne Vranica, "Visa Seeks to Usurp Cash as King," *Wall Street Journal*, March 2, 2009.

26

and policy environments shape credit regimes' permissiveness and households' access to credit. The chapter proceeds by introducing the social policy dimension of credit markets, arguing that individuals borrow money to address social risks and use credit as a form of bounded investment. It also explains how the constellation of credit regime and welfare state structures shapes patterns of indebtedness across and within countries. Credit substitutes for or complements welfare states, or fulfills no social policy function if credit markets are restrictive. I conclude by discussing the fundamental transformation of social rights, social responsibilities, and resource allocations as financial markets emerge as private alternatives to the welfare state.

HOW WELFARE STATES AND CREDIT MARKETS SHAPE PATTERNS OF INDEBTEDNESS

The core argument of this book is that the constellation of two sets of institutions shapes the role of credit as a private coping strategy: welfare state policies that insulate individuals from social risks and provide them with social opportunities, on the one hand, and regulatory institutions and policy choices around capital and credit markets on the other. The less comprehensive welfare states are in addressing social risks such as unemployment or sickness and in providing social investment in education, childcare, or family policies, the more financially exposed households become. When public support is limited, households turn to private alternatives such as credit markets or savings. The availability of private alternatives depends crucially on the nature of what I call a country's *credit regime*: the bundle of regulatory institutions and policy choices governing capital and credit markets that make households' access to credit easier or more difficult. In this section, I develop this argument in greater detail. I explain how welfare states and social policies have responded to changing employment patterns and life course trajectories and what financial shortfalls arise as a result of such responses. I then turn to the role of credit regimes and the ease with which households can tap into credit markets to borrow money.

Welfare States and Financial Shortfalls

Welfare states fulfill three main functions. First, they redistribute resources across individuals, typically across income groups from high-income to low-income. As early as the English "poor laws," established in 1601 to target individuals most desperately in need, welfare states have both offered different forms of poverty relief and helped reduce social exclusion. Most welfare states today provide baseline subsistence support to their citizens and utilize redistributive policies such as social assistance in order to reduce income inequality. Second, welfare states provide insurance against the financial impact of various forms of social risks. This income-smoothing function constitutes the bulk of governments' social policy spending. Perhaps the most prominent policies are insurance against unemployment and sickness as well as old-age pensions to smooth consumption. Benefits are typically financed by either individuals' prior contributions or, alternatively, through general tax revenues. While social insurance policies have redistributive elements that reduce income inequality, they are fundamentally about redistribution across risk and income groups (Baldwin 1990; Rehm, Hacker and Schlesinger 2012). What these policies have in common is that they "socialize" risks. These first two policies are often called passive *social consumption policies* because they aim to maintain income and, in some cases, socioeconomic status through government transfers. Finally, welfare states enable and promote social opportunity and social mobility through public investment in education, childcare, or various programs that allow family members to take time off work for parental leave. In this case, social policies can take the form of income-supporting government transfers or in-kind benefits such as free childcare or education. The literature refers to these types of policies as active *social investment policies*, as they tend to be future-oriented and typically seek to improve individuals' employability and promote investment in human capital through education, retraining, and family policies.[2] In contrast to welfare states' redistributive "Robin Hood" function, which transfers resources across individuals, the latter two insurance and investment functions resemble in Barr's words a "piggy bank" because they redistribute resources over the life cycle (Barr 2001).

Some countries have shifted away from social consumption and toward social investment policies, most notably in the form of the "embedded flexibilization" approach of the Scandinavian countries (Thelen 2014). In many countries, however, welfare institutions have become at odds with individuals' employment patterns and life course choices. More frequent employment disruptions, growing income volatility, and higher expenditures have placed new financial burdens on individuals' shoulders, while welfare state retrenchment and policy drift have weakened social policy support and created financial gaps in individuals' daily lives.

Financial Consequences of Disrupted Employment Patterns

The transition of Fordist economies into flexible knowledge economies has affected labor markets and welfare states and left deep marks on households' financial lives (Boix 2019; Iversen and Soskice 2019). Deindustrialization and the growth of the service sector brought non-standard forms of employment, increasingly "fissured" workplaces (Weil 2014), and more frequent spells of unemployment, which disrupted employment patterns and made incomes more volatile (Emmenegger et al. 2012; Schmid 2002). The integration of trade

---

[2] On the distinction between social consumption and social investment policies, see, for example, Ansell and Gingrich (2015); Hemerijck (2013); Morel, Palier, and Palme (2012), and the contributions in Beramendi et al. (2015).

and capital markets and the resulting increase in international competition have put more pressure on labor markets, particularly in the manufacturing sector, to compete for prices and flexibility (Autor, Dorn, and Hanson 2013; Feenstra 2010). Facing pressure from competitive markets, employers' preferences, and partisan ideology, policymakers across the advanced economies began to deregulate labor markets in an attempt to make them more flexible and allow for faster labor turnover (Palier and Thelen 2010). In many countries, the flexibility of labor markets comes at the expense of more frequent job switching, higher income volatility, and more precarious jobs (with unstable and shorter work hours) in the low-skill and low-pay segments.

These changes have profound implications on households' income trajectories. Unemployment, one of the most severe disruptions in employment patterns, has become a systematic and enduring problem in many OECD countries. In addition to long-term unemployment, more individuals have begun to experience more frequent transitions in and out of employment, resulting in shorter spells of unemployment (Kalleberg 2009; Schmid 2002). Yet job loss is not the only source of income volatility. Jobs that demand flexibility often feature less predictable work schedules and more volatile work hours, which can disrupt incomes because job tenure rates decline and individuals switch jobs more frequently. This is particularly pronounced in the United States, as Morduch and Schneider (2017) show, but also increasingly common in other European countries. In all these cases, individuals and their families experience unexpected, exogenous income losses that result in larger financial burdens.

Life Course Trajectories and Social Opportunities

But labor markets are only one domain that puts pressure on households' financial lives. Changing life course trajectories, including choices about taking time off work, educational attainment, and child-rearing and family arrangements, is another area that has a considerable impact on households' finances. The traditional single-breadwinner family of the Fordist era has given way to more varied family arrangements such as dual-earner couples and single-parent households. The increase in female employment rates clearly reflects these changes (Iversen and Rosenbluth 2010). While the growth in female employment has reduced income volatility for dual-earner married couples, two sources of income no longer provide the same financial buffer as they once did. Instead, many families crucially *depend* on dual incomes as living costs and expenses have grown (Warren and Tyagi 2003).

Choosing to have children also comes with important financial considerations and can lead to income losses and larger financial burdens.[3] As more

---

[3] On the various financial and economic costs of parenthood, see, among others, Adda, Dustmann, and Stevens (2017); Blau and Kahn (2017); Goldin (2014); and Olivetti and Petrongolo (2016).

women join the workforce and have full-time jobs, families have to find new arrangements to take care of children. Countries that offer significant public in-cash or in-kind subsidies require families to make only minimal contributions to the costs of formal childcare (e.g., daycare, preschool, and kindergarten), which becomes prohibitively expensive in countries with limited or no public support. Alternatively, family members temporarily take time off work or draw on informal childcare options through networks of relatives, friends, or community centers.

Educational choices – although not part of the empirical investigation of this book – follow a similar logic. Individuals are less likely to enroll in college or other educational programs if the opportunity costs to do so are higher than starting a job or taking a leave of absence from their current job.[4]

The Changing Nature of the Welfare State

Social consumption policies, typically associated with a Fordist economy, have come under pressure, in part because of economic and fiscal constraints as well as increasing demands due to rising long-term unemployment. Policy-makers attempted to address these challenges with two strategies. On the one hand, they began to retrench social consumption policies by both cutting benefit levels and entitlement periods and tightening eligibility criteria for ben-efits. Requiring longer, often uninterrupted employment histories to be eligible for benefits disqualified those individuals who either had non-standard work arrangements with fewer work hours or who switched jobs more frequently. Means-tested programs, already more common in liberal market economies, found their ways into other welfare states as well. These restrictions made more individuals ineligible for benefits and further weakened their financial situations.

On the other hand, policymakers adopted social investment policies that focus on employability, education and retraining, and supporting families through subsidized leave programs and childcare (Bonoli 2013). At the same time, they also privatized other domains of social policies and replaced publicly provided services with private market-based solutions. Defined-contribution pension schemes and private health insurance plans have become alternatives to defined-benefit plans and publicly provided health insurance, which, again, shift the financial burden of insurances or pensions onto individuals (Gingrich 2011; Hacker 2004; Häusermann 2010). These provisions and services, which are often less generous than the public alternative, often add additional costs for beneficiaries.

The modern postindustrial economy has also created new types of social risks and social opportunities, which existing welfare programs only partially

---

[4] Despite the evidence that having a college degree on average leads to higher incomes and better-quality jobs in the future, the *cost* of attending college can outweigh these benefits.

cover, if at all. Examples include the rise of precarious types of jobs that no longer provide the same employment security and social benefits as standard full-time jobs, or more frequent job switches that increase earnings volatility. These new employment patterns expose households to greater economic and financial risks than before (Eichhorst and Marx 2016). But the flexibility of many modern economies also offers opportunities for families who choose to take leaves of absence from work to take care of children or to get more training and education. Social investment policies that offer free or subsidized childcare, paid parental leave schemes, or opportunities for education and retraining are part of governments' efforts to help families seize these social opportunities.

In many cases, the lack of coverage for new types of social risks and opportunities is the result of political inaction. Policymakers have failed to adapt social policies to new labor market and life course realities, a process known as "policy drift" (Hacker 2004; Streeck and Thelen 2005; Thelen 2004). Consider the example of more frequent job switches. Individuals more often move from one job to another without being unemployed in between. But in many cases they earn *less* in their new jobs than in their previous ones (Schmid 2002). For some, lower pay in a new job is a temporary setback that can be compensated for with a higher-paying job in the future. For others, however, fluctuating incomes due to job switches are a persistent and harmful problem (Morduch and Schneider 2017). Concerns about unstable earnings caused by job switches have led policymakers and academics to consider wage insurance schemes that would provide financial assistance to workers who lost their jobs but cannot find new ones with similar earnings (see, for example, LaLonde 2007).[5] Yet to date, no welfare state in the OECD has public insurance programs in its toolkit that could absorb parts of such income losses.

Fragmented employment patterns and changing life course trajectories make incomes more volatile and add new expenditures to households' budgets, while at the same time welfare states no longer provide either sufficient coverage against social risks or supports to seize social opportunities. The degrees of the resulting financial shortfalls vary considerably across countries, as I will show in greater detail for Denmark, Germany, and the United States in Chapter 3. The weaker social policies are, the more individuals have to draw on private means to smooth income losses and finance higher expenditures. Whether individuals tap into savings or cut expenses, or whether they borrow money and go into debt depends on the structure of domestic credit markets.

---

[5] In the United States, wage insurance for workers who lost their jobs to foreign workers was introduced under President George W. Bush and extended under President Obama. See also Robert J. Shiller, "How Wage Insurance Could Ease Economic Inequality," *New York Times*, March 11, 2016, or President Obama's 2016 State of the Union Address.

Credit Regimes and the Ease of Borrowing

Credit markets have become central institutions that shape the allocation of resources such as access to education and housing and financial liquidity, thus determining distributional outcomes and life chances (Fourcade and Healy 2013; Krippner 2017; Streeck 2011; Thurston 2018). While borrowing conditions for many households have improved across OECD countries, especially as the influence of credit markets has grown, there are significant cross-national differences in the availability of credit and the purposes for which households borrow money. Countries have unique bundles of regulatory and fiscal policy configurations and institutional structures – I call them *credit regimes* – that influence the allocation of credit between households and businesses and, as a consequence, determine households' access to credit markets.

Scholars have long recognized important cross-national differences in the structure of national financial markets, most famously classifying financial systems as bank-based or market-based (Allen and Gale 2000; Culpepper 2005; La Porta, Lopez-De-Silanes, and Shleifer 1999; Zysman 1983). The liberalization of financial systems since the 1970s lifted restrictions on bank lending activities and cross-border capital flows, paving the way for more financialized economies in which credit markets play a much more important role in economic and political domains (van der Zwan 2014). Most of these accounts, however, do not shed light on either the degrees to which these structural differences influence *households'* access to credit or how (bank) credit is allocated within a country.

More recent research has taken important steps to address these shortcomings. Engelen and Konings (2010), for example, identify three distinct trajectories of financialization: institutional configurations and political struggles between actors in the financial sphere are either consensual (enabling high degrees of capital mobility, financial market openness, and financial innovation), contested (protective of too much exposure to financial markets), or compartmentalized (large financial sectors coexist with corporatist labor markets and welfare regimes). Others have focused specifically on structural differences in national mortgage markets by showing the degrees to which OECD countries deviate from the US ideal-type model with high ownership rates, high levels of securitized mortgage debt, and low transaction costs (Fuller 2015; Schwartz 2008). Yet the distinction between bank-based versus market-based financial systems based on different corporate governance rules and the size of housing and mortgage markets alone cannot explain why some countries are more financialized and provide households with easier access to credit than others. Moreover, existing work emphasizes country typologies and "national models" when, in fact, the institutional and policy configurations of credit regimes may be more fluid and not necessarily complementary (Fuller 2015). As Krippner (2011) shows in the United States, policy outcomes in the domain of credit markets are more often the result of unintended consequences than deliberate choices. Lastly, and most importantly, we lack empirical measures of the different facets of countries' credit regimes (beyond idiosyncratic characteristics of borrowers such as age, income, and employment status) that capture the institutional environment that shapes the degrees to which households can tap into credit markets.

To rectify these shortcomings, I offer a comprehensive analytical framework of credit regimes that jointly considers the breadth and depth of the pool of capital and credit within a country; the institutional interrelationship between banks, households, and businesses; and supporting regulatory and fiscal policy choices that shape not only the sectoral allocation of credit between households and businesses but also households' incentives to borrow money. Permissive credit regimes combine open financial markets with large pools of capital that tend to be allocated disproportionately toward households. This institutional structure gives households easier access to credit markets to borrow money. Restrictive credit regimes, by contrast, are less open to global financial markets with smaller pools of capital that tend to be allocated toward the business sector, which, in turn, makes borrowing by households more difficult.

What Makes a Credit Regime?

Credit regimes consist of three dimensions that, together, influence who gets credit in the economy and how easily individuals can borrow money during periods of financial distress. The first dimension is the depth and breadth of financial markets, specifically the size of the pool of capital that can be channeled toward households and businesses. Institutional investors such as pension funds and insurance companies are important drivers behind the expansion of financial markets, aided by the shift from defined-benefit to defined-contribution pension plans (Fligstein and Goldstein 2015; Hassel, Naczyk, and Wiß 2019). Most countries have privatized and marketized their pension systems, albeit to different degrees (Häusermann 2010). As institutional investors draw families deeper into financial markets, they also need investment opportunities and, therefore, promote and depend on liquid financial markets. The distribution of households' financial assets in part reflects these institutional arrangements and households' own role as active market participants. For example, households in Germany and Japan are more likely to hold cash in bank deposits – 39% and 51% of households' total financial assets, respectively – than in shares and equity (11%). In other countries, the distribution is reversed. American, Danish, and Dutch households have fewer bank deposits (13% in the United States and 16% each in the Netherlands and Denmark) but much higher share and equity ownership (34% in the United States and 24% in Denmark), whereas the Netherlands also stands out with similarly low levels of equity ownership (11%) (OECD 2020b). A second factor that influences the domestic pool of capital is the firms' funding needs. If firms can rely on market-based external funding options such as equity and bond markets, banks have more capital at their disposal that they can lend to other actors such as households. By contrast, if firms use bank loans to finance their investments, equity and bond markets are less important and tend to be underdeveloped (Engelen and Konings 2010). Lastly, securitization practices further expand the scope of financial markets. Lenders disperse their credit risks by pooling illiquid debt contracts into securities whose tranches and derivatives can be sold to other investors, thus improving lenders' fundraising capacities by freeing up resources on their balance sheets that they can turn into more loans.[6] Together, institutional investors, firms' funding needs, and securitization markets influence the breadth and depth of capital markets.

The second dimension in my analytical framework of credit regimes concerns the allocation of capital between households and businesses – something that has received less attention in the literature. The institutional relationships between banks and businesses on the one hand, and between banks and households on the other, are core drivers of credit flows in the economy. Firms' corporate governance structure and financial needs strongly shape these relationships. In countries where nonmarket relationships and relational contracting are the norm and ownership of firms is concentrated, banks have developed closer ties with firms to fund their business activities and operate as a "house bank" by providing firms with long-term, patient capital (Cioffi 2006; Hall and Soskice 2001). Since strong lending ties between banks and businesses push credit flows toward firms, capital markets for mortgages and pension assets are weakly developed (Engelen and Konings 2010; Schwartz 2012). But recent changes in financial markets have undermined the role of banks as providers of patient capital since ownership networks have dissolved, domestic stock markets have become more international, and commercial banks have shifted toward market-based banking. In part because of declining labor shares of income, non-financial firms have begun to rely on retained earnings to finance investment, thus reducing their dependence on external capital (Braun and Deeg 2019; Culpepper 2005; Deeg 2009; Hardie et al. 2013). By contrast, in countries where hierarchical and competitive market arrangements and formal contracting prevail and ownership of firms is dispersed, close relationships and cross-holdings between banks and businesses are rare. Instead, arm's-length financial markets underpin corporate governance models and satisfy firms' funding requirements. Since businesses tend to fund themselves through equity and bond markets, banks and other lenders turn to household-related capital markets as alternative sources of lending activities, as I show in Chapter 4. Highly developed and liquid mortgage markets and capitalized

---

[6] In light of the excessive securitization – particularly in the United States and the United Kingdom – that contributed to the surge in subprime loans and the financial crisis of 2007–08, a more skeptical view has emerged that emphasizes the distortionary effects of securitization (see, for example, Mian and Sufi 2009; Shin 2009).

defined-contribution pension systems based on individuals' investments in private pension savings funds emerge as a result of abundant capital flows and credit that are not tied up in business lending.

The third and final dimension in my analytical framework of credit regimes concerns regulatory and fiscal policies that create, promote, and sustain the institutional links mentioned earlier and shape incentives for household borrowing. Governments can encourage banks to lend to households by regulating lending volumes and lending-associated risks through collateral requirements, loan-to-value ratios, rules about securitization practices, and the types of financial products available to prospective borrowers. Governments can also incentivize households to borrow through tax provisions that give preferential treatment to interest payments, for example on mortgages that are often part of a broader political agenda to encourage homeownership. In combination with collateralized borrowing (e.g., home equity loans), these policy choices promote credit flows toward households. But alleviating individuals' credit constraints also reduces savings rates because households can tap into credit markets more easily (Jappelli and Pagano 1994). Consider the example of housing markets. In the United States, the government intervenes much more forcefully in housing policies compared with Denmark and Germany (IMF 2011). Policies include subsidies to low- and middle-income homebuyers, subsidized mortgage guarantees by government-sponsored enterprises, and the tax deductibility of mortgage interest payments. A broad range of government-sponsored enterprises in the United States further promotes access to (and the growth of) mortgage markets. The Federal Housing Administration (FHA) and the Federal National Mortgage Association (FNMA, or Fannie Mae), and later Ginnie Mae and Freddie Mac, offered mortgage insurance and created a liquid secondary market for mortgage loans through securitization. Denmark also allows homeowners to deduct interest payments from their tax liabilities, whereas Germany, which has no tax benefits for debt-financed homeownership, instead offers interest subsidies to buyers through savings accounts (Bausparverträge). The structure of housing markets is central to understanding the extent to which the housing and real estate sectors absorb capital, shaping the allocation of credit toward households and inflating the balance sheet of households and banks.

Together, the size of the pool of capital, the allocation of credit toward households and businesses, and the regulatory and fiscal policies that incentivize or repress household borrowing shape the permissiveness of credit regimes and the ease with which households can borrow money.

Credit Regime Permissiveness and Welfare State Structures
In contrast to other work, I argue that we should think of credit regimes and their degree of permissiveness as occupying positions on a continuous spectrum rather than falling into discrete typological clusters. Some elements of a

TABLE 2.1 *Dimensions of credit regimes*

	More restrictive credit regimes	More permissive credit regimes
(1) Depth of financial markets	o Weak markets for pensions, insurances, and household financial assets o Weak corporate bonds markets o Limited securitization practices	o Deep markets for pensions, insurances, and household financial assets o Deep corporate bonds markets o Strong securitization practices
(2) Allocation of capital and credit	o Strong institutional ties between banks and businesses o Firms rely on banks for long-term patient capital	o Strong institutional ties between banks and households o Firms rely on capital markets and non-bank investors for funding
(3) Political incentives to borrow	o Saving is incentivized through regulatory and fiscal policies o Limited range of financial products for households o Weak mortgage markets	o Borrowing is incentivized through regulatory and fiscal policies o Broad range of financial products for households o Deep mortgage markets

country's credit regime complement each other and increase the institutional stability and complementarity of its particular configuration. However, this does not mean that credit regimes are static entities, falling on either end of the spectrum between permissiveness and restrictiveness. Change in one area can, albeit slowly, make the overall credit regime more or less permissive. As I show empirically in Chapter 4, credit regimes do not map onto existing comparative political economy frameworks such as *Varieties of Capitalism* (Hall and Soskice 2001). It is more fruitful, both theoretically and empirically, to conceptualize the permissiveness of a country's credit regime as a continuous spectrum, bearing in mind that different institutional configurations in one domain can limit and constrain changes in other domains. Table 2.1 summarizes the previous discussion of how the three elements of credit regimes – depth of financial markets, allocation of credit, and regulatory and fiscal incentives to borrow – map onto observable implications along the credit regime permissiveness spectrum. In Chapter 4, I develop an empirical measure of credit regime permissiveness and describe in greater detail the credit regimes of Denmark, the United States, and Germany to shed light on households' ease of access to credit in each regime.

Figure 2.1 illustrates how the constellation of welfare states and credit regimes shapes households' coping strategies and, in turn, patterns of indebtedness. When welfare states are comprehensive, experiencing social risks and harnessing social opportunities do not necessarily expand household borrowing since social policies provide in-cash or in-kind support. In these cases, the structure of the credit regime matters little. Take the example of job loss: When unemployment insurance benefits replace a large fraction of prior earnings, the welfare state mitigates the financial consequences of social risks and limits

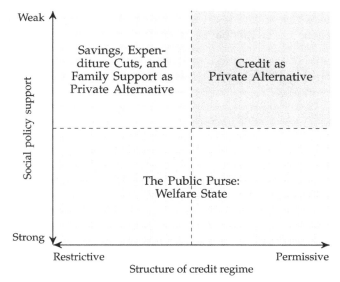

FIGURE 2.1 Micro perspective: How households address financial shortfalls
Note: This figure shows the dominant coping strategies when social policy support is either weak or strong or restrictive.

the gap between earnings losses and government transfers. When the welfare state subsidizes parental leave, it enables social opportunities and, as before, reduces households' needs to draw on private alternatives. Whether the credit regime provides households with sufficient and easy access to credit is less relevant for households' financial well-being in this case because the welfare state absorbs risks and guarantees opportunities. By contrast, when welfare states are weak, households are left to seek private alternatives to address the financial impact of disrupted employment patterns and fragmented life course choices. In these cases, the nature of the credit regime is important because it determines whether credit markets can compensate for financial gaps. In restrictive credit regimes, households have limited access to credit and are unable to borrow money to fill financial gaps. Instead, they internalize costs and income losses, for example through savings, expenditure cuts, and family support. Only in permissive credit regimes does credit emerge as a private alternative to the welfare state. In this case, credit markets help households bridge financial shortfalls due to disrupted employment patterns and life course trajectories. Note that this stylized model allows for various forms of diverging social policy support. Some welfare states differentiate their generosity by income groups, while others segment benefits between labor market insiders (in protected jobs) and labor market outsiders (in more precarious employment situations) (Rueda 2007). Regardless of how welfare states stratify access to and amount of benefits across individuals, the point I want to emphasize here is that groups which receive fewer benefits are forced to rely on private coping strategies, whose availability varies based on the structure of the credit regime.

COPING WITH RISKS AND SEIZING OPPORTUNITIES: THE ROLE OF CREDIT

The institutional configurations between welfare states and credit regimes shape and constrain individuals' everyday behaviors and borrowing choices. They influence how individuals address the financial consequences of social risks and life course choices. Incomes, for example, are rarely stable across the life cycle. Individuals lose their jobs and face periods of unemployment. Individuals take time off work to care for children, pay for childcare, or opt out of the labor force to get more training. More generally, financial shortfalls arise when incomes drop from one period to another while expenditures remain the same, when expenditures increase from one period to another while incomes remain the same, or when incomes drop and expenditures rise. To be sure, expenditures can rise for many reasons, including luxury spending. What concerns me here are expenditures that are necessary to make a living and keep the status quo or to invest in personal assets such as education or childcare and financial assets such as housing. So how do individuals cope with income volatility and higher expenditures?

There are three ways in which households address social risks and fund social opportunities: publicly through social policies and government transfers, privately through savings and expenditure cuts, or privately by borrowing money from credit markets. Figure 2.2 illustrates in a simple two-period model

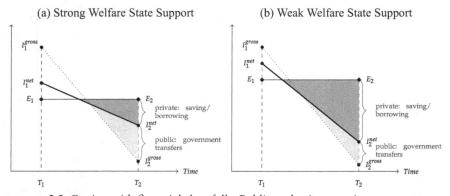

FIGURE 2.2 Coping with financial shortfalls: Public and private options

Notes: A person experiences income losses from period T_1 to T_2, for example due to unemployment or parental leave. I_1^{gross} and I_2^{gross} indicate gross income, I_1^{net} and I_2^{net} indicate net income, and E_1 and E_2 indicate expenditures in time periods one and two, respectively. The shaded areas indicate the *primary* public and private support mechanisms. The welfare state provides larger financial support in panel (a) compared to panel (b).

the ways in which households can, for example, cope with income losses while maintaining their expenditure levels. Panels (a) and (b) depict strong and weak welfare state scenarios, respectively. Net incomes (I_1^{net}) are lower in a strong welfare state due to a larger tax burden, which reduces gross incomes (I_1^{gross}) more than in a weaker welfare state with a lower tax burden. Expenditures are slightly higher in a weak welfare state because individuals have to spend more money on goods and services that are covered by the welfare state in panel (a). Now consider the example of unemployment in period T_2. Gross income declines from I_1^{gross} to I_2^{gross}, but what matters from a person's financial perspective is the decline in *net* income from I_1^{net} to I_2^{net}. Social policies cushion the effect of gross income loss by providing government transfers such as unemployment benefits. If these public transfers are not large enough to maintain the prior expenditure level E_1, there is a shortfall between net income and prior expenditures. To make up for that shortfall, individuals can draw on private means by either accessing liquid savings (e.g., money in their bank accounts) or selling parts of their stock portfolios. They can also use credit markets and borrow money using credit cards, personal loans and payday loans, and home equity lines of credit. One implication of this simple two-period model is that various forms of labor market risks (e.g., unemployment) and life course choices (e.g., parental leave and education) – which are often treated differently in the social policy literature – have similar impacts when viewed through the lens of households' finances.

My focus is on the institutional features of welfare states and credit regimes that determine the size of financial shortfalls as well as the ways in which individuals address such shortfalls. First, the structure of the welfare state (and, implicitly, the structure of taxation) influences the gap between gross and net incomes and, crucially, the size of public government transfers. In countries where the welfare state provides more generous financial support during times of income losses, illustrated in Figure 2.2a, the financial shortfalls are smaller (the distance between I_1^{net} and E_1) and households need fewer private resources to meet their prior expenditure levels. If, however, the welfare state is less generous, illustrated in Figure 2.2b, financial support through public means is much smaller. This exposes households to much larger shortfalls that have to be addressed privately if households want to maintain their status quo without cutting expenses. Consumption levels are lower in Figure 2.2a compared to Figure 2.2b because the welfare state provides more benefits and services.

Not everyone, however, has accumulated enough savings in prior periods (the distance between I_1^{net} and E_1) to smooth income shocks, nor can everyone easily access credit markets to borrow money. These private options depend, secondly, on the structure of the domestic credit regime and the ways in which it interacts with welfare institutions. Credit regimes can be either more permissive and grant individuals easy access to credit, or more restrictive and suppress households' abilities to cover income losses or finance expenditures by borrowing money. Before I discuss different types of borrowing, in the next section I first conceptualize how exactly credit markets have social policy functions and for what reasons individuals borrow money.

Conceptualizing the Social Policy Dimensions of Credit Markets

Credit markets are rarely seen as part of the welfare regime. Esping-Andersen's path-breaking typology of welfare regimes (1990; 1999), for example, does not feature financial markets and private borrowing as possible alternatives for addressing financial shortfalls due to fragmented employment patterns and life course trajectories. But as credit has become a central component of many people's economic lives, its allocation not only shapes economic citizenship and personal well-being but also affects individuals' abilities to address socioeconomic risks and harness social opportunity and economic mobility.

An important justification for government intervention and thus welfare states' existence is market failure. When markets suffer from imperfect competition, information asymmetries, and, consequently, moral hazard, governments step in when private markets fail to provide public goods or insure against uncertainties (Arrow 1963; Barr 2001). As financial markets in general and credit markets in particular have become larger, more efficient, and more accessible – not least because "big data" has allowed lenders to differentiate risks on a much more fine-grained basis – this logic has changed. Credit markets have become more likely to fulfill redistributive and insurance functions and can substitute for government intervention through the welfare state. This does not mean, however, that credit markets operate in a (political) vacuum. They still depend on a minimum level of government support and intervention. Governments can directly facilitate and stabilize credit markets by either subsidizing interest rates or loans or guaranteeing loans when borrowers default. But what is less obvious is that the welfare state itself can sustain credit markets and help them run efficiently. Protection against risks – for example through unemployment or sickness insurance – makes banks and other lenders more likely to lend to individuals precisely because income transfers ensure that these borrowers are able to repay their loans even if they lose their jobs. In the absence of strong welfare state coverage, these individuals would have limited access to credit.

How then can we conceptualize that credit markets fulfill functions that are similar to the welfare state? It may seem surprising at first to think that credit markets can fulfill functions that are similar to social policies, not least because welfare states were in many cases designed to alleviate the detrimental consequences of market fluctuations. But credit markets mirror welfare states' functions in several key ways. Fundamentally, credit markets also redistribute resources – although, crucially, not across individuals but through time. They move resources from the borrower's future self into the present.[7] Credit, or

---

[7] To be sure, credit markets transfer financial resources from savers to borrowers, which makes it an intra-person transfer. But from the perspective of the borrower and in contrast to government transfers, this form of redistribution hinges on repayment in the future.

to be more precise, the resulting debt burden from borrowing, ties debtors to their own future income streams, thus increasing their dependence on stable jobs and other sources of income. Much like social policies can be divided into consumption and investment purposes, I argue that we can conceptualize credit markets' functions in similar ways. Credit can be used to address social risks by smoothing income losses. It can also help finance social investment. But whether borrowing yields upside gains is shaped and bounded by the structure of the welfare state. It is worth emphasizing, however, that this does not mean that credit markets are perfect substitutes for social policies. I will return to this point later.

Credit to Address Social Risks

One key social policy function of credit markets is to provide financial liquidity, which allows individuals to cope with the financial consequences of social risks. We can think of this type of borrowing as the private equivalent to social consumption policies. Individuals go into debt to maintain their current living standards in the face of income losses triggered by unemployment or sickness. As the palette of financial products expands, individuals can use credit cards, take out regular bank loans from formal lenders or high-cost loans from payday lenders or pawnshops. Homeowners can tap into their housing wealth and take out home equity loans. Much like social insurance, credit markets provide liquidity to smooth income losses. But the crucial difference is that credit markets *privatize* risks, requiring borrowers to repay their loans with interest.

To be sure, individuals can deal with these types of income losses through other private means, including drawing on savings, cutting consumption, or selling their homes and moving to a cheaper one. These options, however, are often easier said than done. The life-cycle theory of savings in economics assumes that rational, forward-looking individuals want to smooth consumption over their lifetime and therefore reach optimal decisions about how much of their income to save and how much to consume.[8] Decisions to accumulate savings, however, are demanding and require individuals to gather information and make assumptions about their future income trajectories and risks of income losses. Individuals might be unable to compute the correct amount of savings, for example because of financial illiteracy (Lusardi 2008; Lusardi and Mitchell 2007) or because they are myopic and underestimate risk (Benartzi and Thaler 1995). Even if individuals correctly estimate their savings rates, many lack self-control or fail to put aside savings (Ameriks, Caplin and Leahy 2003; Gathergood 2012; Heidhues and Kőszegi 2010). For these reasons, households' savings rates are smaller than predicted by the life-cycle theory. Cutting expenses, by

---

[8] For a review of the literature on the life-cycle model, see Browning and Crossley (2001).

contrast, presumes that individuals have excess expenditures to cut. Often, this is not the case, as many individuals increasingly live paycheck to paycheck (Kaplan, Violante, and Weidner 2014; Morduch and Schneider 2017). Since moving is financially and emotionally costly, borrowing money can be a viable alternative if income losses are expected to be only temporary.

Credit as Bounded Social Investment

Another key social policy function of credit markets is to enable individuals to invest in personal and financial assets. There are several reasons why families go into debt, such as paying for childcare (e.g., Banerjee, Friedline and Phipps 2017), smoothing income losses during parental leave, or reconciling work and family obligations for dual-career couples. Individuals invest in human capital by taking out loans for education and other training programs, which in the United States and the United Kingdom has led to ballooning levels of student debt.[9] And individuals compensate for temporary pay cuts when they switch from one job to another, perhaps assuming that the new job is a temporary step to a more rewarding career in the future. Credit markets also help individuals obtain financial assets such as their own home – typically the largest financial asset individuals acquire during their lifetime – by taking out mortgages. Traditionally a place of shelter, homeownership has increasingly become a vehicle for dispersing home equity loans on the basis of the underlying property's value, for accessing good school districts, and for creating wealth and a nest egg during retirement. Much like social investment policies (e.g., education, childcare and parental leave, and training and job-search assistance) seek to improve individuals' welfare and investment in skills through public benefits and services, credit can fulfill similar functions by privately providing individuals with the financial means to do so.

When individuals borrow money to cope with social risks, they are retroactively responding to financial shocks, in many cases to maintain their living standards. Using credit as an investment, by contrast, is often prospective, at least in its intent. Credit helps individuals address both the direct opportunity costs of expenditures for childcare, education, and housing and the indirect opportunity costs of forgone income while outside the labor force. Consider the case of childcare. Families may weigh the cost of childcare against the cost of leaving the workforce and forgoing current incomes and potentially take a hit with regard to future incomes upon returning to work. From one perspective, decisions to take parental leave or pay for childcare are forms of human capital investments in early childhood, improving children's skills and cognitive development through parental presence or professional childcare (Heckman and Mosso 2014). Access to childcare can also help parents balance family and work obligations in order to "invest" in their own careers. While

---

[9] On investment in human capital as personal assets, see Becker (1976).

childcare allows parents to keep their jobs and careers, it also comes with significant financial costs, especially if childcare is insufficiently subsidized or not subsidized at all. For many families, having one parent stay at home to take care of children is no longer a feasible option because the family depends on the combined income from two earners – not for economic luxury but for financial necessity (Warren and Tyagi 2003). Similarly, in the case of education, prospective students weigh the cost of education (i.e., tuition fees, living expenses, and forgone earnings by delaying work or leaving the workforce) against better career options and a higher future earnings potential (Oreopoulos and Petronijevic 2013). These examples suggest that individuals borrow money because they not only seek to maintain living standards in light of forgone incomes but also expect future upward gains – higher incomes through more education and training, childcare arrangements that reconcile work and family obligations, job switching flexibility – and, ultimately, upward mobility.

But who engages in credit-financed social investment and whether expectations of upward gains are realized depend crucially on the structure of opportunity costs. Weak social policy support increases the opportunity costs of borrowing money to invest in education, childcare, and taking time off work. When childcare is not publicly subsidized and prohibitively expensive, only households with sufficiently high incomes or wealth will be able to send their children into care in the first place. When education and training programs are prohibitively expensive, students from less affluent backgrounds are less likely to consider going to university or taking time off work to get more training. Social policy support levels the playing field by reducing entry costs and enabling more individuals to participate. Some groups will realize upside gains from credit-based social investments in childcare, education and training, and career changes that lead to higher incomes and upward mobility in the future. Others, however, will not. When a lack of public support forces parents to take unpaid time off work to take care of a sick child or to borrow money to address the resulting financial shortfalls, they will just end up smoothing income losses and not realizing any upside gains.

This is why I call this type of borrowing "bounded" social investment. The returns to credit-financed social investment are bounded and constrained by how leveled the social policy playing field is, and what types of opportunity costs are associated with it. For example, in the absence of paid and job-protecting parental leave, taking time off work not only reduces net incomes – sometimes all the way to zero – but might also negatively affect current and future job prospects through forgone earnings, disrupted work history, and interrupted social insurance contributions, which can make individuals ineligible for social insurance programs. For single parents or minimum-wage hourly workers, opting out of the workforce can simply be impossible. In these cases, opportunity costs are so high that they turn life course choices into social risks. Borrowing money enables households financially either to spend time with their children or to combine career and family obligations by

TABLE 2.2 *Social policy dimensions of welfare states and credit markets*

Domain	Mechanisms	
	Welfare State	Credit Market
(1) Redistribution	Redistribution across individuals	Redistribution within individuals across time
(2) Labor Market and Social Risk	Public insurance against sickness, unemployment, and old age	Private provision of financial liquidity
(3) Life Course and Social Investment	Public investment in education, housing, and family policies	Private investment in personal and financial assets

paying for childcare. Unless public policies reduce these opportunity costs, for example through job protection, free or subsidized childcare, and other forms of financial support, certain life course choices will be limited to households with the requisite jobs, incomes, and wealth. Others may not even consider these options. In a similar vein, the prospects of steep tuition fees and living costs in addition to forgone incomes while in training increase the opportunity costs of education, often to prohibitively high levels. When the lack of public support increases opportunity costs for educational attainment, borrowing money to go to university or get further training can result in a bifurcated and bounded investment. Individuals who are both able and willing to incur such high opportunity costs and take out loans to finance education may reap the benefits of their investment in the form of future employment and high incomes. Others, however, struggle to manage their debt burdens even if they land secure jobs, and they face financial constraints that affect other life choices such as having children, getting married, or buying a home (Addo, Houle and Sassler 2019; Mezza et al. 2020). Forgone incomes and additional expenditures increase opportunity costs in both cases, partly because social policies fail to distribute such opportunity costs more evenly across society. As a consequence, high opportunity costs shape whether credit-financed social investment yields outside gains or simply resembles income smoothing without any upside gain because borrowing is a financial necessity. This allows some groups to "hoard opportunities," reinforcing "winner-take-all" socioeconomic structures.[10]

In sum, by providing financial liquidity to smooth income losses, credit markets can help individuals both address social risks and harness social opportunity and economic mobility through credit-financed social investment. Table 2.2 summarizes these functional similarities between welfare states and credit markets.

---

[10] See Tilly (1998) on opportunity hoarding and Grusky, Hall, and Markus (2019) on opportunity markets.

CREDIT MARKETS AND WELFARE STATES:
A COMPLEMENTARY OR SUBSTITUTIVE RELATIONSHIP?

The ways in which credit regimes and welfare states interact shape patterns of indebtedness across and within countries. When welfare states are limited and credit regimes permissive, households go into debt and borrow money to address social risks and finance social investments. These institutional configurations, in turn, influence not only cross-national variation in the reasons why individuals borrow money as shown earlier in this chapter, but also what "types" of individuals borrow. This has implications for the overall relationship between credit and welfare. In welfare states that sufficiently insulate specific groups (e.g., low-income individuals) from social risks, experiencing such risk does not necessarily expand household borrowing. Borrowing is concentrated among middle- and high-income groups who receive less support from the welfare state but access private alternatives such as credit markets. In contrast to much of the literature on the credit-welfare nexus, in this case the relationship between credit and welfare is primarily complementary, not purely substitutive. Different individuals rely on welfare states and credit markets for their economic welfare, creating a complementary and symbiotic relationship between credit and welfare. Put differently, credit markets coexist with welfare states and complement each other in the provision of financial support, either privately through access to credit or publicly through government transfers.[11] By contrast, in less comprehensive and weaker welfare states, more groups, including vulnerable ones, rely on debt in a substitutive way. The structure of the credit regime is the key determinant that influences whether individuals use credit or savings and expenditure cuts as private alternatives to public spending. Permissive credit regimes enable complementary and substitutive functions depending on which groups are protected by social policies. Restrictive credit regimes, however, foreclose the borrowing option and force individuals to draw on savings and cut expenditures.

Although most of the argument of this book and its empirical edifice focus on unsecured debt, the framework can be generalized and expanded to include mortgage debt. As the large body of work discussed in Chapter 1 suggests, homeownership, financed through mortgages, is often seen as another substitute for the welfare state. However, homeownership and mortgages can also complement the welfare state: when more affluent groups use home equity loans to supplement social benefits, or when some groups rely on private, mortgaged-financed homes while others rely on social housing. It is no coincidence that a country like Germany has one of the lowest rates of homeownership in the OECD. It is also a country with a fairly restrictive credit regime, as I will show in Chapter 4.

---

[11] My use of the concept of complementary does not entail the notion that an increase in the use of good *A* increases the use of another good *B*.

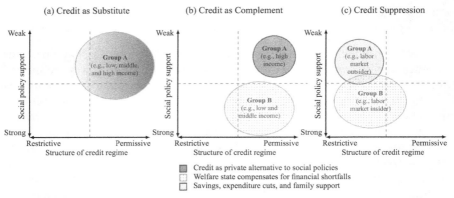

FIGURE 2.3 Macro perspective: How the structure of welfare and credit regimes shapes coping strategies

Notes: The panels show how the structure of welfare states and credit regimes shapes the distribution of coping mechanisms and the role of credit vis-à-vis the welfare state in countries with permissive credit regimes and residual welfare states (panel [a]) and comprehensive welfare states (panel [b]) as well as in countries with restrictive credit regimes (panel [c]).

Building on the micro-level perspective outlined in Figure 2.1, each panel in Figure 2.3 shows a stylized model of how the structure of the welfare state – weak or strong social support – interacts with the structure of the credit regime – restrictive or permissive – to produce variation in coping strategies and, in turn, patterns of indebtedness *within* a given country. Figure 2.4 takes a broader macro-perspective to show what constellation of coping strategies prevails in each of the three countries I study in greater depth in this book. The vertices of the triangle represent three ways to address social risks and finance social investment, thus defining the universe of coping strategies represented by the area inside the triangle. The sides of the triangle map onto the panels in Figure 2.3 and indicate which dominant model results from the interaction between welfare states and credit regimes: (1) credit markets substitute for limited or nonexistent welfare states; (2) credit markets are layered on top of existing welfare states, thus complementing social policies; and (3) credit markets are suppressed, and households rely on a combination of welfare state support and private savings or expenditure cuts. Let me discuss each of these constellations in turn.

Credit as a Substitute for the Welfare State

In countries with limited welfare states and permissive credit regimes, individuals rely considerably on private resources to address social policy-related financial shortfalls. This is the constellation depicted in Figure 2.3a. Credit markets and access to loans play a central role in this model. Households heavily use credit cards to smooth income losses during unemployment and

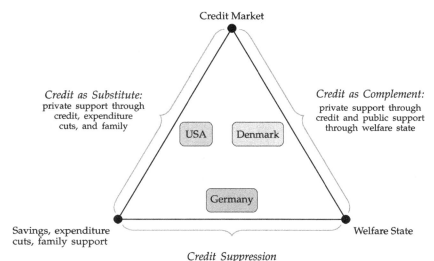

FIGURE 2.4 Macro perspective: Country-level constellations of coping strategies

Notes: This figure shows what constellation of coping mechanisms prevails in Denmark, the United States, and Germany. The vertices represent three ways to address social risks and finance social investment, defining the universe of coping strategies represented by the area inside the triangle. The sides of the triangle indicate the dominant model that results from the particular constellation between welfare states and credit regimes.

to pay for unexpected expenses (indicated by Group *A*). With tax-incentivized mortgages, people purchase homes that provide not only shelter but also access to good schools and jobs, home equity loans, and assets for retirement. While parents must decide how to pay for childcare, financing education – including pre-school, private tutoring, training, and tertiary education – depends increasingly on the abilities of both parents and children to borrow money. Savings rates tend to be low in such countries, in large part precisely because credit markets are easily accessible.

Individuals across the income spectrum draw on credit markets, but the types of debt they use are heavily stratified. For example, low-income and less wealthy groups are more likely to draw on what I call *consumption debt*, which allows them to address labor market risks and related income losses. High-income and more wealthy groups, by contrast, tend to rely on *investment debt*, which enables them to invest in child-rearing, education, and housing. Social services and government transfers are much less important in this model as both risks and opportunities are largely privatized. This raises the opportunity costs for low-income individuals because there is no financial cushion that offers a safety net to allow everyone to make debt repayments even in times of financial distress. Those with limited access to credit markets or those who have already taken on too much debt are often forced to cut expenditures or deplete savings, if possible. The latter is an important and consequential precondition to be eligible for social assistance programs with strict asset requirements.

It is important to emphasize that credit markets can only operate as a substitute for social policies because governments create and enable permissive credit regimes. Governments subsidize interest rates, guarantee loans as in the case of student debt, intervene in secondary markets through government-sponsored enterprises, and set a regulatory framework allowing a liberal use of interest rates and, more importantly, fees to entice lenders to offer loans to borrowers who might otherwise be excluded from credit markets (Fergus 2018).[12] An example of this model is the United States with its permissive credit regime and limited welfare state.

Credit as a Complement to the Welfare State

In countries with comprehensive but stratified welfare states and permissive credit regimes, social policies address labor market risks and provide social investment in families and children and education. But social protection and support is often divided and stratified, for example by income or labor market status, resulting in different degrees of coverage. Figure 2.3b illustrates this constellation. There are two stylized groups in society, one with strong and comprehensive social policy coverage (the circle with the gray dotted pattern [Group *B*]) and another group with weaker social policy coverage (the dark gray circle [Group *A*]). In this case, a permissive credit regime, which is layered on top of the existing welfare state, complements social policies for segments of society that are incompletely covered by the welfare state (e.g., when unemployment benefits are generous and comprehensive for low-income groups but more limited for high-income groups). In other words, credit markets and welfare states complement each other in providing financial liquidity for different groups, either publicly through the welfare state (Group *B*) or privately through credit (Group *A*).

This discrepancy further results in a diverging use of credit markets. Low-income groups rely heavily on generous financial support from the welfare state, whereas high-income groups tap into credit markets to complement less generous support from the welfare state. Credit markets provide financial support for people who move in and out of the labor market, which is rarely or incompletely covered by the welfare state.

---

[12] Howard (1997) considers tax expenditures such as the home mortgage interest deduction part of the "hidden" welfare state. But they only serve social policy purposes to the extent that individuals act on them and borrow money to acquire a home. Tax incentives themselves do not grant social protection. Instead, it is more useful to view the effects of such borrowing incentives through the lens of permissive credit regimes, which, facilitated by such tax incentives, enable credit markets to substitute for direct welfare spending.

Credit regimes in this model are permissive, allowing individuals to shift financial means from the future to the present instead of using savings or reducing expenses during economic hardship. Two critical features set this credit regime apart from the previous, full-substitution model. First, credit markets are more relevant for individuals who are incompletely covered by the welfare state (Group *A* in Figure 2.3b). This affects a very different segment of society compared with the case of a full substitution, in which low-income individuals borrow to much greater degrees. Second, credit markets similarly require a baseline level of government support and intervention to operate smoothly. Whereas governments intervene in credit markets (directly and indirectly) in the previous model, here the welfare state itself fulfills this stabilizing function in this model. Social insurance and other income transfer programs facilitate credit markets' breadth and depth because they ensure that prospective borrowers can continue to service their debt in the event of income losses. An example of this model is Denmark, which combines "flexicurity" in labor markets and social policies with a permissive credit regime. In this system, credit markets are willing to lend generously *because* of the welfare state, which guarantees income streams even in the event of unemployment and thus facilitates continuous and uninterrupted debt repayment.

Suppressed Credit

In the final constellation, shown in Figure 2.3c, the welfare state protects and supports individuals, but it also stratifies individuals, not necessarily by income but by labor market status. It reflects and amplifies status segmentation in the labor market and society, offering comprehensive protection and income support for employees in the core of the economy with long-term employment, but only limited protection for those marginally employed in non-standard or flexible jobs on the periphery. Figure 2.3c illustrates this segmented welfare state with two groups, *A* and *B*, that represent labor market outsiders and insiders, respectively.[13] Social investment policies tend to be more limited compared with the other models. Whereas different groups go into debt and borrow money to address social risks and seize social opportunities in the substitutive and complementary models, this model features a *restrictive* credit regime that limits individuals' access to credit. It relies on fiscal and regulatory policies and institutional arrangements to incentivize citizens to accrue savings and access other forms of private, non-debt-based coping strategies while also placing a strong emphasis on the family as a safety net. Therefore, credit markets in this model rarely, if at all, have a social policy function. To address economic hardship, households that fall outside the boundaries of the welfare

---

[13] Examples of the "core" include manufacturing workers in Germany, whereas those employed in so-called *mini-* or *midi*-jobs with limited work hours and benefits are in the economic "periphery" (Eichhorst and Tobsch 2015). I will discuss these issues in more detail in Chapter 3.

states have to draw on their own, private financial cushions by tapping into savings, cutting back on expenses, or relying on other family members (Group *B* in Figure 2.3c). This model, in other words, combines social responsibility through the welfare state with personal responsibility through savings and the family. Implicitly, there is a strong temporal focus on the present as well as on past savings rather than on future investment and income streams through credit markets. Germany is a good example of this model, because it combines a Bismarckian, family-oriented welfare state with a restrictive credit regime.

In more extreme cases in which welfare states are residual *and* credit regimes are restrictive – countries in the bottom left part of the triangle in Figure 2.4 and individuals in the top left quadrant in Figure 2.1 – households are more likely to both rely on intergenerational transfers through family networks and borrow informally from family and friends or payday lenders and pawnshops in fringe markets (see, for example, Albertini and Kohli 2013; Baradaran 2015).

SHIFTING RISKS, SHIFTING RESPONSIBILITIES

Credit markets, much like social policies, provide households with financial liquidity to address income losses and enhance social prospects and opportunities. But despite functional similarities, credit markets differ in several dimensions from publicly financed social policies; they expose some households to even greater economic risks; and they shape social solidarity and public support for the welfare state. It would be a mistake to regard credit markets and welfare states as equivalent. There are fundamental differences between relying on credit markets instead of social policies to address financial shortfalls that arise due to labor market risks and life course choices. These four differences concern temporality, the flow of resources, access and eligibility rules, and the allocation of risk.

Temporality

One important difference between relying on credit markets rather than on social policies to address financial shortfalls lies in the temporal dimension as depicted in Figure 2.5. Social policies base their provision of legally defined income support and services on entitlements from insurance contributions ("claims to the past") or social rights such as citizenship ("claims to the present"). Credit markets, by contrast, rest on financial streams from the future based on the promise and the expectation that the debtor will repay the borrowed amount with interest. Publicly funded social policies rely on social responsibility and solidarity, either through tax-funded redistribution or contribution-funded insurance. Credit, however, can drive a wedge between individuals and shift responsibility from society to individuals for addressing financial shortfalls related to both labor markets and life course trajectories. Debt, in other words, creates a stronger bond with one's future self than with

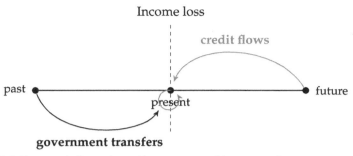

FIGURE 2.5 Temporal dimension of income-smoothing strategies

Notes: This figure illustrates that individuals can address income losses by relying on government transfers on the basis of insurance contribution ("past") and social rights ("present") or drawing on credit markets and borrowing money ("future").

others, erecting social boundaries and imposing social control by trying to discipline the borrower to pay back the loan (Cooper 2017; Dwyer 2018).

The shift toward a privatized welfare regime that grants financial support on the basis of creditors' expectations and debtors' promises to repay borrowed money in the future (i.e., through credit) instead of welfare state's entitlements and guaranteed claims (i.e., through social policies) favors some households over others and has significant downstream consequences for social stratification and public opinion toward the welfare state. For some, credit is a welcome opportunity to opt out of the public provision of goods and services and instead safeguard the returns to their private investments in housing, education, and/or children, or to smooth consumption. Yet for others who have no savings and need to fill financial shortfalls in light of withering social support, borrowing money is the last resort. These two different modes of using credit as a private alternative to welfare programs lead to very different expectations about government social policies and may influence notions of social solidarity, as I show in Chapter 7.

Flow of Resources

The two "models" of coping with financial shortfalls – either publicly through the welfare state or privately through credit markets – differ further in their flows of resources as illustrated in Figure 2.6. In the case of publicly provided social policies such as unemployment and sickness benefits or paid parental leave (Figure 2.6a), tax and contribution payers are paying a share of their incomes into a larger pool of resources from which payouts to eligible beneficiaries are made. Fiscal resources first flow from tax and contribution payers to the common pool, and from there back to benefit recipients. If the tax rate is progressive, high-income individuals pay more into the resource pool than low-income ones, both in absolute and relative terms. A politically determined set

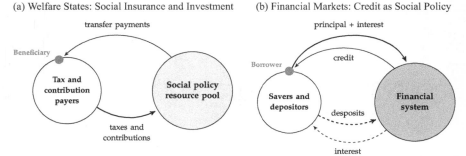

FIGURE 2.6 Two "models" of addressing financial shortfalls

Notes: This figure illustrates how resources flow through the welfare state from taxpayers to social policy beneficiaries (panel [a]) and through the financial system from savers and depositors to borrowers (panel [b]).

of eligibility criteria, which can range from means-tested programs to universal benefits, defines who can draw on these resources and whether beneficiaries are also members of the group who contributes to the resource pool (Bradley et al. 2003; Esping-Andersen 1999). In the case of social insurance programs such as unemployment benefits, recipients are in almost all cases also payees since they are only entitled to benefits if they previously contributed to the unemployment insurance system. In contrast, most redistributive programs such as social assistance base their provision of benefits on social rights. Therefore, some program beneficiaries (i.e., claimants who never held jobs and thus never paid taxes) may not be part of the pool of payees. How much individuals "get out" of the welfare state compared to how much they "pay in," that is, whether individuals are net beneficiaries or net contributors, depends on how often they draw on benefits and on the amount of contributions payed into the system.[14] In the welfare state model of public social insurance and redistributive policies, costs are typically spread widely among taxpayers, while benefits are limited to those who are eligible. If new sources of risk arise, policymakers have to either raise taxes, contribution levels, or both, or finance higher expenditures through deficit spending.

Now consider the case where credit serves social policy functions (Figure 2.6b). Instead of distributing fiscal resources from taxpayers to benefit recipients through the welfare system, financial flows are distributed in the form of credit through the financial system, in which high-income individuals accumulate financial wealth by lending their deposits to the rest (Kumhof, Rancière, and Winant 2015; Mian, Straub and Sufi 2020). When individuals

---

[14] Publicly funded education or healthcare systems are important examples of a large overlap between payees and recipients, but here I limit the discussion to income-supporting policies such as unemployment insurance or paid parental leave.

borrow money, they have to repay not only the principal (i.e., the original amount borrowed) but also the interest, which compensates lenders for their services and risks. Yet credit is *not* an insurance; debtors will pay more than the amount they initially borrowed. Instead, credit is an inter-temporal financial obligation that transfers resources from the borrower's future self into the present through the financial system. Costs and benefits are in most cases targeted to and borne by the same actor: the debtor. The only cases in which costs are no longer borne by borrowers are when debtors default and when banks become illiquid or insolvent and need to be bailed out with taxpayer money. Unlike in the case of public social (insurance) policies, those who rely on credit are not necessarily contributing to the financial system in the form of deposits, nor are they required to do so. Credit is generated by banks, domestic savings, and international capital flows (Passari and Rey 2015; Schularick and Taylor 2012).

Access and Eligibility Rules

A third domain where credit markets and social policies differ is with respect to their access and eligibility rules. The public insurance and redistribution model is based on politically set eligibility criteria that grant access, define conditions under which claims can be made, and constitute legally enforceable rights. It is the political process that decides, in the famous words of Lasswell (1950), "who gets what, when, and how." In the financial system, however, it is private lenders who determine "eligibility" and creditworthiness; that is, whether individuals can borrow money and at what cost, according to business considerations.[15] The political and institutional framework only offers broad guidelines, for example to maintain a competitive and fair playing field or to prevent outright discriminatory behavior. Whereas access to and eligibility for social benefits are politically determined and known ex ante, the cost of credit varies by household type (e.g., based on current income, employment status, assets ownership, geographical location, and family status) and by broader monetary and macro-economic conditions. Credit can be more expensive for those who might need it the most (e.g., low-income or younger households) and less available during economic downturns (e.g., when unemployment is rising but lending is drying up). Yet households that own assets, in particular property, may enjoy privileged access to parts of the credit market. Asset ownership not only influences both the probability of accessing credit and its price, but it also opens access to a set of financial products that require collateral such as home equity loans or home equity lines of credit. Credit markets, in other words, offer unequal access to credit and price loans differently, thereby

---

[15] The dominant goal of private lenders is to maximize profit. In the case of public lenders, government mandates may overrule profit considerations by adding different lending criteria such as serving the local economy or disadvantaged societal groups.

potentially excluding from lending markets those households that would like to borrow to compensate for financial shortfalls.[16] As welfare states' financial support shrinks in many countries, differential access to and cost of credit undermines the "safety net function" of credit for those individuals and families who previously relied on public social policies rather than credit markets to address income losses. While welfare states are built on social rights, credit markets are not.

Risk Allocation

Perhaps the most consequential difference is that welfare states and credit markets allocate risk and economic responsibility in different ways. The welfare state provides redistributive functions across income groups, social insurance functions to protect individuals from social and economic risks (e.g., job loss, sickness, or to invest in highly specific occupational skills), and social investment functions (e.g., education or childcare). Welfare states "socialize" risks by shifting them from the individual onto society – either to all taxpayers or only to those who pay into the insurance pool. Benefits provide a secure stream of financial support and alleviate, to varying degrees, financial constraints. As with any insurance program, social policies work counter-cyclically, supporting individuals financially when their economic circumstances deteriorate.

When individuals use credit as a safety net, however, risks are *not* transferred to society as with public insurance programs, but stay with the borrower and are only deferred to the future. Social insurance is a forward-looking contract, covering expected risks in the future, whereas borrowing money is a response to economic risks *after* they happen. At its heart, credit markets "privatize" both costs and gains since only the borrower pays for a loan and benefits from it. However, relying on credit is more than the privatization of risks because credit markets do not pool risks among those who pay into a private insurance system, as is the case with private health insurance (Hacker 2004) or private unemployment insurance programs.[17] The financial and economic risks of income loss, for example due to unemployment, still rest with prospective borrowers, even though they can rely on credit markets to compensate for financial shortfalls. Credit markets do not transfer risks in the way social policies do; rather, they *amplify* borrowers' exposures to risks if interest rates change or further income shocks threaten or undermine borrowers' capacities to make regular debt repayments. Whether taking on debt to

---

[16] Informal lending markets such as payday loans are increasingly important in countries like the United States or the United Kingdom (Baradaran 2015; Morduch and Schneider 2017; Servon 2017), but they are less important in other countries such as Denmark or Germany. Payday loans are beyond the scope of this book.

[17] Some companies in the United States such as the Great American Insurance Company offer private supplemental unemployment insurance that charges a risk premium on the basis of the beneficiary's state of residence, industry or sector of work, and current salary in exchange for a share of the pretax salary adjusted for the state's unemployment benefits.

bridge income losses will lead to higher economic risks in the future therefore depends on the economic situation of the borrower. Low-income households are at greater risk of default than high-income ones since they already devote a larger share of their incomes to debt payments.

By contrast, social insurance policies are financed through flat-rate or progressive tax and contribution payments, thereby placing larger fiscal burdens on high-income rather than on low-income earners. Unless events associated with income losses such as unemployment, sickness, or childbirth, are positively correlated with income, social insurance policies and their funding structures are not "risk-adjusted." While social policies aim to free individuals from markets and protect them from negative outcomes, debt *increases* individuals' reliance on the market, further constrains individuals' financial situations, and exposes them to new types of risk. Credit markets operate counter-cyclically and provide easy access to credit only in times of economic growth and to "creditworthy" individuals.

The upshot is that credit is *not* a true substitute for the welfare state nor an insurance – despite observational and functional similarities. Welfare states, in Esping-Andersen's words, "de-commodify" individuals by allowing them to maintain socially acceptable living standards independent of market participation (Esping-Andersen 1990). Credit markets, however, turn this logic upside down by *re-commodifying* individuals. In order to keep up with debt repayments, borrowers depend on stable future income streams. At a more fundamental level, the rise of credit as a private alternative to welfare states reflects and reveals a profound transformation of social rights and social responsibilities and consequential shifts in the allocation of risks and opportunities between individuals in the modern economy.

SUMMARY AND EXPECTATIONS

In this chapter, I offer a new perspective on how credit markets shape political economies and reach into individuals' daily lives. The "social policy theory of everyday borrowing" argues that the interaction of welfare institutions and credit regimes produces and reproduces cross-national variation in patterns of indebtedness that reflects the ways in which households cope with the financial consequences of disrupted employment patterns and life course trajectories. Table 2.3 summarizes the empirical implications of this framework. Each column shows a specific constellation that corresponds to one of the panels in Figure 2.3.

Over the course of this book, I will systematically test the empirical implications outlined in Table 2.3. In Chapter 3, I document the size of the financial shortfalls that arise between, on the one hand, higher expenditures and income losses because of fragmented and disrupted employment patterns and life course trajectories and, on the other hand, weaker and incomplete social policy

TABLE 2.3 *Empirical implications of the argument*

	Relationship between Credit Markets and Welfare States		
	Credit as a Substitute	*Credit as a Complement*	*Credit Suppression*
Welfare State Support	Limited social support across most groups	Segmented welfare state • Strong support for low-income groups • Limited support for high-income groups	Segmented welfare state • Strong support for insiders • Limited support for outsiders
Social Opportunity costs	High	Low	Medium
Structure of Credit Regime	Permissive	Permissive	Restrictive
Patterns of Indebtedness	• Both investment & consumption debt • High indebtedness across most groups	• Focus on investment debt • High indebtedness among high-income groups	• Limited investment & consumption debt • Low indebtedness among most groups

support due to welfare state retrenchment and policy drift. In Chapter 4, I develop a novel empirical measure of credit regimes. This measure highlights the considerable cross-national variation in the degrees of permissiveness and helps us understand how access to credit and patterns of indebtedness differ across and within countries. Chapters 5 and 6 are the two main empirical chapters that study how the structures of credit regimes and welfare states in Denmark, the United States, and Germany shape the degrees to which households go into debt to cope with two different types of financial short-falls. Chapter 5 investigates when and how credit addresses social risks that emerge from disrupted employment patterns, while Chapter 6 focuses on the role of credit as a bounded investment during the life course. In Chapter 7, I turn to the socioeconomic and political consequences of easier access to credit and growing indebtedness on economic insecurity and social policy preferences across welfare regimes.

3

Financial Shortfalls and the Role of Welfare States

> "The times in which we live and work are changing dramatically. The workers of our parents' generation typically had one job, one skill, one career – often with one company that provided health care and a pension [...] Today, workers change jobs, even careers, many times during their lives."
> – George W. Bush, Republican National Convention, 2004

In 2004, President George W. Bush identified what in his view had become one of the dominant sources of anxiety among voters in the United States and other OECD countries – job insecurity. In the Fordist economies of the 1970s, stable and long-term employment was the norm. Today, this no longer holds true for many people. Employment patterns have become more fragmented and disrupted, in part because of shorter but more frequent unemployment spells, temporary jobs with limited, if any, benefits, fluctuating work hours, and job switches with fluctuating earnings. Bush's focus on labor markets, however, glossed over two other crucial factors that contribute to growing economic and financial insecurity and influence people's financial lives. First, fragmentation and disruption have also affected people's life course trajectories, a concept I borrow from sociology to capture individuals' movements between various life stages, from employment to pursuing education and training, to raising children, to planning for retirement and taking care of the elderly (see Brückner and Mayer 2005; Mayer 2009). People temporarily leave their jobs to take care of children, to go to university, or to get more training. Life course events such as divorces or childbirth can strain people's finances (DiPrete 2002). The backdrop is a combination of changing family norms and rising female labor market participation, which led to the breakdown of the old single-breadwinner family model and the rise of dual-earner couples and single parents, as well as changing skill requirements in the modern knowledge economy. The disintegration and fragmentation of employment patterns and life course trajectories affect people differently, creating winners and losers. For some it is a boon: high-skilled workers harness the opportunities of new forms of employment, take time off work to raise a family, and get education and more training. For others, however, the flexibility of modern labor markets, the growing demands for certain skills, or the challenges of balancing work and family obligations are a burden.

The second crucial factor that influences people's financial lives is that fragmented employment patterns and life course trajectories increase the financial burden that individuals and their families have to shoulder because welfare states have often not kept up with the shift from Fordist to post-industrial economies (e.g., Hacker 2019). Social policy programs, ranging from unemployment insurance to childcare support, are key financial pillars that help people to not only address and mitigate labor market risks but also seize social opportunities and promote upward mobility. In some countries, governments have responded to structural changes in the economy by shifting toward social investment policies that target people's employability and focus on education, retraining, and family policies (Thelen 2014). But in other countries, government transfers and social services are at odds with people's employment patterns and life course choices. Retrenchment has been the most visible form of change in welfare states and social policies. But it would be misleading to think of the changing landscape of welfare states only as a story about reduced benefits and stricter eligibility rules. Policymakers have also failed to either adapt existing programs to new realities or introduce new programs to meet changing demands. These processes of "policy drift" are less visible but equally consequential in shifting the financial burden from society onto the shoulders of households.

The mismatch between, on the one hand, higher expenditures and income losses that households have to absorb because of fragmented and disrupted employment patterns and life course trajectories and, on the other hand, weaker and incomplete social policy support due to welfare state retrenchment and policy drift causes severe financial shortfalls in people's daily lives. These shortfalls are crucial to helping us understand why households increasingly go into debt and borrow money in some countries but not in others.

In this chapter, I analyze the financial consequences of changes in labor markets, life course trajectories, and welfare states on individuals and their families by comparing the difference between households' gross and net income volatility as a measure of financial shortfalls. I document financial shortfalls across countries and how they have changed over time, and I map these shortfalls to employment disruptions and life course choices. Empirically, I draw on panel data from Denmark, the United States, and Germany to show how income volatility and financial shortfalls vary across these countries as well as across households within these countries as a function of the cause of income loss.

The Danish welfare state provides the most comprehensive buffering function of all three countries, absorbing large amounts of gross income volatility that the flexible labor market produces. Financial shortfalls have grown mildly, especially since the 2000s, and there is more variation in income volatility across households. The United States, by contrast, has an equally flexible labor market but very limited buffering capacities through the welfare state. Gross and net income volatility have increased nearly in tandem, indicating that more households are affected by financial shortfalls because earnings volatility rose while social policies remained weak and limited. Nearly a quarter of households in 2010 experienced a decline in their net incomes by 25 percent or more. In Germany, the welfare state also absorbs a sizable share of gross income volatility, and it has kept the net share of households with annual income losses of more than 25 percent relatively stable. Unlike in Denmark, however, gross income volatility declined slightly since the mid-2000s, while net income volatility increased during the Hartz reform period of the early 2000s. The growing labor market segmentation into a protected core of long-term employment and an exposed periphery of more precarious employment conditions is at least partially mirrored in lower variation of net income volatility across households.

Even more revealing than the sheer size of financial shortfalls are its sources. In Denmark, income losses due to unemployment or sickness have increased, but the far more important driver of income losses are life course events such as taking time off work to raise a family or to get training and education. This is also true in the United States, where the financial impact of life course choices affects more people and is larger than involuntary employment disruptions. But even those who have full-time jobs have seen their incomes become more volatile over time. In Germany, by contrast, more households experience income losses due to unemployment or sickness rather than life course choices, but much like in Denmark and the United States, the latter is gaining slightly more prominence. In sum, the size of the financial shortfalls and their variation across countries and households are the result of changes in labor markets, life course trajectories, and welfare states.

MEASURING FINANCIAL SHORTFALLS

How can we operationalize and measure the size of financial shortfalls and its variation across countries and households? In this chapter, I focus on the income side of households' financial lives.[1] Specifically, I use income volatility before and after taxes and transfers as a measure of financial shortfalls. Income volatility is an important driver of financial security and economic risks. Disruptions of individuals' employment patterns and life course trajectories make gross incomes – in most cases earnings – more unstable. For example, involuntary job losses, flexible work hours, or taking time off work for parental leave

---

[1] One could complement the income side with data on individuals' expenditures and consumption to get a full picture of both earnings and expenditures, but this is beyond the scope of this chapter.

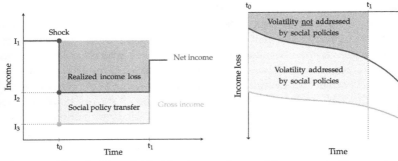

FIGURE 3.1 Stylized model linking income loss and income volatility

Notes: Panel (a) illustrates the extent to which an income shock reduces a person's gross and net income as a function of social policy support in a two-period scenario. Panel (b) shows how individual-level income shocks translate into gross and net income volatility at the country-specific macro level.

and childcare result in volatile incomes. Moreover, changes in family composition such as divorce or childbirth can also increase the instability of *household* incomes. A growing body of work, mostly focused on the United States, has documented substantial increases in the volatility of household incomes since the 1970s and male earnings since the 1990s.[2] Yet we know little about the *composition* of income volatility before and after government transfers as well as its variation across and within countries.[3]

One approach to measure the degree to which welfare states and tax expenditures mitigate financial shocks is to compare fluctuation in *gross* income (i.e., *before* taxes and transfers ["pre-government"]) and *net* income (i.e., *after* taxes and transfers ["post-government"]). Social policies reduce or "soak up" parts of the volatility in gross income, for example by providing income support through unemployment insurance or child benefits.[4] Analytically, the difference between the volatility of gross and net incomes, therefore, reflects the financial shortfall between, on the one hand, households' income and expenditure levels before any kind of financial shock and, on the other hand, the welfare state's financial support through social insurance benefits (e.g., during

---

[2] See, for example, Dahl, DeLeire, and Schwabish (2011); Dynan, Elmendorf, and Sichel (2012); Gorbachev (2011); Gottschalk and Moffitt (2009); Gottschalk et al. (1994); Hacker (2019); Shin and Solon (2011).

[3] An important exception is the cross-national work on income risks, including income inequality and income volatility, by Nichols and Rehm (2014).

[4] The difference between gross and net income is the sum of public transfers minus taxes. In addition to public transfers that smooth out fluctuating incomes, taxes affect the difference between gross and net income volatility if tax rates, tax brackets, or tax reimbursement schedules such as tax credits change. In the US case, tax credits such as the earned income tax credit (EITC) play a large role as part of the "hidden" welfare state (see, for example, Howard 1997).

unemployment or sickness) and social investment benefits (e.g., subsidized childcare and other forms of family support, paid parental leave, or education and training expenditures). Figure 3.1 illustrates this approach. The micro-level perspective of Figure 3.1a decomposes the income trajectory of a person into gross income and net income. That person was employed with income of I_1 and loses her job in t_0. If there were no social policy support, her *gross* income would drop from I_1 to I_3. But since she is able to draw on unemployment benefits, her *net* income only falls to I_2, limiting her realized income loss to the dark shaded area. In other words, the welfare state mitigates the effect of job loss during the period t_0 to t_1 on her net income by providing financial support in the form of unemployment benefits.

For each head of household, I calculate the annual volatility of households' gross and net incomes and aggregate it to the macro level to get a broader picture of households' income fluctuations and the resulting size of the gap at the country level as illustrated in Figure 3.1b. The light shaded area shows how much the welfare state reduces gross income volatility. Social policies typically do not address the full share of fluctuations, leaving households with some residual volatility, indicated by the dark shaded area. In this particular example, net income volatility increases over time due to higher gross income volatility, less comprehensive social policies, or a combination of both. In other words, the dark shaded area is the share of income volatility that is *not* addressed by social policies and therefore constitutes the financial burden that households have to shoulder themselves.

Volatility, measured as the variability in incomes over time, entails both positive and negative movements. It can result from unemployment or sickness, from moving between temporary jobs with lower incomes, or from taking time off from work for education or childcare. There is no clear consensus in the literature on the best way to measure or estimate volatility. Some studies opt for simple and transparent statistics such as the variance and dispersion of earnings, while other studies attempt to isolate transitory income changes from permanent ones using parametric time-series decomposition techniques.[5] These latter models, however, have proven to be very sensitive to modeling choices and the underlying econometric assumptions (see Nichols and Rehm 2014; Shin and Solon 2011). Given my primary interest in comparing trends in net and gross income volatility across and within countries, I opt for a more transparent approach and follow Dynan, Elmendorf, and Sichel (2012) by measuring the volatility of income Y_{it} as the arc percentage change in annual income as $\Delta Y_{it} = 100 \cdot \left(\frac{Y_{it} - Y_{it-1}}{\frac{1}{2}(Y_{it} + Y_{it-1})} \right)$. The arc percentage change is naturally bound between ± 200 and less biased by outliers than simple percentage

[5] For an excellent review of conceptual and measurement issues, see Gottschalk and Moffitt (2009).

changes, which makes it a commonly used measure of income volatility. Note that this measure of income volatility captures both upward and downward volatility. To isolate *downward*, negative volatility, I only consider households that experience income *losses* from one year to another. I follow prior work on income volatility and economic insecurity and focus on households that lose 25 percent or more of their income from one year to another.[6] Using this measure of negative income volatility, I calculate cross-sectional summary measures such as the share of households that experience income losses of at least 25 percent, the average size of these income losses, and the standard deviation using this micro-level volatility measure. While some work has studied the volatility of labor market earnings, I follow more recent studies and take a broader perspective by focusing on the volatility of *household* income. The household is an adequate unit of analysis for my purposes because financial and economic insecurity depends on available household resources. Studying individual-level earnings volatility of a single earner would miss mitigating effects of a second earner in the household.

I estimate income volatility for Denmark, Germany, and the United States using data from Danish full population administrative records, the German Socio-Economic Panel (SOEP), and the Panel Study of Income Dynamics (PSID) in the United States.[7] The Danish administrative records are extremely comprehensive and provide detailed information on all income components. The SOEP and PSID are the longest-running nationally representative surveys of German and US households, respectively, and they are ideal empirical sources for tracking longitudinal changes in households' incomes.[8] While the Danish and German data are available on an annual basis, the PSID switched to a biannual survey in 1997. I harmonize the data sets such that gross and net household incomes follow the same definitions.[9] To capture the working population, the final data sets are a subset of households for which the household head is between sixteen and sixty-five years old. I exclude self-employed individuals and deflate nominal income data into real 2010 local currencies.

One limitation of these data sets is that they only capture annual snapshots. As other work has shown, measuring income volatility from year-to-year can mask variation *during* the year. For example, Morduch and Schneider (2017) followed a sample of American households in their *Financial Diaries* project and recorded on a monthly basis households' earnings, incomes, and borrowing patterns at a more fine-grain level, documenting considerable variability

---

[6] See, for example, Dynan, Elmendorf, and Sichel (2012); Hacker et al. (2014); Morduch and Schneider (2017).

[7] For detailed information about the data sources, please refer to Section A in the Appendix.

[8] On some of the methodological issues associated with the PSID, see Shin and Solon (2011).

[9] Specifically, I draw on the Cross-National Equivalent File (CNEF) for the SOEP and the PSID, which contains harmonized income variables. The Danish administrative records are detailed enough to allow me to replicate the same definition of gross and net income as in the CNEF.

of earnings and incomes within the year. While this level of granularity would be ideal, comparative, long-term panel data at monthly intervals do not exist for most countries. The annual variation documented in the later sections can therefore be taken as a conservative baseline of households' income volatility, bearing in mind that intra-year variability is likely to be higher.

MAPPING FINANCIAL SHORTFALLS

How do disruptions in employment patterns and life course trajectories influence income volatility? To what extent do welfare states mitigate and absorb the financial impact of such disruptions? And how does volatility vary across and within countries? This section translates the stylized model of Figure 3.1 into empirical reality. The panels in Figure 3.2 show the prevalence and extent of income volatility across households in Denmark, the United States, and Germany. Figure 3.2a plots the share of households that experience a decline in gross and net incomes of 25 percent or more from one year to another. The circles show the annual share of households that experience an annual income loss of 25 percent or more in gross income, that is, before taxes and transfers ("pre-government"). The triangles show the annual share of households that experience an annual income loss of 25 percent or more in net income, that is, after taxes and transfers ("post-government"). The lines are fitted trend lines based on locally smoothed polynomials.

Consider first the cross-national variation in households' gross income volatility. Across and within countries, households' gross incomes fluctuate considerably. In Denmark, over 15 percent of all households lose more than a quarter of their gross income annually, with mild increases in the early 1990s, the early 2000s, and again in the aftermath of the financial crisis of 2007–08. Germany follows a similar but more volatile pattern as the share of affected households grew during the 1990s and early 2000s to almost 20 percent, with a slight drop in the late 1990s. Note, however, that the share fell to around 15 percent during the 2000s. The United States, by contrast, stands out as the country where many more households experience significant fluctuations in their incomes. Since the late 1980s, the share of households with annual income drops of more than 25 percent has doubled from around 15 percent to around 30 percent in the aftermath of the financial crisis. Disruptions of employment patterns and life course trajectories drive growing volatility of gross incomes, as I will document in greater detail later in the chapter. These disruptions reflect in part more flexible labor market structures and weaker employment protection, which facilitate higher job turnover rates and more frequent spells of unemployment. But they also reflect individuals' choices about job switches and taking time off work for education or to raise families.

Households are more concerned, however, with how these fluctuations affect their *net* incomes – that is, *after* taxes, tax credits, and government transfers – than the volatility of their gross incomes (mostly earnings). The triangles in Figure 3.2a indicate the share of households that lose 25 percent or more

(a) Share of Households with Income Losses of 25% or More

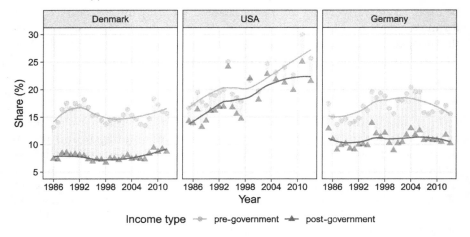

(b) Variation in Income Volatility across Households

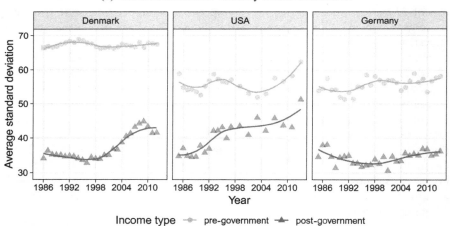

FIGURE 3.2 Income volatility across countries and households

Notes: Panel (a): the circles and triangles show the annual share of households that experience an annual income loss of 25 percent or more in gross and net income, respectively. The shaded vertical bars illustrate the absorbing effect of the welfare state. Panel (b): the circles and triangles show the standard deviation of the average size of the income loss for all households that experience a drop in income of 25 percent or more from one year to another. The lines in both panels are fitted locally smoothed polynomial trend lines. The graphs for the United States and Germany use survey sampling weights; the graphs for Denmark are based on the entire population. *Sources:* PSID (USA), SOEP (Germany), and administrative records (Denmark).

of their *net, post-government* income. Welfare states absorb to varying degrees the effects of such income losses through social consumption and social investment policies. This mitigating effect of the welfare state is captured by the difference between gross and net income volatility, indicated by the vertical shaded bars in Figure 3.2a. In other words, net income volatility is a measure of fluctuations in incomes after taxes and transfers, and it thus reflects the real financial burden households have to shoulder.

Among the three country cases, the Danish welfare state absorbs the largest share of households' income losses. During the 1990s, around 7 percent of households experienced a *net* income loss of 25 percent or more. Since the early 2000s, however, the share of households affected by these significant net income losses has climbed to almost 10 percent. In Germany, around 10 percent of households lost a quarter or more of their net income from one year to another, with a strong, temporary increase in the mid-1990s and the early 2000s. By contrast, households in the United States are considerably worse off. A higher and growing share of households is already exposed to fluctuations in gross incomes, but the welfare state does little to reduce the effect of income losses. The share of households that lose at least a quarter of their *net* income is only slightly smaller compared to gross income volatility data, illustrating the limited absorptive capacity of the US welfare state. As household gross incomes have become more volatile over time, the welfare state has done very little to address income losses.

The averages displayed in Figure 3.2a, however, mask significant differences within countries and across households. Figure 3.2b shows the dispersion of the micro-level volatility of households' gross and net income by calculating the annual cross-sectional standard deviation. Denmark has the largest degree of variation across households' *gross* income volatility among the three cases, which changes only slightly over time. Since the late-1990s, the Danish welfare state has increasingly differentiated across households how much of gross income volatility it addresses, indicated by the growing standard deviation of net income volatility and the shrinking difference between gross and net income volatility. This suggests that some households receive fewer government transfers than others, increasing the variability in net income volatility. In the United States there is less variation in households' gross income volatility compared to the Danish case, but the variation in gross and particularly net income volatility has overall increased. The larger exposure of American households to income shocks is reflected in the growing differentiation by the welfare state. In Germany, by contrast, the variation in both gross and net income volatility across households has only mildly increased since the 2000s, in line with the status-segmenting outcomes associated with the German welfare state (Esping-Andersen 1999; Palier 2010). In Denmark and the United States, the variation in households' *net* income volatility increased markedly, suggesting that their respective welfare states differentiate more and more among groups of people.

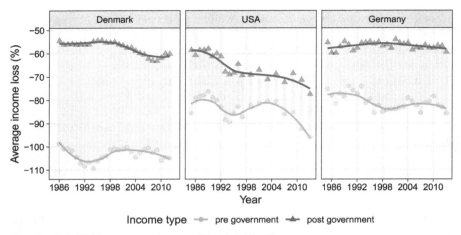

FIGURE 3.3 Welfare states' degree of financial buffer

Notes: The circles and triangles show the average household income loss (negative values), defined as the annual percentage change in income, for all households that experience a more than 25 percent decline in income from one year to another. The lines are fitted locally smoothed polynomials. The vertical shaded bars illustrate the effect of the welfare state. The graphs for the United States and Germany use survey sampling weights; the graphs for Denmark are based on the entire population. *Sources:* PSID (USA), SOEP (Germany), and administrative records (Denmark).

Welfare States as Financial Buffers

How large is the financial burden that these households experience? Figure 3.3 plots the average income loss – again for gross and net income – for all households that experience a decline in income of 25 percent or more from one year to another. As before, the difference in the volatility of gross and net incomes, indicated by the vertical shaded bars, captures the effect of social policies and tax expenditures in reducing gross income volatility. Across the three country cases, Danish households lose by far the largest amount in gross incomes. The economic recession of the early 1990s led to more volatile incomes, peaking at an average loss of around 110 percent, followed by a period of declining volatility.[10] However, gross income volatility has grown since the mid-2000s. In the United States and particularly in Germany, the average gross income loss is smaller than in Denmark, but households in both countries are losing more income annually than in past decades. Since the early 2000s, American households have experienced strong increases in income losses, up from an average of 80 percent to almost 100 percent loss.

The triangles and corresponding lines show the size of households' *net*, post-government income volatility, indicating how much of households' gross income volatility welfare states absorb through government transfers and tax

---

[10] Values can exceed 100% because the measures are based on the arc percentage change, which is bound by ± 200.

expenditures. Complementing the findings of the panels in Figure 3.2, the shaded bars indicate that the Danish welfare state reduces the burden of income volatility the most, followed by the German and American welfare states.

Comparing the three country cases, a few noteworthy trends stand out. The volatility of gross incomes of Danish households has grown slightly in the past decade, while the absorptive capacity of the welfare state has weakened, resulting in growing net income volatility between the late 1990s and the mid-2000s. By contrast, the gross incomes of German households have become more volatile, but the welfare state absorbed these increases and kept net income volatility fairly stable. In the United States, not only does the welfare state address a smaller share of gross income volatility, but its effectiveness has also been declining since the 1990s.[11]

How Employment Disruptions and Life Course Choices Drive Income Volatility

There are two main drivers behind the patterns of income volatility in the three country cases in Figures 3.2 and 3.3. On the one hand, the combination of flexible labor markets and weak employment protection in Denmark and the United States makes gross incomes more volatile compared to Germany, but a more generous welfare state absorbs a larger share of this volatility in Denmark than in the United States. This reflects key institutional differences across the three countries, such as the "flexicurity" model of Denmark and the market-oriented and employment-dependent model (with limited provision of social support) of the United States. On the other hand, income volatility also reflects changes in individuals' life course choices, such as taking time off work for education and training and to raise a family.

In this and the following sections, I only focus on net, post-government income as I examine the degrees to which employment disruptions and life course choices shape income volatility across countries and households. Involuntary disruptions of employment patterns, for example due to unemployment or sickness, cause considerable income losses that, to varying degrees, are mitigated by social insurance policies. But households also make life course choices, such as temporarily taking time off work for education or child-rearing, that similarly result in income losses or come with higher expenses.[12]

I decompose income losses and volatility on the basis of three sources. First, incomes can become volatile because of job switches and fluctuations in work

---

[11] Figure A.3.1 in the Appendix combines Figure 3.2a and Figure 3.3 by weighting the average size of income loss by the share of households experiencing such income loss.

[12] In this chapter, I focus on the volatility of incomes but do not study fluctuations in expenses or consumption. For work on the latter domain, see, for example, Blundell and Pistaferri (2003); Gorbachev (2011); Johnson, Parker, and Souleles (2006).

hours or pay despite regular, consistent employment. Second, volatility can be driven by unexpected, in large part involuntary and temporary employment disruptions such as job loss or sickness. Finally, income losses can be caused by life course choices such as taking time off work for parental leave, sabbaticals, education and training, and other family-related reasons. For the purpose of the analysis that follows, I label these three categories *employment*, *employment disruptions*, and *life course choices*, respectively. Table A.3.1 in the Appendix shows the exact definition of the sources of income volatility for each country. As before, I use the micro-level measure of net income volatility but now split households into their respective source of income loss in a given year, which I sort on the basis of the employment status of the household head. For example, if the household head becomes unemployed in a given year, that household would fall into the *employment disruptions* category in that year. If the household head moved from one job to another in the next year and experienced a decline in earnings, the household would be in the *employment* category for that year.

The panels in Figure 3.4 show how many households are affected by these three sources of income loss as well as the average size of such income losses. As before, the lines in each panel are smoothed trend lines that are less noisy than the underlying data points.

Figure 3.4a shows the share of households whose net income drops by 25 percent or more by income loss category. Consider first households where the household head remains in regular employment. In Denmark and Germany, the share of households whose income drops because of job switches, part-time work, or employment-related earnings fluctuations such as changes in work hours remained relatively stable at around 7 percent and 10 percent, respectively. In the United States, by contrast, the income volatility of households in regular employment doubled from 10 percent in the late-1980s to almost 20 percent in 2010. One explanation for this strong increase in the share of households that are affected by employment-driven income losses is the growth of shorter and fluctuating work hours and more frequent job switches (without unemployment in-between) in the United States (Golden 2015). Second, the share of households experiencing income losses because of involuntary employment disruptions, including unemployment and sickness, has almost doubled in Denmark and the United States since the late-1980s, rising to 20 percent and 40 percent, respectively. In Germany, by contrast, the number of households affected by these types of income losses has slightly declined. Finally, life course choices such as taking time off work for education and child-related reasons affect the largest share of households in Denmark and the United States, outpacing the other two categories. Life course choices that result in income losses affect more households in all three countries since the late 1980s, and have grown even stronger than income losses caused by fragmented employment patterns in Germany and the United States.

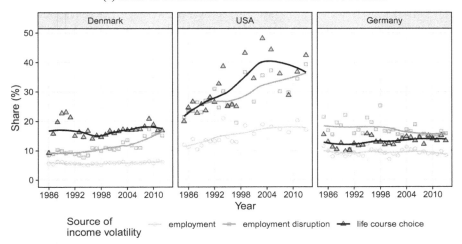

(a) Share of Households with Income Loss of 25% or More

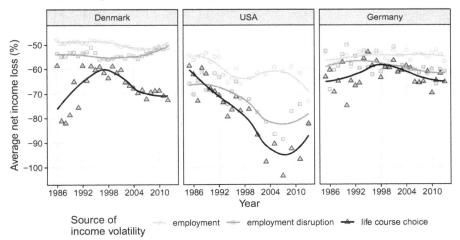

(b) Average Income Loss Among Households with Income Loss of 25% or More

FIGURE 3.4 Employment disruption, life course choices, and net income volatility

Notes: Panel (a): the shapes show the annual share of households that experience an annual income loss of 25 percent or more for different sources of income loss. Panel (b): the shapes show the average household income loss (negative values), defined as the annual percentage change in income for all households that experience a drop in income of 25 percent or more from one year to another for different sources of income loss. The lines in both panels are fitted locally smoothed polynomials. *Employment disruptions* include unemployment, sickness, and disability. *Life course choices* include education (student and retraining), various forms of leaves, and "homemaking." The employment status of the household is based on the status of the household head. For details, see Table A.3.1 in the Appendix. Note that mini and midi jobs in Germany, which are job categories with limited work hours and benefits introduced as part of a labor market reform, are classified as *employment disruptions*. The graphs for the United States and Germany use survey sampling weights; the graphs for Denmark are based on the entire population. *Sources:* PSID (USA), SOEP (Germany), and administrative records (Denmark).

Employment disruptions and life course choices impose considerable financial burdens on households. Figure 3.4b shows the average size of the financial burden for households that experience one of the three sources of income loss. Life course choices in all three countries place the largest costs on households, followed by involuntary employment disruption and employment-related losses. Income losses caused by life course choices have grown since the late 1990s from around 60 percent to around 70 percent for Danish households and to around 65 percent for German households – after a period of declining losses in the 1990s. Even more strikingly, while American households lost around 60 percent of their incomes to life course choices in the late 1980s, this number increased to almost 100 percent by the mid-2000s. To put these numbers into context, this amounts to a hypothetical decline of an annual income from $60,000 to $20,000. In Denmark and Germany, income losses related to employment fluctuations have remained fairly stable, while losses caused by involuntary employment disruptions have slightly declined in Denmark and slightly increased in Germany. By contrast, employment-related income volatility (e.g., shorter or fluctuating work hours and more frequent job switches) and involuntary employment disruptions (e.g., unemployment or sickness leave) have created significant financial burdens for American households since the late 1980s.

In sum, the panels in Figure 3.4 suggest that life course choices are even more financially consequential than employment disruptions at both the macro level (i.e., they affect a large share of households) and the micro level (i.e., households' financial burdens from income losses have grown considerably). In Denmark and particularly in the United States, more households experience larger income losses. In Germany, involuntary income losses, largely caused by unemployment, are more important in terms of both the numbers of affected households and (at least during the 2000s) the size of the financial burden.[13] In the following section, I turn to the drivers behind the variation in income volatility and financial shortfalls across and within countries, focusing on Denmark, the United States, and Germany.

THE DRIVERS BEHIND SHORTFALLS: CHANGING LABOR MARKETS, LIFE COURSE TRAJECTORIES, AND WELFARE STATES

The similarities between janitors who work for many large companies today and a couple of decades ago often go no further than the title of their job and the inflation-adjusted hourly wage. For Gail Evans, a janitor in the 1980s at Kodak in Rochester, New York, the inflation-adjusted hourly pay was about the same as Marta Ramos's, who in 2017 worked as a janitor at Apple in

---

[13] Figure A.3.2 in the Appendix combines both panels by weighting the average size of income loss by the share of households experiencing such income loss.

Cupertino, California.[14] But this is where the similarities end. Gail Evans was a full-time employee for Kodak, with over four weeks of paid vacation per year, tuition assistance for part-time college, and bonus pay. Even when the facility she worked in was shut down, Kodak retrained her to cut film. Contrast this to Marta Ramos, the janitor at Apple, who was hired by Apple as a contractor with essentially no benefits. She has no paid vacation days and does not take any unpaid days off because she needs her wage income. Part-time educational opportunities, retraining, or in-house promotions are not available to Marta. By emphasizing employer-based benefits rather than focusing on the public provision of social services as in many other OECD countries, the United States stands out. From the financial perspective of households, it is the combination of changes in labor markets and the nature of work as well as retrenchment and policy drift in the social policy domain that drive economic instability and financial insecurity.

Labor Markets and Social Insurance Policies

The transformation of Fordist production regimes into post-industrial economies made many people's working lives and the structure of their employment patterns more flexible, less predictable, and more prone to disruption. Three big trends contribute to employment instability. First, the decline of manufacturing and the rise of the service industry helped pave the way toward modern economies. Manufacturing had provided relatively stable jobs for low-skilled, blue-collar workers. Yet new jobs for low-skilled workers in the service sector are often poorly paid and tend to be less stable (Wren 2013). The growth of the service sector went along with a decline of several unions' powers to negotiate traditional job arrangements (Ahlquist 2017; Rosenfeld 2014). Overall, the workplace has become increasingly "fissured" (Weil 2014) as firms outsource larger shares of their production and construct extensive networks of subcontracting and franchising that allow them to streamline operations and cut costs, in particular labor costs.

Second, as international trade is gluing economies together, firms face growing foreign competition and pressure to compete for prices and flexibility. Downsizing and cutting wages and work hours were the primary tools to lower labor costs, but technological change, most notably automation, provided firms with new opportunities to demand more flexibility from their workers or replace them (Autor and Dorn 2013). How much countries are affected by these trends, however, depends on how deeply they are integrated into global markets (Autor, Dorn, and Hanson 2013; Feenstra 2010). Under pressure from competitive markets, employers' preferences, and partisan ideology, policymakers across the advanced economies began to deregulate labor

---

[14] See Neil Irwin, "To Understand Rising Inequality, Consider the Janitors at Two Top Companies, Then and Now," *New York Times*, September 3, 2017.

markets in an attempt to make them more flexible and allow for faster labor turnover (Palier and Thelen 2010). In countries where labor markets were already flexible, skill-based wage inequality further amplified the difference between high-skilled workers seizing high-quality jobs and low-skilled workers ending up in low-quality jobs, often with limited social benefits. By contrast, in countries with more regulated labor markets, policymakers began to segment labor markets into a protected core of "insiders" in standard, long-term employment and a growing, exposed periphery of "outsiders" in non-standard employment and flexible or temporary jobs with fixed-term contracts (DiPrete et al. 2006; Emmenegger et al. 2012; Rueda 2007).

Finally, the transition from the stakeholder to the shareholder model of corporate governance shifted the power from managers to shareholders, and the focus from long-term interests such as stable firm–worker relationships to short-term considerations such as stock prices (Gospel and Pendleton 2005).

Together, these trends have reduced employment stability, increased labor markets' volatility and selectivity, and made movements into and out of employment more frequent and protracted (Schmid 2002). For many people, non-standard work – including temporary work, contract work, and part-time employment – as well as shorter and fluctuating work hours, have become the new reality.

Disrupted Employment Patterns

The structure of national labor markets, in particular employees' tenure rates, labor market turnover, and employment protection, shapes the degrees of employment disruptions. More people began to experience more frequent transitions in and out of employment, resulting in shorter spells of unemployment (Kalleberg 2009; Schmid 2002). The flexibility demanded in many jobs leads to further disruptions in incomes, for example because job tenure rates have declined and individuals switch jobs more frequently or because work schedules are less predictable and working hours more volatile. This is particularly pronounced in the United States but also increasingly common in other European countries. Employment tenure rates and labor market fluidity have diverged considerably between Germany, where long-term employment rose during the late 1990s and 2000s, and Denmark and the United States, where employment stability declined. The share of German employees who had been working for their current employer for ten years or longer had climbed from 35% in 1995 to almost 45% in the mid-2000s. By contrast, in Denmark that number has fallen over the same period from 33 percent to around 25%, while long-term employment in the United States stagnated at around 27%. Low rates of long-term employment are often mirrored in higher rates of labor turnover, or churning rates, among those with tenure of less than one year. Labor mobility is much higher in Denmark and the United States, where in 2011 around 20 percent of workers lost their jobs within one year, compared to Germany, where only 15% of workers remained in their job for less than a year. Skill levels often amplify these trends. In Denmark and Germany, high-skilled people fare much better than low-skilled people, but the skill divergence is especially pronounced in Germany (OECD 2013, ch. 3).

Labor market fluctuation rates, a measure of short-term labor market mobility, show that Germany has relatively low and steady levels of turnover of around 30%. In Denmark, turnover was already over 40% in the early 1990s and increased to over 50% by the late 2000s (Rhein 2010).[15] The divergence in employment stability reflects, in part, the more flexible and deregulated labor markets (with weak employment protection) of Denmark and the United States. This weak employment protection affects in particular temporary workers. In the United States, hiring and firing at will makes the labor market extremely flexible and the distinction between regular and temporary employment less relevant, since employers can easily sack employees. In Germany, differences and changes in employment protection reflect the growing labor market segmentation and dualization into protected insiders and exposed outsiders.

But high labor market fluidity can also lead to shorter unemployment spells because people are more likely to find new jobs. During the past few decades, the nature of unemployment, one of the biggest economic and financial risks for employees, also changed. Under Fordism, unemployment was considered a cyclical response to swings in the business cycle. Workers lost their jobs when business was slow but got rehired or found new jobs when production took off again. With the economic crisis of the 1970s, however, unemployment became a persistent, long-term structural problem rather than a temporary phenomenon. While cyclical unemployment temporarily disrupted employment and earnings, social insurance programs such as unemployment benefits mitigated such interruptions. Yet structural unemployment is much harder to address with existing programs, and overcoming it might require additional steps such as retraining and relocation. The German labor market, more than any other, was and to a certain degree still is affected by long-term unemployment, whereas the more flexible labor markets of Denmark and the United States tend to move unemployed workers into new employment at much higher rates, as shown in Figure 3.5. The United States stands out with a high fraction of unemployed individuals experiencing very short unemployment spells. During the 1980s and 1990s, an average of 30 percent of spells lasted between one and three months. While unemployment has always been a short-term phenomenon, *long-term* unemployment has become a more widespread problem in the aftermath of the financial crisis. In Germany, by contrast, the share

---

[15] Rhein (2010) calculates the labor market fluctuation rate as the sum of the number of newly recruited employees who have been employed at their establishment for less than a year and the number of employees who have left the establishment where they were employed a year before in the course of the last twelve months, divided by the average total number of employees in a given year.

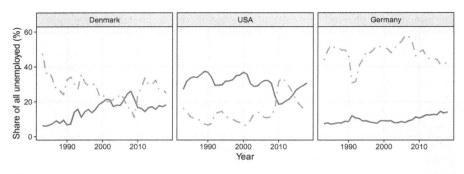

Duration of unemployment — less than 3 months · — 1 year and more

FIGURE 3.5 Share of unemployed individuals by duration of unemployment
Notes: Share of unemployed individuals (ages 25–54) who experience unemployment spells of less than six months, six months to less than twelve months, or more than one year. It is expressed as a share of the total unemployed population. Self-employed individuals are excluded. *Source*: OECD Labor Force Statistics. 2020.

of long-term unemployed individuals has almost doubled during the 1990s and early 2000s, and the share of shorter-term spells is also growing. In the mid-2000s, more than half of all unemployed people in Germany were long-term unemployed (i.e., unemployed for more than one year). In Denmark, unemployed individuals experience increasingly shorter spells, particularly since the mid-1990s. By the late 2000s, the distribution of unemployment spells had begun to resemble the distribution of the United States. The German case shows that strong employment protection discourages not only firing but also hiring, thus amplifying division between protected insiders with long-term job tenures and exposed outsiders who find it much harder to (re-)enter the labor market.

The Decline of Social Insurance Policies
Welfare states and social insurance programs are the most important sources of financial support during unemployment or sickness. These policies are often referred to as "social consumption policies" because their main goal is to help individuals maintain their incomes. As we saw earlier in this chapter, welfare states have different capacities to address and mitigate economic and financial risks. Esping-Andersen's typology of welfare regimes based on shared institutional complementarities and degrees of "de-commodification" remains one of the most influential frameworks for understanding the logic of different social policy designs and their durability through time (Esping-Andersen 1990, 1999).[16] Liberal welfare regimes such as the United States or the United Kingdom share a very narrow definition of eligibility and a limited

---

[16] For more recent debates about this typology, see, for example, Emmenegger et al. (2015) and the other contributions in the *Journal of European Social Policy*'s same special issue.

definition of "social risk," and both countries emphasize private market-based solutions over publicly provided benefits. They offer modest means-tested benefits and targeted social assistance and rely on a combination of public and private insurance schemes that are often "hidden" in various de facto welfare programs such as the Earned Income Tax Credit in the United States and other subsidized programs (Howard 1997, Mettler 2011). By contrast, Social Democratic welfare regimes, often associated with the Nordic countries, are based on the logic of universalism and egalitarianism in which eligibility is determined by citizenship. Most risks are socialized and addressed through generous benefits, while other social policies such as active labor market policies aim to increase the employability of individuals. The third group in this typology consists of Conservative welfare regimes, typically found in continental Europe. These are characterized by status segmentation that privileges long-term employees and civil servants, as well as familialism that privileges the single (often male) breadwinner model, in which parents – in most cases women – are responsible for childcare. These regimes discourage private markets from providing welfare, although some private solutions, for example in the domain of pensions, have made inroads due to fiscal pressures. Unlike Social Democratic regimes, the Conservative welfare regimes manage employment passively through generous unemployment insurance and early retirement schemes (Palier 2010).

Social consumption policies firmly rest on a clear separation of life phases, namely childhood, education, employment, and retirement, a single-breadwinner model with separate roles for men and women within the nuclear family, and uninterrupted careers of full-time work. But with employment stability crumbling, the nature of jobs changing, and non-standard forms of work on the rise, the reach and the adequacy of traditional income-maintaining social consumption policies have been called into question. In many countries, welfare states are increasingly at odds with new employment patterns in the post-industrial economy. The reasons for this mismatch are twofold. First, deliberate cuts and retrenchment of benefit amounts and duration periods have lowered levels of financial support, while tighter eligibility criteria exclude a growing share of individuals who in the past were dependent on welfare benefits (Hemerijck 2013). Individuals in non-standard forms of employment, with fewer and fluctuating work hours and more frequent job switches, can more easily fall through the cracks of the safety net if they do not meet these eligibility criteria. Means-tested programs, already more common in liberal market economies, have grown in other welfare states as well, for example in Germany where earnings-related unemployment benefits were replaced with means-tested flat-rate benefits in 2005. These restrictions made more individuals ineligible for benefits, which further weakened their financial situations.

Second, policymakers have often failed to adapt existing programs to changing circumstances, leading to policy drift and a growing mismatch between welfare programs and employment realities (Hacker 2004; Thelen 2004).

Many OECD countries have scaled back social consumption policies and have instead begun to focus on social investment policies. As I will explain in more detail in the next section, these are future-oriented supply-side policies that aim to increase productivity by investing in education, active labor market programs that emphasize retraining and employability, and family policies that provide financial support for periods of leave and childcare.[17] The Nordic countries, in particular Denmark, have devoted fewer resources toward unemployment insurance and more toward active labor markets policies (ALMP) in the 2010s than two decades before. The continental welfare states such as Germany or the Netherlands have changed much less and still emphasize passive unemployment support, while liberal welfare states like the United States and the United Kingdom have changed little over time and spend less on both active and passive policies.

The combination of disrupted work patterns and rising employment instability on the one hand and declining scope and breadth of social policy programs on the other leads to incomplete financial support from the welfare state. In some cases, new types of risks such as fluctuating earnings or job switches with earnings losses have emerged that are not addressed by social policies at all.

Life Course Trajectories and Social Investment Policies

As employment patterns have become more disrupted since the late 1970s, a second trend has been underway. The life course trajectories of individuals and their families also became less stable and orderly and more flexible and fragmented (Brückner and Mayer 2005; Mayer 2009). New forms of life course trajectories are the result of choices about family structures, whether to take time off from work to raise a family or take a sabbatical, whether to get more education and further training or to move from one job to another. Female employment rates have gone up in many countries during the past four decades, often associated with more jobs in the public sector (for example in the Nordics) or in the low-skilled or part-time service sector (for example in Germany) (Iversen and Rosenbluth 2010). Family arrangements are more varied, including dual-earner couples, families with one full-time and one part-time earner, and single-parent households.

The disintegration of life course trajectories often comes with significant financial costs. Switching jobs, family obligations, and periods of leave expose households to earnings volatility, temporary income losses, and higher expenditures. Childcare or educational programs, for example, are expensive – without the help of public in-cash or in-kind support, households themselves shoulder most of the financial burden. For example, in the United States and

---

[17] On the distinction between social consumption and social investment policies see, for example, Ansell and Gingrich (2015), Morel, Palier, and Palme (2012), and the contributions in Beramendi et al. (2015).

United Kingdom, childcare costs for single parents account for 53 percent and 42 percent of their net incomes, respectively, whereas in Denmark and Sweden the costs are less than 4 percent, in large part because municipalities are legally obliged to offer publicly subsidized childcare for young children (OECD 2016, p. 29). While the growth in female employment has reduced income volatility for dual-earner married couples, having two sources of income no longer provides families with the same financial buffers as it once did. Instead, many families *depend* on dual incomes to pay for increased living costs and expenses (Warren and Tyagi 2003).

For some groups, the transformation of life course trajectories poses new social risks (Bonoli and Natali 2012; Taylor-Gooby 2004). Low-skilled or otherwise economically disadvantaged people can easily fall through the cracks of the flexible labor market and end up in non-standard jobs with limited or no benefits. For others, however, it opens up new opportunities. Highly skilled people, for example, are better equipped to harness opportunities in the modern economy and can move from job to job, knowing that their career trajectory is much more likely to yield higher incomes in the future. Taking time off work to take care of children or get more education and training is an investment in human capital that is likely to pay off in the future even though it comes with financial costs in the present. To be sure, even highly skilled individuals face economic and financial risks in the post-industrial economy, but the skill premium puts them in a much better position compared with low-skilled individuals (Autor, Levy, and Murnane 2003).

Whether life course choices result in another layer of social risk or translate into social opportunity, investment, and upward mobility depends on the size of the opportunity costs, which is largely shaped by the structure of existing social policies. Taking time off work not only reduces earnings and incomes – sometimes all the way to zero – but also comes with potentially large opportunity costs such as foregone earnings, interrupted pension contributions, and disrupted work history that can make individuals ineligible for social insurance programs. For single parents, opting out of the workforce can simply be impossible. Unless public policies reduce these opportunity costs, for example through job protection, free or subsidized childcare, or other forms of financial support, certain life course choices will be limited to households with the requisite skills, jobs, and assets. Others may not even consider them.

The choice of having children also comes with important financial considerations and can lead to income losses and larger financial burdens.[18] In the male-breadwinner model, women typically provide unpaid childcare services by staying at home with their children (Esping-Andersen 1999, ch. 4). With more women now working full-time, this option has become less attractive or feasible for many families, who opt to take care of their children by temporarily

---

[18] On the various financial and economic costs of parenthood see, among others, Adda, Dustmann, and Stevens (2017); Blau and Kahn (2017); Goldin (2014); Olivetti and Petrongolo (2016).

taking time off work, sending them to daycare, pre-school, and kindergarten, or drawing on informal networks of relatives, friends, or community centers. The first two options, however, can incur high opportunity costs and therefore exclude some families from considering these options. Families may have to cope with income losses when parents take time off work for parental leave. How generous welfare states or employers are with regard to financial support during periods of leave determines the size of the income loss and the overall financial burden. If parents decide to send their children to care facilities, the financial burden is a function of the cost of childcare services, which similarly varies by how much these services are publicly subsidized. Taking time off work or financing childcare is expensive when publicly subsidized parental leave schemes or childcare programs are lacking, or when employment regulations do not mandate job-protected parental leaves (paid or unpaid). Only if families consider the opportunity costs worthwhile – for example if neither partner wants to give up their career or because the family depends on two sources of income – will they choose to accept income losses.

Some OECD countries have responded to structural changes in life course trajectories by adapting their social policy toolkits and expanding social investment policies that aim to promote education, strengthen family policies, and bolster active labor market policies. Despite some changes, social investment policies often provide incomplete financial support or legal protection throughout individuals' life course trajectories.

Fragmented Life Course Trajectories
Here I focus on changing family and career structures as important drivers behind the fragmentation of life course trajectories. The increase in women's labor force participation and the breakdown of stable nuclear family structures – often characterized by single-breadwinner models – and the subsequent rise of more diverse family structures (e.g., single-parent households and dual-earner couples (Blossfeld and Drobniéc 2001; Goldin 2006; Lewis 2001)) have created new financial constraints and demands on families, for example due to childcare arrangements and couples' career choices.

The female employment rate had already reached 55 percent in Denmark in 1967, but women did not reach this percentage until 1978 in the UK and 1998 in Germany (Bonoli 2013, p. 115). The gap between male and female employment has shrunk since the 1970s but began to level out in Denmark and Germany in the 2000s. Women in Denmark and other Nordic countries entered the labor market much earlier than in the rest of the OECD. But even Germany, with its more family-oriented society, and the United States have both experienced considerable increases in women's share in the labor market. German unification led to an aggregate increase in female labor market participation since more women in East Germany had already been employed. The rise of dual-earner couples and single-earner households has several downstream consequences: the type of households that children are born into; demand for childcare; and deciding whether one partner should

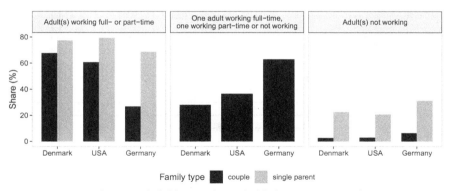

FIGURE 3.6 Distribution of children in households by parents' employment status in 2018

Notes: Children under the age of fourteen living in couple-parent households. Part-time employment is defined as less than thirty hours per week of regular weekly hours in the main job, and full-time employment as thirty or more hours per week of regular weekly hours in the main job. The US data are for children under 17 and do not distinguish between part-time and full-time work. *Sources*: OECD Family Database. 2020 (Table LMF1.1).

take time off work to raise children. Despite overall increases in women's labor force participation, family arrangements still differ across countries. Figure 3.6 shows the distribution of children in couple and single-parent households by their parents' employment status in 2018. Around one-quarter of children in Germany grew up in couple households in which both parents worked full-time, while that share is 61% and 68% in the United States and Denmark, respectively. It is more common in Germany for one partner to work part-time or not at all (63% of couples). In both Denmark and the United States, nearly 80% of single parents work full- or part-time. These numbers in part reflect different social policy environments. In Denmark, subsidized childcare allows single parents to work, whereas in the United States the absence or prohibitively high costs of childcare often leave single parents no choice but to work full-time. By contrast, 31% of single parents were not working at all in Germany in 2018, compared to 22% in Denmark and 20% in the United States (OECD 2020*a*).

These differences are related to and have consequences for the provision and costs of childcare arrangements. The panels in Figure 3.7 show cross-national variation in total public expenditures on family policies and the use and cost of childcare. Denmark has the highest level of public expenditures on family policies as a share of GDP of all three case countries at 3.5% compared to 3% and 1.1% for the United States and Germany in 2015, respectively. Denmark's welfare state provides child-related cash transfers to families with children, public spending on services for families with children, and other financial support for families. Germany and Denmark spend over three times more than the United States on families. Both countries have also increased their spending share over the past decade, whereas the share in the United States has fallen (Figure 3.7a).

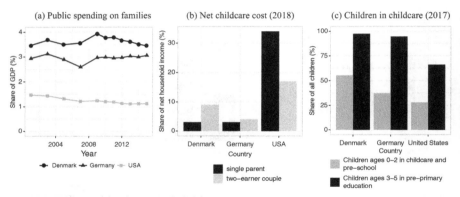

FIGURE 3.7 Family policies and childcare costs

Notes: Panel (a): public spending for families includes, for example, child payments and allowances, parental leave benefits, and childcare support. Panel (b): share of children of either ages 0–2 enrolled in formal childcare and pre-school and ages 3–5 enrolled in pre-primary education or primary school. Data on children ages 0–2 enrolled in formal childcare and pre-school in the United States are from 2011. Panel (c): Net childcare costs for parents using full-time center-based childcare. Calculations are for couples and single parents with two children aged 2 and 3 and assume full-time work for all parents. For couples, the parents earns 100% and 67% of the average wage, respectively. For single parents, the adult earns 67% of the average wage. *Sources*: Panels (a) and (c): OECD Family Database 2020. Panel (b): OECD Social and Welfare Statistic. 2020.

Higher public spending and more affordable childcare are part of the reasons why enrollment in formal childcare is much higher in Denmark and, more recently, in Germany compared to the United States. American families shoulder a much higher financial burden for childcare. On average, the percentage of net household incomes spent on childcare in the United States is 17% for two-earner couples and 34% for single parents. The picture looks quite different in Germany and Denmark, where families spend 10% or less on childcare. Unlike in the United States, single parents are financially more protected and spend less on childcare than couples (Figure 3.7b). These spending differences have consequences for the use of childcare. Figure 3.7c shows that 55% of all children under two years old and nearly all children between 3 and 5 years old in Denmark are in childcare, reflecting that country's large share of dual-earner couples. In Germany, enrollment rates of 0- to 2-year-old children have more than tripled from 10% in the mid-2000s to 37% in 2017. But with only 22% of children growing up in dual-earner households, it is not surprising that enrollment rates are lower compared to Denmark. The differences between Denmark and the United States, however, are more telling. With similar shares of two-earner couples with children, affordability plays a key role in access to childcare.

The traditional sequence of life stages – from education to employment to retirement – has turned into fragmented and non-standard life course trajectories. These new trajectories are varied, whereby some individuals access more education and training after periods of work, some leave employment temporarily to take care of children and elderly family members or take sabbaticals, others frequently change jobs and occupations later on in life, and some interrupt their work for longer periods of family and leisure time. This fragmentation increases families' financial burdens. First, expenditures for childcare and education have grown over time, adding additional costs to households' finances. For example, rising college tuition fees in the United States (and, more recently, in the United Kingdom) led to a near tripling of its outstanding student loan debt from $364bn in 2004 to $966bn in 2012 (Eaton et al. 2016). Second, individuals lose incomes and forgo earnings during periods of leave. They also experience much higher income volatility as they move from one job to another, often with less pay than the previous job. Finally, these interruptions in employment history can make some individuals ineligible for social insurance programs such as unemployment benefits or pension benefits later in life.

For many households with a high proportion of fixed expenditures such as spending on housing, transportation, and food, there is little room for income fluctuations and outright losses, for example when one spouse leaves the labor market. Social policies absorb only some, if any, of the financial consequences of more flexible and disrupted life course trajectories such as high (and often rising) costs for childcare, income losses during periods of leave from work, and earning fluctuations due to job switches.

The Turn to Social Investment Policies

In contrast to passive social consumption policies, which aim to maintain income and labor market status through government transfers, social investment policies are future-oriented and focus on families, education, and active labor market policies as discussed earlier. These policies typically seek to improve individuals' employability and promote investment in human capital. For example, free or subsidized childcare allows parents to reconcile family and work obligations, which has been shown to positively influence child development and school performance later on, especially for disadvantaged children (Esping-Andersen 2009; Olivetti and Petrongolo 2017). Paid and job-protected parental leave improves job continuity for women and increases the rate of return to full-time employment after childbirth. Yet these employment effects only apply to short-term leave, as longer periods of leave can negatively influence women's earnings, employment, and career advancement (Baker and Milligan 2008; Kluve and Tamm 2013; Rossin-Slater 2017). Support for education and training equips workers with new skills, while activation policies with retraining elements help unemployed individuals match their skill sets to new job opportunities.

Here I focus on family policies, including childcare programs and parental leave policies, as well as policies that facilitate transitions between different life

(a) Preferred Funder for Childcare

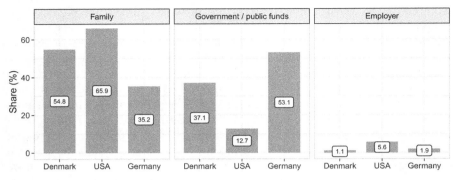

(b) Preferred Funder for Paid Leave after Childbirth

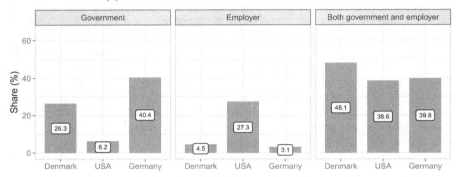

FIGURE 3.8 Preferences for funding of childcare and paid parental leave in 2012
Notes: Panel (a): question: "Who do you think should primarily cover the costs of childcare for children under school age?" Panel (b): Question: "Consider a couple who both work full-time and now have a newborn child. One of them stops working for some time to care for their child. Who should pay for this leave?" Weighted survey responses. *Source*: International Social Survey Programme (ISSP) 2012. Family and Changing Gender Roles IV.

course stages. In light of changing life course trajectories and more dual-career households, financial support for families and more flexible work arrangements have become important political issues in almost all OECD countries. Yet perceptions about the role of the government in funding various programs and corresponding political demands differ across countries. In 2012, almost two-thirds of Americans said that families should primarily cover the costs for childcare, whereas only 13 percent see it as the responsibility of the government (Figure 3.8a). In Germany, by contrast, over half of all respondents stated that cost should be covered by the public purse. Danes occupy a middle position, with more than half seeing the family and more than a third the government as the bearer of costs. Employers play a negligible role in Denmark and Germany and a higher but still small role in the United States. Americans have much stronger preferences for employer-based funding of the costs for paid leave from work for families with newborn children than Germans and, to a lesser degree, Danes, who both prefer the government to assume more financial responsibility for paid leave. Still, almost half of Americans and around 40% of Danes and Germans say it should be a funding mix between the government and employers (Figure 3.8b).

The cross-national variation in family policy design mirrors at least partly the different attitudes among the people in the three country cases. Denmark has a much stronger focus on publicly funded childcare and leave policies, whereas the United States puts a much greater burden on employers but mostly on families themselves. In Germany, norms and policies have only recently changed from a family-based model with very little government interference to more public support for childcare and parental leave. Governments have responded to changing family arrangements by instituting family policies such as providing subsidies for childcare, establishing public childcare facilities, and offering paid parental leave, but many families still struggle financially with income losses and high expenditures. For example, data from the ISSP (2012) show that over half of Germans and almost one-third of Danes agree or strongly agree that children are a financial burden on their parents.[19]

The financial support from welfare states strongly influences how much income individuals lose when they take time off work or how large family- or education-related expenditures will be. Consider two extreme cases: on one end is Denmark, where paid maternity leave is available to all women and the financial support ranges from 100% of prior earnings for public employees and those in jobs in which collective labor agreements stipulate full earning replacements, to income-dependent maternity leave payments similar to unemployment benefits. On the other end is the United States, where publicly financed parental leave is almost non-existent. There is no federal paid parental leave policy in the United States. Some states have introduced paid family leave policies that vary in their duration and replacement rates or offer partial wage-replacement benefits for pregnant women under "temporary disability" insurance programs.[20] Only around one-fourth of private employers in the United States offer some form of paid parental leave (Kaiser Family Foundation 2020). If parents decide to leave work temporarily, it will often be unpaid. The financial costs and the legal protection of employment during and after leave periods depend to a great extent on the social policy framework.

The contrast between family leave policies in the United States and Denmark is illuminating. American families face much larger financial shortfalls than

---

[19] International Social Survey Programme (ISSP) 2012 Family and Changing Gender Roles IV. Question: "To what extent do you agree or disagree with the following question: Children are a financial burden on their parents." Weighted survey shares.

[20] Currently, California, Connecticut, Massachusetts, New Jersey, New York, Oregon, Rhode Island, Washington, and the District of Columbia have state-mandated paid leave plans in place, funded through employer and/or employee payroll contributions.

Danish families because *publicly* financed paid leave policies, especially at the national level, are virtually non-existent in the United States. For low-income families, taking time off to take care of children becomes prohibitively expensive and results in very high opportunity costs, both financially and because in many cases employees are ineligible for unpaid leave. Despite the Family and Medical Leave Act (FMLA), which allows families with newborn children or family members with serious medical conditions to take unpaid job-protected leave, around 40 percent of workers are ineligible for family leave because their employment history is too short or the FMLA does not apply to their employer (Jorgensen and Appelbaum 2014). The lack of public financial support exposes families to difficult choices between their careers and their caregiving responsibilities. Estimates suggest that about 45 percent of FMLA-eligible employees do not take leave because they could not afford unpaid leave, and about a third of them do not take the full leave period because of lost wages (Department of Labor 2014). Middle- and high-income families, on the other hand, often rely on two incomes and work in jobs that grant periods of leave (though often unpaid), thus reducing the opportunity costs of parental leave. Yet they, too, might face a large financial burden because support from the welfare state is incomplete or lacking. Increasingly, parents turn to credit markets and borrow money to compensate for income losses and cover child-related expenditures as I will show in Chapter 6. For Danish families, by contrast, the opportunity costs of taking parental leave are low, regardless of income, because the country's comprehensive welfare and labor market regime provides more generous leave compensation and employment protection.[21]

Welfare states and their support for families have changed considerably during the past decades. Before modern welfare states were created, the family itself was the most important source of protection against economic risks. As welfare states grew, social programs "de-commodified" individuals from the labor market by providing income support independent of market participation (Esping-Andersen 1990). But these social programs also made them less dependent on family structures for economic support. With increasingly fragmented employment patterns and life course trajectories, individuals and families incur financial shortfalls because support from the welfare state is incomplete. But the family, once a source of stability and economic protection, is increasingly unable to fulfill these functions. There are many more dual-earner households that depend on two sources of income out of financial necessity rather than economic luxury (Hacker 2019; Warren and Tyagi 2003). Households increasingly manage their growing financial burdens by taking on debt and borrowing money to pay for basic social services. This is the focus of the remainder of this book.

---

[21] The size of the shortfall still varies across households because government transfers are, in many cases, income-dependent.

DISCUSSION

In this chapter, I document the consequences of changing labor markets, life course trajectories, and welfare states on households' financial lives. The fragmented and disrupted employment patterns and life course trajectories lead to income volatility and income losses due to unemployment, fluctuating work hours, non-standard employment contracts, and time off work as well as higher expenditures for childcare, education, and housing. In many cases, welfare states are at odds with new financial demands, thereby shifting the financial burden onto the shoulders of households. The empirical evidence presented in this chapter shows sizable differences in households' financial shortfalls among the three country cases, measured as the difference in gross and net income volatility. Denmark and the United States both have flexible labor markets and considerable volatility of gross incomes, but fewer precarious types of jobs and a more comprehensive welfare state make net incomes less volatile in Denmark than in the United States. In 2013, around 9% of Danish households and 10% of German households experienced a net income loss of 25% or more, compared with 22% in the United States.

What is even more revealing is the degree to which employment disruptions and life course choices drive income volatility. A larger share of households in both Denmark and the United States experience income volatility because of life course choices – such as taking time off work to raise a family, get an education, or other forms of leave – rather than unemployment or sickness. This is not the case among German households. These fragmented employment patterns and segmented life course trajectories, consequences of the shift from Fordism to flexible knowledge economies, have increased many households' financial burdens. Earnings have become more volatile and expenses have increased, while social policies in many cases no longer provide financial support as they once did.

How then do people address social risks and seize social opportunities? And which types of people are affected most by financial shortfalls? The core argument of this book is that the ways in which welfare states distribute social benefits across individuals and credit markets shape people's access to credit affect how people cope with the resulting financial consequences. This chapter documents cross-national variation in financial shortfalls caused by changes in labor markets, life course trajectories, and welfare states. But to understand whether people draw on credit markets as a private coping strategy depends on the structure of a country's credit regime. This is the focus of the next chapter.

4

Credit Regimes and Patterns of Household Indebtedness

"Today credit [...] has become the lubricant of economic life [and] a driving force for economic growth and the well-being of consumers."
– European Commission (2002)

Financial markets affect our everyday lives. They help us get mortgages to join the club of homeowners, and they allow students to take out loans to go to university. They have become central institutions that shape financial liquidity and the allocation of economic resources as well as determine distributional outcomes and life chances for socioeconomic mobility (Fourcade and Healy 2013; Krippner 2017; Quinn 2019; Streeck 2011). But as debt piles up, financial markets can also drive people into economic insecurity when debt repayments become untenable and drag countries into economic recessions when credit booms go bust (Schularick and Taylor 2012). The financial crisis of 2007–08 shifted the attention of policymakers, activists such as Occupy Wall Street, and scholars toward the political and economic causes behind the growing influence of the financial sector and credit markets on the economy and society.[1] The "financialization" of different spheres of the economy and society is one of the most consequential economic and societal developments over the past decades. But we should not mistake the global reach of finance with uniform impact across and within countries. The domestic regulation of financial markets, the palette of financial products, and the ease of access to credit vary considerably across countries. While financial markets have deeply and systematically influenced and altered the lives of many if not most Americans (Fligstein and Goldstein 2015; Langley 2008), the experience of households in other countries is quite different. Danish and American households for most of the past few decades have had much easier access to credit markets and

[1] See, for example, Carruthers and Kim (2011); Dwyer (2018); Krippner (2011); van der Zwan (2014).

a broad range of financial products than their German counterparts. Perhaps the most striking example is the use of credit cards, which are ubiquitous in the Anglo-Saxon world but much less prevalent and important in Germany's predominantly cash-based economy.

Recent work has provided us with systematic ways of thinking about variation in financial markets across countries, focusing on structural differences in national mortgage markets (Schwartz 2008) and distinct trajectories of financialization and underlying political struggles (Engelen and Konings 2010). Others have highlighted regulatory and fiscal policies that shape degrees of "credit encouragement" and "credit mitigation" (Fuller 2015; Johnston, Fuller, and Regan 2020) and historical legacies that determined whether countries developed bond-based or deposit-based finance systems (Blackwell and Kohl 2018). However, this body of research still falls short of developing a theoretical and empirically testable concept of cross-national variation in credit regimes beyond housing markets. In Chapter 2, I introduce the conceptual framework of "credit regimes" to address these shortcomings. I define credit regimes as the institutional and policy configurations that shape the extent to which credit is allocated either toward households or toward businesses. Credit regimes are characterized by three dimensions: the size of the pool of capital and credit in the economy, the way in which capital and credit is distributed between the business and household sectors, and the regulatory and fiscal policies that incentivize borrowing by households.

In this chapter, I develop a novel empirical measure of credit regime permissiveness for a set of seventeen OECD countries spanning the period from 2000 to 2017. I first identify a set of indicators that map onto the three dimensions of a country's credit regime and use them to derive country-specific credit regime permissiveness scores using principal component analysis. The key observable implication of more permissive credit regimes is that households can more easily access credit and borrow money to address financial shortfalls. To be clear, socioeconomic characteristics of prospective borrowers such as income, labor market status, and credit scores determine credit access at the margin in all countries. But as will become clear throughout this chapter, the structure of a country's credit regime sets the overall boundary conditions that, on average, make it more or less easy for households to borrow money. For example, middle-income Germans find it much more difficult to borrow money because of Germany's restrictive credit regime compared with middle-income Danes who find themselves in a much more permissive credit regime. After introducing this measure, I then turn to Denmark and the United States as cases of permissive credit regimes as well as Germany with a more restrictive one and describe their credit regimes in greater detail. Next, I show that credit regimes condition how easily households can borrow money and shape – from a supply-side perspective – the distribution of debt across and within countries. The final part of the chapter provides a first empirical glimpse at the various ways households in different countries cope with social risks. I first draw on cross-national survey data to show that in countries with permissive credit regimes such as Sweden and the United Kingdom, households are more likely to go into debt to address unexpected income losses than in restrictive regimes such as Germany or Italy. I then use my own credit permissiveness scores to demonstrate that households only go into debt to compensate for weak unemployment insurance (UI) generosity when credit regimes are permissive.

CROSS-NATIONAL DIFFERENCES IN FINANCIAL MARKET STRUCTURES

Scholars have long recognized that there are important cross-national differences in the structure of national financial markets. Gerschenkron (1962) was among the first to suggest that economic factors determine the structure of financial markets. For "moderately backward" economies in the late nineteenth century, the capital requirements of these late industrializers pushed banks to the forefront because only they were able to mobilize large amounts of capital to finance large-scale industrial activity. Bank-based systems such as Germany's allowed its universal banks to develop close ties with industrial firms in order to meet their financial needs, whereas market-based systems like the United Kingdom's at that time were less conducive to such close relationships (see also Allen and Gale 2000; Zysman 1983).

While influential for decades, the explanatory power of economic backwardness as a direct or at least proximate cause of financial development has been called into question. After all, backwardness may be the consequence rather than the cause of muted financial development. In response, scholars have argued that legal, regulatory, and political factors instead of economic conditions directly influence the development and structures of financial systems. During the twentieth century, government regulation in Germany promoted and protected large universal banks while suppressing the development of securities markets, whereas regulatory limits on banking operations in the United States had the opposite effect and spurred financial market growth (Dietl 1998; Fohlin 2007). Others point to different legal frameworks and corporate governance rules protecting shareholders and minority investors as another determinant of financial market structures. Weak investor protections, either de jure or de facto, tend to deter arm's-length markets and instead foster banking practices that allow banks to monitor firms, exercise control, and protect investors' interests. In seminal work, La Porta, Lopez-De-Silanes, and Shleifer (1999) and La Porta et al. (1997) tied minority investor protection to legal traditions and argued that countries with a common law origin such as the United States or the United Kingdom have better minority investor protection and more highly developed capital markets, whereas French civil law systems tend to have weaker investor protection, weakly developed capital markets, and more concentrated ownership.

The long shadow of the colonial era certainly shapes legal traditions. But present-day regulatory environments and the enactment of laws are beyond its reach and, in most cases, endogenous to legal and political conditions since policymakers can change the law if they choose to do so. Contrary to La Porta, Lopez-De-Silanes, and Shleifer (1999), Rajan and Zingales (2003) show that countries with common law systems were *not* more financially developed in 1913, suggesting that structural theories such as those in the legal tradition are incomplete. Instead, they offer a political economy argument of financial development. Incumbents with vested interests in the financial and business sectors will be hostile to stronger arm's-length markets because these markets breed competition. When trade and capital flows can easily cross borders, however, it mutes the ability of incumbents to fight financial development. Others have pointed to the role of political institutions and the degree of centralization. Calomiris and Haber (2014) argue that the structure of a country's banking regime is the outcome of a political "game of bank bargain" between banks and governments over conflicting interests. Governments not only supervise and regulate banks and enforce credit contracts but also depend on banks as powerful financial and political supporters. The results of the bargains depend on how powerful these interests are and whether governments can credibly commit to abide by their agreements. For example, nationally centralized banking policy in Canada was less amenable to local rent-seeking than decentralized banking policy in the United States, where historically states held jurisdictional powers. Verdier (2002) suggests that centralized institutions empower financial centers that deprive peripheral local economies of their financial resources and leave behind aggrieved local constituencies, including borrowers and lenders. Universal banking arose when political centralization was strong enough to create a central bank that could function as a lender-of-last-resort but, at the same time, was limited enough to allow secondary banks and segmented deposit markets in the economic periphery. And Rosenbluth and Schaap (2003) present an electoral regime logic to explain regulatory differences in bank regulation, banking outcomes, and differential costs of borrowing for consumers. Countries with proportional representation or mixed electoral systems such as Germany or Japan tend to have higher levels of protection for banks from market competition and lower levels of prudential regulation, which increases the cost of borrowing. By contrast, countries with majoritarian electoral systems such as the United States and the United Kingdom have more competitive markets and prudential rules that keep borrowing costs lower.

A final set of arguments emphasizes electoral politics as a force shaping corporate governance structures. In this view, firms have to strike a balance of power between their own interests and those of their investors and employees, as weaker investor protection often goes together with stronger employment protection, and vice versa (Gourevitch and Shinn 2005; Pagano and Volpin 2005). When ownership is concentrated, firms want low investor protections in order to extract larger rents from private control of their company and buy support from workers in exchange for stronger job security (stakeholder model). When ownership is dispersed, firms favor stronger shareholder protections to appease minority investors at the expense of weaker employment protections (shareholder model). Proportional electoral systems facilitate stakeholder models because parties can cater to social groups with homogeneous preferences such as entrepreneurs and employees. By contrast, majoritarian electoral systems favor shareholder models because competition is based on winning pivotal districts rather than on ideology (Pagano and Volpin 2005). Roe (2003) expands this logic to party politics, suggesting that Social Democratic coalitions tend to both protect the interests of workers through codetermination of employment protection laws and appease owners by granting them larger shareholdings to counter pressures from workers in order to stabilize employment and focus on growth.

Arguments about the relative influence of legal and regulatory policies and how the interests of organized groups shape financial market structures have advanced our understanding of cross-national differences. Yet most of these accounts fall short on one important dimension: the degrees to which these structural differences influence how easily households can borrow money. Such a household perspective on credit markets is important because it helps us understand why financialization has been a dominant social force in some countries and a rather muted one in others. It also reveals that the structure of financial markets – even in cases where their primary target is the business sector – has downstream consequences for the financial well-being of households and the overall economy.

Schwartz (2008) and Schwartz and Seabrooke (2008) were among the first to pivot the discussion toward a more comprehensive assessment of the drivers behind capital allocation between the business and household sectors. Focusing on housing and mortgage markets, they identify two ideal-type systems depending on how closely countries resemble features of the US housing system, including securitized lending, low transaction costs, and mortgage debt levels and homeownership rates. Blackwell and Kohl (2018) expand this view into a long-term historical perspective, arguing that late-industrial development and capital mobilization are key drivers in the emergence of different national housing finance systems. These approaches, however, mask considerable variation within those ideal types as well as across different finance-related policy domains. Fuller (2015) proposes an alternative perspective that classifies countries depending on the degrees of "credit encouragement" and "credit mitigation." What drives credit encouragement and mitigation is a set of regulations and policy choices that include interest rate restrictions on household borrowing, rules about capital gains for transferring housing assets, restrictions on overall lending volumes relative to assets, the size of mortgage subsidies, and the existence of secondary debt markets. Using this framework, Johnston, Fuller, and Regan (2020) show that strong trade unions and collective bargaining institutions enable more household borrowing in the presence of housing finance institutions that encourage mortgage lending, suggesting a positive correlation between institutions that prop up wages and provide credit access.

Existing accounts, however, tend to focus on differences in mortgage markets, corporate governance regimes, or bank-based versus market-based systems, thus assuming that each sphere is independent of the other. This comes at the expense of a comprehensive analytical framework that captures the size of pools of capital and the institutional and policy configurations that shape the extent to which credit is allocated toward households or businesses. Moreover, the tendency to focus on country typologies and national models obscures the fact that the institutional and policy configurations of credit regimes may be fluid rather than static. Fuller (2015) points out that domestic policies toward credit markets can even be contradictory, while Krippner (2011) reminds us that policy outcomes in the domain of credit markets are more often the result of unintended consequences than deliberate political choices. But most importantly, we lack empirical measures of the different facets of countries' credit regimes that *jointly* capture the institutional and policy environments that shape households' access to credit. In the following pages, I address these shortcomings by developing an empirical measure of credit regimes' degrees of permissiveness.

THE LANDSCAPE OF CREDIT REGIMES

We can think of *credit regimes* as the institutional and policy configurations that shape the degrees to which credit is allocated toward either the household or the business sector. Permissive credit regimes combine open financial markets with large pools of capital that tend to be allocated toward households and, therefore, make it easier for individuals to tap into credit markets and borrow money. Restrictive credit regimes, by contrast, are less open to global financial markets and have smaller pools of capital that tend to be allocated toward the business sector, which, in turn, makes borrowing by households much harder.

In this section, I identify a set of indicators that map onto the three main dimensions of credit regimes introduced in Chapter 2 to develop a novel empirical measure of credit regime permissiveness: the size of the pool of capital; the allocation of capital and credit between households and firms; and regulatory and fiscal policy incentives to borrow money. I then draw on a principal component analysis (PCA) to derive country-specific credit regime permissiveness scores. PCA is a dimension-reduction technique that projects high-dimensional data into a low-dimensional space. The resulting principal components reflect the underlying structure of the data, capturing the directions of the data space with the most variance. This is a useful technique to project the different indicators of credit regimes onto a single dimension to distill credit regimes' degrees of permissiveness.[2]

Measuring Credit Regimes

I collect data for six empirical indicators – two for each of the three dimensions – that jointly influence the permissiveness of a country's credit regime. The final sample contains seventeen North American and Western European countries spanning the period from 2000 to 2017. Here I describe each indicator and the logic for relying on it in detail.[3]

Breadth and Depth of Financial Markets
The first dimension relates to factors that shape the size of the pool of capital that can be channeled toward either households or businesses. This reflects how well financial markets are developed, to what degree institutional investors such as pension funds or insurance companies drive financialization, and to what extent households themselves are active participants in these markets. First, I measure the liquidity of equity markets and the size and prevalence of publicly traded firms using stock market capitalization as a share of GDP. This indicator reflects how firms meet their funding needs as well as potential investment opportunities for households and institutional investors. Second, I measure the overall size of private and public pension assets in capitalized pension funds using the size of pension assets as a share of GDP. This measure captures the role of a set of institutional investors, pension funds, whose investment needs not only drive financialization but also influence the marketization of households' assets (Clark 2000). Both indicators gauge the breadth and depth of financial markets, thus capturing the availability of and demand for capital that lenders can distribute between households and businesses.

Allocation of Capital and Credit between Households and Businesses
The second dimension has received much less attention in the literature; it captures institutional as well as political factors that shape the allocation of capital and credit between households and businesses. To provide a sense of the relevance of this dimension, the panels in Figure 4.1 reveal crucial differences between banks' lending volumes to businesses and the distribution of bank credit across recipients within the economy, averaged over the period from 1994 to 2005. Figure 4.1a shows total bank credit in the economy that goes

---

[2] My credit permissiveness measure differs from Fuller (2015) and Johnston, Fuller, and Regan (2020) in the following ways: it draws on a different set of indicators that are based on objective measures instead of subject ratings; it relies on PCA as a systematic approach to uncover a latent dimension and to allow for differential importance of each factor; and it measures variation in country's credit permissiveness over time until 2017.

[3] A list of all six indicators and data sources appears in Table 4.1.

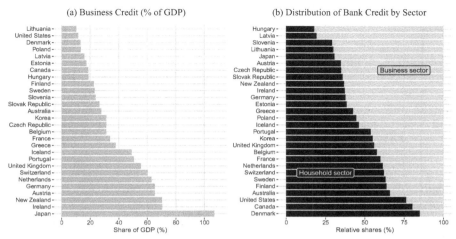

FIGURE 4.1 Credit flows in OECD countries, averages for 1994 to 2005

Notes: Panel (a) shows total credit to the business sector as a share of GDP. Panel (b) shows the relative shares of bank credit that go to either the household or business sector. *Source*: Beck et al. (2012, Table 1).

toward the business sector, measured as a share of GDP. In Japan, credit to businesses makes up an average of 107 percent of GDP, while in Lithuania, the United States, and Denmark bank credit to businesses accounts for less than 13 percent of GDP. But the structure of credit regimes only becomes visible once we disaggregate bank credit flows by recipient sector. Figure 4.1b plots the relative share of credit that flows toward households and businesses. Countries like the United States, Canada, and Denmark stand out because they channel 75 percent or more of all bank credit toward households. In Germany, by contrast, less than half of that share (38 percent) goes toward households while almost two-thirds of credit flows toward the business sector.

I use two indicators to capture institutional and political factors that shape the allocation of capital and credit between households and businesses. First, I measure the amount of bank lending that goes toward the business sector as a share of total lending to both businesses and households. This captures the allocation of bank capital between households and businesses and in part reflects the underlying structure of firm funding. In corporate governance systems based on long-term funding through so-called patient capital, which is less driven by the desire for immediate profits than gains in the long run, banks lend more money to the business sector than to households. In market-based systems, on the other hand, banks play a much smaller role in funding firms' activities and, instead, direct their lending toward the household sector (Beck et al. 2012). Second, I measure governments' influence over lending decisions and the portfolio composition of banks using the share of government-owned banks in the economy. When governments want to promote economic policies such as export-led growth models, political control over banks is a useful instrument to direct capital in line with overarching policy objectives. For example, in consumption-driven growth models, politicians aim to facilitate easy access to credit, whereas in export-driven growth models, politicians seek to suppress consumer lending and direct funds toward the export-oriented sector (Baccaro and Pontusson 2016). Government ownership also allows banks to deviate from a strictly profit-maximizing orientation and seek public investment instead, as is the case with savings banks such as *Sparkassen* in Germany and, at least prior to the financial crisis, *Cajas* in Spain.

Regulatory and Fiscal Incentives for Credit Formation in the Housing Market

The final two indicators involve regulatory and fiscal policy incentives of credit formation in the housing market. Both are important elements of domestic credit regimes because they have downstream consequences on the overall provision of credit to households (Schwartz and Seabrooke 2009). First, I use the average observable maximum loan-to-value (LTV) ratio, which measures the value of mortgage debt relative to the value of the underlying asset. LTV ratios of 100 percent or more, common during the years leading up to the financial crisis in 2007–08, meant that lenders would finance the total value of a property without a down payment. This indicator is partially a measure of risk aversion, as higher LTVs make lending riskier because the collateral that lenders can seize in the event of default is small relative to the loaned amount. It is also an indirect factor that drives the overall level of mortgage debt in the economy. As Fuller (2015) points out, higher LTV ratios indicate "greater acceptance of high debt loads" for the creditors, debtors, and regulators (Fuller 2015, p. 254).

Second, I complement the regulatory LTV measure with a binary fiscal policy indicator of whether a country has tax relief on the debt financing cost of homeownership.[4] Permissive credit regimes incentivize credit formation in the housing market through low LTV ratios and fiscal incentives to take out mortgages. But low homeownership rates have downstream consequences that go beyond weaker demand for mortgages. Countries with smaller mortgage markets are more likely to operate defined-benefit pension systems because capitalized pension funds lack deep mortgage markets as investment opportunities (Schwartz and Seabrooke 2009). House prices tend to appreciate less because there are fewer investors and regular buyers who want to turn over houses quickly to make financial gains. And financial products that depend on liquid housing markets such as home equity loans are limited or nonexistent, reducing the ability to generate loans on the basis of housing assets.

Pension systems, housing-finance systems, and financial markets are strongly correlated. Institutional investors such as pension funds require and

---

[4] Measures capturing the size of tax relief exist for only a few countries and selected years.

TABLE 4.1 *Credit regime indicators: Measurement and data sources*

Dimension	Measure	Data Sources
(1) Financial market depth	○ Stock market capitalization (% GDP)	CEIC (2019); World Bank (2017)
	○ Total pension fund assets (% GDP)	OECD (2018*b*)
(2) Allocation of credit between businesses and households	○ Lending to the household sector (% of total lending)	BIS (2019)
	○ Share of government-owned banks	World Bank (2019)
(3) Regulatory and fiscal incentives for credit formation in the housing market	○ Maximum loan-to-value (LTV) ratios	Catte et al. (2005); Cerutti, Dagher and Dell'Ariccia (2017); ESRB (2019); IMF (2011, 2020)
	○ Tax relief for debt-financed homeownership	OECD (2018*a*)

Notes: Data from the World Bank's Bank Regulation and Supervision Survey (World Bank 2019) I use for the share of government-owned banks has missing observations for nine country-years, which I impute. Lending to household sector as a share of total lending is calculated as lending to households and nonprofit institutions serving households (NPISHs) over the sum of lending to households, NPISHs, and the total nonfinancial sector. Data for binary tax relief for debt-financed homeownership indicator is coded based on data from OECD (2018*a*).

demand deep and liquid financial markets. This suggests that capitalized pension systems tend to go together with deep mortgage markets, while defined-benefit pensions (so-called pay-go systems) are more likely to be found in bank-based financial systems (Schwartz 2012; Toporowski 2000). This strengthens the argument that we need to consider all dimensions of a credit regime jointly in order to understand how easily households can access credit markets. Table 4.1 provides an overview of the three dimensions of credit regimes and their indicators as well as their respective data sources.[5]

Credit Regime Permissiveness

Based on the set of six indicators, I use a PCA to derive credit regime permissiveness scores for each country and year from 2000 to 2017. PCA identifies latent dimensions that jointly explain the variance of all indicators. The first and second principal components account for over two-thirds of the variation across all countries in the sample, explaining 43 percent and 29 percent of

---

[5] Figure A.4.1 in the Appendix shows the average value for each indicator by country.

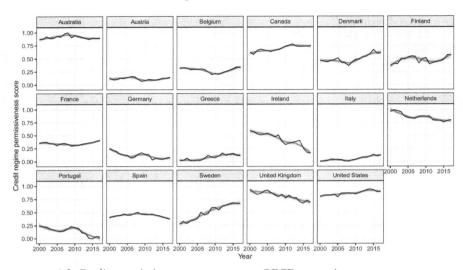

FIGURE 4.2 Credit permissiveness scores across OECD countries

Notes: For each country, the darker-colored line plots the estimated scores and the lighter-colored line shows the smoothed trend. Scores are normalized and range between 0 and 1. Higher scores indicate a more permissive credit regime.

the variation, respectively.[6] I use a PCA model with one dimension to derive scores for countries' credit regime permissiveness, which I normalize to range between 0 (most restrictive) and 1 (most permissive).

Figure 4.2 shows considerable variation in credit permissiveness scores across and within countries from 2000 to 2017 in ways that are not correlated with any widely used typologies of political economies (e.g., Hall and Soskice 2001). The Anglo-Saxon economies except for Ireland have the most permissive credit regimes. But so do the Netherlands and two Scandinavian countries, Denmark and Sweden, which became considerably more permissive throughout the last two decades. In those countries, people enjoy relatively easy access to credit. On the other end of the spectrum lie countries in Southern Europe, Germany, and Austria, with more restrictive credit regimes that make it more difficult for people to take out loans. Figure 4.3 ranks each of the seventeen countries based on their average credit permissiveness score from 2000 to 2017.

Before delving into the relationships between credit regime permissiveness, access to credit and indebtedness, and households' abilities to address social risks, I want to provide a more in-depth background about the credit regimes

---

[6] Figure A.4.2 in the Appendix shows the distribution of countries along the first two principal components, together with the predictive power of each indicator.

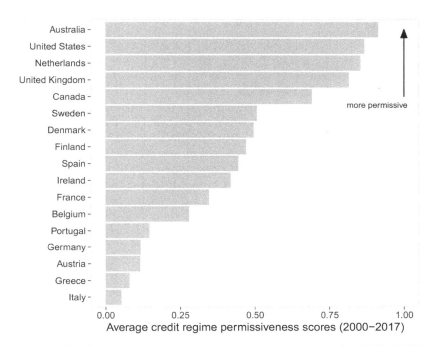

FIGURE 4.3 Credit regime permissiveness scores, ranked averages for 2000–2017
Notes: Scores are normalized and range between 0 and 1. Higher scores indicate a more permissive credit regime.

of Denmark, the United States, and Germany – three countries that vary both in their credit permissiveness and their degrees of welfare state support.

CREDIT REGIMES IN DENMARK, THE UNITED STATES, AND GERMANY

The United States has one of the most permissive credit regimes in the sample of seventeen OECD countries that I examine in this book. Denmark also has a fairly permissive credit regime, yet it has a much more comprehensive welfare regime than the United States. While the permissive credit regimes in both countries allow households to easily borrow money, the German credit regime, by contrast, is much more restrictive and makes it much harder for households to obtain loans. These differences in credit regimes and access to loans have downstream consequences both for the distribution of household debt across and within countries, as we will see in Chapters 5 and 6, and regarding the ability of households to borrow money to address financial shortfalls due to disrupted employment patterns and life course trajectories.

Denmark: A Permissive Credit Regime

Since the 1990s, Denmark has developed a more permissive credit regime, under which households have both gained easier access to credit and become more and more indebted. Until the 1980s, the Danish financial system was heavily regulated. Capital flows into the country were heavily restricted and financial authorities imposed direct limits on loan volumes and lending and deposit rates. The wave of deregulation of cross-border portfolio investments and capital account transactions in the late-1970s and 1980s led to a strong growth in capital inflows.[7] Domestically, the conservative Schlüter government began to dismantle lending ceilings for mortgage credit institutions and banks in the early 1980s. In 1982, the government abolished the regulatory separation of the businesses of insurance companies, pension funds, and banks and granted Danish financial institutions direct access to global capital markets. It also introduced index-linked mortgages, which reduced inflation risks, and increased maximum LTV ratios from 40 percent to 80 percent (Lunde 1997). In the following decades, commercial lending by residents and nonresidents increased considerably.

Denmark opened its cross-border capital flows at a time when many OECD countries liberalized their capital accounts (Simmons and Elkins 2004). As a small open trading nation, Denmark's export-oriented firms favored access to global capital markets to finance business activities (Katzenstein 1985). The government not only responded to the demands of firms and banks to ease access to international capital markets but also deregulated and lifted restrictions on credit flows with the explicit goal of stimulating the economy during recessions and times of economic stagnation (Abildgren 2007; Vastrup 2009). This growth in bank lending since the 1980s was not offset by growth in banks' equity, however, which increased banks' leverage and exposure to fluctuations in international financial markets. By the early 2000s, Danish banks had amassed such large deposit deficits that they had to issue bonds and draw on capital from foreign banks as well as international capital and money markets to finance their deficits (Abildgren, Andersen, and Thomsen 2010, ch. 4).[8] Much like the United States, the Danish financial system took in foreign capital and recycled it into credit toward consumers.

The Danish case also highlights the limits of the dichotomy between liberal and coordinated market economies advanced by the *Varieties of Capitalism* approach (Hall and Soskice 2001). Denmark strongly resembles the liberal Anglo-Saxon economies in the realm of finance, even though the institutional

---

[7] On the deregulation of financial markets in the Nordic countries and resulting "policy overshooting" see Ornston (2018).

[8] For an in-depth account of the role of Danish banks prior to the financial crisis of 2007–08 see the report by the *Committee on the Causes of the Financial Crisis*, "The Financial Crisis in Denmark: Causes, Consequences and Lessons."

configuration of other parts of its economy – most notably the welfare state – are more similar to coordinated market economies or, in Esping-Andersen's (1999) classification, Social-Democratic welfare regimes.

Institutional Linkages

The Danish banking sector has forged close ties with households because of weak institutional relationships with the business sector. Large firms tend to rely on equity and bond markets for capital, whereas small and medium-sized enterprises (SMEs), but also large firms, draw on foundations as "patient owners" for funding, which provide long-term funding that is not driven by the expectation of immediate but rather long-term returns.[9] Strong ties between banks and firms, common in Japan or Germany, were formally prohibited in the Banking Act of 1930 following a severe banking crisis (Rose and Mejer 2003). In the 1960s, when manufacturing exports for the first time exceeded agricultural exports, the growing capital demands of the expanding manufacturing sector were stifled because traditional sectors such as farming and agrarian export industries had much stronger political representation than the export-oriented manufacturing sector. More importantly, the legal prohibition and thus absence of strong linkages between finance and industry, which were present in Sweden but not Denmark, at that time forced Danish firms to turn to international capital markets for financing (Marcussen 1997). After another banking crisis in the late 1980s, a wave of mergers among banks but also across sectors such as savings and commercial banks, mortgage institutions, and insurance companies considerably reduced the number of lenders in Denmark and strengthened the power of the remaining players (Woll 2014, ch. 7). The historical legacy of the absence of formal ties between banks and businesses, the late industrialization and turn of manufacturing exporters to international financial markets, and the importance of foundations in providing patient capital limited banks' role in funding firms' activities. Instead, this environment allowed banks to direct credit flows toward the household sector.

Strong institutional relationships between banks and households influence the depth and liquidity of mortgage markets and pension system as additional sources of lending and investment activities in two ways. First, Denmark has an easily accessible mortgage finance system with a high degree of securitization through covered bonds, the world's largest market both in absolute and relative size (Andersen et al. 2015).[10] Second, Denmark operates a multi-pillar

---

[9] In 1999, almost 20 percent of Denmark's 100 largest companies were in majority ownership by foundations such as Carlsberg, A.P. Moeller, Novo Nordisk, and Lundbeck (Rose and Mejer 2003).

[10] Covered bonds are obligations of mortgage lenders that are collateralized by pools of mortgages. The Danish Mortgage Credit Act sets the regulatory framework for the mortgage market and stipulates in the "balance principle" that each new mortgage liability (i.e., issued mortgage)

pension system that consists of limited government-provided defined-benefit plans with flat-rate minimum benefits, occupational pensions, and capitalized private defined-contribution plans through employers or individual retirement accounts. This pension system depends on deep and liquid financial markets as sources of investment in private pension funds. In sum, banks and other private lenders channel credit flows toward the household sector, thereby providing households with easy access to credit and strengthening mortgage markets and capital-based pension funds.

Policies and the Political Environment

A set of policies that incentivizes households to become market participants and go into debt rather than increase their savings facilitates and sustains the institutional structure that ties together banks and households through financial flows. In many cases, these policies were implemented as part of a larger demand-side policy approach, driven by consumption and fueled by debt (Campbell and Pedersen 2007; Kjær and Pedersen 2001).

The most consequential regulatory policy choices occurred in mortgage markets. By the mid-1980s, the Danish government had already liberalized and deregulated the market for housing finance and mortgages. Today, the Danish mortgage market is one of the most liquid in the OECD. Regulatory policies limit the maximum LTV ratio in Denmark to 80 percent, and the remaining 20 percent typically comes from regular bank loans. Through a set of legal changes, the government further eased access to credit in the 1990s and 2000s. In 1992, the government introduced home equity loans, allowing homeowners for the first time to use housing equity as collateral for nonhousing loans. The limit for these loans was set to 80 percent of the house value. The main impetus for the home equity reform was a demand-side and consumption-driven economic stimulus in response to the economic recession of the early 1990s (Jensen, Leth-Petersen, and Nanda 2014; Leth-Petersen 2010).

Fueled by regulatory reforms that liberalized access to credit, Danish banks expanded their activities throughout the 1990s by introducing new financial products that allowed them to considerably increase lending. In 1996, the government permitted lenders to issue variable-rate mortgage loans, which quickly began to replace fixed-rate mortgage loans that had provided planning certainty for both lenders and borrowers. Between 1999 and 2014, the share of mortgages with adjustable rates increased from 5 percent to 70 percent of the total lending volume, as households took advantage of falling interest rates to refinance existing mortgage loans. In 2003, the government made credit even more readily available. It allowed banks to offer deferred amortization loans, so-called interest-only loans, for which borrowers first pay the interest on a

has to be funded by mortgage bonds that match the underlying liability in cash flow and maturity. In other words, inflows and outflows of mortgage-originating banks must match, which, together with strict lending rules, limits banks' risk exposure. For more details on the Danish mortgage system see IMF (2007) and Andersen et al. (2015).

loan for a specified period of time, typically up to ten years, and only there-after start to repay the principal. For such loans, debt repayment is lighter during the interest-only period but increases considerably once the principal needs to be amortized. As Wood (2019) shows, these policies were in large part designed to stimulate the economy through privatized house-price Keynesian-ism and to gain macroeconomic policy autonomy. Similar to the experience of the United States, the Danish banking sector rode the wave of credit liberaliza-tion and capital inflows and expanded lending to households. But the surge in private loans by far exceeded banks' own deposits. In the decade leading up to the financial crisis, banks became dependent on global capital and inter-bank markets for continuous refinancing of their growing deposit deficits. This pro-credit political environment – with the mortgage market as the spearhead of financialization – also allowed unsecured debt to rise. It is very easy for Danes to borrow money from banks as well as through marketing-intense web-based (so-called quick loans) and SMS loans, especially popular among young adults (Hohnen, Gram, and Jakobsen 2020). Loans from non-deposit-taking institu-tions grew by 50 percent from 14 billion Danish kroner in 2003 to 21 billion Danish kroner ($4.2 billion) in 2013. Web-based and SMS loans grew from 5.1 billion Danish kroner to 8.7 billion Danish kroner ($1.74 billion) over the same time period (Jørgensen 2014).

While regulatory policy choices helped expand the supply of credit and channel capital flows toward the household sector, fiscal policies further incen-tivized households to use easily available credit, in particular for mortgage-financed homeownership. Tax reforms between 1994 and 1998 gradually reduced deductible mortgage interest payments to 46 percent in the 1990s and 33 percent in 2002. But Denmark still has the third most-generous interest-related tax deduction in the OECD world after the Netherlands and the Czech Republic (Andrews, Caldera Sánchez, and Johansson 2011, p. 40). In 2001, the conservative government initiated a property tax freeze, which fixed the taxable property value at its assessed level in 2001. This enabled a sizable growth in credit as the tax freeze effectively prevented rising house prices from translating into higher tax payments. The tax freeze favored existing home-owners, who could reap the benefits of rising asset values and take out home equity loans without paying additional taxes on the property value (Mortensen and Seabrooke 2008). In contrast to Germany, Denmark does not offer fiscal incentives for contractual savings except for pension funds – a point I will return to later.

The Danish business and banking sectors both have vested interests in open capital flows and access to international capital markets, although for different reasons. Firms, especially in the export-oriented manufacturing sector, depend on global capital markets as a primary source of funding, while banks tap into capital markets to finance their lending activities to households. But unlike German banks, which can draw on the deposits of their savers, Danish banks need international financial markets as crucial sources of liquidity to offset their growing deposit deficits (Abildgren, Andersen, and Thomsen 2010, ch. 4).

At the same time, more Danish households participate in the market as home-owners with mortgages, as shareholders in pension funds, or as creditors with personal loans. The "finance culture" that Fligstein and Goldstein (2015) diagnose among American households is also on the rise among Danish households.

The regulatory and fiscal policies that promoted easy access to credit have created political constituencies with vested interests in a permissive credit regime. The coalition of homeowners and middle- and higher-income house-holds that use credit more than lower-income households has become a politically powerful constituency. In 2005, for example, the Socialist People's Party (*Socialistisk Folkeparti*, or *SF*) and the Red-Green Alliance (*Enhedslisten*) almost fell prey to the anger of this coalition when they began to contemplate increasing the property tax rate and reducing property sales costs. The day before the national election in 2007, *SF* reversed its electoral stance regarding the proposed property tax increase because it feared electoral punishment at the ballot box. In the next day's election, *SF* gained more power and bolstered its leadership under the conservative-liberal *Venstre* party. The election results were widely interpreted as a sign that any increases in property taxes are politically not feasible (Mortensen and Seabrooke 2008, p. 313).

The United States: A Permissive Credit Regime

Like their Danish peers, American households can also relatively easily tap into deep and liquid credit markets. One of the reasons for such easy access to credit is the permissiveness of the US credit regime and its orientation toward households. The United States is often characterized as a market-based financial system in which financial markets, in particular securities markets, are equally if not more important than banks in allocating capital, mobilizing savings, and exerting corporate control (Zysman 1983). In 1974, the United States was the first country to dismantle capital controls in order to promote a more liberal financial system that would preserve its policy autonomy and allow the United States to access international capital markets to finance its current account deficit (Helleiner 1995; Simmons 1999). The deregulation of financial markets and the growth of the US dollar as the world's leading reserve currency created strong capital inflows into the United States. Households were among the main beneficiaries of growing credit flows as consumer lending shifted from being a way to facilitate purchases to a profitable end in itself. By the 1980s, most banks had reoriented their business activities to household lending – and household debt was on the rise (Hyman 2011, ch. 7).

Institutional Linkages

In the postwar years, US corporate governance was based on a stakeholder model with managerial dominance, high levels of unionized workers, and tightly regulated markets. Yet during the 1980s, corporate governance shifted toward the shareholder model and firms began to turn to markets to finance their business activities (Cioffi 2006; Davis 2009). By the 1990s, deregulated financial and labor markets and the shareholder value model had formed close institutional alliances (Deeg 2014; O'Sullivan 2000). Commercial banks lost much of their primary market for loan origination because of the growing availability of market-based funding sources to businesses, which forced them to begin reorienting their lending activities toward households. As Figure 4.1 shows, less than a quarter of all bank lending from 1994 to 2005 went toward the business sector – and only about 15 percent of GDP – in part because firms cover a large share of their funding needs through capital markets.

America's deep and liquid financial markets reflect in part an institutional environment with a highly developed mortgage market that is codependent on a capitalized pension system (Schwartz 2012). In response to the Great Depression, the federal government had intervened in the housing finance market and created the Home Owner's Loan Corporation (HOLC), the Federal Housing Administration (FHA), and the Federal National Mortgage Association (FNMA, or Fannie Mae). The FHA offered mortgage insurance that made it less risky for investors to purchase mortgage bonds, while Fannie Mae created a liquid secondary market for mortgage loans, which enabled lenders to issue more loans at lower costs. The creation of the government-sponsored enterprises (GSEs) Ginnie Mae and Freddie Mac under the Housing and Urban Development Act of 1968 consolidated the flourishing secondary market for FHA mortgages. Freddie Mac securitized mortgages and Ginnie Mae provided mortgage insurance through government-backed guarantee, thus further fueling the growth of mortgage markets (Green and Wachter 2005). In a similar turn toward financial markets, the US pension system began to increasingly rely on privately managed financial investment accounts such as 401(k) defined-contribution plans, which in turn depend on liquid financial markets for pension funds to invest their assets. By contrast, Social Security, a government-funded pension scheme, only provides a relatively low retirement income compared with other defined-benefit pension systems in Europe (Langley 2008, ch. 3). The upshot is that both mortgage markets and capitalized pension funds turn people into active market participants.

Policies and the Political Environment
Regulatory and fiscal policies further help create and sustain the permissiveness of the US credit regime. Consumer credit has a long history in the United States, where it was embraced much earlier than in other countries.[11] Already in the 1950s, at the height of tight regulation of small loans, consumer

---

[11] For historical accounts of consumer credit in the United States see, for example, Trumbull (2014) and Hyman (2011).

borrowing expanded rapidly. During the 1960s and 1970s, citizens and progressive groups became concerned about social inclusion and access to credit and homeownership for previously excluded groups such as women and minorities (particularly poor, urban Black Americans) (Thurston 2018). Joined by the National Welfare Rights Organization, these groups began to push for greater availability of credit under the umbrella of "economic citizenship" as a way to turn the question of access to credit into one of economic rights instead of economic welfare (Trumbull 2014, ch. 2). Those efforts culminated in 1974 in the Equal Credit Opportunity Act, which paved the way to tackle discriminatory practices in lending markets.

The early rise in bank lending, particularly in credit and debit card markets, resulted in large part from attempts to strengthen oversight of financial institutions, drive out loan sharks, and improve the ability of all societal groups to get loans on the basis of social justice (Hyman 2011). By the 1970s, access to credit was perceived as an economic right for all Americans (Logemann 2012). Federal Reserve board member Mark Olson portrayed these developments in light of financial market deregulation and the growth of financial products as the "democratization of credit."[12] A wave of deregulatory decisions in the 1980s and 1990s made consumer credit even more easily available. The Supreme Court Marquette Ruling of 1978 eliminated state usury laws on unsecured loans. The Depository Institutions Deregulation Act of 1980 phased out interest rate controls under Regulation Q.[13] Loan markets, previously dominated by a few institutions, were liberalized and became more competitive as more financial institutions entered. US states lost much of their powers to regulate financial products by out-of-state firms but retained controls over LTV limits (McCarty et al. 2010). And lending standards and credit requirements were relaxed considerably, making more households eligible for credit cards and consumer loans. In combination with a significant increase in credit card limits and better techniques for risk-based pricing and credit scoring, consumer debt grew strongly during the late 1990s and 2000s (Wolff 2013). While debt levels fell slightly in the wake of the financial crisis of 2007–08, household debt is now above pre-crisis levels again.

Mortgage markets expanded also during this period, aided by several regulatory and product-level innovations. Securitization practices became more common as mortgages were increasingly funded by capital markets instead of savers' deposits, amplifying the growth of long-term residential mortgages. The standardization of mortgages and the introduction of securitized products such as mortgage-backed securities (MBS) significantly reduced the cost of credit for borrowers as well as the credit risk for lenders. In 2008, over two-thirds of all

---

[12] Remarks by Federal Reserve Governor Mark W. Olson at the America's Community Bankers 2003 National Compliance and Attorneys Conference and Marketplace, San Antonio, Texas, September 22, 2003.

[13] For more details on financial market deregulation in the United States see, for example, Krippner (2011).

residential loans were MBS, the highest share in the OECD. Automated under-writing, with computer-based algorithms determining whether banks should approve loans, and securitization not only reduced the cost of borrowing for consumers but also made subprime loans financially lucrative for lenders. In the wake of a low-interest environment in the 1970s, lenders started to offer floating, adjustable interest rates, which made lending more profitable because it shifted the risk of rising interest rates (and thus the burden of higher costs) onto borrowers and off the books of lenders. With rising house prices and growing home equity since the 1970s, households began to make ample use of home equity loans. Coupled with adjustable interest rates, these loans provided banks with sources to cover their funding costs irrespective of the broader interest environment and with secure collateral if borrowers defaulted (Hyman 2011, ch. 7). During the 1990s and early 2000s, credit requirements for new prospective homeowners were further relaxed and more loans were issued that did not require borrowers to completely document their assets or income history.[14]

Lenient regulations of LTV ratios, which determine how much households can borrow relative to the value of the underlying asset, made credit even more easily available. LTV ratios often exceeded 100 percent in the 2000s, allowing individuals to finance their house purchases without down payments, paving the way for subprime mortgages (IMF 2011, p. 117). American homeowners also heavily relied on the option to refinance their primary homes without fees or penalties. The United States, together with Denmark, is one of the few countries that allows prepayment without penalty (Green and Wachter 2005). The overall cost of mortgage refinancing declined significantly since the early 1990s. Home equity withdrawal became the preferred means for financing home improvements and personal consumption (Klyuev and Mills 2007). Bolstered by rising house prices, many homeowners increased their outstanding mortgage principal by refinancing and extracting more equity from their homes.

The government intervened not only in lending markets through indirect guarantees and GSEs but also through fiscal policy incentives that reduced the cost of borrowing and incentivized households to take on debt. Until 1986, the US tax code had allowed Americans to deduct all interest payments, but the Tax Reform Act of 1986 phased out deductions for most non-mortgage-related interest payments. This made mortgage debt – including home equity loans and home equity lines of credit – fiscally attractive (Dunsky and Follain 2000). The 2017 Tax Cuts and Jobs Act reduced from $1 million to $750,000 the amount of interest on qualified residence loans that taxpayers could deduct from their mortgage and home equity debt.

The shifting norms in corporate finance strongly influenced the deregulation of financial markets in the 1970s and 1980s. During the 1980s, the United

---

[14] Some of these loans were called NINJA loans ("No Income, No Job or Assets").

States had moved from a stakeholder model of corporate governance toward a shareholder model of governance, resulting in the growing dominance of markets and financial values. This move was driven by corporate managers and court rulings regarding taxation and executive compensation and accompanied by corporate attempts to weaken the power of labor (Davis 2009; Hacker and Pierson 2010). The Reagan and Clinton administrations rallied support for neoliberal and finance-friendly policies (Abramowitz and Saunders 1998), while the financial industry and the Federal Reserve under its chair Alan Greenspan successfully influenced legislative decisions and promoted a deregulatory agenda (McCarty, Poole, and Rosenthal 2013; Suárez, and Kolodny 2011). During the 2000s, the mortgage industry lobbied US representatives from districts with a large fraction of subprime borrowers, seeking to influence congressional voting behavior on housing-related legislation (Mian, Sufi, and Trebbi 2013). Both political parties have generally favorable positions toward finance and the financial industry. Republicans sought to promote an agenda of "free-market conservatism" and a homeowner society through various congressional acts, including the National Affordable Housing Act (1990) and the Federal Housing Enterprises Financial Safety and Soundness Act (1992). For Democrats, increasing homeownership, particularly among low-income Americans and minorities, was perceived as a political instrument of redistributive egalitarianism. The American Homeownership and Economic Opportunity Act of 2000 eased financing of mortgages, and the American Dream Downpayment Act of 2003 assisted low-income families with mortgage down payments (McCarty et al. 2010). The set of policies that allowed finance to thrive in the United States not only changed Wall Street but also affected Main Street. Most American households are now part of the market – as investors they buy stocks, pension funds, and mutual funds, and as debtors they owe mortgage payments, credit card debt, and student loans, culminating in what Fligstein and Goldstein (2015) term the rise of a "financial culture" (see also Langley 2008). With ample capital inflows, a large pool of capital, and institutional relationships and a policy environment that channel credit flows toward households, the United States has one of the most permissive credit regimes.

Germany: A Restrictive Credit Regime

Denmark and the United States are cases of permissive credit regimes that provide households with relatively easy access to credit. Germany, by contrast, has a much more restrictive credit regime that tends to channel credit flows *away* from households and toward the business sector, making access to credit much harder for German households compared with their Danish and American peers.

Germany is often classified as a traditional bank-based financial system, in which banks rather than securities markets are the dominant pathway of financial intermediation (Krahnen and Schmidt 2004; Zysman 1983). When most OECD countries began to liberalize their capital accounts in the 1970s, Germany, together with Japan, only half-heartedly lifted cross-border restrictions on capital flows. Until 1979, it regulated foreign transactions to manage exchange rate fluctuations. The tighter regulatory grip on international capital flows and the limited depth and breadth of Germany's domestic financial system reflect an institutional and political environment that promotes the primary role of banks as taking deposits from German savers and lending capital to firms. Even today, financial markets are not very influential in Germany. Securities markets are relatively underdeveloped, despite several political attempts to encourage households to participate in the stock market. Capitalized pension funds, hedge funds, or private equity funds also remain less important. Credit cards, one of the most important sources of liquid capital in other countries, especially in the United States, have grown only slowly in Germany since the 1990s and have had little impact on overall borrowing behavior. In Germany's cash-based economy, credit cards are not widely used and typically take the form of "charge cards" that have to be repaid in full at the end of each monthly billing cycle. In other words, the true credit function is largely missing or rarely utilized. On the other hand, Germans frequently use overdraft lending facilities to address their financial liquidity needs, although at very high interest rates and for much smaller amounts compared with American credit cards. Germany's restrictive credit regime can be traced back to two factors. First, banks in Germany predominantly lend to industries, particularly to SMEs. Second, the country's policy choices and institutional structures incentivize savings and direct fiscal subsidies over loans.

Institutional Linkages

The German financial system is dominated by publicly owned savings banks and cooperative banks, which in 2009 had a combined market share of 82% and held about 44 percent of all banking assets (OECD 2010). Both types of banks are not strictly profit-oriented – they are required by law to serve the liquidity and credit needs of their local and regional constituencies (and in the case of cooperative banks the interests of their members, typically farmers and craftspeople but also private individuals). The savings and cooperative banking sectors provide the vast majority of lending services to SMEs, the backbone of the German economy (Hackethal 2004). SMEs have established close banking relationships with "house banks" (*Hausbanken*) that supply long-term debt financing through patient capital. Firms are embedded in dense business networks with banks, suppliers, and clients and depend for their corporate strategies on tax provision, tight securities regulation, and cross-shareholdings (Culpepper 2005; Hall and Soskice 2001). Patient capital allows firms to retain a skilled workforce throughout the business cycle and invest in long-term projects. Unlike the shareholder models of corporate governance in which access to funding depends on publicly available financial data or current returns, in Germany's stakeholder model of corporate governance with concentrated ownership such access depends on information gathered through formal and informal networks and monitoring. In contrast to firms in the United States or the United Kingdom, the debt leverage of German firms is much lower (Bannier and Grote 2008; Vitols 2001). The close relationship between banks and firms, especially SMEs, makes lending to households less profitable and, in turn, a lower priority.

The Bundesbank, Germany's central bank traditionally, favored savers and asset owners by targeting price stability and low inflation and making credit more expensive by enacting restrictive stabilizing policies with high minimum reserve requirements (Allen 1989; Henning 1994). Germany's corporatist structure further dampened inflationary wage increases, helping to keep the export-oriented industrial sector competitive.[15]

The liberalization of financial markets also affected the relationship between firms and banks – but not in ways that would alter the fundamental flows of credit toward the business sector. Large private banks began to reorient their business models away from the traditional provision of credit lines toward the more profitable investment banking model (Lütz 2005). Large firms similarly saw international capital markets as new sources of funding and began to shift their corporate governance frameworks toward profitability and shareholder values (Höpner and Krempel 2004). The Deutschland AG (Germany, Inc.), a term often used to describe the close ties and cross-holdings between large private banks and large firms, began to disintegrate during the 2000s. Recent changes in financial markets have undermined banks' abilities to provide patient capital because ownership networks have dissolved, domestic stock markets have become more international, and commercial banks have shifted toward market-based banking. Non-financial firms have begun to finance their investments through retained earnings, in part because of declining labor shares of income, thus reducing their dependence on external capital (Braun and Deeg 2019; Deeg 2009; Hardie et al. 2013).

But these developments did not turn Germany's financial system into an Anglo-Saxon shareholder model. New long-term investors such as mutual and pension funds have filled the gap left by banks and become new stakeholders in large companies. With relatively long-term outlooks, they help shield companies against hostile takeovers. More importantly, financial liberalization did not greatly affect the relationship between SMEs, smaller banks, and the public and cooperative banking sectors (including the state-owned *Landesbanken*), which is still based on the structural features of the stakeholder model. SMEs retain close relationships with one key medium-sized bank, and evidence suggests that they are still satisfied with the existing banking structure

[15] For an in-depth account of the history of consumer credit in Germany, see Mertens (2015).

and do not demand access to market-based finance (Deeg 2009). As international financial markets became more closely linked, especially with the European Union, foreign banks began to enter the German lending market in the 2000s, resulting in growing competition and declining credit standards. But domestic household borrowing increased only mildly as German banks used their domestic deposits to lend to households in other European countries (Detzer et al. 2017, ch. 2). Despite the liberalization of financial markets and the entry of foreign lenders, credit still tends to flow heavily toward the business sector, leaving German households with much more restricted access to credit than their Danish and American counterparts. Relatively low rates of credit card usage in Germany illustrates this point well. Only a third of Germans over the age of fifteen have a credit card, compared to nearly two-thirds in the United States. The flip side of a restrictive credit regime is a stronger focus on savings. By now it is almost common knowledge that the German word *Schuld* not only means "debt" in the economic sense but also "guilt," thus carrying a moral obligation. This has led some commentators to root Germany's aversion to borrowing and its focus on savings in language and culture. However, as Garon (2012) points out, to portray the proclivity to either borrow or save as the result of indigenous traditions that are part of a country's national character and culture would heavily discount the role of institutions and deliberate policy choices that create and promote savings institutions.

Policies and the Political Environment
During the postwar era, the German government established an institutional framework on the basis of an ordoliberal "social market economy" and a strong focus on export-oriented industrialization.[16] This "export-savings regime," as Mertens (2015, ch. 4) refers to it, rested on a set of political and institutional factors that aimed to push households to save and accumulate deposits with banks. The latter then turned deposits into long-term credit to industrial sectors. Banks were closely associated with industrial policies to promote growth or even fund government spending (Story and Walter 1997, ch. 6). The broad spirit of banks in Germany has always been and still remains to service business interests, in particular to finance and support export activities. In the 1990s, the conservative government passed three Financial Market Promotion Acts that aimed to bolster Germany's underdeveloped securities markets. It is noteworthy that these reform efforts were *not* concerned with improving credit supply to households. Instead, their goal was to inject households' assets – which in most cases were bank deposits – as capital into the domestic financial market (Mertens 2015, ch. 4). If anything,

---

[16] Ordoliberalism is an economic doctrine based on the idea that a free market can only flourish when the government guarantees order and stability by maintaining price stability, ensuring fair competition, and enforcing economic liability (see, for example, Peacock and Willgerodt 1989).

households became more integrated into the financial market through their bank deposits and, since the 2000s, through fledgling private supplementary pensions, but not through more credit or lending activities like in Denmark or the United States.

The expansion of the German mortgage market – in stark contrast to developments in Denmark and the United States – was much more limited because of regulatory policies. Compared with other OECD countries, Germany has one of the most restrictive LTV ratios (Andrews, Caldera Sánchez, and Johansson 2011). Primary housing loans cannot exceed 60 percent of the underlying value, although this regulatory limit can be extended by another 20 percent through second-order housing loans with higher interest rates offered by building societies. Regulations further require lenders to determine loan amounts – for not only mortgage applications but also unsecured credit – primarily on the basis of prospective borrowers' current incomes and their abilities to repay their loans. For property-based loans such as mortgages, the value of the underlying asset is less important and follows conservative appraisal rules that do not allow for continuous reassessment (Geiger, Muellbauer, and Rupprecht 2016). German mortgage loans have an initial maturity of twenty-five to thirty years with a fixed interest rate. Unlike mortgages in the United States or Denmark, German mortgages carry a prepayment penalty, which discourages expensive refinancing (Green and Wachter 2005). For example, nearly all mortgage loans in 2003 were fixed-interest. Interest-only loans or home equity loans, common in the United States and Denmark, are not available to German households and homeowners, further restricting their access to credit.

The regulatory environment of low LTVs, conservative asset evaluation, and the prevalence of fixed interest rate loans with costly prepayment options reflects the long-term, stability-oriented nature of the German financial system. In stark contrast to the United States and Denmark, this significantly limits homeowners' abilities to refinance their mortgages or take out home equity loans in order to benefit from rising house prices. The path dependency of Germany's institutional relationships and policy environment surfaced in the 2000s when the German mortgage system and its financial market came under pressure from the European Commission's Lisbon strategy, which pushed for regulatory harmonization of national mortgage markets within the EU. The commission sought to eliminate what it perceived to be the protective and credit-constraining elements of the German covered bond market: the low LTV ratios based on conservative appraisals of house values and the prepayment penalty. Yet the German government, strongly lobbied for by the German banking associations, successfully defended the restrictive character of its mortgage system (Mertens 2015, ch. 5).[17]

---

[17] See also the European Commission's Green Paper on Mortgage Credit in the EU (2003) and White Paper on the Integration of EU Mortgage Credit Markets (2007).

Fiscal policies are the final elements that supplement this regulatory policy environment by disincentivizing individuals to borrow and, instead, encouraging them to save. The deductibility of mortgage interest payments was removed in 1986 and replaced with far less valuable tax breaks that are limited to first-time buyers. In the 2000s, these tax breaks were halved and later fully abolished (Geiger, Muellbauer, and Rupprecht 2016). Whereas preferential treatment of debt in the Danish and US tax codes eases access to credit by making borrowing cheaper, the German tax code has no such provisions. Instead, fiscal policies focus on direct subsidies for new homeowners (*Eigenheimzulage*) or subsidies and tax-favored contractual savings plans (Mertens 2015, ch. 8). Moreover, fiscal policies tend to favor corporate profits at the expense of household consumption. Tax rates on corporate profits have declined, whereas value-added taxes have risen (Turner 2016, ch. 11). Politicians in consumption-driven economies aim to facilitate easy access to credit, whereas politicians in export-driven economies such as Germany seek to suppress consumer lending and direct funds toward the export-oriented sector (Baccaro and Pontusson 2016).

The close alliance between banks and businesses and a policy environment that focuses on export-driven growth while stifling consumer borrowing yields a restrictive credit regime in which access to and use of credit is limited.

CREDIT ACCESS AND PATTERNS OF HOUSEHOLD INDEBTEDNESS

The structure of credit regimes reflects the size of the capital pool in the economy, the allocation of credit and capital across different actors and sectors, and the regulatory and fiscal policies that incentivize households to borrow money. In Denmark and the United States, firms rely on funding through capital markets and private foundations (more common in Denmark) rather than banks, which instead target households for their lending activities. Liquid mortgage markets and capitalized pension funds further draw households into markets. Regulatory policies promote rather than curtail borrowing through lower LTVs, forward-looking asset appraisals, and widespread securitization practices. Fiscal policies in Denmark and the United States offer much stronger incentives for borrowing than for saving. Germany, by contrast, has a restrictive credit regime in which banks have close relationships with the business sector through dense business networks, cross-holdings (albeit shrinking), and, perhaps most importantly, the provision of long-term patient capital. Bank lending is primarily directed toward firms, which comes at the expense of more restricted access to credit for many households. These close relationships between banks and firms are created and sustained through conservative regulatory policies that make lending to households costly and through fiscal policies that incentivize contractual savings and disincentive household borrowing.

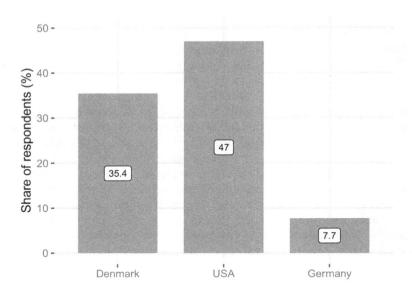

FIGURE 4.4 Share of households with easy access to credit, averages for 2000–2010
Notes: For the United States, the bar plots the share of respondents responding "no" to the question of whether a loan application has been turned down. For Denmark and Germany, the bars plot the share of respondents who report that it is "very easy to borrow money." Weighted survey responses. *Sources:* Own calculations based on Survey of Consumer Finances (United States) and European Social Survey (Denmark and Germany).

These structural differences in credit regimes' permissiveness affect people's access to credit and, in turn, how patterns of indebtedness vary across and within countries. Figure 4.4 shows survey-based access to credit for households in Denmark, the United States, and Germany, averaged over the period from 2000 to 2010. These surveys show that 47 percent of American households, 35 percent of Danish households, but fewer than 8 percent of German households say they can easily tap into credit markets. This finding supports the categorization of Denmark and the United States as permissive credit regimes and Germany as a restrictive credit regime. These patterns also reflect the broader macro-credit flows in the economy as shown in Figure 4.1. In Denmark and the United States, a much larger share of credit goes toward households as opposed to the business sector, whereas in Germany the picture is the opposite with almost two-thirds of bank credit flowing toward the business sector.

How do credit regimes then shape the distribution of household debt across and within countries? During the past few decades, household indebtedness has increased, on average, across many OECD countries. These aggregate trends, however, often mask considerable variation of debt levels *within* countries and across households – something that has received much less attention in the literature. Focusing on the distribution of indebtedness is important because households with higher incomes or more assets can shoulder larger amounts of debt and often pay lower interest rates. But indebtedness can easily turn into financial insecurity when debt repayments become difficult to maintain, for example because of income losses or interest rate changes. Low-income households with few assets are particularly exposed to debt-related economic insecurity.

One reason why we lack comparative studies on the distribution of household indebtedness across *and* within countries is that there is very limited comparative and long-run micro-level data on households' assets and liabilities. Where such data exists, it is often very difficult to access and obtain. I address these challenges by using longitudinal administrative registry-based data in Denmark as well as survey data from the Survey of Consumer Finances in the United States, and the SAVE study in Germany.[18] All three datasets contain information on both secured and unsecured debt measured at the individual or household level. Secured debt includes loans guaranteed by collateral such as real estate property or cars that lenders can seize in the case of default. Mortgage loans are typically the single largest liability. Home equity lines of credit are another type of secure loan that is based on the underlying value of the house, which serves as collateral. Unsecured debt, by contrast, typically includes revolving debt such as credit card loans, overdrafts, or other non-collateralized loans from financial institutions such as personal loans, deferred payments on bills, or educational loans. Ideally, we would only rely on data from government or bank records with high degrees of accuracy. But since only a few countries collect and make such data available, the second-best solution is to use data from surveys of individuals.

If differences in credit regimes' degree of permissiveness influence households' access to credit and their demands for loans, we should also observe strong differences in the patterns of indebtedness across and within countries. To see if these patterns are borne out in the data, I calculate a households' debt leverage, which is a common measure that scales debt by net income. This is a meaningful measure if we are interested in households' exposure to debt as a function of their income. A high debt leverage means that households spend a higher proportion of their incomes servicing debt. The panels in Figure 4.5 show the development of households' debt leverage in Denmark, the United States, and Germany over time. Figures 4.5a and 4.5b document trends for unsecured and secured debt, respectively. The panels show the distribution of debt leverage by net income deciles in each country to provide a more nuanced picture of the variation in debt leverage across households. The lines

---

[18] For details on data sources and variable construction, see section A in the Appendix.

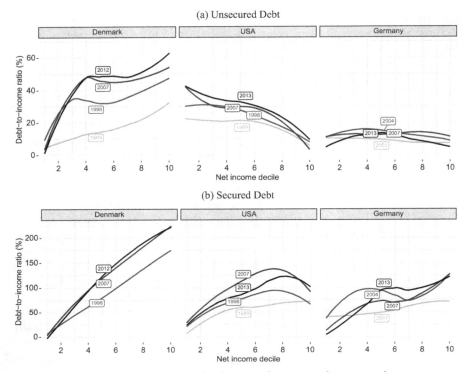

FIGURE 4.5 Debt burden in Denmark, the United States, and Germany by income
Notes: Unsecured and secured household debt as a share of disposable income by household net income deciles. The lines are weighted locally smoothed polynomial regressions (LOESS lines). Unsecured debt in each country consists of the following categories. Denmark: bank loans, credit card debt (included since 1990), and student loans (included since 1991). Bank loans may include a fraction of mortgage debt because of financing requirements of Danish mortgage lenders. Individuals who take out a mortgage have to finance part of the mortgage, often the down payment, through a bank loan. This fraction is typically less than 20 percent of the total purchase value. To address this issue, unsecured debt is based on the non-homeowning population. United States: installment loans, credit card balances, other debts, other lines of credit. Germany: loans from banks, loans from family and friends, and other bank loans. The plots for the United States and Germany are constructed using sampling weights; the plot for Denmark is based on the full population. *Sources:* Denmark: full population administrative records; United States: Survey of Consumer Finances; Germany: SAVE Study.

are smoothed weighted local polynomial regressions fitted to the data points to highlight broader trends.

Debt trajectories differ significantly across and within countries. Three striking patterns stand out in Figure 4.5a. First, unsecured debt leverage is positively correlated with income in Denmark, negatively correlated with income in the United States, and virtually uncorrelated with income in Germany. Second, low-income Americans and middle- and high-income Danes have the highest debt leverages in their respective countries, while in Germany debt leverage is low, irrespective of income levels. And third, debt leverage has also grown to different degrees across these countries. In the United States, the increase in unsecured debt leverage was mostly concentrated among lower-income households, whereas in Denmark it was more evenly distributed across the income spectrum (although slightly more concentrated among middle- and higher-income households). In Germany, by contrast, households only moderately increased their unsecured debt levels relative to incomes. In the countries that saw an increase in debt leverage, it was almost entirely driven by faster growth in debt levels that exceeded growth in incomes. Among the three countries, Denmark saw the most dramatic increase in unsecured debt leverage. For a household at the median of the income distribution, their unsecured debt leverage increased from 14% in 1989 to 32% in 1998 and 48% in 2012. In the United States, debt leverage for a similar median-income household grew from 21% in 1989 to 28% in 1998 and 33% in 2013. In Germany, the corresponding figures for a median-income household ranged between 9% and 13% over the years between 2001 and 2013.

It may seem surprising that unsecured debt leverage among high-income Americans is relatively small, especially compared to high-income Danish households. One explanation is that the income distribution in Denmark is more compressed than in the United States. High-income Americans are much richer than high-income Danes, which increases the denominator for debt leverage in the United States. For example, in Denmark, the top 10% took 21% of the total disposable income share in 2014 (or 35% of the disposable income share for the top 20%), whereas in the United States the top 10% took 29% of the total disposable income in the same year (or 45% of the disposable income share for the top 20 percent). The ratio of the bottom 90 percent over the top 10 percent in disposable income in the United States is more than twice as large in the United States (6.3) than in Denmark (2.9).[19]

In all three countries, secured debt leverage is positively correlated with income (Figure 4.5b). Compared with the other countries, the relationship is much stronger in Denmark, where the debt leverage of high-income households is more than ten times larger than that of low-income households. This suggests that borrowing in Denmark, especially for mortgages, is heavily concentrated among the middle- and upper-middle-classes, which tend to have more stable finances. When the housing bubble burst in the wake of the financial crisis, bankruptcies and foreclosures were fairly limited despite large loan volumes. This is an important contrast to the American experience in the decade leading up to the Great Recession. The debt boom in the United States was largely fueled by subprime mortgage loans and resulted in much larger

---

[19] Figures based on data from the OECD Income Distribution Database (2018) and OECD Income Inequality Update (2016).

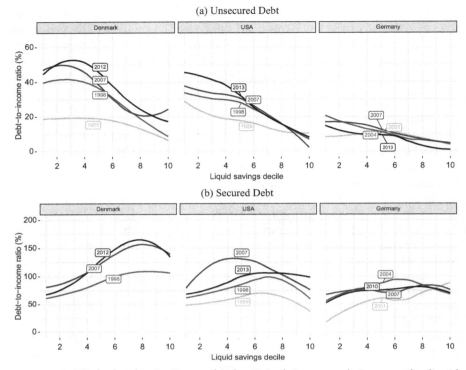

FIGURE 4.6 Debt burden in Denmark, the United States, and Germany by liquid savings

Notes: Unsecured and secured household debt as a share of disposable income by liquid savings deciles. The lines are weighted local polynomial regressions (LOESS lines). Liquid savings are defined as cash and savings in bank accounts as well as equities and stocks. For the debt definitions and data sources, refer to the notes in Figure 4.5.

numbers of foreclosures and bankruptcies than in Denmark (Berg, Nielsen, and Vickery 2018).

An important alternative for households facing financial shortfalls would be to draw on savings as a source of financial liquidity. We would therefore expect that households with more liquid assets would use their savings before drawing on credit markets to address financial gaps, whereas those with limited savings would be more likely to draw on credit markets.[20] The panels in Figure 4.6 confirm this relationship. Danish and American households with more liquid savings have smaller unsecured debt leverage ratios, suggesting that those with more savings have less demand for credit. Even in Germany, there is a weakly negative correlation between debt leverage and savings. Debt

---

[20] Liquid savings refer to assets that families can draw on immediately such as cash, deposits in checking or savings accounts, or stock ownership. Illiquid assets such as pension funds or real estate are harder to access and costlier to liquidate.

leverage increased the most among Danish and American families with less savings, but only moderately, if at all, in Germany. Secured debt became much more concentrated among Danish households with more liquid assets, especially since the mid-2000s (Figure 4.6b). In the United States, by contrast, secured debt increased more among those with fewer liquid assets, reflecting the expansion of subprime loans in the years leading up to the financial crisis. In Germany, liquid savings have become much less predictive of secured debt in recent years.

COPING WITH SOCIAL RISKS

What explains the striking differences in debt-to-income ratios across and within countries? The main argument of this book is that two factors drive these patterns. The first factor is the size of financial shortfalls that arise between, on the one hand, higher expenditures and income losses because of fragmented and disrupted employment patterns and life course trajectories and, on the other hand, weaker and incomplete social policy support due to welfare state retrenchment and policy drift. Chapter 3 documents that income volatility is on average growing in all three country cases, but that households within these countries are affected differently. The buffering function of the welfare state strongly influences these differences. But to fully understand how households in different countries cope with the financial gaps that arise between households' financial needs and welfare states' financial support, we have to consider a second factor: the permissiveness of a country's credit regime and the ease with which households can borrow money to address these shortfalls.

In the following section, I first provide empirical support for the claim that there is considerable cross-national variation in households' approaches to address income losses. I then link the structure of credit regimes to the generosity of welfare states and provide empirical evidence under what circumstances credit markets emerge as alternatives to welfare states. In the next two chapters, I turn to more detailed micro-level evidence about credit as a form of social insurance (Chapter 5) and bounded social investment (Chapter 6).

How Do Households Address Income Losses?

I begin with data from the second wave of the Life in Transition Survey (LITS II), conducted by the European Bank for Reconstruction and Development in 2010. The survey is based on a stratified random sample of 1,000 to 1,500 adult respondents in five Western European countries as well as Eastern European and Central Asian countries (Sanfey 2013). I draw on all five Western European countries in LITS – Germany, Italy, France, Sweden, and the United Kingdom. These countries represent a wide range of cases with varying levels of credit permissiveness and social policy generosity. Unfortunately, LITS does not include Denmark and the United States. In the wake of the

financial crisis of 2007–08, LITS asked respondents to indicate which coping mechanisms they or anyone else in their household drew on in the two
years preceding the survey (i.e., in 2008 and 2009). The options included
drawing on government transfers, reducing consumption, selling assets, delaying payments, and borrowing money from banks as well as from family or
friends. Respondents could select multiple coping strategies. This survey offers
a unique setup to study cross-national differences in coping mechanisms.

Figure 1.2 in Chapter 1 shows the share of individuals in each country
indicating they would use government transfers, reduce expenses, or borrow
money from banks, confirming the initial hypothesis that in countries with
restrictive credit regimes, such as Germany and Italy, households cut expenditures or draw on savings to address income losses and other economic
difficulties. But when the credit regime is permissive as in Sweden and the
United Kingdom, households are more likely to tap into credit markets and
borrow money to cope with financial losses.

I now investigate more systematically whether respondents in a given country are indeed more likely to address income losses by drawing on public
benefits, cutting consumption, or borrowing money from banks by estimating
the following mixed-effects logistic regression model:

$$Y_{i[c]} = \alpha_c + \mathbf{X}'_{i[c]}\gamma + \epsilon_{i[c]} \tag{4.1}$$

This is an adequate modeling strategy since the data contain individuals
i nested within countries c. It allows me to estimate the country-specific
probability of using a given coping strategy conditional on respondent-level
characteristics. For each coping strategy, I estimate a separate model that
includes individual-level covariates $(\mathbf{X}_{i[c]})$ such as homeowner status, income,
employment status, education levels, marital status, gender, age group, and
number of children in the household as fixed effects as well as random
intercepts for countries.

Figure 4.7 shows the odds ratios for the country-specific random intercepts,
taking into account respondents' socioeconomic characteristics. In countries
with more permissive credit regimes such as Sweden and the United Kingdom,
households are much more likely to borrow money from a bank to address
economic difficulties and income losses, compared to restrictive regimes such
as Germany and Italy. Government transfers play the largest role in Sweden
and Germany and the smallest in Italy, whereas cuts in expenditures are most
likely in Italy and France and least likely in Sweden. The results map onto the
three stylized coping models introduced in Chapter 2: the Nordics, exemplified
by Sweden, combine public benefits and private credit markets; Germany combines public benefits, savings, and cuts in expenditures; and the Anglo-Saxon
world, represented by the United Kingdom, where borrowing is more heavily
utilized by individuals compared to government transfers.

These findings have two important implications. First, they indicate that
credit markets can serve as a coping strategy that complements resources

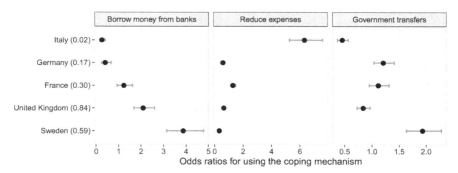

FIGURE 4.7 Odds ratios for coping strategies, country intercepts

Notes: Odds ratios from a generalized linear mixed-effects model with country random effects. For comparison, country-specific credit permissiveness scores from 2009 are in parentheses. Questions: "In the past two years [i.e., 2008 and 2009], have you or anyone else in your household had to take any of the following measures as the result of a decline in income or other economic difficulty? In the past two years, have you or any member of your household tried to borrow money from anyone? (e.g., a friend, other person or institution)." Table A.4.1 in the Appendix shows the full results, including the fixed effects.

offered by the welfare state, even in countries with comprehensive welfare states such as Sweden. Second, the results also show that some countries such as Italy have both restrictive credit regimes and limited social support. In these extreme cases, intergenerational transfers through family support networks and informal credit mechanisms become more important. Albertini and Kohli (2013), for example, show that in Southern Europe a large percentage of adult children live with their parents, which results in more intergenerational financial transfers and resource sharing, whereas Nordic countries rely more heavily on the welfare state, residential autonomy, and few family transfers. Continental Europe has some degree of co-residency and a mix of family transfers and public benefits. This suggests that in countries with limited access to both welfare benefits and credit markets, for example, Italy and, to some degree, Germany, intergenerational transfers are another private coping strategy.

Credit Permissiveness, Welfare State Generosity, and Household Debt

The results from the LITS survey document considerable cross-national variation in how individuals and their families cope with income losses. But they cannot answer why people in some countries are more likely to borrow money to address income losses, whereas in others people tend to either use their savings or cut consumption. I argue that the cross-national differences in coping strategies and, in turn, patterns of indebtedness are the downstream consequences of welfare institutions' interactions with credit regimes. Where credit regimes are permissive and allow easy access to credit, households go into debt to address social policy-related financial shortfalls.

If true, we would expect the relationship between household indebtedness and welfare state generosity to vary as a function of a country's credit regime permissiveness. I test this hypothesis using the previously constructed credit permissiveness scores. I draw on a commonly used measure of UI generosity from the Comparative Welfare Entitlements Dataset, which takes into account UI replacement rates and duration periods (Scruggs, Jahn, and Kuitto 2017). I used data on household debt from the BIS Credit Statistics, measured as total credit to the household sector as a share of GDP.[21] I estimate the relationship between UI generosity and household debt as a function of credit regime permissiveness in the following fixed-effect regression framework:

$$Y_{it} = \beta_1 UI_{gen,it} + \beta_2 CP_{it} + \beta_3 \left(UI_{gen,it} \cdot CP_{it} \right) + \gamma X'_{it} + \alpha_i + \delta_t + \epsilon_{it} \quad (4.2)$$

where Y_{it} is the household debt-to-GDP ratio in country i in year t. $UI_{gen,it}$ is the unemployment insurance generosity measure. CP_{it} is the credit regime permissiveness measure, ranging from 0 (most restrictive) to 1 (most permissive). β_3 captures the interaction effect of UI generosity at different levels of credit regime permissiveness. X_{it} is a matrix of country-level macroeconomic covariates, including GDP (log), real GDP growth, capital account openness, and the unemployment rate to capture business cycle effects. I also control for government expenditures and deficits, the share of service sector employment, and the Gini index. Since the BIS debt measure comprises both secured and unsecured debt, I further include real house prices as a potential confounder and cyclical driver of indebtedness. α_i and δ_t are country and year fixed effects, controlling for time-invariant unobserved heterogeneity across countries and common aggregate time shocks, respectively.[22]

Figure 4.8 plots predicted values for the relationship between UI generosity and household debt in restrictive credit regimes (i.e., those in the bottom quintile of the credit permissiveness score distribution) and permissive regimes (i.e., those in the distribution's top quintile). The results show that only in permissive credit regimes do we see a strong negative and substantively meaningful effect of the relationship between UI generosity and household debt. A one standard deviation–decline in UI generosity is associated with an increase in debt-to-GDP ratios by around 30 percentage points. By contrast, in more restrictive credit regimes, changes in UI generosity have virtually no substantive and statistically significant effect on debt-to-GDP ratios. This suggests that households only go into debt to compensate for less generous UI systems when the structure of a country's credit regime permits easy access to credit. In restrictive regimes, households do not borrow when benefits are weak.

We might be concerned that business cycle effects or financial crises are confounding the results. While controlling for GDP growth and house prices

---

[21] Bank for International Settlement, Total Credit Statistics 2020.
[22] Full regression results appear in Table A.4.2 in the Appendix.

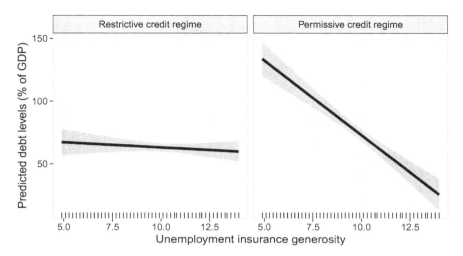

FIGURE 4.8 Predicted effect of unemployment insurance generosity on household debt by credit regime permissiveness

Notes: Predicted effects with 95 percent confidence intervals based on standard errors clustered at the country level. Results are based on the model in column (4) in Table A.4.2 in the Appendix. Restrictive regimes are those at the bottom quintile of the credit permissiveness score distribution, permissive regimes those at the top quintile.

addresses part of that concern, I conduct two further robustness checks. First, to pick up short-term fluctuations in the business cycle I include lagged dependent variables that take into account prior debt levels. In this model, country fixed effects are omitted because OLS estimates are biased in the presence of a lagged dependent variable and fixed effects. Second, I include dummy variables for banking and systemic crises which could influence the results beyond cyclical patterns.[23] Tables A.4.3 and A.4.4 in the Appendix show that the results remain substantively unchanged with these two robustness checks.

DISCUSSION

This chapter develops a novel empirical measure of credit regime permissiveness across OECD countries from 2000 to 2017. The measure is based on the size of the pool of capital, the allocation of credit between households and the business sector, and political incentives for households to borrow money. The Anglo-Saxon countries, the Nordics, and the Netherlands have the most permissive credit regimes in my sample of seventeen OECD countries. On the

---

[23] The data come from Reinhart et al.'s Global Crises Data available at www.hbs.edu/behavioral-finance-and-financial-stability/data/Pages/global.aspx.

TABLE 4.2 *Credit and welfare institutions: Summary by country cases*

	Credit regime	Welfare state	Debt/income ratios
Denmark	Permissive	Comprehensive	High for high-income groups
United States	Permissive	Limited	High for low-income groups
Germany	Restrictive	Segmented	Low for all income groups

more restrictive end of the spectrum are Southern European countries as well as Germany and Austria.

I then take a closer look at the structure of credit regimes in Denmark, the United States, and Germany. Denmark and the United States both have permissive credit regimes. Firms in both countries tend to rely on funding through private foundations and capital markets, which leads banks to form closer ties with households as targets for their lending activities. These relationships are created and sustained through regulatory and fiscal policies that promote borrowing through lower LTVs, forward-looking assets appraisal, widespread securitization practices, and strong tax incentives. Germany, on the other hand, has a more restrictive credit regime in which banks have close relationships with firms through dense business networks, shrinking but still intact cross-holdings, and the provision of long-term patient capital. Unlike in permissive credit regimes, this arrangement diverts bank capital away from households, further restricting households' access to bank credit. Conservative regulatory policies that make lending to households costly and fiscal policies that incentivize contractual savings sustain the restrictive nature of Germany's credit regime.

Variation in households' access to credit and patterns of indebtedness reflect the nature of these credit regimes. Households in Germany find it much harder to borrow money than households in Denmark and the United States. Germany has much lower levels of unsecured debt (both in terms of overall amounts and as a share of disposable income) than the two countries with more permissive credit regimes. While unsecured debt leverage is positively correlated with income in Denmark, it is negatively correlated with income in the United States. In other words, lower-income Americans are more indebted than lower-income Danes. Table 4.2 summarizes the main results.

The chapter concludes with two pieces of empirical evidence that highlight how approaches to address social risks vary considerably across countries, and, specifically, how households access credit to address income losses when social policies are weak. Results from the LITS survey demonstrate that households facing economic difficulties rely on public transfers in most countries, but *private* means such as drawing on savings, cutting consumption, or borrowing money vary considerably. The concept of credit regimes allows us to make sense of cross-national variation in how people cope with income losses.

The macro-level findings indicate that in the context of weak UI generosity, only households in permissive credit regimes go into debt to address financial shortfalls. While the results (despite country and year fixed effects) should be viewed as correlational rather than causal, they provide strong support for the argument that credit only emerges as a substitute for social policies when credit regimes are permissive.

The findings offer support for the *macro-level* part of this book's argument but do not shed light on the *micro-level* questions I raised in Chapters 1 and 2. Under what circumstances do households take on debt, and what explains the variation in debt levels across and within countries? And how does the size and type of financial shortfall – caused by labor market risks or life course trajectories – shape patterns of indebtedness? This is the focus of Chapters 5 and 6, in which I turn to micro-level data to answer these questions.

5

Borrowing to Address Labor Market Risks

In 2012, the *New York Times* profiled Frank Walsh, a forty-nine-year-old electrician from Annapolis, Maryland.[1] When he lost his job in 2011, Walsh and his family supported themselves through a combination of unemployment benefits and various odd jobs. In his state, unemployment benefits paid about half of the weekly average wage up to a maximum of around $380 for up to twenty-six weeks. During this time, Walsh ran up about $20,000 in credit card debt to make ends meet. Now consider a counterfactual scenario for a moment. Had Frank Walsh lived in Denmark instead of his native Maryland, his unemployment benefits would have been between 80 to 90 percent of his prior wage and would have lasted for up to twenty-four months.[2] Perhaps even more consequential, he most likely would not have gotten deep into credit card debt as he did in the United States, because the Danish welfare state would have compensated a large portion of his income loss.

The story of Frank Walsh and his hypothetical Danish persona illustrates that the financial burden of job loss varies significantly across countries. There is also considerable variation *within* countries. The American welfare state distributes much fewer resources to low-income households and exposes households to larger financial shortfalls (the difference between prior income levels and social policies' financial support) than the Danish welfare state. Often considered one of the most comprehensive welfare states, Denmark protects low-income households but exposes high-income households to larger financial shortfalls. In light of limited support from the welfare state, credit markets have become an important financial lifeline for many individuals to bridge unexpected as well as discretionary income losses.

---

[1] The story of Frank Walsh has been reported by Binyamin Applebaum in "The Vanishing Male Worker: How America Fell Behind," *New York Times*, December 11, 2014.

[2] This assumes that Mr. Walsh's income falls in a low-income category, which is around two-thirds of the median income in both the United States and Denmark.

In this chapter, I focus on financial shortfalls that are related to labor market risks and disrupted employment patterns and show under what circumstances households borrow money to address these shortfalls. To do so empirically, I track households in Denmark, the United States, and Germany over time and use policy reforms that resemble quasi-natural experiments to shed light on how changes in social policies affect household indebtedness. This and the following chapter assemble a range of individual-level data sources for each of the three cases to test the empirical implications of the argument. For Denmark, I use administrative records that cover the entire population since the late 1980s. For the German and US cases, I draw on several panel datasets that contain information on labor market status as well as income, assets, and liabilities. Specifically, I use the Survey of Income and Program Participation, the Survey of Consumer Finances, and the Panel Survey of Income Dynamics for the US case, and the SAVE Panel and the German Socio-Economic Panel for the German case.[3]

I begin by studying the links between income losses and household debt in Denmark, where mostly high-income households smooth income losses by borrowing money when facing unemployment because they experience larger financial shortfalls than low-income households. I then turn to the United States, where shrinking government transfers and more frequent disruptions in employment patterns (e.g., fluctuating work hours, temporary work, or job losses) affect the low- and middle-income households the most. These households tap into credit markets to bridge these large financial shortfalls. Lastly, the German case adds an important comparison to the Danish and US cases for two reasons: Germany's restrictive credit regime discourages individuals from borrowing money because it channels capital flows toward the business sector and, instead, incentivizes individuals to save. The labor market centers around a protected core of workers with long-term, stable employment, but since the 2000s Germany has begun to develop a periphery of workers with non-standard and marginal forms of employment. When individuals experience unemployment and income losses, they rarely borrow money to address financial shortfalls because they cannot easily tap into credit markets. While credit cards – wide-spread and heavily used in the United States – are much less common in Germany, overdraft lending facilities (*Dispokredit*) serve a similar but smaller and less important function to help households address financial gaps.

This chapter also highlights how political choices affect the relationship between social policies and household debt. On the one hand, the generosity of the social safety net directly influences households' financial needs and their decisions to borrow money. Using exogenous variation in the generosity of unemployment insurance (UI) benefits across US states and over time, I show that individuals struck by unemployment borrow more in those US states that

---

[3] I describe the data sources in greater detail in section A in the Appendix.

have less generous UI benefits. In Germany, the Hartz labor market reforms of 2005 significantly cut social benefits to the long-term unemployed, which increased the financial shortfall but did *not* increase debt levels for affected households because access to credit remained restrictive. On the other hand, policymakers can also influence individuals' access to credit. When the Danish government in 1992 for the first time allowed homeowners to use home equity loans to borrow against the value of their houses, households that previously had little savings began to draw heavily on these loans to address financial shortfalls.

The different pieces of evidence in this chapter show that when welfare states insulate a broader range of groups from social risks, including economically disadvantaged groups, permissive credit regimes coexist with and complement welfare states in the provision of financial liquidity. By contrast, when social policies are limited and expose disadvantaged groups to social risks, permissive credit regimes substitute for welfare states as more people go into debt to address financial shortfalls. As the scope and breadth of social policies and the resulting financial shortfalls vary across and within countries, so do households' borrowing patterns. This has considerable downstream consequences on households' economic and financial security. High-income households in Denmark repay their debt within a few years after the onset of unemployment. Their more secure economic position makes it much more likely that they can repay their loans without falling into arrears or bankruptcy even if they experience income volatility. By contrast, the more vulnerable low-income households in the United States take on debt to compensate for income losses, which in the case of another income shock in the future increases their likelihood of falling into arrears and facing defaults.

Cross-National Variation in the Financial Costs of Unemployment

As I document in Chapter 3, many OECD countries have begun to deregulate their labor markets in the late 1980s. For some individuals, these policy shifts resulted in shorter employment tenures, more frequent job switches, and more frequent spells of unemployment. But for others, these developments have had less impact on the stability of their employment trajectories. The length of employment tenures provides a useful measure to compare the disruption of employment patterns, for example, due to unemployment, frequent job switches, or short-term temporary employment.

The top panel of Table 5.1 shows that weak employment protection and flexible labor markets in Denmark and the United States are associated with much shorter tenure rates, whereas the more rigid German labor market keeps employees much longer in their jobs. Over 40 percent of Germans have had the same job or employer for ten years or longer, while in Denmark and the United States only 26 percent of employees have equally long tenures. Disrupted employment patterns take different forms, but job loss is still the most

TABLE 5.1 *Average employment tenure and duration of unemployment in 2015 (in percent)*

	Employment Tenure		
	<6 months	1–3 years	≥ 10 years
Denmark	13.6	17.9	26.3
USA	20.2	10.7	26.2
Germany	8	14.3	41.8
	Duration of Unemployment		
	<3 months	6–12 months	≥ 12 months
Denmark	31.5	16.8	32.4
USA	42.2	10.2	20.5
Germany	24.6	15.9	44.3

Notes: Top panel: the cell numbers show the share of employed individuals by their average employment tenure in 2014. Tenure is defined as the number of months or years employees have been in their current or main job or with their current employer. Bottom panel: The cell numbers show the share of unemployed individuals that experience an unemployment spell of a given duration in 2015. *Sources:* OECD Labor Force Statistics. 2017.

common and financially consequential form of disruption. As the case of Frank Walsh illustrates, unemployment is a very different experience across countries. The bottom panel of Table 5.1 shows that unemployed Americans and Danes tend to have shorter spells of unemployment than their peers in Germany, who tend to be unemployed much longer.

These statistics reflect two sides of the same coin. Weak employment protection produces higher labor market turnover and more frequent spells of unemployment, but the flexible labor market channels unemployed individuals into new jobs at higher rates. Stronger employment regulation, by contrast, protects employees and facilitates long-term employment, but it also makes it more difficult for those who leave the workforce – voluntarily or involuntarily – to return to full-time employment.

Once out of work, each country's UI system provides different degrees of financial support and varies according to eligibility, size of benefits, and entitlement period.[4] A common indicator to compare the generosity of UI systems is the replacement rate, which measures the share of prior labor income that unemployment insurance benefits replace in the event of job loss. For example,

---

[4] The three cases have been associated with different types of welfare regimes (see, for example, Esping-Andersen 1990, 1999). These welfare regimes encapsulate, among other aspects, different logics of social policy design.

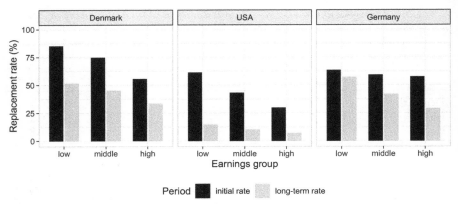

FIGURE 5.1 Initial and long-term unemployment replacement rates in 2016

Notes: Earnings groups are defined as follows: low-income households are at 67 percent of a country's average wage, middle-income at the average wage, and high-income at 150 percent of the average wage. The family type is a single-earner couple household. *Source*: Own calculations based on OECD Tax-Benefit Model. 2017.

a rate of 50 percent means that unemployed individuals receive government transfers amounting to half of their earnings prior to unemployment. Figure 5.1 shows initial and long-term UI replacement rates for single-earner couple households in low-, middle-, and high-earnings groups in Denmark, the United States, and Germany. On average, Denmark has the most generous UI system, followed by Germany and the United States. But the key difference is that benefits in Denmark and (albeit to a lesser degree) the United States vary significantly across income groups. For low-income Danes, initial benefits replace around 85 percent of their prior earnings, but the benefits for high-income Danes are less than half of their prior earnings and smaller than benefits for middle-earner Americans. In contrast, the German UI system initially replaces around 60 percent of prior earnings for individuals virtually regardless of income. These differences become even more striking when we consider long-term rates after five years of unemployment. Low-income single-earner households still receive 52 percent of prior earnings in Denmark, 57 percent in Germany, but only 15 percent in the United States.

The United States and Denmark therefore make for a useful comparison since they share similarly flexible labor markets but provide very different degrees of income support through their respective social safety nets. As a result, households face very different degrees of financial shortfalls when their work hours and earnings fluctuate or when household members lose their jobs. In the following sections, I study how private indebtedness across households in Denmark, the United States, and Germany varies as a result of exogenous income losses due to disrupted employment patterns.

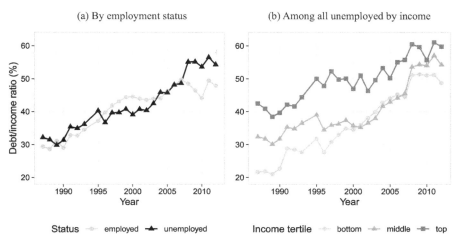

FIGURE 5.2 Average unsecured debt-to-income ratios among the unemployed in Denmark

Notes: The figure shows unsecured debt as a share of disposable income based on the employment status of the household head. Unemployment includes individuals in activation programs. Income tertiles are based on household disposable income. *Source:* Danish full population administrative register data.

LABOR MARKET RISKS AND DEBT IN DENMARK

Denmark exemplifies a case that combines a flexible labor market, a comprehensive welfare state (in particular for low-income households), and a permissive credit regime that grants individuals easy access to credit. Over the last two decades, Danish households on average more than doubled their non-mortgage debts relative to their incomes.

Unemployment

To shed light on whether households borrow money in response to income losses due to unemployment, I begin by comparing unsecured debt leverage (i.e., the ratio of debt to income) in two types of households: when the household head is either unemployed or in an activation program,[5] and when the household head is full-time employed. This is a useful comparison because it reflects broader trends in household debt among Danish households with regularly employed spouses and shows to what extent households with an unemployed member deviate from these trends. Panel (a) of Figure 5.2 shows that until the mid-1990s, households in which the head is unemployed had slightly higher levels of debt relative to their incomes compared to when the

---

[5] Labor market activation programs aim to help the unemployed to find work, for example, through public employment services, training schemes, and employment subsidies.

head is full-time employed. In the following decade, unemployed households had a *smaller* debt leverage than employed households, but in the aftermath of the financial crisis, the debt burden of unemployed households surpassed that of employed ones.

Panel (b) focuses on households in which the head is unemployed or in activation and plots the debt burden for households across different income tertiles. High-income households carry the most debt relative to their incomes, followed by middle- and low-income unemployed households. The debt burden grew for households across the income spectrum, but middle- and particularly low-income households have increased their debt leverage faster than high-income households during the last two decades. By the mid-2010s, low-income households in which the head is unemployed had a debt leverage almost three times as high as in the late 1980s.

Figure 5.2 suggests that high-income households are the ones that experience the largest financial shortfalls in the case of unemployment and thus carry more debt because they borrow money to address these financial gaps. Yet it also shows that debt leverage among both low- and middle-income households has grown even more during the past decades. These trends may reflect a general increase in the availability of credit for these groups and but can also be a response to social policy reforms that lowered overall benefit generosity by restricting access to benefits and shortening entitlement periods.

These descriptive figures support the overall argument of this book but cannot provide conclusive evidence that the size of the welfare state-driven financial shortfall drives the changes in debt among households in which the head becomes unemployed. Households tap into credit markets for a variety of reasons, and addressing income shortfalls is just one of them. In the following sections, I draw on an event study framework to dynamically estimate changes in debt levels before and after unemployment in order to study the borrowing behavior of Danish households that experience income losses due to unemployment. I expect that the weaker the welfare state's financial support is the more debt households accumulate. Since high-income households shoulder more of the financial responsibility during unemployment, these households face a larger financial gap and should rely more on credit markets to bridge finance gaps, compared with their peers from middle- and low-income households.

Event Study Framework

I study the effect of unemployment on debt levels in an event study framework. This design is based on sharp changes in the outcome of interest, Y_{it}, in response to an event such as unemployment occurring in year $\bar{t}_i$ for individual i. The event study estimates the outcome relative to the year prior to the event, essentially making comparisons about changes in outcomes relative to the time before the event. The model captures the effect of each year before and after the event happens in year $\bar{t}_i = 0$ by defining an event-dummy vector for each individual i ranging from L years before and F years after the event happens such that

$$\mathcal{L} = T = \{-L, \ldots, -2, 0, 1, \ldots, F\}$$

For example, if a person becomes unemployed in 2004, this year will receive a value of zero in the event-year matrix, the next year a value of one, and the year prior a value of minus one, and so forth. I chose the event window to range from five years before to five years after the event occurs, resulting in a matrix of eleven event-years per individual. The year prior to the event ($L = T = -1$) serves as the omitted baseline category such that all estimated coefficients are relative to that year.

This design is well suited for high-quality administrative records with a long time frame since the estimation requires sufficient individual-year observations before and after the event to draw inference over such a long time. In the Danish full population data, I observe all individuals before and after such an event occurs and can estimate to what extent individuals borrow to address income losses caused by unemployment in the years following the event. I code individuals as unemployed in a given year if they were unemployed for 40 weeks or longer. I consider household heads who were employed for at least two consecutive years before unemployment to cleanly identify the effect. I select the first year the head becomes unemployed as the beginning of the spell and then construct a balanced panel of individuals who are observed for at least five years before and five years after unemployment began ($T = -5$ to $T = +5$). I then estimate the following ordinary least squares (OLS) regression model:

$$Y_{it} = \sum_{\ell \in \mathcal{L}} \left(\beta_\ell \cdot \mathbb{1}\{t = \bar{t}_i + \ell\} \right) + \mathbf{X}'_{it}\gamma + \alpha_t + \delta_{c[i]} + \sigma_{z[i]} + \epsilon_{it} \tag{5.1}$$

where Y_{it} is the log unsecured debt level of individuals i in year t.[6] $\mathbf{X}'_{it}$ is a vector of time- and individual-varying controls including education dummies, the savings-to-income ratio, income quintiles, age squared, a measure of how many days the individual was unemployed in a given year, gender, marital status, number of children, and unemployment insurance membership.

---

[6] Households' assets and liabilities are highly skewed, but a natural log transformation is problematic since it is undefined at zero. But since many households have zero debt, it is important to keep these households in the sample. To address this problem, I resort to a commonly used inverse hyperbolic sine transformation (IHS) defined for variable z as $sinh^{-1}z = ln(z + \sqrt{1 + z^2})$ in which negative values and zero in z are defined. This transformation is linear around the origin, approximates a log transformation at the right tail, and can be interpreted as a standard logarithmic variable (Pence 2006). I use this IHS transformation throughout for all income, asset, and liability variables.

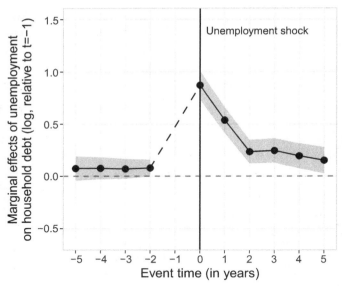

FIGURE 5.3 Baseline effect of unemployment on unsecured debt in Denmark

Notes: Event-year marginal effect coefficients relative to the year prior to unemployment based on Equation 5.1. The year prior to the event ($t = -1$) is the omitted baseline. The shaded areas are 95 percent confidence intervals based on robust standard errors clustered at the household level. The regression model is based on a balanced sample of households whose household head experiences his or her first unemployment spell between 1992 and 2007, such that households are observed during the entire period between five years before and after unemployment.

α_t, δ_c, and σ_z, are year, birth-year, and ZIP code fixed effects, respectively. Year fixed effects control for time trends such as the business cycle, national interest rates, and asset prices, or wage inflation that can otherwise drive borrowing behavior. Birth-year fixed effects control for life cycle and cohort effects as well as trends in individuals' career progression and address other concerns (e.g., that younger adults may have more debt than older ones). ZIP code–year trends allow for heterogeneous effects across ZIP code areas over time. ϵ_{it} is the idiosyncratic error term.

Figure 5.3 shows the event-year coefficients of debt levels in response to unemployment on the basis of the baseline event study model in Equation 5.1. In the years prior to unemployment, debt levels follow a flat path. Yet once the household head becomes unemployed ($t = 0$), debt levels increase sharply by almost 150 percent relative to the level in the year before the unemployment spell began. Note that the year prior to the event ($t = -1$) is the model's baseline and therefore omitted. Two years after the unemployment spell began, debt levels have declined, even if not

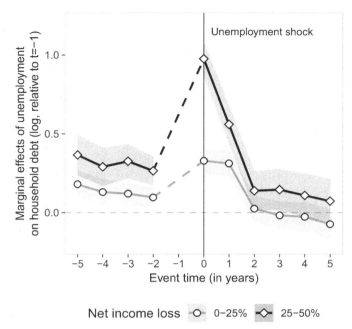

FIGURE 5.4 Effect of unemployment on unsecured debt by financial shortfall in Denmark

Notes: Event-year marginal effect coefficients relative to the year prior to unemployment estimated from Equation 5.1, estimated separately for both income-loss groups. The dark shaded areas are 95 percent confidence intervals based on robust standard errors clustered at the household level. The financial gap is measured as the size of the income loss and calculated as the change in household disposable income from $t = -1$ to $t = 0$. The regression model is based on the same balanced sample of households as in the model in Equation 5.1.

completely to pre-unemployment levels, supporting the argument that households are borrowing money to address temporary income losses caused by unemployment.

This event study model shows that households take on more debt in response to unemployment, but it does not reveal the links between debt and the size of income losses and supports from social policies. Since the net amount of income replacement during unemployment varies by households' prior incomes, we would expect to see different debt levels after job losses depending on the size of the financial shortfalls. To shed light on this relationship, I calculate how much households' *disposable* incomes decline as a consequence of unemployment. More generous government transfers result in smaller declines in disposable income, whereas less generous government transfers translate into larger declines in disposable income. This approach takes into account government transfers and is a direct measure of financial consequences of unemployment. I divide households into two groups according to the size of their *net* income losses when the household head became unemployed: first, those with net income losses of zero to 25 percent of prior income and, second, those with net income losses between 25 percent and 50 percent. I then separately estimate the event study model for both income-loss groups.

Figure 5.4 shows the event-year coefficients for each income-loss group during the event window. Prior to unemployment, the debt trajectories within each income-loss group follow a similar flat trend, satisfying the parallel trend assumption to ensure unbiased results. Once struck by unemployment, households that experience larger social policy–related financial shortfalls also borrow more. A net income loss of up to 25 percent increases debt levels by 1.7 times relative to levels in the year prior. Yet those losing between 25 percent and 50 percent of prior net income borrow even more, almost three times relative to the baseline. The results remain the same when debt is normalized by income prior to unemployment (see Figure A.5.1 in the Appendix). Similar to Figure 5.3, the event studies show that debt levels return to the pre-unemployment levels after a few years, indicating that households use credit to smooth temporary income losses.

The findings suggest that households that are affected by larger financial shortfalls – measured by the net income losses caused by unemployment – borrow more to address the financial gaps. As mentioned earlier, unemployment replacement rates in Denmark vary across the income distribution. High-income households receive much less financial support than low-income households, in part because of a relatively low benefit cap. To corroborate that higher levels of debt in response to unemployment are indeed concentrated among middle- and high-income households, the groups with the largest financial shortfalls, I estimate the following fixed effects regression model that allows the effect of unemployment on debt to vary by income quintiles:

$$Y_{it} = \beta_1 U_{it} + \beta_2^g \sum_{g \neq 1} G_{it} + \beta_3^g \sum_{g \neq 1} (G_{it} \cdot U_{it}) + X_{it}'\gamma + \alpha_i + \delta_t + \epsilon_{it} \quad (5.2)$$

where Y_{it} is the log unsecured debt level for individual i in year t. U_{it} is a dummy variable indicating unemployment and G_{it} is a dummy variable indicating the households' income quintile (the first quintile is the omitted baseline). X_{it}' is a matrix of time- and individual-varying controls including household income, liquid assets, a set of education dummies, age squared, the number of children living at home, and family type. α_i is a unit-level fixed effect controlling for time-invariant unobserved heterogeneity across households, thereby identifying changes in debt based on changes in employment

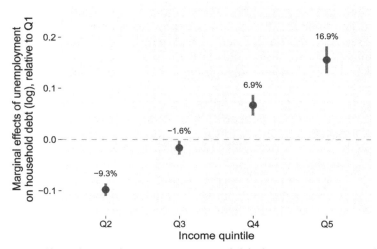

FIGURE 5.5 Effect of unemployment on unsecured debt by income in Denmark
Notes: Marginal effects plot with 95 percent confidence intervals based on Equation 5.2. Households in the bottom income quintile are the omitted baseline. N=29.6m.

status within units. δ_t is a year fixed effect to control for aggregate time trends and ϵ_{it} is the idiosyncratic error term.

Figure 5.5 shows the marginal effects of unemployment on unsecured debt levels by income quintiles, supporting the overall argument that it is upper-middle and high-income households that borrow more in the event of unemployment. Those in the fourth and fifth income quintiles have about 7 percent and 17 percent higher debt levels than those in the bottom quintile, respectively. Combined with Figure 5.4, these findings demonstrate that in Denmark's permissive credit regime, the structure of the welfare state divides the borrowing response to unemployment along the income distribution. Middle- and high-income groups borrow the most because they are less well insulated from social risks and face the largest financial shortfalls compared to low-income groups who are financially protected and have little need to go into debt.

Discussion

Relatively weak employment protection and a flexible labor market make unemployment a common experience for many Danes, but comprehensive social policies help alleviate the financial burdens of job losses. By design, the size of the financial gap is unevenly distributed across the income spectrum because unemployment benefits are more generous for low-income households than for high-income ones. The findings show that the degree of social policy support is an important driver of the extent to which households go into debt to bridge financial shortfalls. Since the replacement rate of unemployment benefits is much lower for households in the upper rather than the lower part of Denmark's income distribution, high-income households borrow more during job losses.

In recent years, however, social policy reforms have reduced the overall generosity of unemployment benefits by enacting more restrictive eligibility criteria, lower benefit amounts, and shorter entitlement periods, thus increasing the financial shortfall between labor market–related income losses and the welfare state's financial support for low-income households (Abrahamson 2015). The steeper growth in debt-to-income ratios among low- and middle-income households (Figure 5.2) reflects in part a response to widening financial gaps caused by these social policy reforms and in part better access to credit and stronger incentives to take out loans, for example, due to the introduction of interest-only loans in 2003.

The reasons why households borrow money and how the resulting debt is distributed across households have significant downstream consequences for households' exposure to economic risks. Despite recent social policy reforms, the Danish welfare state and its social safety net still protect economically disadvantaged households from the economic and financial risks of disrupted employment patterns. High-income households, by contrast, receive less financial support through the welfare state and increasingly turn to credit markets as a private alternative to social policies. Growing debt leverage decreases households' financial leeway and increases their risks of default in the event of future income losses. As the event studies show, debt-induced risk is low because households tend to use credit to *temporarily* bridge financial gaps caused by unemployment. Moreover, most debt is concentrated among high-income households who tend to be more economically secure and thus are less likely to default. Yet the recent increase in debt leverage among low-income households during unemployment can expose these households to economic risks in the future, even though the welfare state protects these individuals to much larger degrees compared with the United States, as I show in the next section.

LABOR MARKET RISKS AND DEBT IN THE UNITED STATES

The United States, much like Denmark, exemplifies a case of a flexible labor market and a permissive credit regime that grants households easy access to credit. The crucial difference, however, is that the American welfare state provides less extensive unemployment and sickness benefits than the Danish welfare state. As a result, because of limited social policy support disrupted employment patterns such as job losses and fluctuating work hours lead to larger financial shortfalls, which pose a significant financial burden to many American households. Employment protection in the US labor market is even weaker than in Denmark and results in shorter employment tenures and more frequent job switches (Golden 2015). Employment patterns are increasingly fragmented, which when paired with an incomplete and shrinking social policy safety net has led to more income volatility and financial gaps. In this situation, many families like Frank Walsh's draw on credit markets to fill the void left by the welfare state – a trend that is enabled and amplified by a permissive credit regime that incentivizes lending to consumers and provides ample and easy access to credit.

Layoff from Work

In this section, I provide a detailed picture of when and under what circumstances households rely on borrowing to address income losses related to labor market shocks and changes in employment patterns. I use data from the Survey of Income and Program Participation (SIPP), a household-based survey designed as a continuous series of national panels of multi-year periods.[7] Individuals and their household members are followed for one panel, which lasts three to six years, and are interviewed every four months for the duration of the panel. Each interview ("wave") covers a four-month window and consists of a core questionnaire and rotating topical module. I combine the annual topic modules on assets and liabilities with the main survey for the panels of 1996, 2001, 2004, and 2008. The SIPP records households' total unsecured debt, which includes credit card debt, unsecured loans from financial institutions, outstanding bills including medical bills, loans from individuals, and educational loans.

Similar to the Danish case, I begin by comparing the debt burden of households in which the household head is unemployed with households where the head is employed full-time. Panel (a) of Figure 5.6 shows that unemployed households carry on average *more* debt relative to their income than employed households, especially since the 2000s. The differences to Denmark, where unemployed households only began to carry more debt than employed households since the late-2000s, are even more pronounced in panel (b), which splits debt leverage among unemployed households by income tertile. Already in the mid-1990s, low-income households where the head is unemployed were carrying *more* debt relative to their incomes than households in the middle- and upper-income distribution segments. By 2010, the debt burden of unemployed low-income American households was over 50 percent larger than that of unemployed high-income households. These debt trajectories are in stark contrast to the Danish case, where over the past decades high-income households

---

[7] For a detailed description of the data and how I construct the variables, see Section A in the Appendix.

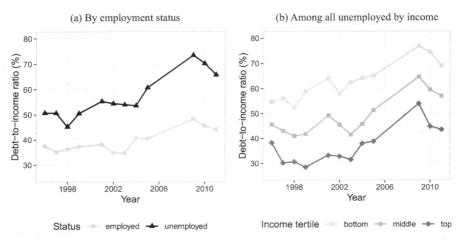

FIGURE 5.6 Average unsecured debt-to-income ratios among the unemployed in the United States

Notes: The figure shows unsecured debt as a share of disposable income based on the employment status of the household head. Income tertiles are based on household disposable income. *Source:* SIPP.

were the ones that had the highest debt-to-income ratio, and point to important differences in the reasons why households in these countries borrow money.

To what extent do Americans take on debt when they get laid off or are absent from work because of illness, childcare, or other reasons? I begin by estimating the level of unsecured debt as a function of households' different employment statuses in the following fixed effects regression framework:

$$Y_{it} = \sum_{e}^{E} \beta_e E_{it} + X'_{it}\gamma + \alpha_i + \delta_t + \epsilon_{it} \qquad (5.3)$$

where Y_{it} is the log unsecured debt for household head i in year t. E_{it} is a vector of e employment statuses of individual i, including layoff, absent from work without layoff, without a job but also not looking, and full-time employed, which serves as the omitted baseline. X'_{it} is a matrix of time-varying individual-level covariates such as education, age, number of children, marital status, homeowner status, race, savings, and interest rate on mortgage payments. I also add controls for households' total incomes as well as for savings constraints, which I define as households with less than one-and-a-half times their monthly income in savings (see Johnson, Parker, and Souleles 2006; Zeldes 1989). α_i and δ_t are household and year fixed effects, respectively.

I find that when individuals are laid off from full employment or when they leave work without being laid off, for example, due to sickness or to care for family members, their unsecured debt increases by 124 percent and 130 percent ($p < 0.001$), respectively. People who do not have jobs, are not laid

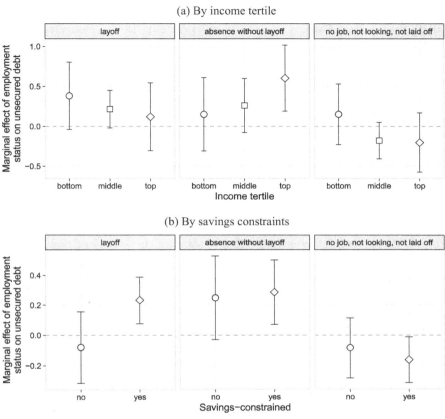

FIGURE 5.7 Variation in unsecured debt levels by employment status in the United States

Notes: Households where the head is full-time employed are the omitted baseline. All coefficients are relative to that baseline. In panel (b), households are savings-constrained if they have less than 1.5 times their monthly income in savings.

off, and are not actively looking for new jobs have less debt than those who are employed full-time, although the difference is statistically insignificant.

In the panels in Figure 5.7, I split the sample into different income tertiles (panel [a]) and savings-constrained households (panel [b]), allowing the effect of employment status to vary across income groups and households' abilities to draw on savings in order to address income losses. Outright job losses are associated with higher levels of unsecured debt across all income groups, but are particularly strong among low- and middle-income groups. Borrowing in response to absence from work without being laid off, however, is concentrated among middle- and high-income groups. As I show later, this reflects the combination of more voluntary forms of labor market exit and the associated opportunity costs with leaving work, typically temporarily, for reasons unrelated to job losses. Those who are not working but also not actively looking have less debt than those who are employed full-time.

We might expect that households do not have to borrow money if they have sufficient savings that would allow them to address income losses associated with disrupted employment patterns. The findings in panel (b) support this claim, showing that unsecured debt levels are considerably higher among savings-constrained households in which the head is laid off, compared to those with full-time employment. For those who are absent from work without being laid off, debt levels are higher relative to those who are employed, but the differences between households with strong and weak financial cushions becomes negligible, suggesting that households in this category borrow regardless of the amount of their private savings.

Savings rates have plummeted across many OECD countries, but the United States stands out with extremely low savings rates. Lusardi, Schneider, and Tufano (2011) find that over 25 percent of respondents, including high-income households, could not come up with $2,000 within thirty days for an unanticipated expense such as a major car repair or a large medical co-payment, and that another 19 percent could only cover such expense through payday loans or selling items for money at pawnshops. Almost half of all American respondents indicated that they could "certainly not" or "probably not" come up with the financial resources to address a financial shock of this magnitude. The Federal Reserve's annual report on the economic well-being of US households echoes these findings, showing that in 2015, 46 percent of adults in their survey could not cover emergency expenses of $400 without selling assets or borrowing money (Federal Reserve 2016). This makes the findings in panel (b) particularly relevant since a large share of Americans across the income spectrum are heavily savings constrained.

The findings thus far suggest that low- and middle-income households borrow the most money to address financial shortfalls caused by layoffs, whereas middle- and high-income households are more likely to take on debt when they leave work without being laid off. The limited social safety net in the United States is an important reason why households rely on credit to substitute for financial support from the government. In the next section, I test the extent to which the *generosity* of the support from social policies and the resulting financial shortfalls caused by unemployment are important drivers of households' debt levels. I leverage the fact that unemployment benefits vary across states and over time, therefore providing differential income support to unemployed individuals and exposing them to various degrees of financial shortfalls.

Variation in Unemployment Insurance Generosity across US States

Unemployment insurance alleviates the financial consequences of job losses by providing income transfers. In the United States, each state has a large degree of freedom to set benefit levels and maximum duration periods.[8] As a consequence, the generosity of UI benefits and the financial ramifications of unemployment vary significantly across states and over time, resulting in strong differences in the financial burdens that households have to shoulder. US states therefore provide fertile ground to shed light on the extent to which households across states go into debt to address such welfare state–driven financial shortfalls. I estimate the impact of variation in UI benefits on debt levels with a novel measure of unemployment insurance generosity based on legislative information on per person benefit levels and maximum duration periods in each US state. This measure is preferable to pure expenditure measures because it captures policy choices regarding the maximum amount and duration for which an unemployed person can receive benefits. Unlike expenditures, which are driven by both supply *and* demand, the UI benefit generosity measure is solely a supply-side measure and therefore well-suited to measure changes in social policymaking.

I collect state-level UI benefit levels and duration periods from the US Department of Labor's Employment and Training Administration, which publishes annual overview documents of "significant provisions of state unemployment insurance laws."[9] These documents contain detailed state-wide information on major categories of unemployment insurance laws, including benefits, coverage, and taxes. Specifically, they provide information on the weekly dollar amount and the maximum annual duration of unemployment insurance a person can receive. On the basis of that information, I compute the maximum UI benefit generosity by multiplying the maximum weekly benefit amount with the maximum amount of benefit weeks for each state and year (see also Hsu, Matsa, and Melzer 2018).[10] This measure is advantageous for my research purpose because it is beyond the influence of households and varies considerably across states and over time, as Figure 5.8 shows. For example, maximum UI generosity ranged from $5,924 in Mississippi to $27,253 in Massachusetts in 2011.

To estimate the extent to which differences in UI benefit generosity are linked to differences in household indebtedness, I use data from the 1996, 2001, 2004, and 2008 panels of the SIPP. In annual topic modules on assets and liabilities, the SIPP asks respondents about household-level secured debt, which includes mortgage debt and car title loans, and unsecured debt, which includes credit card debt, unsecured loans from financial institutions, outstanding bills such as medical bills, loans from individuals, and educational loans.

---

[8] For an overview on US unemployment insurance see Woodbury (2014) and US Department of Labor's Employment and Training Administration (see https://workforcesecurity.doleta.gov/unemploy/uifactsheet.asp).

[9] For more information see https://ows.doleta.gov/unemploy/laws.asp.

[10] If the documents included a range for the maximum weekly benefit amount or the maximum number of weeks, I chose the upper limit.

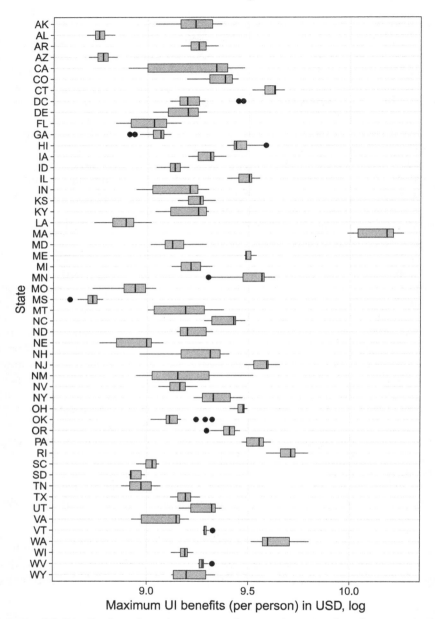

FIGURE 5.8 Distribution of maximum unemployment insurance benefit generosity in US states, 1996–2011

Notes: The boxplots show the per person unemployment insurance benefit generosity levels (log USD, adjusted for inflation) between 1996 and 2011 across states. Whiskers indicate variability outside the upper and lower quartiles, and dots indicate outlier years. *Source:* Own calculations based on US Department of Labor's Employment and Training Administration, Office of Unemployment Insurance, and the Census Bureau's Census of Government Finances and Annual Survey of Local Government Finances.

I merge the main survey with these annual topic modules, creating the final dataset that spans from 1996 to 2011 (the last year when respondents were interviewed for the assets and liabilities topic module) and includes households whose heads of household are sixteen- to sixty-five-year-olds. I winsorize unsecured debt at the 99th percentile.[11]

The variation in unemployment insurance generosity across states and over time allows me to identify whether households in which the head becomes unemployed borrow more money in states where UI benefits are less generous using the following generalized difference-in-differences (DID) model:

$$Y_{it} = \beta_1 Gen_{st} + \beta_2 UI_{it} + \beta_3 (Gen_{st} \cdot UI_{it}) + \mathbf{X}'_{it}\gamma + \mathbf{Z}'_{st}\lambda + \alpha_i + \delta_t + \epsilon_{it}$$

(5.4)

where Y_{it} is the log unsecured household debt of individual i at time t.[12] Gen_{st} is the log maximum amount of per capita unemployment insurance benefits in state s at time t – my measure of generosity. UI_{it} is a dummy variable indicating whether individual i received unemployment benefits in year t. Since not all unemployed individuals receive UI benefits, this approach ensures that we estimate the effect among those who actually receive benefits. $\mathbf{X}'_{it}$ is a matrix of individual-level covariates, including highest educational degree, age and age squared, number of children, marital status, homeownership, race, savings, and income quintiles. Ideally, I would control for respondents' access to credit, but since the SIPP only asks about mortgage interest rates, I include this variable as a proxy.[13] $\mathbf{Z}'_{st}$ is a matrix of state-level covariates, including per capita gross state product (GSP) and GSP annual growth rates, state unemployment rates, and state per capita expenditures and revenues.[14] Household fixed effects (α_i) capture all time-invariant household characteristics and identify the effect of UI generosity on unsecured debt conditional on any given household member switching into unemployment, thereby leveraging within-household variation. Year fixed effects (δ_t) capture common time shocks. Robust standard errors are clustered at the state level. One concern would be that changes in UI generosity levels correlate with unobserved trends across states that also affect household borrowing. I provide a general check against the possibility that other state-varying factors, such as credit market regulation, influence household debt levels by including state-specific time trends as well as state-by-year fixed effects that take into account time-varying state-level variables.[15]

---

[11] The results are robust to using the full distribution of the debt data.

[12] As before, I use an inverse hyperbolic sine transformation in which negative values and zero in the asset and liability variables are defined.

[13] For those with no mortgage payments this variable is zero.

[14] State-level data comes from Carl Klarner. 2015, *State Economic and Government Finance Data*. Harvard Dataverse 2015.

[15] Full regression results for various model specifications appear in Table A.5.1 in the Appendix.

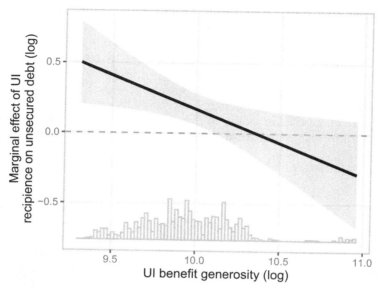

FIGURE 5.9 Effect of unemployment insurance generosity on unsecured debt among unemployment benefit recipients

Notes: Marginal effects of receiving UI benefits on unsecured debt as a function of unemployment insurance generosity with 95 percent confidence intervals based on column 4 in Table A.5.1 in the Appendix. The histogram shows the distribution of UI benefit generosity in the sample.

Figure 5.9 plots the marginal effects of unemployment on debt for different levels of unemployment insurance generosity. The results show a strong negative effect between UI benefit generosity and household debt. In states where UI benefits are less generous, households in which the head becomes unemployed borrow more money than in states where benefits are more generous. In substantive terms, a decline in average unemployment benefits by 20 percent from the samples' average maximum UI benefits of $9,645 increases unsecured debt levels by about 11 percent – about $2,000 of the samples' average unsecured debt level. This is a sizable effect. The findings suggest that households borrow money to fill the financial gap left by weaker UI benefits and use credit as a substitute for government transfers. Put differently, a more generous safety net could potentially alleviate households' need to draw on credit to address financial gaps, thereby reducing overall indebtedness.

Fluctuations in Work Hours

Job loss is one of the most important drivers of income loss, but irregular work hours and interrupted employment schedules have become more common in the United States and, increasingly, in other countries (see Chapter 3 and, for example, Eichhorst and Marx (2016) and Golden (2015)). In 2012, around one-third of SIPP panelists reported that they worked less than thirty-five hours per week. These non-standard employment patterns increase the financial burden on households through two channels. First, earnings become more volatile as individuals switch jobs more frequently and experience short periods of unemployment. Second, disrupted employment patterns can make individuals ineligible for social benefits because they do not meet rigid eligibility criteria (McHugh and Kimball 2015). A recent study of low- and middle-income Americans shows that about half of households' income volatility was due to variation within the same jobs rather than job losses (Morduch and Schneider 2017, ch. 1 & 3). Other research by the JPMorgan Chase Institute, drawing on data of over 2.5 million financial transactions between 2012 and 2014, demonstrates that income volatility is prevalent across all rungs of the income distribution. Almost half of all individuals in their data experience a change in income between 5 percent and 30 percent annually and, notably, all individuals except those in the top quintile do *not* have sufficient liquid savings to address those fluctuations. For example, their findings suggest that middle-income households have only about $3,000 in liquid savings but they need about $4,800 to address their income fluctuations (Farrell and Greig 2015, p. 16).[16]

Variation in hourly pay, fewer work hours, and periods of unpaid absences from work are among the main reasons (besides job loss) why earnings are now more volatile. What separates this type of income volatility from the one caused by unemployment is that in the United States there is no social safety net in place to alleviate the financial burden on households.[17] This leaves households with even larger financial shortfalls than in cases of unemployment. With little savings at their disposal, I expect that many households therefore draw on credit markets and go into debt to address these financial gaps.

Based on the SIPP data, I find that on average a household head who works less than thirty-five hours per week carries 38 percent (±13) more debt than a head who is employed full-time ($p < 0.01$).[18] Yet there are many reasons for fewer and fluctuating work hours. Some individuals deliberately choose to work less than thirty-five hours per week, while others

---

[16] See also Farrell and Greig (2016).

[17] Households may be eligible for the Supplemental Nutrition Assistance Program (SNAP, formerly known as "food stamps"), but there is no social policy program that is specifically designed to counter the consequences of these "new types" of social risks.

[18] From a regression model with unit- and time-fixed effects as displayed in Table A.5.2 in the Appendix.

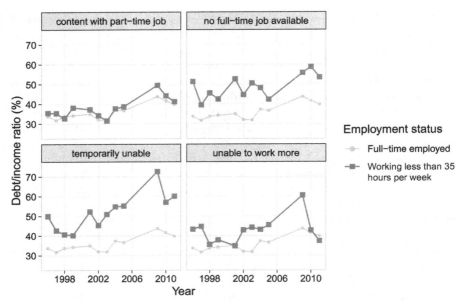

FIGURE 5.10 Fewer work hours and unsecured debt leverage in the United States
Notes: Ratio of unsecured debt to disposable income for households whose head indicates one of the displayed reasons for working less than thirty-five hours per week. The gray lines overlay the debt-to-income ratio for households with a full-time employed household head. *Source:* SIPP.

find themselves with no other choice when full-time jobs are not available, when jobs are paid by the hour and their hours are cut, or when personal circumstances prevent full-time work. The SIPP asks respondents about their reasons for working fewer hours, which allows me to distinguish between those who voluntarily work fewer hours from those who do so involuntarily. Figure 5.10 tracks changes in debt-to-income ratios over time for households whose head indicates that he or she works less than thirty-five hours per week for a given reason. For comparison, the gray lines show the debt-to-income ratio for households in which the head is full-time employed.

Individuals who deliberately choose to work shorter days or fewer hours ("content with part-time job") are *not* carrying more debt relative to income than individuals working full-time. Instead, it is households in which the head is temporarily unable to work full-time that have the largest debt-to-income ratios and saw the strongest increase in this ratio over the last two decades. Much like in the case of unemployment, credit markets have become an important instrument to address income volatility in light of fewer or fluctuating work hours.

These findings also shed doubts on arguments that claim that rising debt levels are the consequence of conspicuous consumption and attempts to "keep up with the Joneses."[19] If this were the case, the debt leverage should be higher for households that voluntarily work fewer hours because these households, according to those arguments, need to finance their conspicuous consumption by taking on more debt. This is not the case. To the contrary, debt leverage is higher for households where the head is *involuntarily* working fewer hours, suggesting that credit helps households address income volatility during temporary declines in work hours. In Chapter 6, I further unpack the reasons for working fewer hours and unpaid absences from work and their effects on households' debt leverage.

Discussion

For many American households, the financial burden of disrupted employment patterns has grown considerably over the past decades. Fluctuating and irregular work schedules, fewer work hours, and frequent periods of unemployment make earnings much more volatile and often lead to significant income losses. The rise in jobs with no or limited benefits makes American households even more vulnerable to economic and financial shocks. But the US welfare state only covers a small set of these risks and provides limited and often declining financial support either because new types of jobs deliberately exclude individuals from the public safety net due to reduced benefits or restrictive eligibility criteria, or because policymakers fail to adapt existing policies to new labor market realities and let policies drift. The result is a rising gap between the financial needs of households that experience income losses and the financial support they receive from social policies. Increasingly, this social policy-related financial shortfall is no longer limited to low-income households but has expanded into middle-income segments of society.

In light of rising financial shortfalls, the American credit regime with easily available credit has turned into a private alternative to publicly financed social policies. Borrowing has become a critical instrument for low- and, increasingly, middle-income households to fill financial gaps left by job losses or fluctuating and fewer work hours. Variation in social policies are an important driver behind financial gaps. Households in which the household head loses his or her job borrow significantly *more* in states that have *less* generous UI benefits. This suggests that credit replaces financial transfers from the public social safety net or, from a public policy perspective, that

---

[19] On conspicuous consumption see, for example, Frank, Levine, and Dijk (2014). On arguments that middle-class Americans finance their conspicuous consumption with debt see, for example, Christen and Morgan (2005) and Frank (2010).

more generous social policies can reduce households' need to draw on credit markets.

The comparative perspective yields important insights: Denmark and the United States share flexible labor markets and permissive credit regimes that grant households easy access to credit, but disruptions in employment patterns and irregular and non-standard work contracts are more prevalent in the United States. Even more important are differences in social policy regimes that influence the financial consequences of labor market risks and their variation across households. The Danish welfare state protects low-income households to a much greater extent than the American welfare state, resulting in very different degrees of financial shortfalls for low-income households. In both countries, households borrow money in response to such social policy-induced shortfalls, but it is different types of households that go into debt. Among households with unemployed members, it is high-income Danish households and low-income American households that carry the most debt relative to their incomes. This outcome matters because low-income households, often with little assets, tend to have much weaker capacities to shoulder debt levels, carry more debt relative to their incomes, and, as a result, are more vulnerable to future income shocks that may interrupt their debt repayment schedules.

LABOR MARKET RISKS AND DEBT IN GERMANY

Germany provides a fruitful comparison to the United States and Denmark. It exemplifies a restrictive credit regime that favors lending to businesses instead of households, making it more difficult for individuals to borrow. The labor market is segmented into a protected core of workers with long-term stable employment trajectories and an exposed periphery of workers with unstable and increasingly marginal forms of employment. Policymakers have introduced labor market and social policy reforms, in particular with the so-called Hartz reforms in the early 2000s, in an attempt to deregulate labor markets and introduce more flexibility. These reforms have exacerbated the dualization of the German labor market mostly by expanding temporary and marginal jobs.

German households on average have lower debt levels and debt-to-income ratios than American or Danish households (see Figure 4.5 in Chapter 4). This is driven in part by the more restrictive credit regime and in part by weaker incentives for individuals to borrow money. I therefore expect that German households are less likely to go into debt and borrow money to address labor market risks and income losses compared with Danish and American households. To empirically test this hypothesis, I draw mainly on data from the German SAVE panel, a longitudinal study that was designed in 2001 in response to the lack of adequate data on assets and liabilities in existing panel

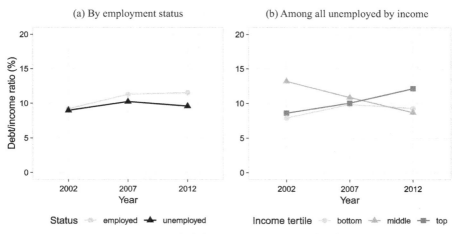

FIGURE 5.11 Average unsecured debt-to-income ratios among the unemployed in Germany

Notes: The figure shows unsecured debt as a share of disposable income based on the employment status of the household head. Marginally employed individuals are those who work in unstable jobs, mini-jobs, and midi-jobs. Mini-jobs are forms of short-term marginal employment with low pay (i.e., below €450 per month). These jobs are exempt from taxes and social insurance contributions, have limited unemployment benefits, and do not entitle employees to pension claims. Midi-job employees earn between €450 and €850 and have reduced social insurance contributions (see also Chapter 3). Income tertiles are based on household disposable income. *Source:* SOEP General Survey and Wealth Supplements (2002, 2007, 2012).

surveys, most notably the German Socio-Economic Panel (SOEP) (Boersch-Supan and Essig 2005).[20] For some descriptive statistics, however, I rely on the SOEP since its sample size is larger than that of the SAVE panel and is more representative of the German population and thus yields more precise estimates.[21]

Unemployment

As in the previous two sections about Denmark and the United States, I begin by comparing the debt leverage of households in which the household head is unemployed with those in which the head is employed full-time. Panel (a) of Figure 5.11 shows that debt levels relative to income are much lower in Germany compared with Denmark (Figure 5.2) and the United States (Figure 5.6) and have remained fairly stable over time. In the early 2000s, the debt ratios of households with an unemployed head of household were similar

---

[20] The SOEP only collects data on assets and liabilities in three wealth supplements in 2002, 2007, and 2012 and is therefore not suitable for analyzing the borrowing response following an income loss.

[21] For data description and variable construction, see section A in the Appendix.

to those of households with an employed head of household, but they declined slightly over the course of the following decade. Among households with an unemployed household head, middle-income households have the largest debt burden, but the size of the debt burden and its differences across households are small compared to Denmark or the United States.

These patterns are the result of Germany's restrictive credit regime, which makes credit much harder to obtain, especially for households that have unemployed members or that lack secure sources of income. Credit cards that only require a minimum payment at the end of the billing cycle – an important financial lifeline for many Americans – are less common in Germany and rarely used.[22] Instead, overdraft facilities on checking accounts are more important for many German households. These overdraft lines allow account holders to overdraw their accounts up to a fixed limit (which is based on income). Since German households face a restrictive credit regime that makes credit much harder to secure, I expect to see a much more muted borrowing response to income losses from unemployment compared with the Danish or American cases.

I begin by estimating how the varying degrees to which a head of household is attached to the labor market affects changes in unsecured debt in the following fixed effects OLS regression:

$$Y_{it} = \sum_{e}^{E} \beta_e E_{it} + X'_{it} \gamma + \alpha_i + \delta_t + \epsilon_{it} \tag{5.5}$$

where Y_{it} is the log unsecured debt for household head i in year t. E_{it} is a vector of e employment statuses of individual i, including unemployment, part-time (15–35 hours per week), part-time (less than 15 hours per week), and sometimes employed. Employed household heads serve as the omitted baseline. X'_{it} is a matrix of time-varying individual-level covariates and α_i and δ_t are unit and year fixed effects, respectively. Table 5.2 shows the marginal effects of different employment statuses on unsecured consumer debt.

The baseline model without covariates in column (1) shows that there is a mild but statistically insignificant increase in debt among those who are unemployed and work part-time with 15–35 hours per week. Adding a full set of covariates in column (2), the effect size increases slightly but still remains statistically insignificant. Households in the sample hold an average of around €2,115 (about $2,375) in unsecured debt. This is a small amount compared to other countries. Fewer work hours in the United States are strongly associated with more borrowing, especially when they are the result of involuntary

---

[22] The vast majority of German credit cards are more akin to charge cards, with which one can spend a limited amount of money over the duration of the billing cycle but has to pay the entire outstanding balance by the end of the billing cycle. On the use of cash versus credit cards see, for example, Kalckreuth, Schmidt, and Stix (2014).

TABLE 5.2 *Effect of degrees of labor market attachment on unsecured debt in Germany*

	Dependent variable	
	Unsecured debt (log)	
	(1)	(2)
Unemployed	0.26	0.32
	(0.21)	(0.21)
Employed part-time (15–35h/week)	0.17	0.21
	(0.26)	(0.26)
Employed part-time (< 15h/week)	0.06	0.12
	(0.26)	(0.26)
Employed: sometimes	−0.13	−0.03
	(0.34)	(0.34)
Controls	–	✓
Unit fixed effects	✓	✓
Year fixed effects	✓	✓
Observations	11,466	11,466
R^2	0.57	0.57
Adjusted R^2	0.48	0.48

Notes: Results from regression models with unit and year fixed effects as well as a set of controls based on Equation 5.5. Robust standard errors clustered at the household level. Full results appear in Table A.5.3 in the Appendix. *p<0.1; **p<0.05; ***p<0.01.

choices. The German data do not allow me to distinguish the reasons for working fewer hours, but, regardless of the reasons, the findings suggest that in Germany fewer work hours are *not* associated with higher debt.

I then estimate the effect of income loss due to unemployment on unsecured debt in the following OLS regression:

$$Y_{it} = \beta_1 U_{it} + \beta_2 I_{it} + \beta_3 (U_{it} \cdot I_{it}) + \mathbf{X}'_{it}\gamma + \alpha_i + \delta_t + \epsilon_{it} \tag{5.6}$$

where Y_{it} is the log unsecured debt for individual i in year t. U_{it} is a dummy indicating if the household head i is unemployed and I_{it} is household income. $\mathbf{X}'_{it}$ is a matrix of time-varying individual-level covariates and α_i and δ_t are unit and year fixed effects, respectively. The results are shown in Table 5.3. Column (1) shows the bivariate model without control variables and similarly finds a mild positive but statistically insignificant effect. Adding a set of control variables (column [2]) increases the effect size slightly but leaves the findings statistically insignificant. Column (3) allows the effect of unemployment to vary by households' disposable incomes and shows that income does not influence debt levels among the unemployed. These findings can be explained by the design of Germany's unemployment insurance system, which only mildly differentiates benefits by income groups, and by Germany's credit regime, which

TABLE 5.3 *Effect of unemployment on unsecured debt in Germany*

	Dependent variable		
	Unsecured debt (log)		
	(1)	(2)	(3)
Unemployed	0.36	0.39	0.36
	(0.26)	(0.26)	(1.85)
Household income (log)			0.25
			(0.16)
Unemployed × Household income (log)			0.01
			(0.18)
Controls	–	✓	✓
Unit fixed effects	✓	✓	✓
Year fixed effects	✓	✓	✓
Observations	6,102	6,102	6,102
R^2	0.61	0.61	0.61
Adjusted R^2	0.51	0.51	0.51

Notes: Results from regression models with unit and year fixed effects as well as a set of controls based on Equation 5.6. Robust standard errors clustered at the household level. The omitted baseline are households where the household head is full-time employed. Full results appear in Table A.5.4 in the Appendix. *p<0.1; **p<0.05; ***p<0.01.

restricts access to credit, particularly for households that cannot show reliable future income streams, for example, because one member is unemployed. The lack of borrowing by households in which the head works fewer hours or loses her job is in stark contrast to the United States and Denmark, where more households take on debt to address financial shortfalls. In the following section, I show if and to what extent overdraft facilities – an important financial lifeline akin to US-style credit cards – help German households bridge income gaps.

Overdraft Lending: Germany's Small Hidden Credit Market
The evidence thus far suggests that in Germany's restrictive credit regime, households rarely tap into formal credit markets in order to borrow money to address income gaps caused by disrupted employment patterns. In this section, I explore the role of overdraft lending, which some households access as an alternative to formal lines of credit in order to mitigate financial shocks.[23] The SAVE study contains a question about individuals' use of overdraft facilities. I create a binary indicator for whether respondents state they either use their overdraft facilities "often or always" or "never." I then estimate whether

[23] On the role of overdraft facilities in Germany, see, for example, Deutsche Bundesbank (2015, p. 20).

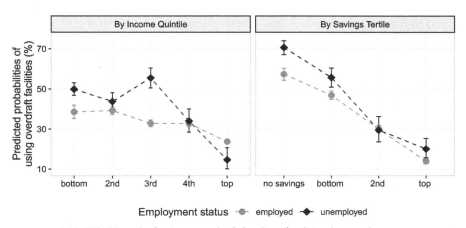

FIGURE 5.12 Likelihood of using overdraft lending facilities by employment status in Germany

Notes: Predicted probabilities with 95 percent confidence intervals from mixed effect logistic regression models. Tables A.5.5 and A.5.6 in the Appendix show the regression results for income and savings groups, respectively.

households in which the household head becomes unemployed use overdraft facilities to address income losses with a mixed effects logistic regression that combines fixed characteristics of each individual and random intercepts for individuals and years, allowing correlations among the latter.

The panels in Figure 5.12 plot the predicted probabilities of using an overdraft facility during unemployment for different income and savings groups. The left panel shows that households in the bottom 60 percent of the income distribution in which the head becomes unemployed have a higher probability of drawing on overdraft facilities than households with a full-time employed head. The differences between employed and unemployed households are about 14 percentage points for the bottom 40% of the income distribution and around 26% for the third income quintile, indicating that low-income households and in particular middle-income ones rely on overdraft facilities in the case of unemployment. The right panel shows the results from the regression model based on savings dummies, suggesting that savings work as an alternative coping mechanism to deal with income losses during unemployment. Households that have no savings and in which the head becomes unemployed have more than 70 percent probability of using overdraft facilities, almost 14 percentage points higher than households with a full-time employed head. For households with more savings, the differences between employed and unemployed groups disappear.

While the findings show that low- and middle-income households and particularly those who have limited or no savings draw on their overdraft facilities during unemployment, the overall magnitude of such borrowing is very small.

The SAVE panel does not ask individuals about the amount of overdraft they have used. Another survey has found that around 12 percent use €1,500 or more in their overdraft lending facility and another 18 percent use an average of €500–1,500 (Statista 2016).[24]

Discussion

The Germany case shows that the nature of the credit regime influences whether households can access and use credit to address financial shortfalls. In contrast to Denmark and the United States, the German credit regime restricts households' access to credit, channels capital flows toward the business sector, and incentivizes households to save. Average debt levels relative to incomes are much smaller in Germany than in the two other cases, reflecting significant differences in credit regimes. With credit being less easily available, households rarely tap into formal credit markets in order to borrow money to address income losses caused by unemployment or fewer work hours. Unlike in the cases of Denmark and the United States, the distribution of debt holdings among unemployed households varies little by income. Overdraft lending, by contrast, is an alternative source of financial liquidity in cases of unemployment, but its importance should not be overstated because households use it for relatively small amounts. German households are much more likely to internalize the financial burden of job losses or fewer work hours, for example, by drawing on savings.

The structure of the German labor market, segmented into a protected core of workers with stable, long-term employment patterns and comprehensive benefits and an exposed periphery with marginal and increasingly precarious jobs with limited benefits, reinforces these borrowing patterns. Formal lending in Germany is strongly determined by the prospective borrower's future income stream. This makes it especially hard for households to borrow if they become unemployed or rely on temporary or marginal forms of employment. While the Danish and American labor markets are much more flexible and fluid, the protected core of the German labor market still enjoys long-term employment tenure with stable incomes. But for individuals with jobs in the exposed periphery, they experience disrupted employment patterns and volatile incomes. Social policy and labor market reforms in the early 2000s have widened the financial shortfalls between households' financial needs and the welfare state's financial support as benefits have been cut while unemployment and job switches became more common.

---

[24] The remaining 64 percent use overdraft lending of up to €500. Six percent of the sample gave no answer.

THE IMPACT OF POLICY REFORMS ON INDEBTEDNESS:
WELFARE STATE RETRENCHMENT AND EASIER ACCESS TO
CREDIT

Political choices can influence the relationship between social policies and
household debt. In this section, I first show how individuals cope with cuts in
social policies after the Hartz labor market reform in Germany in 2005. As this
reform occurred in a restrictive credit regime, I expect that affected individuals
did not borrow money to compensate for financial gaps. I then turn to the
politics of credit and study the impact of an exogenous expansion of access to
credit in Denmark. In 1992, the Danish government for the first time allowed
homeowners to borrow against the value of their houses with home equity
loans. Households that before the reform had little savings to deal with income
losses began to draw heavily on these loans to address financial shortfalls.

The 2005 Hartz Labor Market Reform in Germany

In the early 2000s, the German government adopted a range of labor market and social policy reforms to tackle high unemployment rates and an ailing
economy by addressing what had been diagnosed as the root cause: the inflex-
ible and rigid labor market (Dustmann et al. 2014). In a series of reforms,
implemented in four consecutive laws named *Hartz I* through *IV*, the government enacted one of the most far-reaching labor market and social policy
reform agendas of Germany's postwar welfare state.[25] At the heart of the labor
market reform packages was the fourth labor market law, *Hartz IV*, which
adopted a set of activation policies for unemployed individuals, especially
those who had been unemployed long-term (over one year), and, most importantly, replaced earnings-related unemployment benefits with a means-tested
flat-rate unemployment benefit scheme. The reform, both prominent and con-
troversial, reduced benefit levels for new and existing unemployment insurance
recipients who had been unemployed for more than twelve months.[26]

Under the old system prior to the reform, unemployed individuals could
rely on a two-tiered social policy scheme: individuals who had worked at least
twelve months over the preceding three years were eligible to receive unemployment insurance benefits (*Arbeitslosengeld*) that replaced 60 percent of
their prior earnings (or 67 percent for those with dependent children). Benefit

---

[25] For an overview of the reform package and its impact on labor market outcomes see, for
example, Eichhorst, Kaufmann, and Konle-Seidl (2008); Jacobi and Kluve (2007); Krebs and
Scheffel (2013).

[26] For newspaper coverage of the Hartz reforms, in particular the Hartz IV law, see "German
Labour-Market Reform: Hartz and Minds," *The Economist*, December 29, 2004 and Mark
Landler, "The Heart of the Hartz Commission," *New York Times*, November 26, 2004.

duration was dependent on age and work experience and ranged from a maximum of twelve months for workers under forty-five years old to thirty-two months for those over fifty-seven years old. After these benefits were exhausted, the unemployed could apply for long-term means-tested unemployment assistance (*Arbeitslosenhilfe*) that replaced 53 percent of their prior earnings (or 57 percent for those with dependent children) indefinitely. Those who were ineligible for either unemployment benefits or unemployment assistance could draw on tax-funded means-tested social assistance (*Sozialhilfe*).

The Hartz IV reform law, the centerpiece of the labor market reform agenda, merged long-term unemployment and social assistance, and set the benefit amount at the lower level of social benefits (*Arbeitslosengeld II*). Eligibility criteria were tightened and the amount and duration of unemployment benefits were sharply reduced. Long-term UI benefits are no longer based on prior earnings but consist of flat-rate benefit payments (€345 per month for people in West Germany and €331 for people in former East Germany in 2005) with additional benefits for dependent spouses and children and subsidies for rent and heating. Notably, the reform – effective as of January 1, 2005 – applied to all unemployed individuals and did not grandfather in those who at that time already received benefits.

The process for calculating benefits shifted from a wage-index system to flat-rate payouts, which created a steep loss in unemployment benefits, particularly among high-income earners who had received higher unemployment benefits under the old system. In 2004, the year prior to the reform, 52 percent of all unemployed individuals (about 1.7 million people) were long-term unemployed for twelve months or more, one of the highest rates in the OECD (the OECD average in that year was 31 percent) (Bundesagentur für Arbeit 2017; OECD 2017). The Hartz IV reform therefore affected a large share of unemployed individuals.

Welfare Cuts and Growing Financial Shortfalls in a Restrictive Credit Regime

The implementation of the Hartz IV law on January 1, 2005, led to a significant drop in unemployment benefits among new and existing benefit recipients and therefore increased the financial shortfalls they experienced as a result. To estimate if and how affected individuals responded to the reform by borrowing money to address their financial gaps, I compare debt trajectories of employed and unemployed individuals before and after the reform. Based on the SAVE survey data, Figure 5.13 shows the differences in unsecured debt between employed and unemployed individuals before and after the Harz labor market reform was implemented. Prior to the reform, employed individuals tended to have slightly higher levels of debt than unemployed individuals, although the differences are statistically insignificant. Important for the following analysis, debt trajectories across the two groups follow parallel trends and lessen concerns about pre-treatment confounding differences in debt of

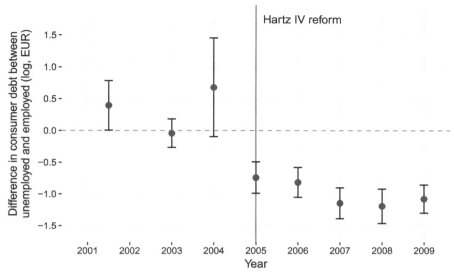

FIGURE 5.13 Differences in unsecured debt between unemployed and employed individuals before and after the German Hartz IV labor market reform
Notes: Differences in unsecured debt between employed and unemployed individuals based on raw SAVE data. Error bars show bootstrapped mean standard errors.

employed and unemployed individuals before the reform was enacted. Once the reform took effect in 2005, debt levels among the unemployed dropped significantly, reversing the patterns of debt holdings. In the years following the reform, unemployed individuals have consistently had less debt than employed individuals.

To corroborate these findings in a statistical framework, I estimate how the cuts in unemployment benefits influenced borrowing choices among unemployed individuals using a difference-in-differences (DID) design. The data unfortunately do not allow me to distinguish between short- and long-term unemployed since I only observe whether or not individual i is unemployed. The marginal effects of the Hartz IV reform on debt therefore capture the average treatment effect among all unemployed individuals. The DID regression model is as follows:

$$Y_{it} = \beta_1 U_{it} + \beta_2 (U_{it} \cdot post) + \mathbf{X}'_{it}\gamma + \alpha_i + \delta_t + \epsilon_{it} \qquad (5.7)$$

where Y_{it} is the log unsecured debt of individual i at time t. U_{it} is a dummy variable indicating unemployment and *post* is a dummy variable for post-Hartz IV reform status coded one for the years from 2005 onward and zero for the years before 2005. $\mathbf{X}'_{it}$ is a vector of time-varying individual-level covariates. α_i is a unit-level fixed effect controlling for any time-invariant unobserved factors, δ_t is a period fixed effect to control for common trends, and ϵ_{it} is the idiosyncratic error term. β_2 captures the DID effect of the Hartz IV reform on

TABLE 5.4 *Effect of the German Hartz IV labor market reform on unsecured debt*

	Dependent variable		
	Unsecured debt (log)		
	Raw data	Entropy-balanced data	
	(1)	(2)	(3)
Unemployed	1.71***	1.89***	1.84***
	(0.62)	(0.66)	(0.66)
Unemployed × Period$_{post}$	−1.19**	−1.26**	−1.26**
	(0.58)	(0.61)	(0.62)
Controls	✓	✓	✓
Unit fixed effects	✓	✓	✓
Year fixed effects	✓	✓	✓
Observations	5,342	5,342	5,342
R^2	0.64	0.64	0.64
Adjusted R^2	0.53	0.54	0.54

Notes: Results from a OLS regression model with unit and year fixed effects and control variables based on Equation 5.7. Robust standard errors are clustered at the household level. In columns 2 and 3, the data is adjusted for imbalances between employed and unemployed respondents using entropy balance based on age, education, number of children living in household, number of people in household, and marital status. Column (3) excludes income and savings as covariates because they may introduce posttreatment bias. The lower-order term *Period$_{post}$* is a time-invariant indicator of reform status and is not identified in the presence of year fixed effects. Full results appear in Table A.5.7 in the Appendix. *p<0.1; **p<0.05; ***p<0.01.

debt levels among the unemployed. While the set of individual and year fixed effects controls for time-invariant unobserved factors of individuals and common time trends, employed and unemployed individuals may still differ along other dimensions. I further use entropy balancing to adjust remaining imbalances between employed and unemployed respondents (Hainmueller 2012).[27] Table 5.4 shows the effect of cuts in unemployment benefits due to the reform on borrowing by the unemployed.

Although the reform brought a significant loss in benefits among the long-term unemployed, debt levels *declined* among the unemployed by over 70 percent in response to the Hartz IV reform. This effect is in stark contrast to the behavior of American households that borrow *more* in response to unemployment, particularly in states where unemployment insurance generosity is lower. The comparison between Germany and the United States also suggests

---

[27] Respondents are balanced on age, education, number of children living in household, number of people in household, and marital status.

that the structure of the credit regime and individuals' ease of credit access shape how households address financial gaps in light of different social policy regimes.

The Hartz IV reform in Germany provides a fruitful policy experiment that shows how a restrictive credit regime prevents households from borrowing money despite growing financial shortfalls driven by welfare state retrenchment.[28] In the next section, I turn to Denmark to study a policy reform that operated on the credit supply side.

The 1992 Home Equity Reform in Denmark

In 1992, the Danish government introduced legislation that allowed lenders to offer home equity loans, thereby enabling homeowners to borrow against the value of their houses without changing their wealth positions. Prior to this reform, homeowners could not borrow against their houses. Yet only homeowners who already had a significant portion of equity in their homes could extract liquidity. This exogenous and unanticipated increase in credit supply for eligible households provides a natural experiment to causally identify the effect of easier access to credit on borrowing.

The home equity reform took effect on May 21, 1992, as part of a larger agenda of liberalizing financial markets and stimulating the ailing economy. It allowed homeowners with sufficient equity to use initially up to 60 percent (and since December 1992 up to 80 percent) of their current real estate wealth as collateral for non-housing-related consumer loans. The reform has two useful features that make it attractive as an "as if" random shock to credit supply. First, it was introduced quickly after a very brief discussion in the Danish parliament, and was therefore not anticipated by the broader public.[29] Second, the reform did not change homeowners' wealth positions and only affected the cost of credit. Since the amount of collateral that homeowners could borrow against was based on the outstanding mortgage amounts at the time of the reform – to great degrees determined by when the house was purchased – we can rule out strategic behavior of homeowners or bias in borrowing responses driven by wealth. Prior evidence suggests that this unexpected increase in liquidity had several significant effects: it "unlocked" an average amount of home equity that could be used as collateral of about $30,000 (Jensen, Leth-Petersen, and Nanda 2014); it increased households' consumption over time (Leth-Petersen 2010); and it reduced overall unemployment insurance uptake (Markwardt, Martinello, and Sándor 2014). We should

---

[28] The data and this research design do not allow me to distinguish whether households *would* borrow if they had access to credit.

[29] Leth-Petersen (2010) shows that not even Danish newspapers reported about the reform until a month before the reform took effect in May 1992.

therefore expect that with easier access to credit, those who become unemployed would compensate their income losses by borrowing more, relative to those who remain employed. This comparison is important since households may use credit for various purposes unrelated to income losses. If the home equity reform allows eligible homeowners to tap into credit markets to increase their spending, there should be no difference among employed and unemployed individuals, or even a stronger effect among the former, knowing that they have a stable job. Yet if those who lost incomes, for example, due to unemployment, are granted better access to credit, we would expect them to borrow more to compensate for income losses.

I used data on the entire Danish population four years before and after the reform (from 1988 to 1996). I first define "savings constraints" as having less than one-and-a-half months' worth of income in liquid savings in 1991, the year prior to the reform. This is a standard measure of savings constraints in the literature (see, for example, Johnson, Parker, and Souleles 2006; Leth-Petersen 2010; Zeldes 1989). The distinction between liquid and illiquid savings is important since the former contain financial assets that households can immediately access, such as deposits in checking or savings accounts or stock ownership. Typically, illiquid savings and assets such as real estate or pension funds cannot be easily converted into money, or it is costly to execute such conversions. Liquid savings are therefore an important financial cushion.

I estimate the effect of the home equity reform on total debt by savings-constrained homeowners who became unemployed in a triple difference-in-differences (DDD) framework. Because of data constraints in the earlier years of the register data, I cannot distinguish between secured and unsecured debt. I therefore use total debt instead. This regression model takes the average change in debt levels for unemployed individuals among those who were savings-constrained (treatment group) and nets out changes in means for unemployed among those who were not savings-constrained (control group) and the changes in means for employed individuals among those who were savings-constrained (treatment group). The DDD estimator controls for potentially confounding trends in changes in employment status of individuals *across* groups who are savings-constrained and those who are not that are orthogonal to the home equity reform. It also controls for changes in employment status of individuals *within* savings-constrained and unconstrained groups that might be related with group-specific factors influencing employment status, for example, income or wealth.

Since unemployed and employed individuals might still differ along other dimensions not accounted for by the DDD design, I use entropy balance as before to adjust remaining imbalances between employed and unemployed respondents.[30] I implement the DDD model in the following fixed effects regression OLS framework:

---

[30] Respondents are balanced on birth year, education (five categories), ZIP code, family type, number of children, and the gender of the household head.

$$Y_{it} = \beta_1 S_{i,91} + \beta_2 post + \beta_3 U_{it} + \beta_4 (S_{i,91} \cdot post) + \beta_5 (S_{i,91} \cdot U_{it})$$
$$+ \beta_6 (post \cdot U_{it}) + \beta_7 (U_{it} \cdot post \cdot S_{i,91}) + X'_{it} \gamma + \alpha_i + \delta_t + \epsilon_{it} \quad (5.8)$$

where Y_{it} is the log total household debt of individual i at time t. $S_{i,91}$ is a dummy variable indicating if individual i's household is savings constrained, defined as having less than one-and-a-half months' worth of income in liquid savings in the year prior to the reform (1991). $post$ is a dummy indicating the post-reform period from 1992 onward, and U_{it} is a dummy variable indicating if individual i was unemployed in year t. X'_{it} is a vector of time-varying individual-level covariates. α_i is a unit fixed effect controlling for any time-invariant unobserved factors among households, δ_t is a year fixed effect controlling for common shocks and trends, and ϵ_{it} is the idiosyncratic error term. β_7 is the coefficient of interest and captures the effect of easier access to credit among those who became unemployed and were savings constrained, relative to those who remained employed.

Panel (a) in Figure 5.14 shows that the increase in credit availability due to the home equity reform had a sizable effect on savings-constrained unemployed compared to employed individuals. After the reform, the amount of debt nearly doubled for savings-constrained employed individuals but more than tripled for savings-constrained unemployed individuals. In other words, unemployed individuals borrowed 80 percent *more* than employed individuals.[31]

I further estimate a fully flexible and dynamic version of Equation 5.8 to estimate the development of debt levels by interacting the dummies for unemployment and savings constraints with year dummies (relative to the year prior to the reform) instead of pooling the pre- and post-reform periods. Panel (b) in Figure 5.14 shows that in the years leading up to the reform there is virtually no difference between savings-constrained employed and unemployed individuals, satisfying the parallel trends assumption. Yet in the years after the reform, unemployed individuals began to borrow more relative to the pre-reform years *and* relative to employed individuals, suggesting that newly gained access to credit provided an opportunity for unemployed individuals to address income losses. Individuals responded to the new possibility of taking out home equity loans by increasing their debt levels, but this occurs with a time lag of one to two years after the parliament passed the reform legislation. This delay can be explained by the time it takes for individuals to decide if they should use and apply for home equity loans and for lenders to process these applications and grant lines of credit.

---

[31] Table A.5.8 in the Appendix shows the full set of regression models based on the unadjusted data as well as models based on the entropy-balanced data. The models based on the entropy-balanced data have slightly smaller values on the lower-order coefficients and the interaction terms, reducing the overall DDD effect. The substantive conclusion remains the same.

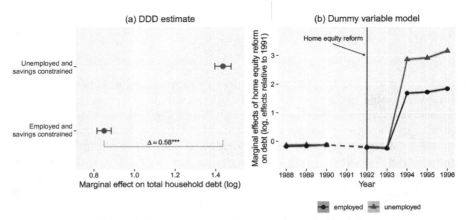

FIGURE 5.14 Effect of home equity reform on household debt among savings-constrained households by employment status in Denmark

Notes: Panel (a) shows the marginal effects of the home equity reform in 1992 among savings-constrained employed and unemployed individuals based on the triple difference-in-differences Equation 5.8 (column 6 in Table A.5.8 in the Appendix). The error bars are 95 percent confidence intervals based on robust standard errors clustered at the household level. Panel (b) shows the marginal effects of the home equity reform among savings-constrained employed and unemployed individuals based on a version of Equation 5.8 where *post* is replaced by year dummies. All results are relative to the year prior to the reform (the omitted baseline). The 95 percent confidence intervals are based on robust standard errors clustered at the household level, although not always clearly visible because of the high precision of the administrative records. N=16.8m.

DISCUSSION

This chapter presents a range of micro-level evidence from Denmark, the United States, and Germany that paints a cohesive picture of credit as a vital private instrument for households to address financial gaps that emerge in the domain of social risks.

The comparative perspective of this chapter suggests that only in countries with permissive credit regimes do households borrow money when welfare states insufficiently address unexpected income losses that are caused by disrupted employment patterns and fluctuating work hours. The situation of Frank Walsh, who ran up $20,000 in credit card debt to make ends meet after he became unemployed, is emblematic of many households in the United States. And yet, it is quite different from the way households in Denmark and Germany experience unemployment. It is the combination of disrupted employment patterns and a declining social safety net that forces many households like Frank Walsh's to turn to credit markets to compensate for financial shortfalls in light of limited financial alternatives. In Denmark, a country with weak employment regulation, a flexible labor market, and a permissive credit regime that incentivizes lending to households, the combination of disrupted employment patterns and comprehensive financial support from the welfare state limits the financial shortfall to upper-middle-income and high-income households. These households have easy access to credit and address such shortfalls by temporarily borrowing money. For low-income households, by contrast, the Danish welfare state provides sufficient financial support and protection from risks, thereby lessening the need to borrow money. Credit markets and social policies complement each other in the provision of financial liquidity. Recent welfare reforms, however, have widened the gap between earnings losses and social policy income support for low-income groups and have increased their reliance on debt to address the resulting financial shortfalls. Social policies in Denmark are, however, still more financially protective than in the United States.

By contrast, in the United States the labor market is similarly flexible but employment protection is even weaker. Employment patterns are more unstable and increasingly more precarious as households face not only more frequent spells of unemployment but also irregular and fewer work hours. The welfare state, however, addresses a much smaller share of these employment disruptions and resulting income losses and provides less financial support compared to the Danish case. As a result, many households ranging from the bottom to the middle of the income distribution experience much larger social policy–related financial shortfalls. In the United States, permissive credit markets are also an important source for households to stem financial gaps, but unlike in Denmark, it is mostly low- and middle-income households that borrow money to compensate for labor market risks and income losses. Germany provides an important comparison to both Denmark and the United States, emphasizing the role of the credit regime and households' access to credit. Regardless of income, German households rarely tap into credit markets when they face income losses caused by disrupted employment patterns. If anything, they rely on small amounts from their overdraft facilities. These findings are reflected in Figure 5.15, which compares debt-to-income ratios among unemployed individuals in the three country cases.

Finally, this chapter draws attention to political choices in the realm of social and credit policies that influence households' debt levels. In the US case, I find that individuals struck by unemployment borrow more in states with less generous benefits. In the Danish case, I demonstrate that after the unexpected introduction of home equity loans in 1992, households that previously had little savings to deal with income losses related to unemployment began to draw heavily on these loans to compensate for financial shortfalls. Both countries have permissive credit regimes that provide easy access to credit and enable households to borrow money to address financial shortfalls that arise as a result of labor market–related income losses and incomplete social policy support. Lastly, I show that the Hartz IV labor market reform in Germany in

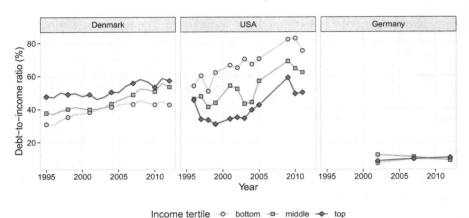

FIGURE 5.15 Average unsecured debt-to-income ratios among the unemployed by income

Notes: Unsecured debt as a share of disposable income. For more details and data sources, see notes for the respective figures in each country section.

2005, which sharply cut long-term unemployment benefits and led to a considerable increase in financial shortfalls, *lowered* household debt among the unemployed. This is because Germany's restrictive credit regime makes credit much harder to obtain for households.

The findings in this chapter show that permissive credit regimes can substitute for social policies in limited welfare states as more people go into debt to address financial shortfalls, pushing economically vulnerable groups into debt. By contrast, when social policies are comprehensive but stratified, permissive credit regimes coexist with and complement welfare states in the provision of financial liquidity, protecting economically disadvantaged groups through government benefits while allowing more affluent but less protected groups to borrow money. It is the interplay of the structure of the welfare state and the resulting financial shortfalls on the one hand and the permissiveness of the credit regime on the other that explains variation in debt levels across households, as summarized in Figure 5.16. At the macro level, the structure of the credit regime plays an important role in restricting or permitting households to tap into credit markets. But the micro-level evidence about how different "types" of households borrow money in response to social policy–related financial shortfalls offers a cautionary conclusion: credit is a double-edged sword. It can help households address temporary income shortfalls during unemployment if they can manage their debt burdens and repay their loans as the case of high-income Danish households suggests. But it can also amplify risks and increase the financial burden on households that are already economically disadvantaged, such as low-income American households. I revisit

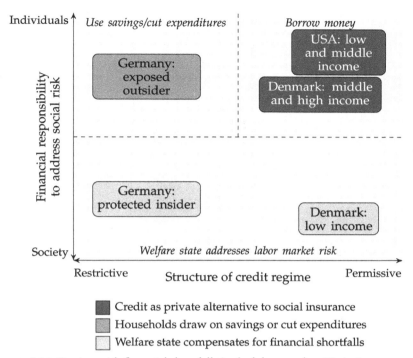

FIGURE 5.16 Coping with financial shortfalls in the labor market: Variation across and within countries

Notes: In Germany, "exposed outsiders" are affected by the Hartz IV labor market reform, and "protected insiders" are unaffected by the reforms (i.e., they are working in stable jobs).

the socioeconomic and political consequences in greater detail in Chapter 7. But first, in Chapter 6 I turn to credit as a form of bounded social investment and study the effect of fragmented life course trajectories on household debt.

6

Borrowing during the Life Course

Meet Mette and Christian Miller-Harris. When the couple was interviewed by a newspaper in 2012, they lived in Copenhagen with their then thirteen-month-old daughter Martha. What makes their life as a dual-earner couple with a child financially viable, they told the reporter, is the affordable cost of childcare and public leave programs.[1] Targeted government policies such as subsidized childcare, paid parental leave, and flexible work hours allow Danish parents such as the Miller-Harrises to take time off work after childbirth and later to enroll their children in childcare, enabling mothers to participate in the labor market, too. "I never once thought about not going back to work after having Martha," says Mette.

When it comes to promoting social investment, economic mobility, and overall social opportunities, the "Scandinavian model" of social policies is often compared favorably with the approaches taken in the United States and Germany. Denmark in particular is known for its education and family policies that invest in its citizens and help them reconcile work and family life. Government support for maternity and paternity leave and publicly subsidized childcare allow both Danish parents to continue to work while their children are in daycare. The numbers speak for themselves: about 92% of children who are between one and two years old and 97% of children between three and five years are in daycare (Kvist 2015). Danish families pay up to a quarter of the cost of daycare; for low-income families and single parents, the costs are even lower. This helps explain why almost all women return to work after taking, on average, one year off following childbirth, and why stay-at-home mothers are extremely rare (Albæk 2008, ch. 8).

Many governments recognize that childcare is an educational investment in children, and it also helps parents, especially mothers, reconcile their career

---

[1] See Lucy Rock, "What Britain Could Learn from Denmark's Childcare Model," *Guardian (US edition)*, February 18, 2012.

aspirations with family obligations. But policy responses and financing options differ considerably across countries. "Early childhood education is one of the most important investments a parent can make. [...] But too often, quality child care is out of reach for middle class families," said Christine Quinn in 2013, who was at that time New York City's Council speaker and mayoral candidate.[2] But instead of following the Danish approach of publicly subsidized places in childcare facilities, she introduced the "Middle Class Child Care Loan Initiative," a subsidized loan program that would cover the costs of daycare and preschool for parents with annual incomes between $80,000 and $200,000 and very good credit scores. This is where credit and debt enter the picture.

But the cost of childcare is only one part of the financial burden that many American families face. Unlike in Denmark, where paid sick days and parental leave allow individuals to take time off work for child-related reasons without large income losses, incomplete or nonexistent public support and varying degrees of employer-based benefits increase the financial burdens for American families with children. Consider the case of Raquell Heredia, who in 2014 lived in Fontana, California, and suffered severe morning sickness after she became pregnant.[3] Yet her job as a waitress and bartender did not provide her with sick leave, and thus she decided to quit and began working at a pharmacy. Her new job, however, offered limited maternity leave, and when her first child was born, she left that job, too. "I think that they should make it a lot easier, like for parents to have holidays off with their kids," she said. Raquell Heredia's situation is not uncommon for many Americans who cannot afford to take time off work to take care of their children because it is prohibitively expensive. For those who have the option of unpaid leave, this too is risky because this type of leave is usually not job-protected. People like Raquell Heredia often have no choice but to go into debt to make ends meet.

This chapter focuses on financial shortfalls that arise during the life course and the role of credit as a means toward social investment. I study the circumstances under which individuals and their families go into debt and borrow money to address the financial consequences of moving in and out of the labor market and hopping from one job to another as well as the costs associated with raising a family. Contrasting the experience of families in Scandinavian countries and the United States illustrates how similar life course choices and family situations can lead to investment in children, careers, and perhaps even upward mobility on the one hand, and to financial uncertainty and economic insecurity on the other. What determines whether the use of credit as a social investment has a "positive yield," to use banking jargon, or is more likely to

---

[2] Quoted in Kim Vesley, "Should Upper Middle Class Tots Get Subsidized Student Loans for Pre-School?" *Observer (UK)*, May 8, 2013.

[3] See Claire Cain Miller and Liz Alderman, "Why U.S. Women Are Leaving Jobs Behind," *New York Times*, December 12, 2014.

resemble a socioeconomic necessity depends on how leveled the social policy playing field is and what types of opportunity costs come with such life course choices. In cases where family policies provide financial support to parents through paid leave and subsidized childcare and legally protect their jobs during periods of leave, the choices to take time off work or to enroll children in daycare are much less dependent on financial considerations compared to cases where no such policies exist and families have to shoulder the financial consequences themselves. Opportunity costs influence whether borrowing money for these life course choices turns into either positive social investment in children and parents' career aspirations or new forms of social risks when unpaid time off work or prohibitively expensive childcare put jobs in jeopardy and increase financial risks.

In Chapter 3, I show that life course trajectories in many OECD countries have become more fragmented as individuals temporarily leave work to raise families and get more education and training, and they also switch jobs more frequently. These disruptions are often very costly. Parents have to cope with outright income losses when they take time off work to take care of children. If they want someone else to take care of their children, some parents opt to pay for daycare. More frequent job switches may reflect new job opportunities or simply the reality of short-term contracts, but in either case these shifts often increase income volatility because earnings in the new job may not necessarily be the same or higher than in the old job.

Welfare states shape how much public support individuals receive during various life course stages, and how much of the costs individuals and their families themselves have to shoulder. Some countries have expanded their social investment policies, but others lag behind. In 2007, the OECD issued a report, aptly titled "Modernising Social Policy for the New Life Course," urging countries to shift toward social investment policies that would address the new working and living realities of households in the knowledge economy (OECD 2007). Denmark and Sweden, two of the countries that turned toward social investment policies early, offer publicly funded subsidies and transfer payments to ameliorate the financial impacts of disrupted life course choices. These policies absorb much of the financial burdens of parental leave and childcare costs and, as a consequence, lower the opportunity costs of taking leaves for education or child-rearing. In other countries such as the United States or the United Kingdom, social investment policies lag behind, requiring individuals to shoulder a larger share of income losses when they take time off work and have to meet (rising) expenditures for childcare, education, or training. Increasingly, individuals in the United States and the United Kingdom stem these financial shortfalls by tapping into credit markets and borrowing money.

I begin this chapter by documenting the broad links between life course trajectories and household indebtedness in Denmark, where mostly middle- and high-income households draw on credit to smooth income losses when they temporarily leave work, for example to take care of children or to pursue (re-)training. In fact, this type of borrowing is more prevalent than tapping into credit markets to cope with labor market-related risks as I show in Chapter 5. I use the home equity reform of 1992, which had eased access to credit considerably, to show that individuals with limited savings who leave the workforce for reasons other than unemployment (e.g., childcare leave or training) are almost twice as likely to go into debt than those who become unemployed. By contrast, the cost of childcare – which is a significant financial burden for many households in the United States that results in more borrowing to stem those costs – does not lead to higher levels of debt in Denmark because considerable government subsidies contain families' expenditures. But job switches, a more frequent phenomenon in the flexible Danish labor market, can further amplify income volatility when the new job does not pay as much as the previous one. I show that individuals who switch jobs and experience a decline in earnings are more likely to borrow money to mitigate those losses than individuals who switch jobs but maintain their prior earning levels.

In the United States, by contrast, there are more individuals who borrow money to address the financial consequences of fragmented life course trajectories and to cover related expenditures. A large and growing number of employees temporarily leave their jobs for a few weeks scattered throughout the year to take care of children, to get training or education, or to take personal days. Unlike in European welfare states, social policies in the United States rarely provide financial support for these forms of leave, which are often unpaid. Family policies such as paid maternity or paternity leave or childcare are less generous than in other OECD countries. If in-cash or in-kind support does exist, it is often unequally distributed or only available through large employers. Some individuals and their families choose to invest in their children, education, and their own careers by borrowing money to pay for childcare, stem additional expenditures for education and training, or smooth out lost income. For others, however, the lack of baseline social support and the high costs of childcare increase the opportunity costs such that borrowing money becomes a financial necessity rather than a social investment. One similarity that the United States shares with Denmark is that individuals also borrow money to address financial gaps caused by job switches that result in lower earnings. In the context of fragmented life course trajectories and limited support from social policies, the permissive credit market has become a private alternative for many Americans to address volatile incomes or higher expenses.

In the final section of this chapter, I turn to Germany, where the growing flexibility of the labor market and changing family structures – including the decline of the single-breadwinner model and the influx of women and young mothers into the labor market – have only recently been met by shifts toward social investment policies. But as we already saw, the German credit regime is far more restrictive than the Danish or American ones. Despite more flexible life course trajectories, more individuals temporarily taking time off work to take care of children, and growing earnings volatility as individuals shift from one job to another, Germans rarely go into debt. With one of the highest savings rates in the OECD, individuals are more likely to tap into savings to smooth income losses and cover related expenditures.

LIFE COURSE TRAJECTORIES AND DEBT IN DENMARK

Denmark and other Scandinavian countries have long been perceived as being role models among OECD countries for their social policies that support households' efforts to reconcile work and family life (Bonoli 2013; OECD 2007). These countries' governments heavily subsidize childcare, which thus rarely poses significant financial burdens for their citizens. Often, however, it is the growing fragmentation of life course trajectories that increases income volatility. Taking time off work to raise a family or get more training takes a financial toll. The amount of financial support from the welfare state depends on individuals' incomes and, in the case of maternity and paternity leave, on employers' contributions.[4] Another type of financial burden for households is due to frequent job changes *without* periods of unemployment, which lead to income volatility if new jobs pay less.

The financial impact of fragmented life course trajectories also varies across households. As I show in Chapters 3 and 5, the Danish welfare state provides more generous support for low-income individuals and families than for high-income ones. This means that income replacement rates during leaves of absence from work are higher for those in the lower rungs of the income distribution compared to those in the upper rungs. Similar to unemployment benefits, parental leave payments are tied to prior earnings and capped at a relatively low level. But unlike social insurance transfers, more individuals receive higher parental leave benefits. These individuals include public sector employees who are paid their full salaries during leave periods as well as private sector employees for whom collective labor agreements guarantee higher pay during leaves than the public (unemployment insurance) rate. The out-of-pocket costs of childcare also vary by household income. Low-income parents can get free or heavily subsidized childcare, whereas high-income parents have to cover up to one-third of the cost of childcare themselves, regardless of employment status. The average cost, however, is one of the lowest in the OECD. Relatively high availability and affordability of care reduce opportunity costs for enrolling children in full-time care centers and help parents reconcile work and career aspirations with family life. In sum, Denmark's permissive credit regime matches the financial needs of individuals and their families in the

---

[4] Public sector employees in Denmark receive full salary compensation during maternity and paternity leave.

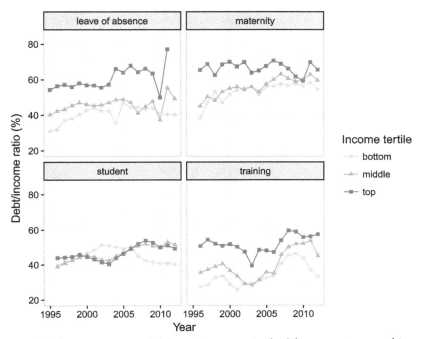

FIGURE 6.1 Average unsecured debt-to-income ratios by life course stages and income in Denmark

Notes: Household-level debt-to-income ratio for households where one member of the household is on a leave of absence, maternity leave, a student, or enrolled in training. *Source:* Danish full population administrative register data.

modern knowledge economy because it allows them to bridge financial gaps and volatile incomes as they move from one life course stage to another.

Borrowing During Life Course Stages

How do debt levels of Danish households change as they move through different phases of their lives? As in Chapter 5, I use Danish full population administrative register data to estimate how different life course stages such as taking leaves of absence and enrolling in educational programs shape households' debt leverage.[5] Figure 6.1 shows the development of debt-to-income ratios over time for households in different life course stages and income tertiles. Across all households where one household member is on a leave of absence, including maternity or paternity leave, or in training, high-income households carry more debt relative to their incomes than middle- and

---

[5] For more details on the data, see Section A in the Appendix.

low-income families. Among households with a member on maternity leave, high-income households consistently had greater debt-to-income ratios than middle- and low-income households, even though debt leverage of the latter two groups has caught up since the mid-1990s. Finally, for households with a member in education, either as a student or in other forms of training, unsecured debt leverage has on average increased since the mid-2000s. Among students, there is a growing divergence between middle- and high-income students whose debt leverage slightly increased and low-income students whose debt leverages considerably decreased. Among those in training, debt leverage increased throughout the income distribution but was greatest for high-income groups. In the aftermath of the financial crisis of 2007–08, low-income groups strongly de-leveraged.

To address concerns that other factors such as changing family structures, age, or income dynamics influence the trends in debt leverage displayed in Figure 6.1, I estimate the effect of different life course stages on household debt across different income quintiles in the following fixed effect regression framework:

$$Y_{it} = \beta_1 L_{it} + \beta_2^g \sum_{g \neq 1} G_{it} + \beta_3^g \sum_{g \neq 1} (G_{it} \cdot L_{it}) + X'_{it}\gamma + \alpha_i + \delta_t + \sigma_z + \epsilon_{it} \quad (6.1)$$

where Y_{it} is the log unsecured household debt for household head i in year t. L_{it} is a dummy variable indicating the respective life course stage (leave of absence, maternity, training, and student). The control group includes households with full-time employed heads of the household. G_{it} is a dummy variable indicating the households' income quintile (the bottom quintile is the omitted baseline category). X'_{it} is a matrix of time- and individual-varying controls including household income, liquid assets, a set of education dummies, age squared, the number of children living at home, and the family type. α_i are unit-level fixed effects controlling for time-invariant unobserved heterogeneity across households, thereby identifying changes in debt on the basis of changes in employment status within units. δ_t are year fixed effects to control for aggregate time trends. σ_z are birth-year fixed effects to control for age and cohort effects. ϵ_{it} is the idiosyncratic error term. I estimate a separate regression for each life course stage.

Figure 6.2 shows the marginal effects of leaves of absence, maternity leave, and being a student on unsecured debt by income quintiles compared to individuals in full-time employment. Households in which one member is on maternity leave are the ones that carry the most debt compared to households with members on other forms of leaves of absence and being a student. In these cases, borrowing is mostly concentrated among middle-income households, in particular those in the second income quintile. These households carry between 70 percent and 110 percent more unsecured debt than those in the bottom income quintile when a household member is on maternity leave, compared to those with full-time working household members. For other types of leaves of

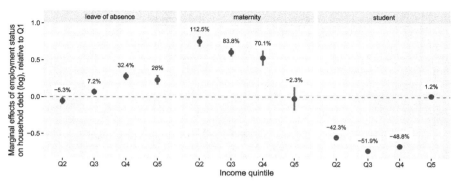

FIGURE 6.2 Effect of life course stages on unsecured debt by income in Denmark
Notes: Marginal effects of life course status on unsecured debt by income quintiles. The bottom quintile (Q1) is the omitted baseline. The numbers show the percentage difference relative to those in the bottom income quintile. Each panel comes from a separate fixed effect regression model with unit, year, and birth-year fixed effects based on Equation 6.1. Full results in Table A.6.1 in the Appendix. *Source:* Danish full population administrative register data.

absence, high-income households tend to take on considerably more debt compared to those in the bottom quintile. Much like in the case of unemployment, documented in Chapter 5, the welfare state supports low-income households to much greater degrees than middle- and higher-income ones, reducing the necessity of low-income households to tap into credit markets.

Children and Household Debt

The decline of the single-breadwinner model and the rise of dual-earner families have increased demand for childcare, funded and organized either publicly or privately, since families have a harder time providing and affording care as they seek to reconcile work and family life. Figure 6.3 compares the net costs of childcare in Denmark, the United States, and Germany for different family types over time. In Denmark and Germany, single parents with two children spend less than 5 percent of their net household income on childcare, one of the lowest rates in the OECD. The United States, by contrast, is one of the most expensive countries for childcare for single parents, who spend over a third of their net household income on childcare. For couples, the Danish and German systems are more expensive because the share of parents' financial childcare contributions increases on the basis of household income. In recent years, however, Germany has improved public subsidies and the provision of childcare, reducing parents' own contributions considerably. Danish couples spend around 11 percent of their income toward childcare, whereas American couples spend nearly double that amount. The stark differences in the affordability of childcare across the OECD but also within countries by family type

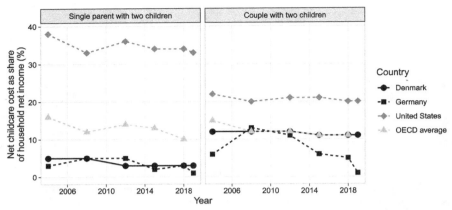

FIGURE 6.3 Net childcare costs as share of household net income across families
Notes: Earnings of the primary adult earner are set at 67 percent of the country's average wage in a particular category. For couples, partner's earnings are set at 67 percent of average wages. *Source:* OECD Tax-Benefit Model. 2020.

and income shape whether families decide to send their children to childcare and how likely it is that mothers are taking up full-time work.

Childcare is relatively affordable in Denmark because it is heavily subsidized by the government, with prices set annually at the municipality level. Parents may end up paying up to one-third of the total cost of care, but reduced rates and subsidies are available for families with lower incomes and with siblings enrolled in public care (Esping-Andersen et al. 2012; Simonsen 2010). Moreover, starting at one-year-olds, the government guarantees that all children have a place in childhood education and care centers. Denmark is also one of the few countries that provide childcare services beyond regular school hours (Flynn 2017). The combination of affordability and comparatively high availability is reflected in high shares of children who are enrolled in full-time care centers as well as high female employment rates, including among young mothers. Almost 80% of all children up to age three, irrespective of parental income, are in childcare (compared to only 20% in Germany), and about 90% of them are in care for thirty hours per week or longer (compared to 44% in Germany). Nearly all four-year-olds are in daycare (Kvist 2015, p. 47–8).

With heavily subsidized childcare costs, many families in Denmark have little or no need to go into debt to pay for childcare. This is in stark contrast to the experience of many young parents in the United States who cannot rely on publicly subsidized low-cost preschools and daycare and thus are more likely to borrow money to finance child-related income volatility and expenses, as I show in later sections.

Easier Access to Credit and Borrowing: The Home Equity Reform of 1992 Revisited

Expenditures for life course choices such as education or childcare tend to be low because the government pays for most of it. It is the income losses that families experience – particularly high-income ones – when they take time off from work for education, training, or family-related leave that lead to borrowing. Since the welfare state provides more support for low-income individuals and families, debt tends to be concentrated among middle- and high-income groups.

In this section, I revisit the effect of easier access to credit when Denmark introduced home equity loans for the first time in 1992.[6] In Chapter 5, I demonstrate that the possibility of borrowing against the value of one's house had a sizable effect among previously savings-constrained homeowners. Did greater credit availability also influence the borrowing behaviors of individuals who are outside the labor force for reasons other than unemployment or sickness? This category includes individuals on leave of absence, including parental leave, and individuals pursuing education or training. I estimate a triple difference-in-differences (DDD) model analogous to the one introduced in Equation 5.8 in Chapter 5, but this time I compare savings-constrained households in which the head was outside the labor force for reasons other than unemployment to those in which the head remained employed. I use employed individuals as an anchor for the size of the effect, as all eligible savings-constrained households are affected by this exogenous ease of credit.

Panel (a) in Figure 6.4 shows that after the reform, easier access to credit more than doubled debt levels among savings-constrained households with a head who is outside the labor market compared to a head who is employed. Substantively, this effect is twice as large as the effect estimated for unemployed individuals in Chapter 5, suggesting that life course trajectories influence borrowing more than unemployment. Panel (b) shows the results from a fully flexible and dynamic version of equation 5.8, which interacts the dummy variables for being outside the labor force and being savings-constrained with year dummy variables (instead of pooling the pre- and post-reform periods). In the years leading up to the reform, there is virtually no difference between savings-constrained households in which the household head is employed compared with household heads who are out of the labor force (but not unemployed). After the reform, however, those who were outside the labor force began to borrow more relative to both employed individuals *and* the pre-reform years, suggesting that newly gained access to credit provided an opportunity for those outside the labor force to address income shortfalls. Easier access to credit increased borrowing among households with household members who had

---

[6] See Chapter 5 for more details on the reform.

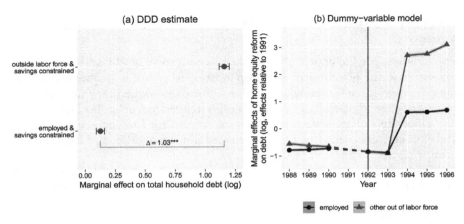

FIGURE 6.4 Effect of home equity reform on household debt among savings-constrained households by employment status in Denmark

Notes: Panel (a) shows the marginal effects of the home equity reform in 1992 among savings-constrained households with a head who is either employed or outside the labor force based on the DDD model in Equation 5.8 in Chapter 5. The error bars are 95 percent confidence intervals based on robust standard errors clustered at the household level. Panel (b) shows the marginal effects of the home equity reform among savings-constrained households with a head who is either employed or outside the labor force based on a version of Equation 5.8 for which *post* is replaced by year dummies. All results are relative to the year prior to the reform (the omitted baseline).

Source: Danish full population administrative register data.

opted out of the labor force for reasons other than unemployment (e.g., child-care, education, or training) to much larger degrees than among households with an unemployed household member.

Job Switches and Income Losses

Social insurance and investment policies aim to both mitigate the consequences of adverse labor market risks and support individuals and their families through various life course stages. While the social policy coverage of these risks varies across countries, some types of risks are not insured at all. Consider how moving from one job to another and earning less in the new job than in the previous one affects income volatility. This form of income fluctuation has increased in many OECD countries during the past few decades. Lower earnings in a new job may be a temporary setback that can be compensated for with a higher-paying job in the future. While some policymakers such as Presidents George W. Bush and Barack Obama have acknowledged that earnings volatility poses a significant financial problem, they fell short of introducing forms of wage insurance that would address these issues.[7] In the absence of welfare state support, employees who move into new jobs with lower pay have to absorb these income losses themselves.

In this section, I show that individuals who are affected by declines in income because of job switches tap into credit markets and borrow money to bridge these income gaps. Analogous to the event study framework used in Chapter 5, I compare individuals who switch jobs and lose some income to those who switch jobs and retain the same income. Using the Danish full population administrative register data, I combine data for when individuals switch jobs *without* becoming unemployed with data on when labor incomes (earnings) change as a result of job switches. I define a decline in earnings as a drop of more than 5 percent from one year to the next.

Figure 6.5 shows the event study coefficients relative to the year prior to the job switch. In the years before the job switch, debt levels, as expected, follow a similar trend among those whose income remains the same after the switch. Once individuals switch jobs, debt levels begin to diverge. Those who experience declines in their incomes take on about 50 percent more debt in the year of the job switch (converted from the logged coefficient) compared to the year before they switch jobs. This effect persists in subsequent years. By contrast, those whose income remains the same do not borrow money. This suggests that credit markets function as a private insurance mechanism, allowing individuals to bridge income gaps when their new jobs pay less than their old ones.

In sum, Danish households are more likely to use credit for social investments to address the financial consequences of life course choices than for social risks such as unemployment. Borrowing tends to be concentrated among middle- and high-income groups who are less well covered by the welfare state. Next, I turn to the United States as a country with a similarly permissive credit regime but a much more limited welfare state, in particular in the social investment domain.

LIFE COURSE TRAJECTORIES AND DEBT IN THE UNITED STATES

When it comes to social investment policies, the United States lags behind many other European countries. Policies such as paid parental leave or subsidized childcare that people from other countries take for granted only exist in a few states. There is no federal law requiring private sector employers to provide paid leave. Instead, individuals and their families to much greater degrees rely on employers to provide benefits that in other countries would be offered publicly through the welfare state. But as the example of

---

[7] In the United States, a specific form of wage insurance for workers who lost their jobs to foreign workers has been introduced under the George W. Bush and Obama administrations. See also Robert J. Shiller "How Wage Insurance Could Ease Economic Inequality," *New York Times*, March 11, 2016, and Obama's 2016 State of the Union address.

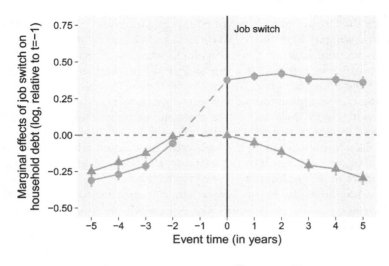

FIGURE 6.5 Job switches, income changes, and unsecured debt in Denmark
Notes: Event-year marginal effect coefficients relative to the year prior to the job switch based on Equation 5.1 in Chapter 5. The year prior to the event ($t=-1$) is the omitted baseline. The error bars are 95 percent confidence intervals based on robust standard errors clustered at the household level. The model is based on a balanced sample of families whose head changes jobs between 1992 and 2007, such that individuals are observed five years before and after job change during this period. *Source:* Danish full population administrative register data.

Raquell Heredia shows, the American "public–private" welfare state, which combines government and private sector support (Hacker 2002; Morgan and Campbell 2011), provides less support for families and addresses fewer risks than it once did. In Chapter 3, I document how deliberate cuts in social policies and failures to adapt policies to changes in families' work and life course realities have further reduced the scope of the American welfare state. An important pillar of the private welfare state, many employers have also not updated their policies to meet new demands. A recent national survey conducted by the Bureau of Labor Statistics found that only 18 percent of private sector employees had access to paid family leave (Donovan 2020).

The lack of public and private financial support has severe consequences as individuals' life course trajectories have become more fragmented. Individuals switch jobs more frequently and leave work temporarily to take care of children or frail elderly relatives and to get more training and education. The number of dual-earner, full-time working parents has increased considerably over the past couple of decades. In the early 1960s, both partners were working in only about 25% of married-couple households with children under eighteen.

In 2012, that number had climbed up to 60%.[8] During the same period, the share of children living with one parent had increased from 9% in 1960 to 26% in 2014.[9] Facing financial costs associated with these life course choices and lacking other options, many individuals turn to the ever-more permissive American credit regime, which offers individuals easy access to credit cards, personal loans, and home equity lines of credit.

Incomplete and declining government support not only raises the financial costs throughout the life course but also increases the opportunity costs of taking time off work, getting training and enrolling in educational programs, or raising a family. When parents have to take unpaid time off work to take care of a sick child and go into debt to address the resulting financial short-falls, they will just end up smoothing income losses rather than realizing any upside gains because such actions are financial necessities, not social invest-ments. Even if companies or state policies offer such benefits, few employees make use of them. For many, the opportunity costs are too high because there can be negative career implications for leaves of absence and because many leave arrangements are unpaid. The playing field on which people make life course choices is not level. Some people are reluctant to attend college or get more training because of the financial costs, including lost incomes and fears of not being able to repay their loans after graduation. For others, credit can help pay for childcare or address income losses during periods of leave, allowing parents to maintain their careers and invest in their children. Doing so might lead to higher incomes and upward mobility, or, as with Raquell Heredia, it might not.

Borrowing during Life Course Stages

Rising debt among American households has received much attention, but the circumstances that lead individuals to take on more debt remain less clear. In this section, I demonstrate how fragmented life course trajectories and the resulting income losses documented in Chapter 3 contribute to growing indebt-edness. As before, I draw on the Survey of Income and Program Participation (SIPP) to track households over time and use the employment status of the household head as the reference point.[10]

Figure 6.6 documents changes over time in debt-to-income ratios, or debt leverage, for households in different income groups and with different degrees of labor market participation. In both employment scenarios, low-income households almost always carry higher debt burdens compared to high-income households. While debt leverage on average has increased for most households

---

[8] "The Rise in Dual Income Households," *Pew Research Center*, June 18, 2015.

[9] "Parenting in America," *Pew Research Center*, December 17, 2015.

[10] For more details on the SIPP, see Section A in the Appendix.

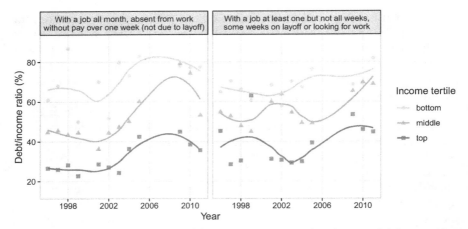

FIGURE 6.6 Average unsecured debt-to-income ratios by degree of labor market participation and income in the United States
Notes: The classifications of labor market participation are based on SIPP codings. Lines are smoothed trends lines. Unsecured debt as a share of disposable income for households in which the head is in a certain life course stage. Income tertiles are based on household disposable income.
Source: SIPP 1996–2012.

across the income distribution, the sharpest expansion occurs with middle-income households in which the head took an unpaid leave from work. These patterns suggest that indebtedness is strongly associated with short-term work interruptions, which are often driven by child-related issues, education and training, or sickness.

Limited and incomplete financial support from both the welfare state and employers force individuals into unpaid leave and part-time work, increasing households' financial shortfalls and pushing them further into debt. Figure 6.7 shows trends in households' debt leverage when the head is either absent from work without pay or working part-time, split by different reasons for doing so. For comparison, the thin light-gray line in each panel indicates debt leverage for households in which the heads are full-time employed. Panel (a) shows that vacation and personal days, illnesses, and child-related issues are among the primary reasons for unpaid absences that have become most strongly associated with higher debt burdens over time. It is important to emphasize that individuals often take unpaid vacation and personal days not for leisure time but to take care of children or of the elderly, in part because the Family and Medical Leave Act (FMLA) grants individuals unpaid leave only after they have used up their sick leave and vacation time.[11] Panel (b) paints a similar

---

[11] The FMLA is the only federal policy that entitles individuals working for larger companies up to twelve weeks of *unpaid* leave.

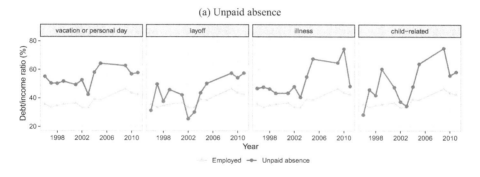

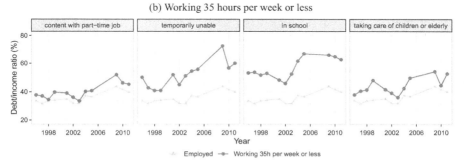

FIGURE 6.7 Average unsecured debt-to-income ratios during unpaid absence and part-time work in the United States

Notes: Unsecured debt as a share of disposable income for different causes of unpaid absence (panel [a]) and part-time work (panel [b]). Income tertiles are based on household disposable income. *Source*: SIPP 1996–2012.

picture. Debt leverage has increased considerably among those who work part-time (i.e., thirty-five hours per week or less) because they are either in school or temporarily unable to work full time. Note that those who are content with their part-time jobs do *not* carry more debt than those who are employed or have other reasons for part-time work. This is a noteworthy pattern because it sheds doubt on arguments that see conspicuous consumption as a main driver behind the rise in debt (e.g., Frank 2010).

Unpaid Absences, Fewer Work Hours, and Indebtedness
If fewer work hours were voluntary choices that reflected individuals' deliberate preferences, we might be less concerned about the financial impact of this form of employment. In many cases, however, the reasons for part-time work and unpaid absences are related to raising a family, illness, and the need to temporarily leave the workforce (Gould and Schieder 2017). To further corroborate the descriptive findings from the previous section, I estimate a series of logistic regression models that allow me to control for sociodemographic

factors such as family structure or income that can influence debt levels and decisions to leave work. The regression models take the following form:

$$Pr(Y_{it} = 1) = logit^{-1}(\beta_1 + \beta_2 S_{it} + \beta_3(S_{it} \cdot G_{it}) + \mathbf{X}'_{it}\gamma) \qquad (6.2)$$

where Y_{it} is the binary response of whether household head i carried unsecured debt in year t. S_{it} is a dummy variable indicating if the respondent was on an unpaid absence from work or, alternatively, a categorical variable indicating the reason for an unpaid absence. G_{it} is individual i's income quintile. $\mathbf{X}'_{it}$ is a matrix of individual-level covariates including liquid savings, education level, age, number of children, family type, homeowner status, and race.

Households in which the head is on unpaid leave have a 32 percent predicted probability of carrying unsecured debt, almost five percentage points higher than households in which the head is full-time employed. When we allow the effect of unpaid absences on debt to vary by income quintiles, the results displayed in the left panel of Figure 6.8a show that there are virtually no differences across the income distribution in the probability of carrying debt during unpaid absences. This is in stark contrast to the comparison group of households in which the head is in full-time employment. Here we see that it is mostly middle-income households that have the highest probability of being in debt. In other words, low- and to a smaller degree high-income groups have a much lower probability of going into debt during unpaid absences from work. Low- and high-income households are likely to have different reasons for why they are absent from work without pay. If Raquell Heredia's experience is more reflective of low-income groups, indebtedness might be indicative of financial necessity. If, however, high-income groups take unpaid absences to invest in their children or advance their career through training, borrowing is more likely to reflect a form of social investment. We can go into more detail by looking at the specific reasons why individuals temporarily leave work without pay. The right panel of Figure 6.8a shows that individuals who take unpaid time off work for personal days and vacation as well as pregnancy and childbirth have a higher probability of carrying debt than those whose unpaid absences are caused by economic factors such as temporary layoffs.

Fewer and fluctuating work hours add an additional layer of financial insecurity onto the shoulders of many Americans (Golden 2015, 2016). I estimate the effect of fewer work hours and the underlying reasons on the probability of indebtedness through a set of simple logistic regressions, using the same set of control variables as in Equation 6.2 as well as dummies for income quintiles. Individuals who are working part-time are on average more likely to carry unsecured debt than those who are regularly, full-time employed. This pattern holds across the income distribution, as the left panel of Figure 6.8b shows. But unlike in the case of unpaid leave for which all income groups are equally affected, middle- and high-income groups have a higher probability of carrying debt. Even more revealing are the results when we look at the reasons for fewer work hours (the right panel of Figure 6.8b). Individuals who worked

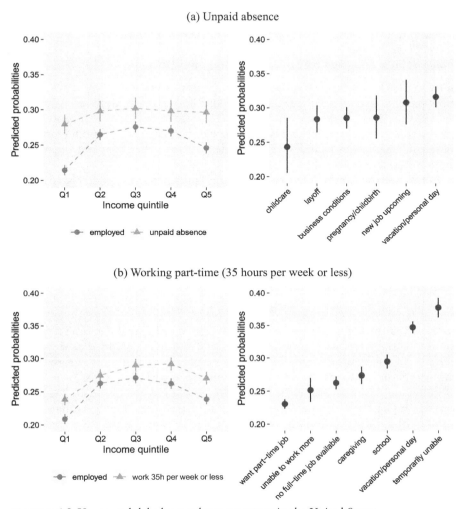

FIGURE 6.8 Unsecured debt by employment status in the United States
Notes: Predicted probabilities based on separate logistic regressions models for each panel. *Source:* SIPP 1996–2012.

fewer hours because they are temporarily unable to work more, took a personal or vacation day, pursued some form of education or training, or took care of children are all more likely to carry debt than those who prefer part-time jobs. Complementing the earlier findings, this further calls into question the argument that luxury consumption fuels indebtedness.

In sum, unpaid leaves and fewer work hours are in no small part the outcomes of incomplete social policy support. In both Denmark and Germany, the welfare state eliminates or at least reduces the need for individuals to take *unpaid* absences for maternity or paternity leave, even though the replacement rate and thus the financial burdens vary across households.

Child-Related Income Losses, Expenditures, and Debt

Since in the United States most private sector employers and many states do not offer paid family leave, unpaid absences and fewer work hours are often the only options for taking time off work to take care of children. As I show in the previous section, because there is limited or non-existent social policy support, many individuals and families go into debt to stem the financial impacts of these life course events.

In this section, I take a closer look at the links between child-related financial costs and household debt. Do families who want to spend time with their children after birth borrow money to absorb income losses during unpaid leaves and pay for additional expenditures? Do childcare costs lead to more indebtedness? And does growing indebtedness lead to more bankruptcies? I answer these questions by first estimating the effect of unpaid absences after the birth of the first child on unsecured debt across different family types in the following regression framework:[12]

$$Y_{it} = \beta_1 B_{it} + \beta_2 U_{it} + \beta_3 (B_{it} \cdot U_{it}) + X'_{it}\gamma + \alpha_i + \delta_t + \epsilon_{it} \tag{6.3}$$

where Y_{it} is the log unsecured household debt of individual i at time t. B_{it} is a dummy variable indicating the period around childbirth, defined as sixty days before and one year after individual i had a child. U_{it} is a dummy variable indicating whether individual i was absent from work without pay. X'_{it} is a matrix of individual-level covariates including household income quintiles, log liquid savings, highest educational degree (five categories), age and age squared, the number of children, a dummy variable indicating renter states, and three race categories. α_i and δ_t are unit and year fixed effects. I estimate separate model for single-parent mothers and married couples.

The results in Table 6.1 show that a single mother who takes unpaid leave during and after her child is born has about 1.8 times more unsecured debt than mothers who are not on unpaid leave during and after childbirth. For a married woman who takes an unpaid leave, the increase in debt is only about 7.3 percent and statistically insignificant. One implication of these findings is that the additional financial cushion that another spouse brings to the table reduces the need to go into debt during periods of unpaid leave. Single mothers, however, have limited financial alternatives and are therefore much more likely to resort to credit markets to smooth income losses during leave periods without pay.

Many parents in the United States take a significant hit to their incomes and forgo earnings when they decide to take time off work to take care of children, in large part because the government and their employers provide little or no

---

[12] I use the birth of the first child only because in these cases the event window around childbirth is not confounded by other child-related borrowing costs.

TABLE 6.1 *Unpaid maternity leave and unsecured debt in the United States*

	Dependent variable:	
	Unsecured debt (log)	
	Single-mother households (1)	Married-couple households (2)
Birth period	−1.24***	−0.19
	(0.44)	(0.16)
Unpaid absence	0.26**	0.25***
	(0.12)	(0.07)
Birth period	2.26***	0.26
× unpaid absence	(0.80)	(0.37)
Observations	51,802	110,971
R^2	0.77	0.72
Adjusted R^2	0.45	0.42

Notes: Results from three separate regression models with unit and year fixed effects and a set of controls that estimate the marginal effects of paying for childcare on log unsecured debt; sample split by household type. Birth period is defined as sixty days prior and one year after the birth of the first child. The model in column (2) is estimated for women only. Robust standard errors are clustered at the household level. Full results appear in Table A.6.2 in the Appendix. *$p<0.1$; **$p<0.05$; ***$p<0.01$.

financial support. But this is not the only financial burden parents face. The cost of childcare itself has increased considerably over the past decades.[13] In 2019, the average cost for center-based childcare for one child ranged from $6,890 in Arkansas (14.6% of a median family's income) to $20,913 in Massachusetts (22.7% of a median family's income), where infant care costs 63.7% (about $8,134) *more* than four-year public college tuition (EPI 2020). Faced with rising costs, families increasingly tap into credit markets to shoulder the financial burden of childcare.

The panels in Figure 6.9 show results using the logistic regression model in Equation 6.2 with the same set of control variables as before. Households that pay for childcare have a 36 percent likelihood of carrying unsecured debt, nearly ten percentage points more than households with children that do not pay for childcare (panel [a]). When we allow the effect to vary across the income distribution (panel [b]), we see that middle- and high-income groups with children are more likely to have debt than those in the bottom quintile. Paying for childcare, however, increases the likelihood of being indebted considerably. The largest difference of fourteen percentage points is among low-income groups, but it is middle-income households that are overall the most likely to carry debt when they pay for childcare (45 percent probability).

---

[13] On the debate about the exact increase in childcare costs over time, see, for example, Herbst (2018) and Laughlin (2013).

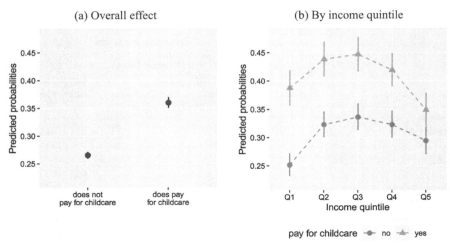

FIGURE 6.9 Unsecured debt and the cost of childcare in the United States
Notes: Predicted probabilities from logistic regression models for having debt when households pay for childcare compared to those who do not. Panel (a) shows the overall effect. Panel (b) splits the results by households' net income quintiles. *Source:* SIPP 1996–2012.

Opportunity costs of enrolling children in childcare are one reason behind the differences in indebtedness across income groups. Many low-income parents cannot afford to enroll their children in kindergarten or daycare and, instead, rely on informal networks of family, friends, or community organizations. For example, the 2002 National Survey of America's Families found that three- to four-year-old children in high-income families are more likely to be enrolled in childcare centers, whereas children from low-income families are more likely to be taken care of by relatives (Minton and Durham 2013). Low-income individuals face particularly high opportunity costs to enroll their children in kindergarten or daycare and rarely rely on credit markets to finance private childcare. Middle-income families, by contrast, are more likely to take on debt to finance private childcare.

As more families take on debt to cope with child-related income losses and rising expenditures, economic risks increase, too, and push families into financial difficulties. Some even fall into bankruptcy (see also Warren and Tyagi 2003). Data from the Survey of Consumer Finances show that over four percent of couples and single parents with children have declared bankruptcy in the past five years. This is nearly twice as high as the rate of single earners without children (see Figure 6.10). These findings show that the lack of comprehensive family policies in the United States, such as paid leave and subsidized childcare, adds large financial burdens to families' budgets and forces

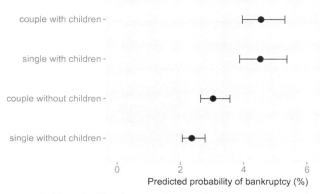

FIGURE 6.10 Likelihood of bankruptcy by family type in the United States
Notes: Predicted probabilities of having declared bankruptcy in the past five years from logistic regression models. The models control for age, gender, completed education degree, race, employment status, homeownership, income, and asset percentiles. N=228,935. *Source:* Survey of Consumer Finances (SCF) Combined Data 1989–2016.

many families to borrow money to address income losses during time off work and childcare expenditures. The results also indicate that households use credit differently over the life course. Those who can rely on childcare are able to invest both in their children's education and in their own careers. In many of these cases, stemming child-related costs through credit is a form of social investment. Others, however, struggle to raise their families while keeping their jobs, and borrowing becomes a financial necessity to fill financial gaps that has little in common with credit-financed social investment.

Job Switches and Income Losses

In Denmark, I show that declining incomes caused by job switches increase borrowing among affected households. Do we see similar patterns in the United States? The SIPP contains detailed information on a month-to-month basis about whether respondents moved from one job to another. This allows me to construct a variable for switching jobs without spells of unemployment. Since liabilities are only reported once every wave instead of every month, I estimate the effect of job switches and income changes on household debt in the following fixed effect regression model:

$$Y_{it} = \beta_1 S_{it} + \beta_2 I_{it} + \beta_3 (S_{it} \cdot I_{it}) + \mathbf{X}'_{it}\gamma + \alpha_i + \delta_t + \epsilon_{ist} \qquad (6.4)$$

where Y_{it} is the log unsecured household debt of individual i at time t. S_{it} is a dummy variable indicating the period after the individual switched her job. I_{it} is a dummy variable indicating whether individual i's income

TABLE 6.2 *Job switches, income changes, and unsecured debt in the United States*

	\multicolumn{4}{c}{Dependent variable}			
	\multicolumn{4}{c}{Total unsecured debt (log)}			
	(1)	(2)	(3)	(4)
Post-period	−0.47***	−0.40**	−0.43***	−0.40**
	(0.15)	(0.16)	(0.16)	(0.16)
Less income (dummy)	−0.17	−0.20	−0.23	−0.20
	(0.24)	(0.25)	(0.25)	(0.25)
Savings-constrained			−0.12	
			(0.11)	
Savings as share of				0.00
pretreatment income				(0.00)
Post-period × Less income	0.34*	0.40**	0.45**	0.40**
	(0.18)	(0.18)	(0.18)	(0.18)
Baseline controls	–	✓	✓	✓
Unit FE	✓	✓	✓	✓
Panel FE	✓	✓	✓	✓
Observations	16,779	16,752	16,428	16,727
R^2	0.70	0.70	0.70	0.70
Adjusted R^2	0.45	0.46	0.46	0.46

Notes: Regression models with unit and panel-year fixed effects. The sample consists of households in which all members of the household are full-time employed and one member switches jobs without a period of unemployment. *Post-period* is a dummy indicating the period after the job switch. *Less income* is a dummy indicating that the job switch led to a decline in income. Robust standard errors in parentheses. Full regression results appear in Table A.6.3 in the Appendix. *p<0.1; **p<0.05; ***p<0.01.

declined in the year when she switched jobs. A decline is defined as a 5 percent decrease in total household income. The comparison group is individuals whose incomes did not decline despite job switches (i.e., either remained the same or increased). X'_{it} is a matrix of individual-level covariates, including highest educational degree (five categories), the number of children, family type (four types), a dummy variable indicating renter status, three race categories, total pretreatment household income quintiles, a dummy variable indicating savings-constraints defined as liquid savings of less than one-and-a-half month's income, or, alternatively, liquid savings as a share of pretreatment household income. α_i and δ_t are unit and panel-year fixed effects. The results for different model specifications appear in Table 6.2.

The simple bivariate model in column (1) shows a positive effect on the interaction term, suggesting that individuals whose incomes declined with job switches have around 40 percent more unsecured debt than those whose incomes did not decline. Adding the set of pre-treatment covariates increases the effect size (column [2]). The model in column (3) adds a dummy variable indicating savings-constraints, which further strengthen the effect size but might introduce post-treatment bias if savings change when incomes decline. To lessen this concern, the model in column (4) scales savings by pretreatment income. The effect remains substantively similar. These findings show that job switches that lower incomes have a strong effect on households' unsecured debt levels, suggesting that credit markets in both Denmark and the United States allow individuals to smooth these income losses when social policy support is absent. In the final part, I turn to Germany to show how households cope with the financial burdens that arise during life course trajectories in a restrictive credit regime.

LIFE COURSE TRAJECTORIES AND DEBT IN GERMANY

Long considered the archetype of a Conservative welfare regime that was centered on a single-breadwinner model (e.g., Esping-Andersen 1999), life course trajectories of German households have become more fluid and fragmented in recent years. As I show in Chapter 3, this is largely driven by growing female labor force participation, especially since the 1990s, changing family structures and norms, and a more flexible labor market. But compared to other Western European countries, these changes set in late. The family-oriented and status-preserving nature of the German welfare state, which promoted employment stability and suppressed women's entry into the labor market for most of the postwar period, has only recently shifted toward a social investment approach (Clasen 2005). Maternity leave benefits, for example, have changed considerably. Such policies have moved away from long duration periods, in many cases job-protected, with comparatively low pay to much shorter but better-paid leave arrangements that resemble the Scandinavian model of parental leave schemes. While the previous approach favored single-earner families, the more recent model opened up opportunities for both partners and especially mothers to return to work. In 2007, the government introduced new parental leave benefits (*Elterngeld*) that allow parents to take between twelve and fourteen months off from work at typically 67% of prior net income (payments range between a minimum of €300 and a maximum of €1,800 per month). The share of full-time working mothers with one- and two-year-old children increased from 32% in 2006 to 43% nearly ten years later. The share of fathers receiving parental leave benefits grew from 21% in 2008 (immediately after new parental leave benefits were introduced) to 34% in 2014. Bergemann and Riphahn (2010) attribute this increase to the availability of parental benefits and find that the share of mothers who intend to return to work after a year of maternity leave increased by fourteen percentage points. Demands for more subsidized places in childcare facilities have increased, too, and gained political momentum in the past couple of years, indicating more support for policies that help to reconcile work and family obligations. These policy shifts reflect the fact that the majority of Germans believe the government should be the primary funder of paid parental leave and childcare centers (see Chapter 3).

More fluid life course trajectories and new family structures have undermined the traditional single-breadwinner model and have had significant consequences on households' finances. Shorter but better-paid parental leave schemes support families and dual-earner couples, helping (and incentivizing) caregivers to return to work after childbirth. But they still leave parents with considerable financial burdens during their leave. As more mothers have entered the labor market, demand for childcare has also grown. In Chapter 3, I show that the fragmented and disrupted life course trajectories caused by taking time off work (e.g., to raise children or to pursue education) drive income volatility as much as unemployment (see Figure 3.4). And according to data from the 2012 International Social Survey Programme (ISSP), over 50 percent of German respondents say that children are a significant financial burden to their parents.[14]

But despite changing life course trajectories, German households rarely go into debt to cope with related financial shortfalls because Germany's restrictive credit regime makes borrowing much harder for individuals and their families. Instead, households "internalize" most of the income losses and higher expenditures by drawing on savings or cutting back expenses. Credit, in other words, plays only a small social investment role. This is in stark contrast to Denmark and especially the United States. Both countries have permissive credit regimes, in which households can easily draw on credit products and are much more likely to borrow money to manage income volatility and rising expenditures from life course choices that are incompletely or not at all covered by the welfare state.

Borrowing during Life Course Stages

As I show in Chapter 4, German households carry much lower levels of debt, both in absolute terms and relative to their incomes, compared to Danish and American households. Moreover, the distribution of debt-to-income ratios across households in different income groups is relatively similar. In this section, I draw on the German Socio-Economic Panel (SOEP), including the supplemental wealth modules that collected information on different types of assets and liabilities in 2002, 2007, and 2012.[15]

As before, I begin by documenting changes in average unsecured debt-to-income ratios over time for different life course stages and income groups.

[14] Own calculation based on the 2012 Social Policy Module from the ISSP.
[15] For more details on the SOEP, see Section A in the Appendix.

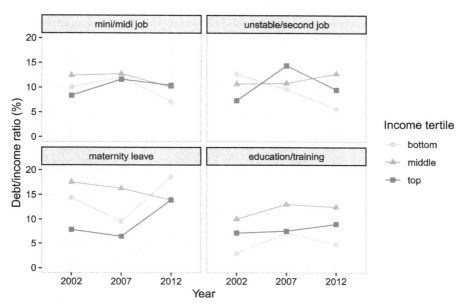

FIGURE 6.11 Average unsecured debt-to-income ratios by life course stages and income in Germany
Notes: Household-level debt-to-income ratios for households in which a spouse is in one of the life course stages displayed in the panel. Mini- and midi-jobs are forms of marginal employment.
Source: SOEP 2002, 2007, and 2012.

While the SOEP is the most comprehensive panel data set in Germany, information on liabilities is only available for three years. Figure 6.11 shows the average debt-to-income ratio for households in different income tertiles on the basis of whether the head is in one of the following life course stages: marginally employed in so-called mini- or midi-jobs, unstable or second job, maternity leave, or education and training. Mini-jobs are part-time jobs with low monthly incomes that cannot exceed €450 per month, while midi-jobs have monthly incomes between €450 and €1,300. Across all life course stages, households carry much smaller levels of debt relative to their incomes than in Denmark and the United States. Between 2002 and 2012, debt leverage remained relatively stable. Differences in debt leverage across income groups are small over that period, often below five percentage points. In contrast, more households in Denmark and the United States borrow money in response to financial gaps that arise due to fragmented life course trajectories. In Denmark, this is mostly concentrated among middle- and high-income households when one of its members temporarily leaves the workforce to care for children. In the United States, borrowing is much more common as families absorb the financial impacts of unpaid leaves of absence and fewer work hours.

Average statistics about changes in debt leverage are informative but do not necessarily tell us whether households tap into credit markets when their life course trajectories become interrupted. Given the restrictive nature of Germany's credit regime and its focus on stable employment and income as criteria for prospective borrowers who want to take out loans, it is much less likely that households go into debt to address financial shortfalls and expenditures caused by life course events. To capture disruption and fragmentation empirically, I create a measure of how many months per year an individual was in a given employment or life course status using the SOEP's monthly labor force dataset. The main dependent variable is a binary indicator: whether a household member is currently paying back loans and interest. I chose this measure because asset and liability amounts are not available on an annual basis. They were only collected in the wealth supplements in 2002, 2007, and 2012. I also create an indicator for whether a household member has taken on *new* debt, which takes the value of one if a household member is repaying debt in year t but did not state that she or he was repaying debt the year before (t_{-1}). While less common, this indicator cannot rule out that households resumed repaying old debts after they stopped making debt payments for a year. Both are imperfect measures of indebtedness since they do not capture the level of debt. Nonetheless, they allow me to estimate the probability of paying back current or new debt in response to fluctuations in employment status and across life course stages. I estimate a series of conditional logistic regressions that make use of the panel structure of the data and stratify by household:

$$Pr(Y_{it} = 1) = logit^{-1}(\beta_1 + \beta_2 E_{it} + \mathbf{X}'_{it}\gamma) \tag{6.5}$$

where Y_{it} indicates if respondent i is paying back either current or new loans and interest in year t. E_{it} is the number of months the respondent was either full-time employed, part-time employed, on maternity leave, in school or university, or in vocational training. For each status, I estimate a separate regression model. $\mathbf{X}'_{it}$ is a matrix of individual-level covariates including household net income (log), monthly savings (log), age and age squared, the number of children in the household, education dummies (six degree categories), marital status, a dummy variable indicating renter status, and a dummy variable indicating if the respondent resides in former East Germany. Similar to a fixed effect regression, the estimated effects in a conditional logistic regression are comparisons within respondents.

Figure 6.12 shows the odds ratios based on these regression models. Across all employment and life course stages, only more months in full-time employment (in a given year) are associated with a slightly higher probability of repaying debts, both existing and new. For respondents either on maternity leave or in training, more months in those statuses are associated with *smaller* likelihoods of carrying debt, but these findings are not statistically significant. The regression models estimating the probability of carrying *new* debt show no effect for maternity leave and an even smaller likelihood for respondents

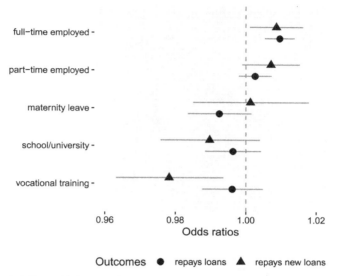

FIGURE 6.12 Effect of labor market status on debt repayment in Germany
Notes: Odds ratios with 95% confidence intervals from separately estimated conditional logistic regression models of months in a given employment status on whether a member of the household currently repays loans and interest or repays *new* loans and interest. Full results appear in Table A.6.4 in the Appendix. *Source:* SOEP.

in school, training, or university, but again these effects (with the exception of vocational training) are not statistically significant. In contrast to Denmark, where middle- and high-income households took on more debt for leaves of absence, including maternity and paternity leave, and the United States, where unpaid absences and fewer work hours are also associated with higher debt levels, German household do not take on debt under any of these circumstances. In the following sections, I show in greater detail that neither child-related absence from work nor income loss because of job switch increases the likelihood of carrying debt.

Child-Related Costs, Absences from Work, and Debt

I document that in the United States, unpaid absence from work for child-related reasons and the cost of private childcare have strong and sizable effects on households' debt levels. Do similar effects exist in Germany? Since daycare has become a prominent political topic, even resulting in the legal right to a place in a public childcare facility, I first estimate whether the cost of daycare influences households' indebtedness. The child supplemental data of the SOEP collected information from 2010 through 2013 about whether parents pay for daycare, and if so, how much. As before, I use annual information on whether households repay loans and interest to test how paying for childcare

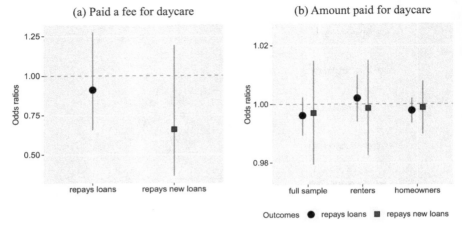

FIGURE 6.13 Childcare costs and debt repayment in Germany

Notes: Odds ratios with 95 percent confidence intervals from separately estimated conditional logistic regression models. The dependent variable is either whether a member of the household currently repays loans and interest or repays *new* loans and interest. Panel (a) shows the effect of paying for childcare versus not paying for it. Panel (b) estimates the effect of the amount paid for childcare. Full results appear in Table A.6.5 in the Appendix. *Source:* SOEP.

affects indebtedness. I estimate a set of conditional logistic regressions akin to Equation 6.5, predicting the probability of repaying loans (existing ones and new ones) on the basis of whether the household pays for daycare. I also estimate the effect of the amount paid for childcare on the probability of repaying loans. To rule out that the effect is only picking up mortgage debt repayments of (younger) families, I split the sample into homeowners and renters and re-estimate the latter model.

Figure 6.13 shows the odds ratios for these models. Panel (a) suggests that those who pay for daycare are about 8 percent less likely to repay loans than those who are not paying for daycare (34 percent less likely to repay new loans), but these effects are not statistically significant. Panel (b) shows that regardless of the specification of the dependent variable, higher costs of daycare do not influence the likelihood of repaying loans. Even when splitting the sample between renters and homeowners, the results remain statistically and substantively insignificant. Childcare costs are not associated with indebtedness.

The SOEP also collects information on whether individuals were absent from work to take care of sick children. Since this may result in income losses, I estimate a conditional logistic regression model to test whether those who are absent from work to take care of sick children have a higher likelihood of carrying debt. The simple bivariate regression in column (1) of Table 6.3 shows that there are no substantive and statistically significant differences between those who were absent compared to those who were not. Adding a set of control variables (column [2]) and estimating the model for repaying *new* debt only (column [3]) does not change the substantive results.

TABLE 6.3 *Absence from work to care for sick children and household debt in Germany*

	Dependent variable		
	Household has debt to pay off (dummy variable)		
	All debt		New debt
	(1)	(2)	(3)
Absent from work to care for sick child	0.99	0.92	0.85
	(1.06)	(1.09)	(1.18)
Controls	–	✓	✓
Observations	59,917	32,893	31,806
R^2	0.00	0.00	0.00
Max. Possible R^2	0.41	0.35	0.14
Log Likelihood	−15,863	−7,136	−2,344
Wald Test	0.01	37.93***	40.05***

Notes: Odds ratios based on conditional maximum likelihood estimates from conditional logistic regressions with unit strata. The models in columns (1) and (2) use the indicator "whether the household repays loans and interest"; the model in column (3) uses the indicator "whether the household repays *new* loans and interest." Full regression results appear in Table A.6.6 in the Appendix. *p<0.1; **p<0.05; ***p<0.01.

In sum, the financial costs of daycare and income volatility caused by child-related absences from work do *not* appear to increase indebtedness among German households, even though half of Germans agree or strongly agree that children are a financial burden on their parents (ISSP 2012). Whereas in the United States, families incur significant child-related expenses that make them more likely to go into debt and even file for bankruptcies, there is no evidence of a similar link between child-related costs and debt in Germany because of its more restrictive credit regime.

Job Switches and Income Losses

Finally, I examine whether individuals who move from one job to another and, as a consequence, have lower earnings than before go into debt to bridge this income loss. Recall that Danish and American households respond to this type of job switch–induced income loss with more borrowing. I test whether a similar pattern occurs in Germany as follows. First, I create a dummy variable to indicate *switching jobs* if the respondent took on a new job within the last thirty days. Among those individuals, I only consider those who were continuously employed in the past year to rule out that individuals found a new job after pursuing education, being unemployed, or concluding other periods of leave. I then define a dummy variable for *less income* if the respondent's

TABLE 6.4 *Job switches, income changes, and indebtedness in Germany*

	Dependent variable			
	Household has debt to pay off (dummy variable)			
	All debt			New debt
	(1)	(2)	(3)	(4)
Switch job	1.00	0.99	0.98	1.12
	(1.03)	(1.03)	(1.03)	(1.06)
Less income	0.97	0.97	1.00	1.02
	(1.01)	(1.01)	(1.02)	(1.04)
Switch job × Less income	1.00	1.00	0.98	0.88
	(1.05)	(1.05)	(1.07)	(1.12)
Baseline controls	–	✓	✓	✓
+ income and savings	–	–	✓	✓
Observations	127,438	121,514	83,249	82,327
R^2	0.00	0.00	0.00	0.00
Max. Possible R^2	0.70	0.70	0.61	0.26
Log Likelihood	−77,005	−73,204	−38,594	−12,469
Wald Test	6.96*	119.40***	296.88***	141.89***

Note: Odds ratios based on conditional maximum likelihood estimates from conditional logistic regressions with unit strata. The models in columns (1) through (3) use the indicator "whether the household repays loans and interest;" the model in column (4) uses the indicator "whether the household repays *new* loans and interest." Full regression results appear in Table A.6.7 in the Appendix. *$p<0.1$; **$p<0.05$; ***$p<0.01$.

household income declines by more than 5 percent. As before, I use debt repayments as an indicator of whether respondents go into debt after switching into lower-paying jobs.

Table 6.4 displays the odds ratios of a series of conditional logistic regression models using the same set of covariates as in the previous model (see notes for Equation 6.5). The bivariate baseline model without controls in column (1) shows that individuals who switch jobs and experience declines in their incomes are as likely to carry debt as those whose incomes do not change or increase. In other words, there is no evidence that these individuals would borrow money to address job-related income losses. Adding baseline sociodemographic controls (column [2]) as well as income and savings (column [3]) leaves the interaction effect virtually unchanged. Unlike in Denmark and the United States, income losses due to job switches do not affect household debt in Germany, suggesting that credit markets do not serve as private alternatives to smooth income losses as individuals move from one job to another.

DISCUSSION

There are many ways to support individuals and their families throughout the life course and to promote social opportunities, for example by investing in childcare and education, providing housing in locations with good jobs and schools, and supporting individuals who take time off work to raise a family or get training. This chapter focuses on the financial shortfalls that arise during the life course and the extent to which individuals go into debt and borrow money to address them when social policy support is weak or incomplete. For people like the Miller-Harrises in Denmark and Raquell Heredia in the United States, the welfare states they live in influence not only the financial costs they face but also the social opportunities they have in various life course stages. While some people use credit to finance social investments in education, children, or their own careers, others may not even consider such options, let alone be able to finance them.

The Scandinavian welfare states provide stronger financial support, compared with the United States, through comprehensive family and educational policies such as childcare services and other in-kind benefits that limit families' financial exposures and lower households' opportunity costs to take time off work, send children to childcare, and pursue education and training programs. It is less the costs of childcare and education per se than the associated income volatility or income losses that can pose financial challenges. Similar to financial protection during unemployment, low-income Danes are better supported financially, whereas middle- and high-income households are the ones that draw on credit to smooth income losses when a spouse temporarily leaves work, for example to take care of children or undergo (re-)training. The Danish home equity reform of 1992, which considerably eased access to credit among eligible homeowners, had a much stronger effect among those who were "outside of the labor force" (i.e., on leave or in training) than on those who remained employed. Moreover, this effect is almost twice the size of the effect among unemployed individuals as I show in Chapter 5, suggesting further that Danes are more likely to use credit as a social investment than to address social risks.

In the United States, by contrast, most of the responsibility for social investment and the financial costs of funding it rests on the shoulders of individuals and families themselves. More individuals, particularly low- and middle-income ones, borrow money to cope with the financial consequences and new expenditures associated with fragmented and disrupted life course trajectories. A large and growing number of employees temporarily leave their jobs for a few weeks throughout the year to take care of children or elderly family members, to get training or education, or because of sickness. Whereas these forms of leave would be supported financially through the welfare state in many European countries, in the United States these types of leave are often unpaid, which puts a considerable financial burden on families' shoulders. I show that debt leverage among individuals who took unpaid leave for reasons *other* than layoffs (e.g., personal days, illness, and to raise a family) increased from around 40 percent in the early 2000s to 68 percent in 2009 – more so than among those who were laid off for the same period. I find similar patterns of growing debt leverage among individuals with fluctuating and fewer work hours because they are temporarily unable to work full-time or are in school. It is worth reiterating that those who are content with their part-time jobs do not carry more debt than those who are employed or have other reasons for part-time work, shedding doubt on arguments that see conspicuous consumption as being behind rising debt levels. Finally, I show that in the United States childbirth and childcare are also related to higher levels of indebtedness. Single mothers on unpaid maternity leave during and after their child is born carry almost twice as much debt as single mothers who are not on unpaid leave during the same time. With soaring costs of childcare and limited, if any, government support, it is unsurprising that households who pay for childcare have a ten percentage points higher probability of carrying debt compared to households with children who do not pay for childcare. In the case of job changes, however, there is no social policy support in either Denmark or the United States. Declining incomes after changing jobs are met with growing debt levels in both countries.

In Germany, life course trajectories have become more fluid and flexible as the traditional single-breadwinner model has declined. Only in recent years has the government increased places in childcare facilities and shifted toward leave policies that resemble those in Scandinavian countries. Although the financial costs associated with education, childcare, and raising a family have risen, Germany's restrictive credit regime makes it much harder for households to borrow money to address income losses and additional expenditures. Across all life course stages, this chapter documents that German households carry much smaller levels of debt relative to their incomes than in Denmark and the United States. Throughout the 2000s, the period for which data are available, debt leverage remained relatively stable, with no discernible differences across income groups. Neither childcare expenses (including the income volatility caused by child-related absences from work) nor job-related income losses (when individuals move to lower-paid jobs) make households more likely to go into debt.

Almost every Danish family has access to and draws on paid family leave and subsidized childcare. While low-income families receive generous government support, middle- and high-income families are more likely to use credit as a social investment to supplement social benefits and government services. In the United States, however, these options are increasingly out of reach for many families because the country lacks a level playing field. Limited social policies increase the opportunity costs associated with education, childcare, and taking time off work to raise a family. For example, American families that can afford to take leaves – paid or unpaid – use credit as a means toward social investment and reap the benefits of their "investments" through upward mobility. Others, however, fear losing their jobs if they were to take time off, and if they do, it is usually unpaid. In these cases, credit becomes another financial lifeline to cope with income losses to make ends meet. It has little to do with social investments. While life course choices are social investments in some countries, they can easily turn into social risks in others.

In the following chapter, I turn to the socioeconomic and political consequences of credit markets, showing how easier access to credit and indebtedness shape individuals' economic insecurity and social policy preferences across welfare regimes.

7

The Political and Socioeconomic Consequences of Credit and Debt

"Until Debt Tear Us Apart"

– Graffiti, Lx Factory, Lisbon, 2017

Walking around the premises of the Lx Factory in Lisbon's Alcântara neighborhood, an old weaving and textile manufacturing complex that has been turned into a commercial and artistic space, a graffiti on a brick wall stands out. In large black letters, it reads, "Until Debt Tear Us Apart." In light of the Eurozone debt crisis that followed the Great Recession and the growing rifts between Northern European lenders, who insist on structural reforms and austerity policies, and Southern European borrowers, who demand debt relief, the graffiti reminds us how contentious and divisive questions around public and private debt have become. It also warns us of debt's potential socioeconomic and political consequences.

Credit markets have become tightly woven into the social fabric of many advanced democracies. They substitute and complement welfare states by offering private alternatives to address social risks and seize social opportunities, as I show throughout this book. But despite these trends, we know surprisingly little about the ways in which credit markets influence individuals' support for the welfare state and how the relationship between access to credit, indebtedness, and political preferences varies across and within countries.[1] One reason is that our micro-level theories of social policy preferences focus largely on income, labor market risks, and assets, but they fail to systematically incorporate the role of credit markets and indebtedness as potential drivers behind welfare state support. Another reason we know little about the relationship between credit markets and the welfare state is that we lack adequate micro-level data that combine information on households' balance sheets

---

[1] For notable exceptions, see, for example, Trumbull (2014) and Prasad (2012).

with political preferences and that cover several countries for comparative analyses.

In this chapter, I address these shortcomings and lay out the socioeconomic and political consequences of easier access to credit and rising indebtedness across welfare regimes. I offer a theoretical framework that explains how access to credit and debt shape social policy preferences. Building on the empirical evidence I assembled in the preceding chapters, we know that credit markets offer private alternatives to welfare states, either substituting for or complementing social policies. But it is not immediately obvious how access to credit and indebtedness influence social policy preferences. Credit and debt not only privatize risks; they also privatize socioeconomic opportunities. Access to credit allows individuals to self-insure against socioeconomic risks. Moreover, credit markets enable individuals to "opt out" of the welfare state by drawing on private, credit-funded options and reaping the benefits of social investments. In both cases, we would expect individuals' support for social insurance to fall because individuals are (or at least perceive themselves to be) self-insured and have the ability to opt out of the welfare state.

Once individuals have borrowed money, however, the risk and investment calculus changes depending on the type of debt. Unsecured debt such as credit card debt or personal loans, which I call *consumption debt* when individuals use it to smooth income losses, might increase demand for social insurance because that type of debt tends to be associated with economic risks. Debtors demand more social support to avoid having to go into debt in the first place, for example during unemployment, and to address future economic risks that could put debt repayments into jeopardy. By contrast, student loans or mortgages, which I label *investment debt*, might decrease demand for social insurance. There are two reasons why investment debt negatively affects social insurance preferences. First, individuals invest in human capital and financial assets because they expect greater job prospects, higher incomes, and upward economic mobility (e.g., through educational credentials and access to good neighborhoods and labor markets) that lower the need for social insurance. Second, individuals opt out of the welfare state by relying on private, potentially higher-quality alternatives, which lowers their demand for public goods and services. This relationship between indebtedness and social policy preferences is amplified and, in many cases, filtered by individuals' existing levels of wealth, which introduces an additional private buffer to address risks, as well as by individuals' values, norms, and beliefs such as attitudes toward borrowing and political ideology.

I test the theoretical implications of my framework using data from an original cross-national survey fielded in nine OECD countries – Canada, Denmark, England, France, Germany, the Netherlands, Spain, Sweden, and the United States – in April and May 2017. The survey contains about 2,000 completed interviews in each country except the United States, where a larger sample of about 5,000 interviews was collected.[2] I use a subset of the data for respondents between the ages of fifteen and sixty-four to capture the working-age population and remove self-employed respondents in order to exclude business-related loans.

This chapter demonstrates that credit markets provide a form of self-insurance but also privatize risks and losses as well as opportunities and gains. These two effects – insurance and privatization – have diverging consequences for individuals' support for social policies depending on the type of debt. Easier access to credit is associated with less support for social insurance – even in the face of future economic risks – because it introduces a private insurance alternative and inflates individuals' sense of wealth. The relationship between indebtedness and social policy support, however, is more complicated. First, I document that unsecured debt, typically associated with consumption and income smoothing, is more likely to increase individuals' economic insecurity than secured debt. Second, individuals who draw on consumption debt are also more likely to demand greater social policy support than individuals who borrow for social investment purposes. These effects vary across countries and are less pronounced in countries that have stronger social safety nets. Finally, I show that rising debt burdens can undermine social solidarity and cohesion by driving apart societal support for the welfare state. Wealth, attitudes toward borrowing, and political ideology become critical filters through which individuals evaluate and update their social policy preferences as their debt burdens increase.

CREDIT MARKETS AND SOCIAL POLICY PREFERENCES: A NEW THEORETICAL FRAMEWORK

Financial markets have become a key part of many people's daily lives. People use financial products to save and accumulate pension assets. They use credit cards, personal loans, and payday loans to smooth income losses and pay for unexpected expenses. And people borrow money to go to college or university and take out mortgages to buy homes. As access to credit markets has become easier over time, individuals spend considerable amounts of money every month paying down outstanding loans and interest. In 2018, household debt relative to disposable income ranged from 87 percent in Italy to 281 percent in Denmark (OECD 2020b). A growing body of work has shown that

---

[2] The survey was designed and implemented together with Jacob Gerner Hariri, Amalie Jensen, and David Dreyer Lassen, whose European Research Council Grant No. 313673 generously funded the survey. We obtained permission from MIT's IRB under protocol number 1701804164. Respondents were contacted through the survey company Epinion. The average response rate across all nine countries was 66 percent. For detailed country-level information about exact numbers of completed interviews and response rates, see Table A.7.1 in the Appendix.

rising indebtedness has severe socioeconomic implications, including prolonging economic downturns and financial crises (Mian and Sufi 2014; Schularick and Taylor 2012) and rising wealth and income inequality (Kumhof, Rancière, and Winant 2015). For individuals, growing debt burdens heighten economic insecurity (Porter 2012*a*; Warren and Tyagi 2003) and negatively affect health outcomes (Sweet et al. 2013; Turunen and Hiilamo 2014) and employment prospects (Bos, Breza, and Liberman 2018; Dobbie et al. 2020; Kiviat 2019). But even though debt is a very salient issue for many individuals – not only for debtors – we know very little about the political consequences of growing indebtedness when it comes to preferences toward the welfare state.

Why People Support the Welfare State

Prior work on the micro-foundations of social policy preferences falls broadly into two camps: individuals' economic positions and ideological predispositions. The first set of arguments identifies individuals' *economic position and material self-interest* as key drivers of preferences for social policies and focuses on income, labor market risks, and – more recently – assets. The canonical Meltzer–Richard model hypothesizes that the median voter will push for more redistributive spending up to the point where the efficiency costs of distortionary taxes outweigh the flat-rate benefits of redistributive spending (Meltzer and Richard 1981; Romer 1975). Individuals' relative position in the income distribution should therefore determine their preferences for redistribution, with higher incomes leading to less support for redistribution. This model, however, has been criticized for its underlying assumptions about rational and knowledgeable individuals, and its predictions are typically not borne out empirically (see, for example, Moffitt, Ribar, and Wilhelm 1998).

Welfare states, however, are not only about redistribution – they also provide social protection and insurance. Individuals' exposure to various kinds of risks is another important driver behind individuals' demand for social policies. Labor market risks such as unemployment or volatile work hours, which in the United States can also affect health insurance coverage, increase economic insecurity and systematically and substantially affect individuals' attitudes toward social policies (Cusack, Iversen, and Soskice 2007; Hacker, Rehm, and Schlesinger 2013; Moene and Wallerstein 2001; Thewissen and Rueda 2019). Individuals tend to become more supportive of redistribution and insurance when risks and insecurity are increasing. Other researchers have focused on the specificity of skills as yet another factor shaping attitudes toward social policies. Individuals who invest in highly specialized skills that are tied to specific industries and cannot easily be transferred to other sectors potentially face longer periods of unemployment and thus more significant declines in income if they lose their jobs (Iversen and Soskice 2001). As a result, these individuals strongly support social policies that protect them against risks associated with skill specificity (see also Estevez-Abe, Iversen, and Soskice 2001; Mares 2003). This insurance logic is not limited to industry-specific risks but also extends to occupational risks as determinants of redistributive preferences (Rehm 2009, 2016). This helps explain why even well-off individuals are willing to support redistribution and in particular social insurance if they expect their incomes to drop or their skill-specific risks to increase in the future.

Finally, more recent work has drawn attention to individuals' participation in financial markets in general and the role of assets as a buffer against income losses in particular. Margalit and Shayo (2020), for example, use a field experiment to document that trading in financial markets increases individuals' familiarity with and trust in markets, which makes them more politically conservative on issues involving inequality and redistribution, the role of luck in determining economic success, and economic fairness. Chwieroth and Walter (2019) show that as individuals, especially in the middle class, become more reliant on financial and credit markets, their demands increase for the government to protect their wealth during financial crises (e.g., through crisis interventions and bank bailouts). While exposure to financial markets can shape social policy preferences by increasing individuals' vested interests in markets and "pro-credit" policies, individuals' support for the welfare state decreases as they accumulate more financial assets. Homeownership, for example, offers a form of private insurance through housing assets as a "nest egg." Rising asset prices increase both the value of houses and homeowners' private wealth buffers, which, in turn, make homeowners less likely to support social insurance (Ansell 2014). In a similar vein, Hariri, Jensen, and Lassen (2020) focus on liquid wealth and show that savings-constrained households are more likely to support social insurance because they lack alternative financial buffers.

A second set of arguments to explain social policy preferences highlights individuals' *ideological predispositions*. Partisan ideology and partisan identification, conceptualized as psychological attachment (Campbell et al. 1960), social identity (Green, Palmquist, and Schickler 2002), or as an informational shortcut about which political party best serves individuals' self-interests (Achen 1992; Downs 1957), have long been identified as forces that shape policy preferences in general and attitudes toward social spending in particular. For most of the twentieth century, support for the welfare state appeared to be much stronger among voters of the Left than those of the Right (Shaw and Shapiro 2002).[3] Others have pointed to the role of values and beliefs about the extent to which individuals have control over their income prospects, the

---

[3] Note that this conceptualization of partisan identification is most likely to hold in the United States' majoritarian two-party system, whereas multiparty systems and coalitional government tend to complicate partisan alignment, yielding ambiguous predictions for partisan identification in these settings.

prevalence of economic opportunities, and the direct or proximate causes of poverty and wealth (see, for example, Alesina and Glaeser 2004; Bean and Papadakis 1998; Bowles and Gintis 2000; Gilens 1999). Beliefs and norms about reciprocity, fairness, and equality of opportunity – combined with varying perceptions of the role of governments in guaranteeing these norms – strongly influence individuals' desired levels of taxation, their demands for publicly provided social policies, and their willingness to support redistribution to the poor (Alesina and Angeletos 2005; Bénabou and Tirole 2006; Cavaillé, and Trump 2015; Fong 2001).[4]

While these accounts help us understand how individuals' economic positions and material interests as well as political attitudes, beliefs, and ideologies shape support for the welfare state, we know very little about how credit and debt influence individuals' preferences toward the welfare state. If credit is a private alternative to publicly provided goods and services, and if credit privatizes both risks and gains, we have every reason to believe that access to credit markets and indebtedness influence social policy preferences.

How Credit Markets Shape Social Policy Preferences: Insurance and Privatization Effects

When individuals borrow money to address income losses during unemployment or time off work, or to finance child- or education-related expenses, they use credit markets to privately address social risks and to invest in human capital and social opportunities. In this section, I argue that having easier access to credit and using credit for insurance and investment has two downstream effects that shape individuals' support for social policies.

The first effect of credit markets is that easier access to credit allows individuals to self-insure against risks. I call this the *insurance effect of credit markets*. Since credit can substitute for social insurance functions by allowing individuals to address social risks and smooth income losses, permissive borrowing conditions – either real or perceived – can *decrease* demand for social insurance. In times of economic hardship, for example when individuals lose their job or face unexpected medical expenses, easy access to credit allows them to borrow money to fill financial gaps or meet higher expenditures. It increases individuals' perceived economic security because they know they can draw on credit lines to smooth income fluctuations, buffer shocks, or afford higher expenditures. Easier access to credit serves as a form of private self-insurance, which suppresses demand for public social insurance.

In addition, easier access to credit may indirectly influence individuals' overall economic circumstances as it allows them to address income losses and higher expenditures and spend beyond their financial means while deferring costs to the future. As a consequence, individuals may *perceive* themselves as

---

[4] For an overview of research on cross-national variation in public attitudes toward the welfare state, see, for example, Svallfors (2010, 2012).

wealthier, even if their actual income and wealth remain unchanged. Note that this perception of credit as being readily available is enough for individuals to believe they are wealthier, even though in reality borrowing money might be more difficult. Such an inflated sense of wealth may lead individuals to believe that they no longer need social insurance.

Both mechanisms – individuals' inflated sense of economic security and wealth – draw on a process of cognitive updating in which access to credit influences individuals' perceived economic self-interest and abilities to address future risks, their positions in the income and wealth distribution, or both. Individuals incorporate new information through a learning and updating process and form new preferences accordingly. When individuals assimilate the new information, they reevaluate their economic positions and their exposures to risks and abilities to address them (e.g., Gerber and Green 1999; Page and Shapiro 1992). Margalit (2013), for example, invokes this updating logic to argue that individuals whose economic circumstances were negatively affected during the economic recession of 2008–09 became more supportive of welfare policies. The preferences of individuals who held opposing political views prior to the recession converged once these individuals were hit by economic shocks.

The second effect of credit markets is that borrowing money privatizes both risks and opportunities. I call this the *privatization effect of credit markets*. On the one hand, individuals can opt out of the welfare state by relying on private, credit-funded options in order to effectively privatize gains. Much like the insurance effect of credit access, the debt-leveraged privatization of gains reduces demand for social insurance. On the other hand, however, indebtedness can also *increase* demand for social insurance when debtors want to avoid going into debt to address inadequately covered social risks in the first place, or when debtors seek protection against future income losses that would make debt repayments more difficult and, therefore, increase economic risks such as falling in arrears and facing bankruptcy. As debt privatizes risks, demand for social insurance increases.

This suggests that once individuals have borrowed money and carry debt, their considerations about the welfare state may change and deviate from the "credit-as-insurance" logic because debt privatizes not only (potential) opportunities and gains but also risks. The two different types of credit use that I document in detail in Chapters 5 and 6 – credit to address social risks and credit as bounded social investment – fall into these two categories and have different implications for debtors' social policy preferences. When individuals use credit purely for consumption purposes (e.g., through credit cards, personal loans, or payday loans), it is often associated with economic risks and might increase demand for social insurance. By contrast, when people use credit as a bounded social investment (e.g., to finance childcare, taking time off work, education, career advancement, and housing), they expect to increase their opportunities and upward mobility, which might lower demand for social insurance.

Consumption Debt and Social Risks

I argue that individuals who rely on unsecured debt as "consumption debt" are more likely to demand social support as indebtedness increases. There are two mechanisms behind this relationship. On the one hand, we might expect that individuals who have had to borrow money to address income losses now prefer a stronger social safety net in order to limit the need to go into debt in the first place, as I demonstrate in Chapter 5. In this retrospective reasoning, rising indebtedness is linked to greater demands for social policies because individuals want to limit their exposure to debt. On the other hand, we might expect debtors to prefer a stronger safety net because debt itself exposes them to new forms of economic risks. Since debt and interest payments require stable incomes, any interruption of this income stream due to unemployment, income volatility, or unpaid time off work can lead to economic distress, falling into arrears, and – at worst – bankruptcies (Porter 2012a). In order to reduce future economic risks, debtors may therefore demand more social policy support if they become unemployed and are unable to pay their existing debts. In this prospective "debt-as-risk" reasoning, rising indebtedness is linked to greater demand for social policies because debtors want to ensure that they can make debt payments in the future (see also Wiedemann 2021).

Economically disadvantaged groups are particularly exposed to debt-related economic risks. They are more likely to have unstable jobs and greater variability of earnings (Morduch and Schneider 2017). They also tend to pay higher interest rates compared to high-income groups and often devote larger shares of their incomes to debt service (Baradaran 2015). For both reasons, these groups are more likely to fall behind on debt payments as their debt leverage increases. But high-income people are not necessarily shielded from debt-related risks. While they may have more stable incomes, they too have often limited savings and live paycheck-to-paycheck (Kaplan, Violante, and Weidner 2014). Both mechanisms are not mutually exclusive and may plausibly operate at the same time.[5]

Investment Debt and Social Opportunity

While debtors who borrow money to cope with social risks and smooth income losses are more likely to increase their support for the welfare state, I argue that debtors who use credit for social investments have very different social policy preferences. There are two reasons to think that "investment debt" will reduce

---

[5] To be sure, pooling credit cards and personal loans with so-called fringe financial services such as payday loans comes at the expense of analytical and empirical nuances. Participants in the fringe financial economy are often members of disadvantaged minorities with limited access to formal banking services who rely on payday lenders or cash-checking services on a more regular basis. Credit card users also differ in why and how they use their cards: while some use credit cards to smooth income losses and incur interest charges, others pay their cards in full at the end of every billing cycle and reap the benefits of their card's reward programs. I choose to pool various types of unsecured credit to offer a unifying category of "consumption" debt that is separate from "investment" debt and to gain statistical power in my empirical analyses.

demand for social insurance: self-insurance and the ability to opt out of the welfare state to reap the benefits of private social investment.

First, credit markets allow individuals to invest in human capital and financial assets in order to privately self-insure against various forms of economic risks. When individuals take out student loans to invest in their education, they expect these educational credentials to pave the way to better-paying and more stable jobs with higher future incomes. Since private investments in human capital are forms of self-insurance that lower future economic risks such as unemployment or income volatility, demand for social insurance declines. Individuals are even less likely to support costly social policies if their higher expected future incomes also increase their tax burdens, especially under progressive tax systems. Investing in childcare can be viewed through the same lens, because it allows parents to maintain their careers and reconcile work and family life. However, whether borrowing money for childcare is indeed a social investment or merely consumption smoothing depends on the overall opportunity costs associated with raising a family as discussed in Chapter 2. Student loans and mortgages may be more clear-cut cases of (social) investment, but borrowing for childcare or taking time off work highlights the bounded and ambivalent nature of the use of credit as a social investment.

Individuals can also use credit to invest in financial assets such as housing. Housing wealth provides another form of self-insurance; individuals can use it as a "nest egg" during retirement and as an additional source of financial liquidity through home equity loans. These direct wealth effects influence support for the welfare state. Ansell (2014), for example, documents that homeowners become more conservative and less likely to support public unemployment insurance when their house values increase, in part because the net worth of their private insurance has grown. Homeownership might also provide indirect insurance through access to neighborhoods with good schools, high-quality jobs, and more upward mobility (Chetty and Hendren 2018; Gingrich and Ansell 2014).

The second reason why investment debt can suppress demand for social insurance is that credit markets allow individuals to opt out of public services. Private alternatives are now available in a range of social policy domains, including capitalized pensions, care for children and the elderly, health, and education (Busemeyer and Iversen 2014; Gingrich 2011; Naczyk and Palier 2014). These private options may be of higher quality than public services. They also align costs and benefits more closely than the tax- and contribution-funded welfare system, where divergence between net beneficiaries and net contributors is larger. Individuals who borrow money to take out mortgages, finance educational programs or college degrees, or pay for private childcare may want to opt out of the public provision of such goods and services because they do not want to pay taxes for public services they do not use. I expect that these individuals have fewer incentives to support tax-financed social policies and resources that would mainly benefit others who use such services from the welfare state. Debtors may therefore prefer less spending on social insurance and fewer redistributive policies because both would undermine future payoffs and returns on their private investments. This form of opting out is most visible in education, for which students and parents can choose between public and private options (Ansell 2010; Busemeyer and Iversen 2014). By tapping into credit markets to privately finance goods and services that alternatively could be offered publicly, including housing, education, childcare, or paid parental leave, individuals essentially opt out of public services and, instead, borrow money that they have to repay.

In addition to facing debt and interest repayments beyond their tax payments, borrowers who took on mortgage debt, student loans, or debts to pay for childcare may perceive these loans as bounded investments with sunk costs whose benefits they want to reap. For example, in 2013 the New York City council ran a pilot program with a credit union – the "Middle Class Child Care Loan Program" – to offer subsidized loans to eligible families with annual incomes between $80,000 to $200,000 to help pay for childcare. In the United Kingdom, NGOs such as the Social Market Foundation have proposed a "National Childcare Contribution Scheme" that would allow parents to borrow up to £10,000 to help them pay for childcare.[6] I therefore expect such borrowers to be less likely to support tax-funded policies that provide similar services to the general public because they want to protect the future rewards of their investments and do not want their taxes going toward services they already paid for privately. If the costs of credit outweigh the tax burdens, and if the gains from opting out of public social services are larger than the expected benefits, individuals who use credit markets to pay for these services should be *less* likely to support publicly funded welfare policies.

Table 7.1 summarizes the key theoretical insights and observable implications of my argument. The first column shows the main credit domains (either accessing credit markets or borrowing for consumption or investment purposes), while the second column indicates whether this behavior privatizes risks or gains and opportunities. The third and fourth columns show the mechanisms through which credit access and borrowing money influence social policy preference formation and their hypothesized impact on support for social insurance. Credit market's insurance and privatization effects yield different predictions about debtors' social policy support depending on the channel and the dominant mechanism for preference formation.

Preference Polarization

Whether credit markets' insurance or privatization effects dominate how debtors form social policy preferences depends on the macro-level relationship

---

[6] Hilary Osborne, "Childcare Loans Scheme Proposed by Thinktank," *Guardian (US edition)*, February 8, 2012.

TABLE 7.1 *Effect of access to credit and indebtedness on social insurance preferences*

Credit Domain	Channel	Mechanism for preference formation	Demand for social insurance
(1) Insurance Effect			
Access to credit	Privatizes risks, gains, and opportunities	• Perceived self-insurance • Perceived wealth effect	Declines
(2) Privatization Effect			
Consumption debt (e.g., credit card debt, personal loans, payday loans)	Privatizes risks	• Retroactive: avoid borrowing to address risk • Prospective: debt as source of (future) risk	Increases
Investment debt (e.g., student loans, mortgages)	Privatizes gains and opportunities	• Self-insurance through investment in human capital and financial assets • Opting out of welfare state through private options	Declines

Notes: This table summarizes the argument's key theoretical insights and empirical implications. The first and second columns show credit markets' main function and whether they privatize risks or gains and opportunities. The third and fourth columns highlight the mechanisms through which credit markets influence social policy preference formation.

between credit markets and the welfare state (i.e., whether it is substitutive or complementary) as well as a set of micro-level factors (e.g., individuals' wealth, political ideology and beliefs, and overall attitudes toward borrowing).

The first micro-level factor that shapes and amplifies the link between indebtedness and social policy preferences is individuals' wealth. Individuals with a lot of assets, in particular liquid assets, are less likely to go into debt to address social risks because they can draw on such assets to buffer risks. Instead, they are more likely to borrow money to invest in human capital or more financial assets. Moreover, even if incomes fluctuate, these individuals may be able to shoulder larger debt-to-income ratios and tolerate income volatility or expenditure shocks because they can tap into savings to keep up with debt repayments. By contrast, individuals with fewer assets are more likely to not only borrow to address social risks but also face future economic risks because they lack financial cushions. I therefore expect the amount of asset holdings to drive individuals' social policy preferences further apart as debt leverage increases.

The second factor that mediates the link between indebtedness and welfare state support is individuals' attitudes toward borrowing. Some people prefer to rely on credit markets instead of public alternatives provided by the welfare state. One reason is that some individuals are more comfortable going into debt than others. Some morally object to borrowing money.[7] Others might have a more favorable stance toward credit markets because they believe that markets are superior to governments, for example because of concerns about efficiency or corruption. And borrowing money might be less cumbersome than claiming social benefits, which comes with administrative costs, time commitments, and psychological frictions and social stigma. For example, many government benefits are means-tested and have strict asset limitations that require prospective claimants to "spend down" their finances, and they have eligibility requirements such as participating in job programs or working a limited number of hours while claiming benefits. By contrast, opportunities to easily access loans are plentiful, as evidenced by the direct mail marketing of pre-approved credit card offers and the growing numbers of online loan providers. Psychological frictions, social stigma, and higher administrative costs can inhibit people from claiming welfare benefits, even if they are entitled to them, and drive them instead toward credit markets (Baumberg 2016; Bertrand, Mullainathan, and Shafir 2006; Bhargava and Manoli 2015; Currie 2006).[8] I therefore expect that overall attitudes toward borrowing further separate social policy preferences among debtors.

The final factor that shapes social policy preferences as debt burdens increase is individuals' political ideology, including norms about personal responsibility. A large body of literature shows that political ideology, typically conceptualized as a set of ideas and issue positions that "go together" in a belief system, shapes public opinion and policy outcomes (e.g., Campbell 2012; Caughey and Warshaw 2018; Converse 1962; Lax and Phillips 2012; Poole 2007; Stimson 2004). The confluence of free-market conservatism and social conservatism was critical in paving the way for credit markets to emerge as private alternatives to social policies. Compared with liberalism, conservatism places greater value on personal autonomy and responsibility, economic freedom, and cultural traditionalism (Ellis and Stimson 2012). Social conservatism, among other characteristics, in particular emphasizes traditional family values and views citizens, families, and communities – not the government – as the driving forces behind thriving societies. It positions itself against paternalistic welfare states, thus favoring limited social policies to reduce dependency on government transfers (Cooper 2017; Mounk 2017). Economic conservatism

---

[7] As has become well known during the discussions about public debt relief in the aftermath of the financial crisis of 2007–08, in German the word *Schuld* means both "debt" and "guilt," implying a moral obligation to repay one's debt.

[8] (Over-)indebtedness, however, carries its own forms of social stigma and social exclusion (e.g., Fahmy 2018; Porter 2012*b*; Schicks 2014).

212   *The Political and Socioeconomic Consequences of Credit and Debt*

favors economic freedom and limited government regulation of market activity. Proponents of this view support private provision of social benefits over government transfers, and they favor lowering taxes and providing fewer regulations and welfare benefits over government-based efforts to equalize economic outcomes (Ellis and Stimson 2012; McCarty, Poole, and Rosenthal 2013, ch. 2).

One particularly relevant angle of political ideology, especially of the conservatism flavor, is the belief in personal responsibility. Responsibility has become a familiar theme in debates about the welfare state and attempts to reform it. In 1996, President Clinton signed the "Personal Responsibility and Work Opportunity Reconciliation Act" (PRWORA), promoting a workfare approach that incentivized individuals to seek work, punished those who remained "dependent" on welfare programs, and, as the name suggests, sought to instill a new norm of personal responsibility for one's economic situation. Nearly a decade later, Chancellor Schröder unveiled Germany's largest labor market and welfare state reform in postwar history in 2003, the *Agenda 2010* (which included the Hartz labor market reforms), and summarized its core principle as follows: "We are going to cut government benefits, promote personal responsibility, and demand more personal contributions from each and every individual."[9] And in 2013, the Danish finance minister Bjarne Corydon echoed a similar perspective, stating that he "believe[s] in the competition state as the modern welfare state" (quoted in Abrahamson 2015, p. 35). These remarks reflect a broader shift in the notion of personal responsibility from a broad understanding of responsibility as duty, often to things outside oneself, to a narrow understanding of responsibility as accountability, that is, taking care of one's own needs to avoid asking things of others, particularly the state (Mounk 2017). In the United States, for example, where households often have limited savings, Sussman and O'Brien (2016) show that people are most likely to turn to high interest rate credit over existing savings because they believe that doing so is the "responsible option" for financial emergencies.

Political ideologies about personal responsibility can affect social policy preferences. Brewer and Stonecash (2015), for example, argue that "Conservatives begin with whether individuals have been responsible in taking care of their lives. If they have and they have achieved, then they should be rewarded and not penalized by higher taxes. Their income should not be taken through taxation to reward those who have been less responsible" (p. 132). This suggests that individuals who go into debt and borrow money might perceive themselves (and be perceived by others) as being personally responsible for their economic and financial well-being and, as a consequence, become less likely to assume social responsibility for other people's economic fates by supporting a tax-funded welfare state. I therefore expect that political ideology

---

[9] Speech by Chancellor Gerhard Schröder in the Bundestag, March 14, 2003 (own translation).

and beliefs in personal responsibility drive another wedge through the social policy preferences space as debt leverage increases.

In the following sections, I test these predictions empirically using original cross-national survey data. I first show the extent to which indebtedness influences individuals' economic insecurity and how strongly this relationship varies across countries. I then turn to credit markets' insurance and privatization effects, revealing considerable divergence of social policy preferences as a result of the different ways people engage with credit markets. In the final section, I show that individuals' wealth position, attitudes toward borrowing, and political ideology and beliefs drive individuals' social policy preferences apart as indebtedness increases, potentially undermining social solidarity.

INDEBTEDNESS AND ECONOMIC INSECURITY

Households' economic and financial insecurities have risen in many OECD countries over the past two decades and have become a growing concern for households and policymakers alike. The list of factors driving economic insecurity is long: job losses, earnings and income volatility, unexpected expenditures, rising costs of living despite stagnating wages, illness and associated healthcare costs, family dynamics such as the birth of a child or divorce, and declining welfare benefits, to name but a few.[10] Meanwhile, rising levels of debt add a new form of risk to households.

Exposure to these risk factors varies across households and across countries depending on the degree to which macro-level institutions such as unemployment insurance, parental leave schemes and childcare support, or healthcare coverage exist to mitigate income losses when people lose their jobs or have children, or to limit out-of-pocket expenditures when individuals become sick.

We can measure economic insecurity in two ways. First, through observable objective factors such as income losses, health insurance coverage, or the amount of assets people hold as a financial buffer (e.g., Hacker, Rehm, and Schlesinger 2013). Hacker et al. (2014), for example, have developed the "Economic Security Index" (ESI), which captures insecurity among Americans as a function of large losses in household income, large spikes in household medical spending, and the adequacy of household financial wealth as a buffer to mitigate these shocks. Alternatively, we can measure economic insecurity by asking respondents about their perceptions of their own economic security. The advantage of the latter approach is that it provides a more nuanced picture of individuals' subjective senses of economic insecurity across different domains. Moreover, self-reported answers to standardized questions enable better cross-national comparisons, since factors such as health insurance coverage are a source of risk in the United States but typically not in European countries.

---

[10] On economic insecurity and its causes, see, among others, Armingeon and Bonoli (2006); Boarini and Osberg (2014); Hacker (2019); Morduch and Schneider (2017); Western et al. (2012).

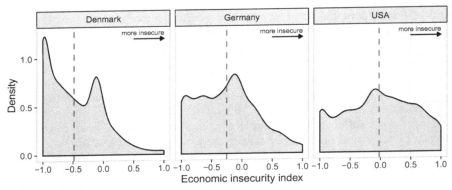

FIGURE 7.1 Distribution of the economic insecurity index

Notes: The economic insecurity index ranges from −1 to 1. Higher values indicate more insecurity. The gray dashed line indicates the country average.

Following this approach, I use five survey items that ask respondents to indicate on a scale from 0 to 10 how worried they are about their job, their health insurance coverage, maintaining their current income, saving enough money for retirement, and getting out of debt. These survey items yield a very rich picture of individuals' economic concerns and can be compared across countries. I then combine these five survey items into an economic insecurity index using principal component analysis. The resulting scores are standardized and range between −1 and 1, where higher values indicate more insecurity.[11] Figure 7.1 shows the distribution of the economic insecurity index in Denmark, Germany, and the United States. Respondents in the United States are on average the most insecure (average of −0.02), followed by respondents in Germany (−0.25) and Denmark (−0.48). In Denmark, the distribution is heavily left-skewed, indicating that many more Danish respondents perceive themselves as economically secure. In the United States, the distribution is more right-skewed than in Germany and Denmark, showing a much stronger prevalence of economic insecurity.

Household debt has become another source of economic and financial insecurity in recent years (Dwyer 2018). Many borrowers devote a considerable share of their disposable incomes to debt service, depending on the interest rate and the outstanding debt balance. Low-income people face particularly high costs since they are typically charged higher interest rates than high-income people and, for a given level of debt, often devote a larger share of their disposable incomes to service their debt burdens. Moreover, debtors are also at higher risk of falling into arrears or even bankruptcy when their incomes fluctuate or suddenly drop. Higher debt leverage, however, does not necessarily lead to higher levels of insecurity. Sufficient liquid savings help individuals

---

[11] Table A.7.2 in the Appendix shows the factor loadings of each survey item.

make monthly debt repayments even if incomes are volatile. When employment is stable and secure, large debt repayments are also more manageable since individuals can count on regular incomes to pay back their loans. But some types of debt are more likely to cause economic and financial trouble than others. Payday loans or credit card debt carry much higher interest rates than other types of debt. Moreover, people tend to be in worse financial circumstances when they take out these loans to smooth income losses or cover financial emergencies. Other types of debt (e.g., mortgages or student loans), however, allow individuals to invest in financial or human capital, which are more likely to yield payoffs in the future. But even these types of debt do not shield individuals from falling off the financial cliff. Job losses, volatile incomes, or stagnating wages can turn most types of debt into sources of financial insecurity. At the macro-level, a range of institutions prevents higher levels of debt from turning into sources of risk. Strong employment protection that guarantees (more) stable employment and comprehensive social policies that provide income support in the case of unemployment or sickness are examples of policies that ensure that households are able to make regular debt payments. Bankruptcy regimes and the ease of debt discharge allow individuals to stop a foreclosure on a house.

How do different types of debt influence households' subjective economic insecurity across different countries? Here I focus on unsecured debt, student loans, and mortgage debt as examples of consumption and investment debt, measured as a share of household income. Debt-to-income ratios are an important metric to gauge the debt burdens households face relative to their incomes, thus capturing their abilities to repay debts over time. I then estimate the effect of debt leverage on individuals' economic insecurity index in the following ordinary least squares (OLS) regression framework:

$$Y_{ic} = \beta_1 UD_{ic} + \beta_2 SD_{ic} + \beta_3 MD_{ic} + \mathbf{X}'_{ic}\gamma + \alpha_c + \epsilon_{ic} \qquad (7.1)$$

where Y_{ic} is the subjective economic insecurity index for respondent i in country c, ranging from -1 to 1. UD_{ic}, SD_{ic}, and MD_{ic} are respondent i's debt-to-income ratios for unsecured debt, student loans, and mortgage debt (including home equity loans), respectively. Unsecured debt consists of credit card debts, personal bank loans, debts from family and friends, overdrafts, and payday loans. I convert these ratios into deciles to make them less sensitive to outliers.[12] $\mathbf{X}'_{ic}$ is a matrix of individual-varying controls including age, gender, dummy variables indicating unemployment and retirement, highest education degree (eight degree-level categories), family status (four categories for single or couple households, with and without children), the number of children at home, net disposable income tertiles, liquid savings (log), a dummy variable indicating homeownership, and an indicator of respondent's willingness

---

[12] Specifically, I split respondents with any debt into nine equally sized groups. Respondents with no debt are allocated to a separate bottom group.

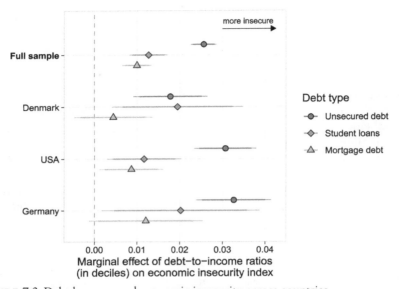

FIGURE 7.2 Debt leverage and economic insecurity across countries
Notes: Regression coefficients with 95 percent confidence intervals based on the model in Equation 7.1. Unsecured debt includes credit card debts, personal bank loans, debts from family and friends, overdrafts, and payday loans. Mortgage debt includes home equity loans. The economic security index ranges from −1 to 1, where higher values indicate more insecurity. The full country sample includes country fixed effects.

to take risks (ten-point scale). α_c are country fixed effects controlling for baseline differences across countries. ϵ_{ic} is the idiosyncratic error term. I estimate regressions for the full country sample, including country fixed effects, as well as for each country separately. Figure 7.2 summarizes the main effects.[13]

Growing debt leverage is associated with more economic insecurity in all countries, but the intensity of this relationship varies across countries and debt types. Unsecured debt is the most important predictor of insecurity in the full sample as well as in the United States and Germany. Student loans are also a more significant driver of insecurity in Denmark and Germany than in the United States. Note that student debt levels in Denmark and Germany, however, are lower overall than in the United States, where debt also covers tuition fees plus room and board instead of just living expenses (especially in Denmark). One explanation why student loans appear to be less associated with economic insecurity in the United States than in the other two countries is that they it may capture different expectations about future economic gains. On average, people with college degrees, even if they are debt-financed, still earn higher incomes and secure better jobs compared to nongraduates,

---

[13] Full regression results appear in Table A.7.3 in the Appendix.

which can explain why perceived economic insecurity is lower among the first group (Cappelli 2020; Hout 2012). Mortgage debt leverage only has a small and statistically insignificant effect on insecurity in Denmark but is a stronger predictor in the United States.

One reason why debt leverage in the two permissive credit regimes – Denmark and the United States – is associated with different levels of economic insecurity is the size and scope of the welfare state. In Denmark, comprehensive coverage and income support through social insurance, especially for low-income groups, helps borrowers keep up with debt repayments during unemployment or sickness. In the United States, however, government transfers are much more limited and provide little financial support during times of economic hardship. This lack of buffer contributes to a growing sense of insecurity as indebtedness, especially due to unsecured debt, grows. In Germany's restrictive credit regime, by contrast, borrowing money is much harder and less widely used and increases insecurity among those who do have to rely on debt.

ACCESS TO CREDIT AS SOCIAL INSURANCE

How does relying on credit as a private alternative to publicly provided social insurance affect individuals' social policy preferences? Individuals may perceive that by having easier access to credit as a form of self-insurance, they are more economically secure and therefore less supportive of the welfare state. Put differently, if individuals can easily tap into credit markets to smooth income losses, then higher expected economic risks such as unemployment may *not* translate into greater demand for unemployment insurance, as standard political economy models would predict.

To test this claim empirically, I use three survey items to estimate whether access to credit mediates the effect of expected unemployment risk on preferences for social insurance. First, I measure support for social insurance by asking respondents a widely used question about whether the government should do more to help the unemployed (five-point answer scale, ranging from strongly disagree to strongly agree). In all three countries, over 60 percent of survey respondents agree or strongly agree that the government should do more to help the unemployed. Second, I measure access to credit using a survey item that asks respondents to rate how easy it would be for them to borrow money from a financial institution if they were to experience financial hardship (five-point answer scale, ranging from very difficult to very easy). The share of individuals who state they can borrow very easily is highest in Denmark, followed by the United States and Germany.[14] Across the three countries, high-income individuals state that they have easier access to credit. However,

[14] In the survey sample, access to credit is higher among German respondents compared with the findings in Chapter 4 using data from the European Social Survey. One explanation for these differences is that both surveys capture different time periods, and access to credit has improved in Germany over time.

low-income Danes are nearly three times more likely to report having very easy access to credit compared to low-income Americans or Germans. One important reason for these differences across income groups is the scope of the welfare state. Since the Danish welfare state protects low-income individuals comparatively well against economic shocks and income losses (see Chapter 3), lenders are more willing to provide credit to this group because they know that these prospective borrowers will be able to repay their loans even when they become unemployed. Very low bankruptcy rates are in line with this argument (Kilborn 2009). Finally, I measure prospective economic risk with a survey item that asks individuals to assess on a 0 to 100 probability scale the probability of becoming unemployed in the next year. The average self-reported risk of unemployment ranges from about 21% in Denmark and Germany to 27% in the United States.[15]

Using these three variables, I estimate the following OLS regression model to test how easy access to credit influences respondents' support for social insurance policies as a function of their subjective risks of future unemployment:

$$Y_{ic} = \beta_1 R_{ic} + \beta_2 C_{ic} + \beta_3 \left(R_{ic} \cdot C_{ic}\right) + \mathbf{X}'_{ic}\gamma + \alpha_c + \epsilon_{ic} \tag{7.2}$$

where Y_{ic} is the support for unemployment insurance of respondent i in country c. R_{ic} is the respondent's probability of becoming unemployed in the following year. C_{ic} is the measure of ease of credit access. $\mathbf{X}'_{ic}$ is the same set of individual-level covariates as in model based on Equation 7.1. α_c are country fixed effects, and ϵ_{ic} is the idiosyncratic error term. Figure 7.3 shows predicted values for the full sample of nine countries.

Among individuals with easy access to credit, greater risk of unemployment is only weakly associated with more demand for social insurance, suggesting that the availability of credit as a private alternative to government transfers suppresses demand for more public insurance. By contrast, those respondents who find it more difficult to borrow money as a private alternative demand more social insurance as the risk of unemployment grows. This suggests that individuals who have subjectively easy access to credit are much less likely to demand more social insurance than households with more difficult access to credit markets. Even in light of a high perceived risk of job loss, in people's minds easier access to credit is a form of private insurance that dampens demand for public unemployment insurance.[16]

---

[15] The exact wording for all questions appears in Table A.7.4 in the Appendix.

[16] One potential concern with this analysis is that respondents might overestimate their perceived access to credit, for example because they are overly optimistic about the future, while also (or as a consequence) underestimating the risk of unemployment. This could potentially introduce bias. To lessen this concern, I estimate the main model using the number of months a respondent was unemployed or out of the labor force in a given year (e.g., sickness, taking care of children and elderly family members, leave of absence) as a measure of objective labor market risk. Moreover, I also include a variable for expected income changes in the next year to capture respondents' overall financial outlook. The results remain substantively similar (see columns 2 through 4 in Table A.7.6 in the Appendix).

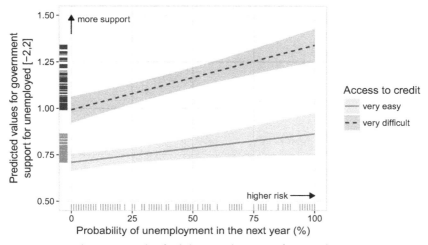

FIGURE 7.3 Credit access, risk of job loss, and support for social insurance
Notes: Marginal effects with 95 percent confidence intervals based on Equation 7.2 and column 1 in Table 7.2. The sample includes nine OECD countries.

As an additional robustness check, I estimate the same model for preferences toward redistribution instead of social insurance. Since we expect credit to serve as a form of self-insurance, we should not see a shift in redistributive preferences. The question I use asks if the government should do more to reduce income differences. Table 7.2 compares the effects of easier access to credit on preferences for unemployment insurance (column 1) and redistribution (column 2) as a function of the risk of job loss in the next year. As expected, the precisely estimated null effect indicates that changes in credit access do not influence redistributive preferences even if unemployment risk grows. This further supports the argument that individuals perceive credit markets as a private alternative to social insurance – but not as an alternative to fiscal redistribution.

PRIVATIZING RISKS AND OPPORTUNITIES: INDEBTEDNESS AND THE POLARIZATION OF SOCIAL POLICY PREFERENCES

So far I demonstrated that access to credit influences the relationship between individuals' exposures to economic risks and their preferences for social policies. When borrowing is difficult, individuals demand more social insurance in light of labor market risks. By contrast, when borrowing is easy, preferences for social insurance remain unchanged, even as risk grows. But what happens to social policy preferences once people have taken out loans and carry debt? While the insurance effect of credit markets might still play a role, other, potentially competing, considerations come to the fore.

TABLE 7.2 *Credit access, risk of job loss, and social policy preferences*

	Dependent variable	
	Unemployment insurance (1)	Redistribution (2)
Ease of credit access	−0.072***	−0.093***
	(0.012)	(0.014)
Probability of unemployment next year	0.207***	0.145***
	(0.035)	(0.040)
Ease of credit access	−0.063***	0.000
× probability of unemployment next year	(0.024)	(0.027)
Constant	1.335***	1.451***
	(0.126)	(0.144)
Observations	7,188	7,181
Controls	✓	✓
Country FE	✓	✓
R^2	0.087	0.115
Adjusted R^2	0.084	0.112

Notes: Regression models are based on the full nine-country sample with country fixed effects and a set of control variables. Full results in columns 1 and 5 in Table A.7.6 in the Appendix. $^*p<0.1$; $^{**}p<0.05$; $^{***}p<0.01$.

Borrowing money and the subsequent monthly debt repayments make indebtedness a salient issue in people's minds. But since credit privatizes both upside gains and downside risks, the effect of indebtedness on social policy preferences depends on which channel operates. Investment debt such as student loans and mortgages is more likely to privatize gains and negatively affect support for social insurance. Consumption debt, however, privatizes risks and may strengthen support for social insurance, either because people borrowed money in response to a weak safety net or because debt itself becomes a source of downstream economic risk.

In this section, I examine how and under what circumstances indebtedness influences support for social insurance. I focus on social insurance because we would not expect an effect on redistributive preferences, as documented earlier. In light of my theory, I expect the links between indebtedness and social policy preferences to vary across consumption and investment debt as well as across countries depending on their welfare and credit regimes. More encompassing welfare states not only limit individuals' needs to borrow money in lieu of social policies but also lessen the degrees to which indebtedness translates into financial insecurity. And finally, I expect that individuals' wealth, attitudes toward borrowing, and political ideologies mediate the link between indebtedness and social policy preferences.

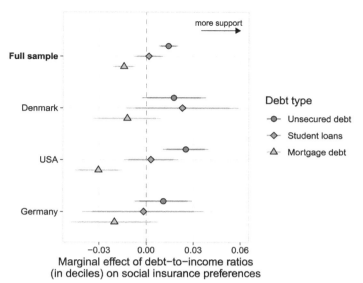

FIGURE 7.4 Debt leverage and support for social insurance across countries

Notes: Regression coefficients with 95 percent confidence intervals based on Equation 7.3. The full nine-country sample model includes country fixed effects. All other coefficients come from separate country-specific regressions. Unsecured debt includes credit card debts, personal bank loans, debts from family and friends, overdrafts, and payday loans. Mortgage debt includes home equity loans. Debt-to-income ratios are measured in country-specific deciles. Full results in Table A.7.7 in the Appendix.

Indebtedness and Social Policy Preferences

I begin by estimating the baseline effect of debt leverage on social insurance preferences in the following OLS regression framework:

$$Y_{ic} = \beta_1 UD_{ic} + \beta_2 SD_{ic} + \beta_3 MD_{ic} + X'_{ic}\gamma + \alpha_c + \epsilon_{ic} \qquad (7.3)$$

where Y_{ic} is the support for unemployment insurance of respondent i in country c. As in the model based on equation 7.1, UD_{ic}, SD_{ic}, and MD_{ic} are respondent i's debt-to-income ratios (measured in deciles) for unsecured debt, student loans, and mortgage debt, respectively. X'_{ic} is the same set of individual-level covariates as before. α_c are country-level fixed effects controlling for baseline differences across countries. ϵ_{ic} is the idiosyncratic error term. I estimate the effect of each of the three types of debt on social insurance preferences for the full nine-country sample and separately for Denmark, Germany, and the United States. Figure 7.4 shows the results.

In the full nine-country sample, higher mortgage debt leverage is associated with less support for social insurance. If individuals perceive mortgage debt as investments in their homes and specific neighborhoods, their expectation of future payoffs from housing wealth, private nest eggs, and even access to better schools and jobs lowers their demands for social insurance because investment debt privatizes gains. This finding dovetails with prior work documenting that homeowners are more conservative than renters and, as their housing wealth rises, prefer less social insurance (Ansell 2014; Davidsson 2018; Gilderbloom and Markham 1995). By contrast, higher unsecured debt leverage is associated with stronger social insurance support. While the data do not allow me to distinguish the reasons why people took on unsecured debt, this finding is consistent with the argument that borrowers adjust their social policy preferences to the fact that this type of debt is more likely to privatize risks. Individuals demand more social insurance when they take on debt in response to weak social safety nets, or because they perceive this debt burden as a source of future economic risk and want to insure against it, or both. Changes in student loan leverage do not influence preferences for social insurance. One explanation for this finding is that students or recent graduates are cross-pressured: on the one hand, student debt might be an investment with expected future rewards (e.g., better jobs, higher income), which should lower demand for social insurance. Yet on the other hand, student debt could also increase support for social insurance if borrowers are uncertain about whether their investments will materialize and whether they will be able to repay their loans (Goldrick-Rab 2017; Zaloom 2019).

Looking at the three country cases separately, mortgage debt has a negative effect in all countries but is only statistically significant (and largest) in the United States. This partly reflects the strong emphasis on housing as part of the US asset-based welfare state (Hay 2013; Sherraden 2005). Student debt has no effect in Germany and the United States but increases support for social insurance in Denmark (although the result is statistically insignificant). Finally, unsecured debt has the strongest effect in the United States – the country where indebtedness is both a consequence of a weak welfare state and a source of economic risk.

Preference Polarization by Wealth, Attitudes toward Borrowing, and Political Ideology

What explains the variation in the strength of the relationship between indebtedness and social policy preferences across countries and debt types? How can we disentangle the fact that debt privatizes both risks and gains and increases insecurity for some but not others, and show how these processes affect welfare state support? To shed light on these questions, I now turn to three mediating factors – assets and economic incentives, attitudes toward borrowing, and political ideologies – that help us understand why some groups demand more support from the welfare state as debt leverage grows, while others demand less.

I first examine how individuals' economic considerations about the costs of debt repayment and the tax burdens in relation to the respective benefits from credit markets and welfare states drive preference divergence by focusing on individuals' wealth position. Assets, in particular liquid assets, are important buffers and alternative private means to address financial gaps that can mitigate individuals' needs to go into debt. I measure respondents' wealth using their total assets, including money in savings and checking accounts, stocks and bonds, as well as home equity. As before, I turn this measure into country-specific quintiles to make it less sensitive to outliers.

The second mediating variable between indebtedness and social policy preferences is respondents' attitudes toward borrowing, which I measure using the following two survey questions. The first asks respondents if they agree or disagree with the statement: "There should be laws to limit how much an individual can borrow." This question captures respondents' willingness to limit their exposures to credit markets, because of either egocentric reasons (e.g., if respondents regard their own debt burden as being too high) or sociotropic concerns (e.g., if respondents perceive indebtedness as a societal or macro-economic problem). It also taps into respondents' views about the balance between free markets on the one hand and government intervention in markets on the other. The second question asks respondents if they agree or disagree with the statement: "Households should save money for purchases instead of borrowing money." This question is less about the government's role in regulating credit access than about individuals' own preferences for saving money and drawing on accumulated resources versus borrowing money and drawing on future resources.

Finally, I broaden the perspective by examining the extent to which respondents filter their social policy preferences in light of changing debt levels through their own political beliefs and ideology. Such beliefs reflect different attitudes about the relative role of markets and governments in the provision of goods and services and to what degree individuals themselves ought to be personally responsible for their own economic fates. I measure political ideology on the basis of respondents' preferences across five policy domains that capture post-material and social issues, economic issues, and attitudes toward immigration and nationalism. I combine respondents' answers to these questions into a joint political ideology index using principal component analysis.[17] This approach is preferable to simply asking people where they fall on a Left–Right ideological spectrum.[18] I standardize this ideology measure such that it ranges from −1 to 1, where higher values indicate more liberal orientations.

I then estimate the degree to which these factors mediate the link between indebtedness and social insurance preferences across respondents and debt types in Denmark, Germany, and the United States in the following OLS regression model:

[17] For details, see Table A.7.5 in the Appendix.
[18] For a similar approach, see, for example, Caughey, O'Grady, and Warshaw (2019).

$$Y_i = \beta_1 D_i + \beta_2 M_i + \beta_3 (D_i \cdot M_i) + \mathbf{X}_i'\gamma + \epsilon_i \qquad (7.4)$$

where, as in the model based on Equation 7.3, Y_i is the support of respondent i for social insurance. D_i is the respondent's debt-to-income ratio (either unsecured debt, student loans, or mortgage debt). M_i is one of the three mediators: a respondent's wealth position, attitude toward borrowing, and political ideology. $\mathbf{X}_i'$ is the same set of individual-level covariates as in the previous models. ϵ_i is the idiosyncratic error term. As before, I estimate separate regression models for each debt type for Denmark, the United States, and Germany.

Wealth Effects

How does wealth influence demands for social insurance as debt-to-income ratios grow, and how does this effect vary across countries? Figure 7.5 shows predicted support for unemployment insurance at low and high debt-to-income ratios (measured as the bottom and top quintiles) for unsecured debt, student debt, and mortgage debt at different levels of wealth in Denmark, the United States, and Germany on the basis of the regression model in Equation 7.4. The solid shapes indicate that the coefficients from the interaction model are statistically significant, while the empty shapes indicate that they are statistically insignificant. I use this symbology in all subsequent figures.

Wealth mediates the relationship between debt burdens and social policy preferences only in a small set of cases. As unsecured debt leverage grows, asset holdings only divide preferences for unemployment insurance in a statistically significant way in the United States and Denmark. Americans with few assets are particularly dependent on credit cards and payday loans to address income losses during unemployment, as I show in Chapter 5. In this case, debtors may demand more welfare state support because they want to avoid borrowing in the first place since they have little savings to rely on otherwise. In addition, such debtors may prefer a safety net to cope with potential downstream economic risks, since future income losses can put debt repayments into jeopardy. We see a similar divergence of policy preferences across households with different levels of wealth in Germany, but the differences are statistically insignificant. By contrast, Danes with small debt burdens and limited assets are more likely to support social insurance than those with lots of assets, but these differences disappear as unsecured debt increases. Higher unsecured debt burdens generate support for social insurance across the wealth distribution.

Growing student debt also creates a wedge between the preferences of wealthy and non-wealthy respondents. In Denmark and Germany, debtors with few assets demand greater support from the welfare state than those with many assets – but the differences are statistically insignificant, in part because of the smaller sample size of wealthy respondents with large amounts of student debts relative to their incomes. In the United States, asset-poor respondents with little student debt are more supportive of social insurance

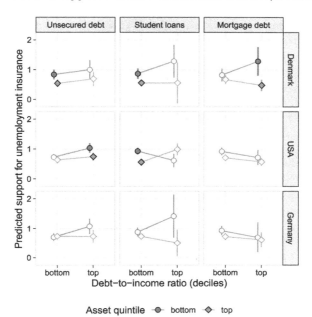

FIGURE 7.5 Wealth, debt leverage, and support for social insurance

Notes: Predicted values from regression models based on Equation 7.4. Results for each panel come from separate regressions that control for individuals' socioeconomic characteristics. 95 percent confidence intervals based on robust standard errors. Solid shapes indicate statistically significant coefficients. Unsecured debt includes credit card debts, personal bank loans, debts from family and friends, overdrafts, and payday loans. Assets include money in savings and checking accounts, stocks and bonds, as well as home equity. Asset quintiles are country-specific.

than asset-rich respondents who carry little student debt. These differences disappear as student debt leverage increases. One explanation for these diverging cross-national patterns is that non-wealthy respondents with student loans have different expectations about employment and income prospects. If borrowers expect to have well-paying and stable jobs, their unemployment risk and demand for social support might both be lower. If, however, respondents are less optimistic about their future economic path, they might demand income protection through social insurance. These findings, however, are statistically underpowered to give us reliable results.

Finally, wealth mediates the link between mortgage debt and social policy preferences in Denmark but not in the United States or Germany. As mortgage debt burdens increase, non-wealthy Danes demand more social support, while wealthy Danes' social policy preferences change only slightly. Such demand for social insurance among highly leveraged debtors with few liquid assets can reflect their desires to cushion against economic risks and their needs to make debt and interest payments. In Germany and the United States, asset holdings have almost no effect on demands for unemployment insurance as debt increases. Debtors with little wealth become slightly more opposed to social insurance than wealthier debtors.

The structure of the welfare state and the tax system as well as the permissiveness of the credit regime help us understand these patterns. As I show in Chapters 3 and 5, Danes with high incomes and many assets face higher tax burdens, receive smaller amounts of social benefits such as unemployment and paid leave relative to their incomes, and (in part as a consequence) carry larger debt burdens to address these financial shortfalls compared to low-income, non-wealthy Danes. One reason for the lack of preference divergence across the wealth distribution as unsecured debt increases is the comprehensive Danish welfare state, which limits exposures to risks for economically disadvantaged people and thus reduces their need to go into debt. This is in stark contrast to the United States, where unsecured debt poses much larger financial risks in the absence of a comprehensive welfare state, especially for people with limited savings. This increases demand for social support among those debtors. In Germany's restrictive credit regime, wealth matters little for social policy preference formation in light of changing debt burdens.

Attitudes toward Borrowing Money

People's underlying attitudes toward saving and borrowing are a second group of factors that mediate support for social policies in the context of growing debt. Some people are more comfortable borrowing money and, as a result, more accepting of debt. Others, however, are wary of indebtedness and prefer to save money before going into debt (Almenberg et al. 2018; Bover et al. 2016). These attitudinal differences also influence how people think about the trade-off between saving and borrowing and shape their demand for limitations (legal or otherwise) on how much people can and should borrow. People who are more likely to accept credit as a means to either address labor market risks by smoothing income losses or seize social opportunities by taking out student loans or getting a mortgage may also be less likely to support social policies as their debt burdens increase compared with those who are less accepting of debt.

Respondents were asked if they agree or disagree with the statement: "There should be laws to limit how much an individual can borrow." In Denmark, half of the respondents agree or strongly agree that borrowing should be limited. The number is slightly higher in the United States (54 percent) and Germany (63 percent), which reflects differences in the permissiveness of credit regimes between Denmark and the United States on the one hand and Germany on the other. These attitudes are positively correlated with social policy preferences. Respondents who favor more restrictions on borrowing

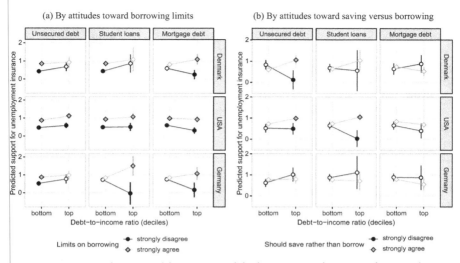

FIGURE 7.6 Attitudes toward borrowing, debt leverage, and support for social insurance

Notes: Predicted values from regression models based on Equation 7.4. Results for each panel come from separate regressions that control for individuals' socioeconomic characteristics. 95 percent confidence intervals based on robust standard errors. Solid shapes indicate statistically significant coefficients. Unsecured debt includes credit card debts, personal bank loans, debts from family and friends, overdrafts, and payday loans. The wording for the questions (using a 5-point answer scale ranging from strongly disagree to strongly agree) is as follows: Panel (a): "There should be laws to limit how much an individual can borrow." Panel (b): "Some people say that households should save money for purchases instead of borrowing money. Do you agree with this statement?"

demand stronger social safety nets, while respondents who are against restrictive borrowing policies are less likely to support social policies. This pattern goes right to the heart of the micro-foundation of the balance between states and markets: Some individuals are willing to give up unlimited access to credit and impose restrictions on lending in exchange for more government support. Across the three country cases, this effect is strongest in Denmark and the United States.

The panels in Figure 7.6 provide a more nuanced picture of how people's attitudes toward debt and their views about states and markets intersect the link between indebtedness and support for the welfare state. The evidence is mixed with regard to how attitudes toward borrowing limits influence social insurance preferences as debt leverage increases (Figure 7.6a). In most cases, respondents who favor limits on borrowing tend to be more supportive of social insurance. But as unsecured debt leverage increases, the differences in social insurance support between those who favor borrowing limits and those who do not disappear in Denmark and Germany but become stronger in the

United States. Growing student debt separates preferences only in Germany and to a smaller degree in the United States, but not in Denmark, where, as before, preferences converge with higher debt leverage. Across all countries, increasing mortgage debt leverage is associated with preference divergence; those who favor borrowing limits become more supportive of social insurance than those who oppose such limits.

These findings lend some support to the idea that those who demand more government regulation of credit markets to curtail private borrowing want more social policy support as indebtedness grows. The patterns are also consistent with the argument that borrowers want to avoid having to take on debt, for example to finance income losses or invest in education or housing, as they do in permissive credit regimes. And finally, these findings suggest that highly leveraged borrowers may want the government to help them reduce their own exposures to debt-induced economic risks by limiting indebtedness and strengthening social support, thus shifting risks from themselves back to society. This can explain why in Denmark and Germany support for unemployment insurance converges between respondents with more and those with less favorable views toward legal limits on borrowing as unsecured debt leverage increases. By contrast, insurance support across the same groups diverges in the United States as more Americans use both credit cards and personal and payday loans during unemployment to make ends meet, thus increasing their exposure to risks.

Figure 7.6b offers a slightly different perspective by focusing on individuals' attitudes toward saving and borrowing. Social insurance preferences diverge considerably among Danish and, albeit to a lesser degree, American respondents as unsecured debt leverage increases. Respondents who agree that one should save rather than borrow become more supportive of social insurance as unsecured debt leverage increases, while those who are more accepting of debt and do not think that people should save become less supportive, as is the case in Denmark, or do not change their level of support, as in the United States. This pattern is absent in Germany. A similar relationship emerges for student debt in the United States but not in Germany or Denmark. American respondents with large student debt leverage are split into two groups: one that views savings as being preferable to borrowing and demands more support from the welfare state; and another that accepts borrowing while demanding less support from the welfare state. Two explanations are consistent with these patterns. Individuals who are more favorable toward borrowing might be opposed to social policies because either their attitudes are conservative and pro-market – I say more on this later – or their willingness to take on debt allows them to opt out of public services and exclude others from such privately obtained services. These mechanisms are less likely to be at play in Denmark and Germany, where higher education is mostly publicly funded and private education options that would allow students and parents to opt out of the public system are much more limited compared with the United States.

Finally, attitudes about the balance between saving and borrowing have little to no substantive and statistically significant influence on social policy preferences as mortgage debt leverage increases. As mortgages are, for most people, the only way to obtain a (first) home, it is perhaps unsurprising that preferences for saving and borrowing are largely irrelevant.

These findings suggest that respondents who are more accepting of borrowing than saving become *less* supportive of social policies as they take on more unsecured debts relative to their incomes. These attitudinal differences point to a more fundamental question about the relative balance between credit markets and welfare states as two ways to distribute resources, address social risks, and seize social opportunities. People who subscribe to a more credit-based perspective and take on debt are also more likely to reject the idea that the government should provide social goods and services. This effect is strongest in Denmark and the United States for unsecured debt, which is often used to smooth income losses, and for student debt in the United States. It may also suggest that individuals who are less accepting of debt but still have high debt burdens are more in favor of welfare states because they borrowed out of necessity, for example to address financial shortfalls and economic hardships.

Political Ideology and Beliefs

Attitudes about borrowing limits and the relative virtue of savings over borrowing are part of a broader bundle of values, norms, and beliefs that shape welfare state support. The final and perhaps most important and powerful lens through which individuals filter their social policy preferences in the context of rising indebtedness is political ideology. Figure 7.7 reveals strong divergence of social policy preferences between political conservatives and liberals – on the basis of the joint political ideology index constructed earlier – as debt leverage increases.

What stands out the most is that political ideology plays a much larger role in the United States and Germany compared with Denmark. In both countries, liberals become overall more supportive of social insurance as debt increases, whereas conservatives either keep their preferences stable or become less supportive of social insurance. Political ideology is the lens through which respondents evaluate their demands on the government as debt burdens grow. By contrast, demands for social insurance increase only slightly among Danish liberals as unsecured debt grows, but any differences across the political spectrum that did exist for low levels of student and mortgage debt leverage fade away as debt leverage rises. In other words, political ideology ceases to structure social policy preference formation in Denmark when investment debt is growing.

One explanation for these patterns is that conservative debtors become opposed to social insurance because they regard borrowing and debt as

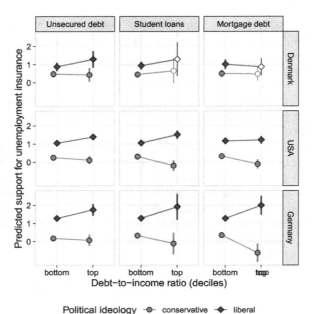

FIGURE 7.7 Political ideology, debt leverage, and support for social insurance

Notes: Predicted values from regression models based on Equation 7.4. Results for each panel come from separate regressions that control for individuals' socioeconomic characteristics. 95 percent confidence intervals based on robust standard errors. Solid shapes indicate statistically significant coefficients. Unsecured debt includes credit card debts, personal bank loans, debts from family and friends, overdrafts, and payday loans. I code respondents at the ends of the political ideology index as "conservative" and "liberal."

behavioral outcomes that are in line with notions of personal responsibility. The aversion to government transfers among conservative borrowers – especially for those with student loans and mortgage debt – reflects the confluence of family values, personal responsibility, and pro-market forces in a neoconservative political ideology: Credit markets are seen as a way to shift responsibility toward individuals and families, often through intergenerational debt as the example of parents' liability for their children's student loans shows (Cooper 2017). Conservatives in Germany only respond to growing mortgage debt leverage by becoming less supportive of social insurance. Politically liberal respondents, by contrast, are less likely to subscribe to rhetoric about personal responsibility and free markets and instead delegate a social responsibility role to the government as debt burdens grow. These findings also support the view that conservatives may see markets as being superior to governments, and therefore they turn to markets and demand less support from welfare states. Liberals, by contrast, are more favorable toward government support as unsecured debt grows, which may reflect either a more interventionist stance to help individuals address debt-related risks or a positive view toward the government and its ability to provide income support and buffer risks. Finally, the fact that political ideology structures preferences much less in Denmark compared with Germany and the United States may reflect a broader cross-class coalition that is committed to government service provision, social responsibility, and easy credit access – all of which are necessary for credit markets to complement and co-exist with Denmark's universalistic welfare state.

DISCUSSION

This chapter offers a new theoretical framework to study the socioeconomic and political consequences of easier access to credit as well as indebtedness. The key insight is that credit markets' insurance and privatization effects shape social policy preferences by affecting debtors' perceptions of economic security and their relationships with the state. Access to credit markets allows individuals to not only self-insure but also opt out of publicly provided goods and services and instead reap the benefits of private alternatives. These insurance and privatization effects reduce individuals' demands for social insurance.

But credit markets privatize both opportunities and risks, or, to put it more concretely, both gains and losses. Once individuals have borrowed money and have to make monthly debt and interest payments, their demands on the welfare state change. On the one hand, indebtedness can increase economic risks and make borrowers vulnerable to income volatility and income losses that could make debt repayments more difficult and result in debtors' falling into arrears or facing bankruptcy. Borrowers who took on unsecured debt to address social risks by smoothing income losses become more supportive of social insurance to limit their exposures to future economic risks. On the other hand, individuals who borrowed money to invest in human capital (e.g., student loans) and financial assets (e.g., housing) are less likely to support social insurance because they expect positive economic gains from their investments through better jobs, higher and stable incomes, and upward economic mobility. Individuals' private wealth, attitudes toward borrowing, and their political ideologies in particular amplify these diverging sets of preferences and drive wedges in the social policy preference space, potentially undermining social solidarity.

In this chapter, I draw on data from an original cross-national survey to empirically test my arguments. Across all nine countries in the data, unsecured debt is associated with more economic insecurity compared to student loans or mortgage debt even after controlling for salient socioeconomic characteristics such as age, employment status, and income. Comparing the United States and Denmark – two countries with permissive credit regimes – I find a much stronger relationship between unsecured debt and demand for social insurance in the United States, where credit markets increasingly substitute for a weak welfare state, than in Denmark, where credit markets complement a comprehensive welfare state, shielding economically disadvantaged groups from financial risks and debt.

This has consequences for debtors' demands for social policy support. First, I show that easier access to credit breaks the link established in the literature between labor market risk and demand for social insurance. The ease with which respondents can borrow money leads to a strong polarization of social policy preferences among respondents with similar levels of unemployment risk: individuals who cannot easily access credit demand more social insurance, while those with ample borrowing opportunities do not. Credit, in other words, operates as a form of self-insurance, suppressing individuals' perceived needs for public protections. Second, I document considerable preference divergence across both different types of debt and countries. When borrowers use "consumption debt" to address social risks (e.g., through credit card debt or personal loans), it increases their support for social insurance, in part because they want to reduce their own debt-induced risk exposures. "Investment debt," by contrast, often has the opposite effect; borrowers who have invested in human capital and financial assets – effectively opting out of the public welfare state – are privately insured against risks and want to reap the benefits of their private investment, which reduces their demands for public insurance.

These differences in the effects of credit access and indebtedness on social policy preferences across and within countries reflect the varied nature of the relationship between credit markets and welfare states that is at the core of this book. When credit markets *substitute* for public goods and services, as is the case in the United States, a much larger part of society relies on credit to address social risks and to invest in human capital and financial assets to seize social opportunity. In the context of a weak and limited welfare state, high debt leverage, especially among economically disadvantaged groups, increases economic risk and strengthens social policy support. For example, unsecured debt through credit cards or personal loans in the United States is associated with more economic insecurity and demand for social insurance than in Denmark. By contrast, when credit *complements* the welfare state, as is the case in Denmark, the subset of society that borrows money for social policy purposes is very different. While the welfare state considerably protects low-income groups, it is mostly middle- and upper-middle- income households that borrow money to supplement public benefits. This suggests that there is broader support for this symbiotic relationship between the credit market and the welfare state in Denmark than in the United States. This is a key reason why political ideology – in particular regarding beliefs about the allocation of responsibilities between individuals, states, and markets – has little impact on social policy preferences in Denmark as indebtedness increases. In Germany and especially the United States, however, politically conservative respondents become less supportive of social insurance as debt burdens grow, whereas liberals become more supportive. Drawing on credit markets and borrowing money aligns with conservatives' views about personal responsibility and free-market efficacy that favors resource allocation through the market instead of government intervention. In addition, respondents who are more accepting of debt and want fewer restrictions on borrowing are also more likely to reject the role of the government in providing social services as they take on more debt.

The findings suggest that the growing influence of credit markets on people's daily lives has strong socioeconomic and political consequences. Wealth, political ideologies, and attitudes about personal responsibility amplify how access to credit and indebtedness shape support for social policies. Indeed, indebtedness has the power to undermine social solidarity and cohesion – a sentiment that is captured well by the graffiti in Portugal: "debt [may] tear us apart."

8

Implications and Conclusion

"Every poor person must be allowed a fair chance to improve his/her economic condition. This can be easily done by ensuring his/her right to credit."
– Muhammad Yunus, 1986[1]

As financial markets are now woven deeply into the fabric of our societies, debt has become a familiar if not always welcome presence in many people's daily lives. This book sheds light on the political causes and consequences of the growing reliance on credit and the rise in household indebtedness across rich democracies, revealing a fundamental transformation of social rights, social responsibilities, and the allocation of resources, risks, and opportunities. I develop a "social policy theory of everyday borrowing" that integrates credit markets and social policies in the study of comparative political economy. The book's main argument is that the constellation of two institutions can explain why patterns of indebtedness vary considerably across and within countries: the first institution is the *structure of a country's welfare state* and the extent to which it addresses social risks and provides social opportunities to different groups. The financial costs associated with fragmented and disrupted employment patterns and life course trajectories that welfare states do not cover create financial shortfalls for many families. In both Denmark and the United States, gross income volatility has grown considerably over time. This shift is partly a result of involuntary employment disruptions such as unemployment or sickness, but it is also increasingly attributable to fragmented life course trajectories as people more frequently switch jobs and take time off work to raise a family and enroll in educational programs. While the American welfare state is doing little to mitigate these financial shocks, the Danish welfare state provides coverage that is more comprehensive for low-income and otherwise economically disadvantaged groups but less generous for high-income groups.

[1] Quoted in Gershman and Morduch (2015, p. 14).

In Germany, the segmented labor market and welfare state splits society into a protected core of long-term employment and an exposed periphery of precarious jobs with unstable and fluctuating work hours. Across all three countries, financial shortfalls increase demands for private coping strategies such as savings, expenditure cuts, and – the focus of this book – borrowing money.

But to systematically understand which private coping strategy prevails, I introduce a second institution: the *structure of a country's credit regime*. This concept captures the institutional relationships between banks, businesses, and households and the supporting regulatory and fiscal policy environments and political coalitions that, together, shape the allocation of credit in the economy and the ease with which households can borrow money. In permissive credit regimes (e.g., many Anglo-Saxon countries and the Netherlands, Denmark, and Sweden), close institutional relationships between banks and households paired with conducive regulatory and fiscal policies encourage lenders to offer a broader range of financial products to households. In restrictive credit regimes (e.g., Southern Europe and Germany), strong institutional relationships between banks and the business sector and regulatory and fiscal policy environments that incentivize households to save inhibit households from easily accessing credit.

Both sets of institutional features – the structure of welfare states and credit regimes – influence patterns of indebtedness. When welfare states offer both comprehensive protection against social risks and support for social investments, individuals rarely borrow money because financial shortfalls are small. However, when social policies are limited, inadequate, or absent, the structure of credit regimes determines which private coping strategies are available. In permissive credit regimes, households go into debt to either address income losses caused by social risks (e.g., unemployment or sickness) or to finance expenditures associated with social investments (e.g., education, childcare, or parental leave).

Studying how individuals address social risks and seize social opportunities within a diverse set of welfare state and credit regime structures has two important distributive implications. At the macro-level, it reveals a more complex relationship between credit markets and welfare states than what current comparative political economy scholarship has identified. When weak welfare states shift the financial costs of social risks and social investments to large parts of society, including economically vulnerable groups, credit markets *substitute* for welfare states. People compensate for insufficient or nonexistent social policies by borrowing money. This is the case in the United States. But when welfare states protect larger parts of society against social risks and provide social investments for education, training, and family supports, credit markets are layered on top of the welfare state and *complement* each other in the provision of financial liquidity. More affluent groups who often receive relatively less support from the welfare state borrow money to access private alternatives, while low-income groups who are protected through social policies have little need to go into debt. Denmark exemplifies this scenario. Finally, in restrictive credit regimes, suppressed credit markets preclude the borrowing option. Households instead rely on a combination of welfare state support and private savings, family support, or expenditure cuts. This is the case in Germany. Perceiving the relationship between financial markets and welfare states in purely substitutive terms is, therefore, incomplete and misleading.

At the micro-level, the book's theoretical framework reveals that we need to pay closer attention to the different reasons and purposes for why individuals use credit. Some borrow money to maintain their standard of living in light of income losses in order to "move onward." Others use credit as a form of bounded social investment, hoping to "move upward" by investing in human capital or financial assets with the expectation of upward mobility and future socioeconomic gains. It is important to emphasize that whether credit-financed social investments either yield positive opportunities and "payoffs" or are simply another form of consumption smoothing is they are bounded and constrained by how level the social policy playing field is and what types of opportunity costs are associated with it. In Chapters 5 and 6, I show that fragmented life course trajectories rather than disrupted employment patterns due to job loss are more consequential for income volatility and borrowing. The introduction of home equity loans in Denmark in 1992 reveals that individuals adjust their borrowing behaviors to cope with income losses when credit constraints (for eligible homeowners) are alleviated. While the reform increased compensatory borrowing among the unemployed, the increase in debt was even larger among individuals who had intentionally left the workforce, for example to get education or training or to raise a family. Danes are more likely to use credit for making social investments than for addressing social risks.

In the United States, by contrast, more people rely on credit markets to cope with the financial consequences of labor market risks and life course choices in light of a weak and often incomplete welfare state. Americans borrow money to address income losses and smooth out income fluctuations caused by unemployment, fewer work hours, and non-standard work arrangements. Regional variation in social policy generosity amplifies these effects. People who become unemployed borrow more in states where unemployment benefits are less generous. And, finally, Americans go into debt when they temporarily leave the workforce, often without pay, to meet family obligations, get training, and pay for childcare. Debt leverage is high across the income distribution but is particularly concentrated among low-income groups, who carry much more debt relative to their incomes than similar groups in Denmark and Germany. In both Denmark and the United States, credit markets also fill gaps that welfare states do not cover. For example, switching from a higher-paying job to a lower-paying job (without a period of unemployment) leads to more borrowing.

Since Germany's restrictive credit regime suppresses access to credit, households tend to rely on a combination of welfare state support, private savings, and expenditure cuts to address income losses. The Hartz IV labor market reform of 2005 reveals how individuals cope with social policy retrenchment in the context of a restrictive credit regime. Unlike in more permissive regimes, cuts in welfare state benefits led to a *decline* in debt leverage rather than an increase in borrowing. People start to repay their loans, perhaps out of fear of falling into arrears or facing bankruptcy, and, instead, draw on savings and cut expenditures to fill financial gaps. There is little change in debt leverage over time, nor is there much difference across income groups. Life course choices – other than buying homes – have no impact on debt leverage, nor is there evidence that paying for childcare increases the probability of carrying debt. Germans rarely use credit markets as private alternatives to social policies.

The final contribution of this book is to document the profound consequences of accessible credit markets and indebtedness on individuals' economic insecurity, social policy preferences, and the future of the welfare state. The crucial insight I want to emphasize is that credit markets privatize risks and losses as well as opportunities and gains. I show that easier access to credit markets lowers individuals' demands for social insurance because it offers the ability to self-insure. Once individuals have borrowed money and become debtors, the social policy calculus changes depending on the way they use credit. On the one hand, individuals who rely on credit for social investments have opted out of the public provision of goods and services, essentially privatizing opportunities and associated gains through credit markets. As a result, demand for social insurance declines. There are two reasons for this. One is that debt and interest payments rival tax payments, which individuals seek to reduce if they are not drawing on public benefits. Another reason is that borrowers expect positive socioeconomic gains and want to reap the benefits of their social investments; they are no longer willing to support public services that would benefit others.

Yet on the other hand, if individuals borrow money to smooth income losses (i.e., "consumption debt"), credit markets privatize economic risks by concentrating the financial burdens on individuals themselves. Indebtedness, regardless of the type of debt, increases borrowers' vulnerabilities to future earning losses and income volatility. But since individuals who use credit to cope with social risks often have limited savings, they are particularly vulnerable to downstream economic shocks. As debt privatizes risks, demand for social insurance increases. Borrowers prefer a more comprehensive welfare state to avoid borrowing money in the first place. And borrowers seek protection against future income losses to avoid falling behind on debt payments and risking bankruptcy.

At its core, this book reveals that the emergence of credit markets as private alternatives to welfare states has gradually but steadily transformed the relationship between individuals, states, and markets in four crucial ways. It has reallocated responsibility for addressing social risks and harnessing social opportunities from society to individuals. It has shifted social rights, account-ability, and eligibility from democratically legitimized institutions such as the welfare state to private, mostly unaccountable lenders as the new gatekeep-ers of equal and fair participation in labor markets, housing markets, and educational opportunities. It has increased individuals' dependence on market participation instead of protecting them and limiting their exposure to adverse market outcomes. And it has amplified existing inequalities and created new ones, bolstering opportunity hoarders in a winner-take-all socioeconomic envi-ronment that is aided, through financial markets, by an increasingly regressive model of resource allocation from very affluent depositors to nonaffluent creditors.

In the remainder of this concluding chapter, I turn to the broader implica-tions of the book's argument and findings. I delineate, necessarily speculatively, the politics behind credit regime structures and reflect on the political coali-tions and dynamics that support complementary and substitutive relationships between credit regimes and welfare states and their implications for the future of the welfare state. I then shed light on how credit markets create new forms of social exclusion and inequality. I end by discussing potential ways to make credit markets and welfare states work together toward a more fair and egalitarian distribution of risks and opportunities in democratic societies.

THE POLITICS OF CREDIT AND DEBT

This book uncovers three dominant ways in which credit regimes interact with welfare states: credit markets substitute for limited or nonexistent wel-fare states; credit markets are layered on top of comprehensive welfare states, thus complementing social policies in the provision of financial liquidity; and when credit markets are suppressed, households rely on a combination of wel-fare state support and private savings, family support, or expenditure cuts. The book's core argument and its focus on the different ways households address social risks and finance social investments raise the question of what politi-cal factors create and sustain these different equilibria, or "coping models." My goal is to conceptually identify and empirically document the existence of such models by focusing on micro-level behaviors within macro-level contexts. Once we understand these facts, we can turn to questions of the political ori-gins of particular credit regime and welfare state constellations and the unique political coalitions that reinforce them.

This book agrees with the argument advanced by Greta Krippner (2011) and others that the concurrent turn to finance and the subsequent rise in credit in many OECD countries is largely the unintended consequence of political responses to limited fiscal resources, too many political demands on the democratic system, and fading confidence in governments' abilities to solve economic problems (see also Davis and Kim 2015). Credit has valuable features for policymakers who face distributional struggles, conflicting societal demands, and fiscal constraints. It allows policymakers to circumvent difficult political choices of allocating scarce resources by shifting such choices onto the market and incentivizing lenders to expand access to credit, subsidize loans, or directly offer credit through government-sponsored enterprises (GSEs). And credit provides financial solutions to pressing problems without immediately adding significant costs to public budgets that are visible to the eyes of taxpayers (Quinn 2019).[2]

This does not suggest, however, that governments, organized interests, or voters have no roles to play in creating and sustaining credit regimes. Across the ideological spectrum, policymakers in many countries embraced financial market liberalization. In the United States, Democrats pushed to "democratize credit" as a form of redistributive egalitarianism, while Republicans sought to stimulate mortgage borrowing to create an "ownership society" and promote personal responsibility through asset ownership (McCarty, Poole, and Rosenthal 2013). In the United Kingdom, various governments privatized the social housing stock, liberalized financial and mortgage markets, and eased credit constraints for borrowers (Hay 2009). Examples include Thatcher's "Right-to-Buy" program, which allows occupants of social housing to buy the council houses they are living in at large discounts, and Cameron's "Help-to-Buy" program, which extends the right-to-buy program to housing association tenants and aims to help individuals, especially first-time buyers, acquire residential properties through mortgage guarantees, equity loans, and share ownership, among others. Central banks, too, are complicit in expanding access to credit by moving interest rates, altering the money supply, and purchasing assets – often amplifying inequities by favoring some economic sectors over others (Jacobs and King 2016; Reisenbichler 2020).

As I document in Chapter 4, permissive credit regimes rest in part on governments' direct interventions in financial markets by subsidizing interest rates and guaranteeing loans through secondary market operations. Perhaps the most prominent examples are GSEs such as Fannie Mae, Ginnie Mae, and Freddie Mac in the United States, which helped turn an otherwise illiquid real estate market into a liquid one by pooling and securitizing large numbers of home mortgages. Market interventions made prices more predictable and reduced information uncertainty for aspiring homeowners while creating stable income streams for issuers. In doing so, Fannie Mae absorbs a large part of the risks associated with home mortgages: the risk of sales price volatility at which issuers ultimately sell pooled mortgages to Fannie Mae, and the risk of defaults of mortgages within that pool (Carruthers and Stinchcombe 1999; Quinn 2019).

Polanyi's (1944) insight that the notion of laissez-faire markets was always an aspirational idea to justify deregulation rather than an empirical reality is as relevant today as it was decades ago. It might be more appropriate to describe the financial system as a "franchise arrangement" backed by the sovereign's

---

[2] The only exception, of course, are large-scale bailouts of overexposed lenders when things go wrong.

full faith and credit in which state and market actors effectively form a public–private partnership (Hockett and Omarova 2016). Governments not only issue public liabilities through currencies and bonds but also "publicly accommodate and monetize private liabilities" by taking on privately issued debt as liabilities of their own (Hockett and Omarova 2016, p. 1147–8). Mazzucato and Wray (2015), for example, estimate that the US federal government in some form backs about one-third of all private debt.

Governments help generate and distribute capital and credit flows through the financial system by directly intervening in financial markets and by writing and underwriting the legal code that sustains the capitalist order (Pistor 2019). But what is perhaps less obvious is the fact that governments can also indirectly create and sustain permissive credit regimes with smoothly running financial markets by operating a comprehensive welfare state. Protection against risks – for example through unemployment or sickness insurance – offers individuals income support and lenders an implicit guarantee that borrowers are able to keep repaying their loans even if they lose their jobs or become sick. In other words, government transfers ensure lenders that debt is much more likely to be repaid. A comprehensive welfare state can in part explain why Danish lenders are willing to extend loans to low-income unemployed people.

By way of concluding, I want to shed light on two additional groups that have vested interests in either permissive or restrictive credit regimes: organized interest groups and economic elites, operating through "quiet politics" (Culpepper 2011); and voters, making their voices heard in the electoral arena. One set of vested interests arises from economic interest groups, most notably the financial, insurance, and real estate (FIRE) sectors, which favor laws and regulations that ensure a permissive credit regime and easy borrowing conditions for households, which, in turn, allow them to operate profitably in the consumer-credit space. Lobbying, political campaign contributions, and revolving doors between private and public sectors, leading to regulatory capture, are powerful tools through which the FIRE sector attempts to shape political outcomes (e.g., Johnson and Kwak 2010; McCarty et al. 2010; Mian, Sufi, and Trebbi 2013). But enthusiasm for financial market liberalization was and still is not always shared widely across societal and business groups. For example, the export industry in Germany is more likely to benefit from suppressed credit access, in part because it boosts Germany's real exchange rate and the overall price competitiveness of the export sector by helping restrain domestic wages and consumption growth (e.g., Baccaro and Pontusson 2016; Braun and Deeg 2019; Johnston and Regan 2016; Stockhammer 2016). Trumbull (2014) has revealed that coalitional support that either favors or opposes credit varies across countries. He shows that American employers, labor unions, and welfare reformers supported credit access as a distinct form of social policy in the early twentieth century, forging coalitions between striking workers who saw consumer credit as a safety net and the banking sector that spotted an opportunity to make inroads into lucrative consumer markets.

In France, however, the political Left and the Catholic Right regarded easier borrowing conditions and rising indebtedness as a threat to social solidarity.

This suggests that there is another group with vested interests in a particular credit regime structure: voters and their demands for pro-credit policies and easy access to credit. Many people, especially in the electorally pivotal middle class, are vested in markets and a financialized economy through, for example, mutual funds, stock trading accounts, and various retirement products (Fligstein and Goldstein 2015; Langley 2008). They also increasingly depend on credit markets to obtain mortgages, home equity lines of credit, student loans, car loans, and credit cards. These trends are particularly pronounced in the United States and the United Kingdom, but also exist in the Netherlands (e.g., Engelen, Konings, and Fernandez 2010) and the Nordic countries (e.g., Belfrage and Kallifatides 2018) – all of which have permissive credit regimes. These vested interests manifest themselves in different ways. As voters' economic lives have become more tied to these markets, they also start holding governments responsible for protecting their assets and wealth from market volatility and financial crises. Chwieroth and Walter (2019) show that voters not only expect banking sector bailouts because financial crises threaten middle-class wealth but also vote incumbents out of office if they fail to do so.[3]

Tax-incentivized mortgages – a key element of permissive credit regimes – and the role of housing more generally are other areas in which voters' vested interests in permissive credit regimes become visible. The US government's consideration to remove the home mortgage interest deduction as part of the 1986 tax reforms was met with public outcry (Ventry 2010). The Danish Socialist People's Party (*Socialistisk Folkeparti*) was forced to reverse course after contemplating increasing the property tax rate to reduce property sales costs, fearing electoral backlash at the ballot box (Mortensen and Seabrooke 2008). And more recently, the Obama administration adopted several measures under the Troubled Asset Relief Program to reduce principal and interest payments of distressed homeowners in the aftermath of the financial crisis of 2007–08. Between 2009 and 2018, the Home Affordable Modification Program restructured about 1.8 million home loans while the Home Affordable Refinance Program helped about 3.5 million underwater and near-underwater homeowners refinance their mortgages.

This book introduces the concept of credit regime permissiveness with two goals in mind: The first is to offer a conceptual framework to think systematically about the institutional and policy factors that shape the allocation of credit in the economy and households' access to credit. The second goal is to provide the basis for an empirical measure that allowes me to document cross-national variation in credit regime permissiveness and its effect on patterns of

---

[3] Rosas (2009), however, argues that electoral accountability makes governments less likely to bail out banks if taxpayers shoulder the costs.

indebtedness. With these conceptual and empirical tools at hand, we can help answer questions about the politics behind credit regimes in order to understand the extent to which governments, organized interests and economic elites through quiet politics, or voters in the electoral arena shape credit regimes' permissiveness.

POLITICAL COALITIONS AND THE FUTURE OF THE WELFARE STATE

The particular constellations of credit regime and welfare state structures rest on and feed back into political cleavage structures and coalitional alignments. In this section, I delineate the contours of two political coalitions that can help sustain such constellations in the context of permissive regimes.

Credit markets' complementary relationships with welfare states may arise in more egalitarian and responsive political systems with a broad cross-class coalition between low- and middle-income voters – who support a comprehensive welfare state – and affluent voters – who demand a permissive credit regime to supplement public benefits by borrowing money. By contrast, when welfare states are weak and limited, credit markets' substitutive role may be the result of more divisive political structures in which middle-class and affluent voters are less likely to support a comprehensive social safety net and, instead, favor a permissive credit regime that provides private alternatives to public options. Not only are low-income groups forced to rely on private means to address financial shortfalls such as borrowing money, but they also have limited political influence to shape (social) policy outcomes. Research from the United States (e.g., Bartels 2010; Gilens 2012) and Europe (e.g., Elsässer, Hense, and Schäfer 2018; Streeck and Schäfer 2013) finds that political influence is tilted toward affluent groups,[4] suggesting that welfare states inadequately support those who depend on them the most if affluent people get their preferences for lower social spending translated into policy outcomes. As high-income groups rely on credit markets instead of welfare states, opting out of the public provision of goods and services such as education, housing, as well as childcare and parental leave might further reduce pressure on policymakers to adapt welfare states to new economic realities.

The political shifts away from welfare states toward private markets are often accompanied by rhetorical shifts that emphasize personal instead of social responsibility (Cooper 2017; Mounk 2017). Credit markets intersect with such rhetoric because they allow individuals to live by the "responsible" option, taking on credit if necessary without relying on government support. In the United States, this notion of personal responsibility is a political "dog whistle," or coded racial language, that resonates with individuals who believe

[4] For an alternative view, see Elkjær and Iversen (2020).

that primarily "undeserving" minority groups use public goods (DeSante 2013; Haney-López 2014). In this context, easier access to credit can undermine support for public spending because it allows prospective borrowers to remove themselves from the imagined group of welfare beneficiaries by opting out of the welfare state. The rhetoric and language around personal responsibility and asset ownership mask the fact that public policies and legal and financial frameworks in the United States deliberately steer people, often in racialized and discriminatory ways, toward homeownership and consumer credit as vehicles for wealth building and consumption (Minow 2012). These rhetorical shifts are not limited to the United States, even though this is where they are most prominent and salient. New Labour's "Third Way" politics in the United Kingdom and the Schröder government in Germany have both invoked norms of personal responsibility to justify welfare retrenchment and privatization efforts (Dwyer 2004; Mau and Sachweh 2014). But while the United Kingdom has embarked on a similar debt-fueled trajectory like the United States, Germany has not.

One question that arises from the discussion of these coalitional dynamics and the book's argument more generally is this: How stable are the complementary and substitutive relationships between credit regimes and welfare states? The growing availability of credit as private means to address social risk and seize social opportunity may change electoral dynamics through feedback effects that can undermine support for universalistic benefits in comprehensive welfare states. Busemeyer and Iversen (2020), for example, show that in the presence of private alternatives, affluent groups prefer limited public insurance with fewer and more targeted benefits to low-income people instead of universal or income-dependent benefits. These dynamics can weaken the broader cross-class support coalition behind the complementary ties between credit and welfare institutions and turn them into substitutive relationships. This results in new electoral cleavages between affluent groups (who benefit from permissive credit regimes and have little interest in supporting a universal welfare state) and economically disadvantaged groups (who are forced to rely on credit markets owing to limited welfare state coverage). For example, by adding more stringent work requirements, the Danish welfare reforms in the early 2000s under the conservative–liberal coalition government have reinforced the cleavages separating middle- and low-income voters.

Political contestation over the provision of and access to social goods and services is likely to play out in two other domains. Although this book only touches upon them in passing, they are critical to the distribution of risks and opportunities between individuals and society: housing and education. Both are key anchors of a modern knowledge economy. Housing provides spatial access to vibrant labor markets, good schools, and desirable neighborhoods – often located in expensive urban areas – while educational credentials help individuals reap these benefits by obtaining high-paying or high-status jobs (Grusky, Hall, and Markus 2019; Le Galès and Pierson 2019). If access to housing and education is privatized or only attainable through private markets, for example by borrowing money, the distribution of socioeconomic opportunities that arises as a result will be skewed and unequal.

Credit markets alter people's relationships with welfare states because they not only offer private alternatives but also affect the salience of public goods provision. "Visible" social policy programs such as unemployment insurance or pension benefits provide financial support and tie individuals more closely to the welfare state, creating powerful policy feedback effects that sustain these programs in the long run (Campbell 2003; Jacobs and Mettler 2018; Pierson 2001). In many countries, however, visible social policies have morphed into more "hidden" (Howard 1997) and "submerged" (Mettler 2011) forms of government policies. For example, recipients do not always recognize tax expenditures (or tax breaks) such as tax credits for childcare or college tuition, particularly common in the United States and the United Kingdom, as being government benefits, and thus they are less supportive of these types of public programs than other, more visible ones (Mettler 2018). Relying on credit as a private alternative to social policies further loosens individuals' ties to the welfare state, potentially undermining trust in government and increasing individuals' perceptions of governments "failing" their citizens because social goods and services are no longer provided by the government but, instead, by individuals' future selves.

This has consequences for political mobilization and participation because the provision of public goods through private means blurs the relationship between beneficiaries and the state. In such an environment, citizens are more likely to attribute benefits to private providers in the marketplace rather than recognizing that the government directly or indirectly creates and sustains such markets. As a result, citizens are less likely to mobilize politically (Thurston 2018).

Indebtedness as the result of engaging in private markets may further stifle political participation because it strains debtors' economic and mental resources. Levine (2015) shows that economic and financial insecurities negatively affect political activism and participation because any rhetoric intended to mobilize individuals around these issues reminds them of their economic fears and socioeconomic constraints. As indebtedness increases perceptions of economic insecurity, it may also lower trust in government (Foster and Frieden 2017; Wroe 2016) and even strengthen support for populist and antiestablishment parties (Mughan, Bean, and McAllister 2003). Welfare states and employment-focused systems of social protection can mitigate the link between economic insecurity and vote choice for populist and anti-establishment parties by dampening economic insecurity (Swank and Betz 2003). By contrast, credit markets have the opposite effect: they create and amplify economic insecurity, especially when households go into debt to fill gaps left by incomplete welfare state support, and further fuel political discontent.

On the other hand, indebtedness may also increase political activism, as demands by the *StrikeDebt!* movement and the *Jubilee Debt Campaign* in the United Kingdom show. These movements sought to grant overindebted individuals more time to settle their debts by amending regulations on lending and debt moratoria. In the United States, activists have pushed states and cities to limit when and how employers can use credit reports under the Fair Credit Reporting Act. Although the issue of student debt has gained some political traction in recent years, especially in electoral campaigns in the United States and the United Kingdom, it remains puzzling why household indebtedness has not become a more salient topic in political campaigns and party platforms. The electoral consequences of rising indebtedness are an area ripe for future research.

CREDIT, DEBT, AND INEQUALITY

In many countries, access to credit is now a prerequisite for full participation and inclusion in what Grusky, Hall, and Markus (2019) call "opportunity markets" for education, housing, and good jobs. This turns credit markets into key sites of T.H. Marshall's notion of "economic citizenship," not least because being excluded from such markets has even greater consequences (Marshall 1964).[5] Individuals with strong credit scores and consistent employment histories and income records can easily borrow money, while those with worse scores and more scattered and volatile work histories are deemed less creditworthy and, therefore, pay higher interest rates to obtain loans. Still others have no access to formal credit markets and banking services and, instead, rely on informal and fringe lending services such as payday lenders and pawnshops (Baradaran 2015).

But credit-related inequalities go beyond issues of access. One source of inequality emerges in the form of debt repayments, since low-income individuals typically spend larger shares of their incomes on debt and interest payments than high-income individuals. The less money one has, the more one pays to use it. Another form of inequality arises because different people borrow money for different reasons. Throughout this book, I emphasize the bifurcated nature of credit. Some individuals borrow money to smooth income losses and compensate for volatile employment patterns, while others rely on credit as bounded social investments in education, housing, childcare, or to take time off work to raise a family. For individuals who find it difficult to access credit markets at reasonable costs, a limited welfare state not only increases opportunity costs but also leaves such individuals with fewer options to address risks and harness opportunities. A final source of inequality are credit scores, which quantify people's credit and repayment histories. No longer do credit

[5] For more on opportunity markets, see, for example, Reeves (2017).

scores reflect only the risk of lending to prospective borrowers – they determine one's prospects for renting an apartment, getting insurance, and, as evidence from the United States and Sweden suggests, acquiring and retaining jobs (Bos, Breza, and Liberman 2018; Dobbie et al. 2020; Kiviat 2019). Recognizing that people with bad credit have fewer labor market chances, the New York City Council in 2015 banned employers from using individuals' consumer credit histories when making employment decisions, joining cities such as Chicago as well as eleven states that already limit how employers can use credit information about prospective employees (Traub and McElwee 2016).

Differences in access to and cost of credit have downstream consequences for social mobility and wealth inequality. Credit can lessen inequalities by providing individuals with financial opportunities they would not have otherwise, for example granting mortgages to buy homes or offering student loans to low-income or economically disadvantaged individuals so they can attend college or university, improving their likelihood of achieving upward social mobility. But credit can also aggravate existing inequalities. Political economies carry their histories with them, and this is most visible in the case of the racialized American economy (see, for example, Dawson and Francis 2016). Biases in financial services have deep historical roots, stretching back to the infamous practice of "redlining" housing areas, in which banks and other lenders systematically discriminated against low-income and minority households on the basis of community demographics (Rothstein 2017; Taylor 2019). Racial injustices are still prevalent in the credit system despite anti-discriminatory regulation. Ross and Yinger (1999) find that in the United States, Black and Latino Americans face higher rejection rates and obtain mortgages with much less favorable terms than White Americans with similar credit and income characteristics. The result is a "dual-mortgage market" (Immergluck 1999) that is divided into prime lending, concentrated in high-income and White communities, and subprime, often predatory lending, concentrated in low-income minority areas (see also Pager and Shepherd 2008). This is no coincidence. Court documents reveal that a number of major American banks, including SunTrust, Wells Fargo, and Bank of America, had engaged in discriminatory lending practices by using race as a central factor to determine both higher fees and interest rates for subprime mortgages during the housing boom preceding the financial crisis of 2007–08. Lenders essentially preyed on minority (subprime) housing debt, which Wells Fargo loan officers pejoratively called "ghetto loans" (Dawson and Francis 2016, p. 39).

Unequal access to credit and outright discrimination set people on diverging wealth-building trajectories. Inequalities of the past resurface in the present. Losing out on the opportunity to acquire financial assets such as a house and to subsequently participate in the increase in home equity is one of the most important factors behind the racial wealth gap in the United States, undermining Black American's ability to accumulate wealth (Baradaran 2017; Chiteji 2010). In 2106, the median net worth of White households was about

$149,703, which is more than ten times higher than that of Black households ($13,024) (Kuhn, Schularick, and Steins 2020; McIntosh et al. 2020).

Lastly, growing indebtedness can also increase economic insecurity by making households more financially vulnerable to sudden income losses or unexpected expenditures. When incomes stagnate – as they have for many individuals at the lower end of the wage scale (OECD 2019) – any increases in debt will lower households' disposable incomes because they have to devote more of their incomes to debt service. This reduces households' financial leeway to cope with future financial shocks. To be sure, not all debtors face similar levels of economic and financial vulnerability. Individuals with sufficient assets, incomes, and secure jobs that provide financial cushions and the ability to regularly pay off debts are economically more secure and better able to shoulder larger levels of debt. But many households do not have enough assets, in particular liquid savings, to weather financial shocks (Lusardi, Schneider, and Tufano 2011).

People's exposure to economic risks also depends on how well macro-level institutions mitigate the prevalence of risky events and the size of financial fallouts if such events occur (DiPrete 2002; Hacker and Rehm 2021). Consider the risk of job loss. In Denmark, the flexible labor market creates a comparatively high risk of job loss, but the welfare state contains the financial consequences by providing relatively generous unemployment support (the so-called flexicurity model), in particular for low-income households, as I document in Chapters 3 and 5. Even in the event of unemployment, Danes are therefore able to meet regular debt and interest payments. By contrast, job loss in the United States has much broader financial ramifications beyond just income shocks. Compared with Denmark, unemployment insurance benefit amounts are lower, duration periods shorter, and eligibility criteria harsher. But perhaps even more consequential is the looming risk of losing other types of social protection such as health insurance, which is often tied to employment. Income volatility or outright income losses quickly spread into other domains and increase debtors' financial insecurity when social benefits that could provide income support are limited. Misfortunes in one domain cascade to increase risks in other domains (Thelen and Wiedemann 2021). Debt becomes a compounding problem as a result of financial volatility, which can easily lead to a downward spiral of risk contagion because weak unemployment insurance benefits are *themselves* a driving force of indebtedness, as I show in Chapter 5. This helps explain why American households are at much higher risk of bankruptcies and foreclosures than Danish households, even though the latter carry on average even higher levels of debt (Porter 2012*a*).

Some scholars argue, however, that higher levels of personal bankruptcy reflect the fact that bankruptcy serves a social insurance function and should therefore be considered part of the social safety net (e.g., Adler, Polak, and Schwartz 2000; Fisher 2019; Hynes 2004; Sullivan, Warren, and Westbrook 2000). In the context of the United States, however, the highly regressive and racialized nature of bankruptcy proceedings and outcomes means that bankruptcy is beneficial for some groups and predatory and exploitative for others (Wise 2020). In this view, a permissive bankruptcy regime substitutes for a more limited welfare state by allowing individuals in economic difficulties easier debt discharge.

MAKING WELFARE STATES AND CREDIT MARKETS WORK TOGETHER

Is it possible to make credit markets and welfare states work together to ensure a more fair and egalitarian financial system and, at the same time, to safeguard and strengthen the social safety net, public investment in social opportunities, and, ultimately, social rights?

Through its comparative perspective, this book demonstrates that the patterns of indebtedness that arise from social policy-related financial shortfalls are far from preordained. They are the results of institutional design and political choices. Governments shape both the supply of credit through the structure of their credit regimes and the demand for credit by regulating labor markets and designing social policies that influence the size of financial burdens pressed upon households. Instead of further individualizing and privatizing risks and opportunities, we should strive for a concerted societal approach that distributes risks *and* opportunities more equitably. This requires us to balance two goals: equal and fair access to credit by altering the structure of credit regimes; and equal and fair distributions of social risks and provisions of social opportunities through the welfare state.

The first goal should be to ensure that all individuals can equally access and fairly engage in credit markets. Suppressing individuals' participation in financial markets (as is the case in restrictive credit regimes) is not the right approach. But neither is excessively relying on credit markets, encouraged and incentivized through fiscal and regulatory policies and securitization practices. Governments have a range of tools at their disposal that could help pave the way toward a more fair and egalitarian financial system. One example is to strengthen public banks and invest in community banking. Baradaran (2012, 2015) suggests bolstering postal banking in the United States, relying on the existing post office framework and infrastructure to extend credit and financial services to underbanked individuals. Publicly mandating some lenders to serve local communities rather than following purely profit-maximizing goals might be another solution. Yet another example is to make lenders share more of the credit risks during periods of economic distress. Mian and Sufi (2014) propose flexible mortgage contracts that tie the principal balances of mortgages and the interest payments to a zip code–specific house price index. If house prices in that zip code fall, the principal balances and interest payments are automatically adjusted downward, providing relief to homeowners when they might need it most.

The second goal should be a renewed effort to invest in two sets of social policy instruments. Policies to address social risks should be designed in ways that protect the most economically vulnerable, and they should be portable across the life course and therefore independent of employment. And more emphasis should be placed on policies that strengthen and expand social investment, in particular through paid and job-protected parental leaves, subsidized childcare, and more affordable education. A stronger welfare state helps level the playing field, broadens the availability of social opportunities, and offers social insurance that allows credit markets to function more equitably and induce less risk to individuals and their families. The potential macro-economic benefits of such social policies are large. Growing evidence suggests that high debt leverage amplifies economic recessions because borrowers cut down on spending, which slowly chokes off the economy (Mian and Sufi 2014). This book shows that an atrophied welfare state has a similar effect. It forces people to take on more debt and provides little financial support during economic downturns. Put differently, a more comprehensive welfare state not only lessens the need for people to go into debt but also ensures that debtors can better manage their finances during times of economic distress, avoiding new debt while being able to repay existing debt. The coronavirus pandemic, raging still as I finish this book, brings this painfully to light.

This perspective is also relevant for debates about whether credit ought to be a right, be it a moral, social, or legal one. Muhammad Yunus, the founder of the Grameen Bank, a micro-finance organization and community development bank serving Bangladesh, and cowinner of the 2006 Nobel Peace Prize, is one of the most prominent advocates for credit to be considered a human right: "Every poor person must be allowed a fair chance to improve his/her economic condition. This can be easily done by ensuring his/her right to credit" (quoted in Gershman and Morduch [2015, p. 14]). This rights-based approach is often grounded in the idea that credit is both an important means for individual and societal economic development and foundational to safeguarding other rights such as private property. Meyer (2018), for example, argues that in a private property–owning society, "non-owners lack sufficient reason to accept such a duty unless a right to credit mitigates the exclusionary character of private property" (p. 305). In this view, it then falls on the state to help prospective borrowers who are not creditworthy become creditworthy. Others, however, are skeptical about whether credit should be a right. Hudon (2009) points to potential negative consequences such as the risks of overindebtedness and abusive financial practices, the infeasibility of granting and guaranteeing such a right, and empirical evidence that sheds doubt on the causal link between access to credit and economic development. Gershman and Morduch (2015) suggest that ensuring nondiscriminatory access to micro-credit instead of turning credit into a (human) right might better serve the goal of economic development.

I share these concerns and skepticism around the notion of credit as a social right. Instead of attempting to create a right to credit, which almost inevitably prompts morally charged and normative views on whether debt is "good" or "bad," it is more useful to ask what outcomes we try to achieve by turning credit into a right. The fundamental question that lies at the heart of this book is this: should the responsibility to address socioeconomic risks and to provide social investments and opportunities lie with individuals, states, or markets? The problem with (credit) markets is that they neither protect the most vulnerable people in our societies nor offer a level playing field for everyone to seize social opportunities. Credit markets, after all, are *not* a form of social insurance. As I show throughout this book, they privatize risks and opportunities, thus re-commodifying individuals by increasing their dependence on markets and stable long-term income streams.

Instead, we should focus on safeguarding and strengthening social rights and claims on the (welfare) state because these goals can be achieved more equitably, democratically, and with fewer downstream risks through social policies instead of credit markets. For example, childcare and education can be publicly funded and provided through taxation or, alternatively, privately funded and operated through markets. People who become unemployed can either draw on government benefits or take on credit card debt. With regard to addressing risks and guaranteeing opportunities, there are two reasons for tilting the balance toward the welfare state instead of credit markets. First, welfare states distribute goods and services according to democratically defined rules and legally enforceable social rights. In credit markets, by contrast, most lenders determine "eligibility" and creditworthiness in order to maximize profits. Moreover, they operate without democratic oversight (within legally defined rules to curb discriminatory behavior), and they are not required to extend loans to all prospective borrowers. Second, welfare states distribute risks and opportunities across individuals, again based on democratically defined criteria, and, crucially, do not add *additional* risks to benefit claimants because funding is based on past and current tax and insurance contributions. Credit markets, however, concentrate risks within individuals because debt constitutes a claim over future resources that needs to be repaid with interest. Both reasons suggest that welfare states are better equipped to both help individuals cope with social risks and provide them with social opportunities.

This book shows that different structures of labor markets, welfare states, and credit regimes, together with the political choices that sustain them, produce and reproduce very different patterns of indebtedness across and within countries. It is not an easy task to strike the right balance between a fair and egalitarian financial system on the one hand, and an equitable distribution of risks, opportunities, and, ultimately, life chances on the other – but it is well worth trying.

Appendix

The data sets used in this book are harmonized according to the following principles. All individual-level data are aggregated to the household level to take into account resource sharing within the household. The household head is, in line with most household-level data sets, the male person of that household. I subset all data sets to working-age individuals between the ages of 15 and 65 and exclude self-employed individuals as this group might have loans for business purposes that cannot be identified separately in the data sets. All data are inflation-adjusted.

Since data on households' assets and liabilities are highly skewed but also contain households with zero assets and liabilities, using a natural log transformation is not an option because it is undefined at zero. To address this problem, I resort to a commonly used inverse hyperbolic sine transformation (IHS) defined for variable z as $sinh^{-1}z = ln(z + \sqrt{1 + z^2})$ in which negative values and zero in z are defined. This transformation is linear around the origin, approximates a log transformation at the right tail, and can be interpreted as a standard logarithmic variable (Pence 2006). I use this IHS transformation for all income, asset, and liability variables.

Danish Administrative Register Data

In the Danish case, I use several high-quality administrative records gathered by Statistics Denmark that cover, for most variables, the entire Danish population since 1987. I link these registers based on unique anonymized personal identification numbers (CPR number) that are assigned at birth. This allows me to combine different registers at the individual level into a large panel data set that spans several decades and contains around 55 million observations or around 4.4 million unique household heads. The registers contain detailed information on individuals' demographic characteristics, household composition, labor market attachment and social policy program participation, income and government transfers, and assets and liabilities. Data on income and wealth are based on administrative tax returns collected by the Danish Tax Agency (SKAT) and supplemented by information from third-party reporting such as banks and other financial institutions reported to the tax authorities at the end of the year. I obtained fine-grained information on individuals' liabilities including bank and mortgage loans as well as complete portfolio information including the value of stock and bond ownership and cash in bank accounts. Labor market information comes from the register-based Labor Force Statistics (RAS) and the Integrated Database for Labor Market Research (IDA). For more information on the Danish registers, see, for example, Petersson, Baadsgaard, and Thygesen 2011.

The data are unique in their quality because they cover the entire Danish population over a very long time horizon. They are not self-reported by individuals and therefore contain minimal measurement error and do not top-code assets, liabilities, and incomes. Unlike in survey-based panels, there is virtually no missing data or attrition.

In the Danish register data, a household is defined as all individuals living at the same address if they are either a registered or married couple and have at least one joint child according to the civil register, or are of the opposite sex with age difference of less than 15 years, unrelated, and live with no other adults. All other adults living at the same address are counted as members of different families. Children are part of a family if they are registered at the same address as at least one parent, are under 25 years old, have never been married or in a civil partnership, do not have children of their own, and are not part of a cohabiting couple. In the US Panel Study of Income Dynamics (PSID) and the German Socio-Economic Panel (SOEP), households are composed of people living together who are related by blood, marriage, or adoption, or permanently living together and sharing income and expenses. I use *household* and *family* interchangeably. To ensure comparability, the default household head in all three countries is the man in the case of a couple (married or not); when the household consists of a woman alone, she is the head.

Survey of Consumer Finance (United States)

The Survey of Consumer Finance (SCF) is a triennial cross-sectional survey of around 6,500 US households sponsored by the Board of Governors of the Federal Reserve System and includes information on households' incomes, assets, and liabilities, as well as demographic characteristics. It oversamples higher-income households to improve representativeness in the right tail of the heavily skewed wealth distribution. The SCF data impute missing values and issue five multiple-imputed data sets to reflect statistical uncertainty. The SCF is considered to collect the most detailed and accurate wealth information and is often used as a benchmark to judge the validity of wealth data collected in other surveys (Eggleston and Klee 2015).

Survey of Income and Program Participation (United States)

The Survey of Income and Program Participation (SIPP) is a household-based survey administered by the Census Bureau and designed as a continuous series of national panels. It uses a two-stage stratified design to produce a nationally representative panel of respondents who are interviewed over a period of approximately three to four years. Within a SIPP panel, the entire sample is interviewed at various waves, generally at four-month intervals. In addition to income, assets, liabilities, and public program participation, the SIPP includes data on other factors of economic well-being, demographics, and household characteristics.

For household debt, I use the SIPP instead of the PSID because it contains data on household liabilities for every year of the wave. Other panel data sets such as the PSID switched to a biannual data collection and are therefore not helpful to study borrowing choices in response to income losses.

Socio-Economic Panel (Germany)

The German SOEP is an annual longitudinal study of German households based on face-to-face interviews with all members of a given survey household aged 16 years and older. It contains a wide range of domains, including household composition, labor market status, and income and government transfers. The SOEP started in 1984, with the new German states added in 1991, and it interviews a sample of around 11,000 households or about 30,000 unique individuals. See Wagner, Frick, and Schupp (2007) for more information on the SOEP. A disadvantage of the SOEP is its lack of regular information on household wealth. The SOEP began to collect detailed information on individuals' assets and liabilities in wealth supplements in 2002, 2007, and 2012 (see Frick, Grabka, and Marcus 2010).

SAVE Study (Germany)

The German SAVE study is a panel data set that was initiated in 2001 and produced by the Mannheim Research Institute for the Economics of Aging (MEA) with the aim to analyze households' saving behavior. It is a response to Germany's limited availability of longitudinal panel data to analyze households' financial behavior. Existing data sources such as the German SOEP only started to collect information on assets and liabilities in 2002, with follow-up waves in 2007 and 2012, making it impossible to study annual changes in households' financial situation. The SAVE study includes detailed information on households' income, assets, and liabilities based on a representative sample of around 1,500 German households annually. For more information, see Boersch-Supan and Essig (2005).

EMPIRICAL APPENDICES

Appendix for Chapter 3

TABLE A.3.1 *Definition of sources of income volatility*

	Employment disruption	Life course choices
Denmark	Unemployed Activation Sickness	Leave of absence Maternity leave Student Training
United States	Unemployed Temporary laid off Disabled	Student Homemaker
Germany	Unemployed Mini-/midi-job	Homemaker Maternity leave Training

Notes: Composition of the groups for the sources of income volatility. The definitions of employment status in each country data set do not match perfectly. Mini- and midi-jobs in Germany have limited work hours and benefits. *Sources:* USA: PSID; Germany: SOEP; Denmark: administrative records.

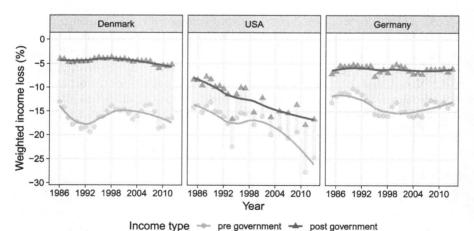

FIGURE A.3.1 Weighted gross and net income volatility
Notes: The dots show the average gross and net household income loss (negative values), defined as the annual percentage change in income, weighted by the share of households that experience a drop in income of 25 percent or greater from one year to another. The lines are fitted locally smoothed polynomial trend lines. The graphs for the United States and Germany use survey sampling weights; the graphs for Denmark are based on the entire population. *Sources:* PSID (USA), SOEP (Germany), and administrative records (Denmark).

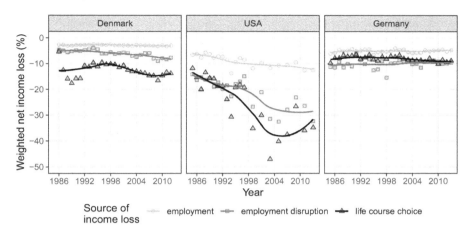

FIGURE A.3.2 Weighted net income volatility by employment status

Notes: The dots show the average net household income loss (negative values), defined as the annual percentage change in income, weighted by the share of households that experience a drop in income of 25 percent or greater from one year to another. The lines are fitted locally smoothed polynomials. *Employment disruptions* include unemployment, sickness, and disability. *Life course choices* include education (student and retraining), various forms of leave such as family leave and homemaking. The employment status of the household is based on the status of the household head. For details, see Table A.3.1 in the Appendix. Note that in the German case, mini- and midi-jobs are classified as employment disruptions. The graphs for the United States and Germany use survey sampling weights; the graphs for Denmark are based on the entire population. *Sources:* PSID (USA), SOEP (Germany), and administrative records (Denmark).

Appendix for Chapter 4

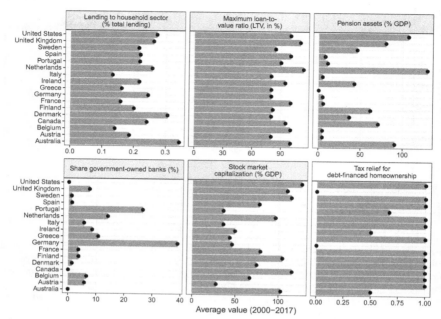

FIGURE A.4.1 Raw values of the credit regime indicators (averages for 2000–17)
Notes: The indicators for government-owned banks and tax relief for debt-financed homeowner-ship are zero for countries that do not have any government-owned banks and do not offer tax relief, respectively. See Table 4.1 for data sources.

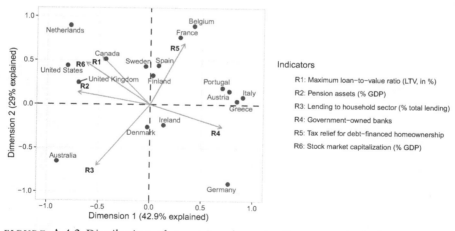

FIGURE A.4.2 Distribution of countries along the first two principal components (averages for 2000–17)
Notes: The plot shows the distribution of countries along the first two factors of the principal component analysis.

TABLE A.4.1 *Coping strategies by country, fixed effect results*

	Dependent variable		
	reduce expenses (1)	borrow from bank (2)	government transfers (3)
Homeowner	−0.25***	0.47***	−0.56***
	(0.07)	(0.15)	(0.08)
Income (deciles)	−0.23***	0.24***	−0.35***
	(0.02)	(0.04)	(0.03)
Employed	0.09	0.34*	−0.34***
	(0.08)	(0.17)	(0.09)
Education level	−0.06***	0.10**	−0.01
	(0.02)	(0.04)	(0.03)
Married	0.10	−0.04	−0.02
	(0.07)	(0.14)	(0.08)
Respondent male	−0.14**	0.15	−0.03
	(0.06)	(0.13)	(0.08)
Age head 25–34	−0.28	0.10	−0.10
	(0.18)	(0.42)	(0.18)
Age head 25–34	−0.12	0.49	−0.28
	(0.18)	(0.40)	(0.18)
Age head 35–44	−0.11	0.43	−0.44**
	(0.17)	(0.40)	(0.18)
Age head 45–54	−0.45**	0.30	−1.11***
	(0.18)	(0.41)	(0.19)
Age head 55–64	−1.10***	0.43	−2.32***
	(0.18)	(0.43)	(0.21)
Age head 65+	0.11***	−0.07	0.25***
	(0.04)	(0.07)	(0.04)
Number of children	2.03***	−5.18***	1.34***
in household	(0.50)	(0.65)	(0.31)
σ_{FR}	0.25	0.21	0.11
σ_{DE}	−0.54	−0.9	0.19
σ_{IT}	1.85	−1.34	−0.78
σ_{SE}	−1.12	1.35	0.66
σ_{UK}	−0.44	0.74	−0.17
Observations	5,445	3,544	5,445
Log Likelihood	−3,116.92	−885.48	−2,227.55
Akaike Inf. Crit.	6,261.85	1,798.96	4,483.09
Bayesian Inf. Crit.	6,354.28	1,885.38	4,575.53

Notes: Fixed effects from a generalized linear mixed-effects model with country random effects. Questions: "In the past two years [i.e., 2008 and 2009], have you or anyone else in your household had to take any of the following measures as the result of a decline in income or other economic difficulties? In the past two years, have you or any member of your household tried to borrow money from anyone (e.g., a friend, other person or institution)?" The random effects are displayed in Figure 4.7. *p<0.1; **p<0.05; ***p<0.01.

TABLE A.4.2 *Marginal effects of unemployment insurance generosity and credit permissiveness on household debt*

	Dependent variable			
	Household debt (share GDP)			
	(1)	(2)	(3)	(4)
Credit permissiveness	222.44*	240.84**	287.10***	240.14***
	(122.65)	(103.70)	(98.91)	(63.90)
UI generosity	7.65	7.39	7.33*	5.23
	(5.85)	(4.86)	(4.26)	(3.26)
Real GDP growth		−0.93***	−0.16	−0.07
		(0.23)	(0.21)	(0.29)
Capital account openness		−28.88	−32.22	−36.29
		(24.22)	(23.75)	(25.00)
Government deficit		−1.04**	0.33	0.69
		(0.46)	(0.47)	(0.56)
Share service sector employment			167.91	159.98
			(111.35)	(96.67)
Unemployment rate			1.04**	1.78**
			(0.47)	(0.69)
Gini			−0.13	−0.39
			(1.00)	(0.92)
Government outlays			1.96***	2.11***
			(0.74)	(0.72)
Real house prices				0.26***
				(0.08)
Credit permissiveness × UI generosity	−19.92*	−22.37**	−26.23***	−22.40***
	(11.70)	(9.92)	(9.17)	(6.23)
Mean DV	67.74	67.74	67.74	67.74
State FE	✓	✓	✓	✓
Year FE	✓	✓	✓	✓
Observations	191	191	191	191
R^2	0.96	0.97	0.97	0.98
Adjusted R^2	0.95	0.96	0.97	0.98

Notes: $^*p<0.1$; $^{**}p<0.05$; $^{***}p<0.01$.

TABLE A.4.3 *Marginal effects of unemployment insurance generosity and credit permissiveness on household debt: robustness to lagged DV*

	Dependent variable	
	Household debt (share GDP)	
	(1)	(2)
Credit permissiveness	8.30**	4.53
	(4.18)	(3.74)
UI generosity	0.16	0.16
	(0.11)	(0.10)
GDP (log)	−1.01***	−0.77***
	(0.23)	(0.21)
Real GDP growth	−0.19**	−0.31***
	(0.09)	(0.06)
Capital account openness	3.65	3.38*
	(2.44)	(1.86)
Government deficit	0.39***	0.30***
	(0.11)	(0.08)
Share service sector employment	26.99***	21.53***
	(7.65)	(6.68)
Unemployment rate	0.07	0.05
	(0.06)	(0.06)
Gini	0.22*	0.16
	(0.13)	(0.10)
Government outlays	−0.02	−0.07
	(0.06)	(0.05)
Real house prices	0.07***	0.04***
	(0.01)	(0.01)
Household debt (share GDP), lagged 1 year	0.99***	1.40***
	(0.01)	(0.08)
Household debt (share GDP), lagged 2 years		−0.41***
		(0.08)
Credit permissiveness × UI generosity	−0.94**	−0.59*
	(0.36)	(0.32)
Mean DV	69.16	70.66
State FE	−	−
Year FE	✓	✓
Observations	175	159
R^2	1.00	1.00
Adjusted R^2	1.00	1.00

Notes: *p<0.1; **p<0.05; ***p<0.01.

TABLE A.4.4 *Marginal effects of unemployment insurance generosity and credit permissiveness on household debt: robustness to crisis dummies*

	Dependent variable	
	Household debt (share GDP)	
	(1)	(2)
Credit permissiveness	239.95***	245.76***
	(62.14)	(67.91)
UI generosity	5.12	5.88*
	(3.17)	(3.35)
Real GDP growth	−0.03	−0.19
	(0.31)	(0.31)
Capital account openness	−33.13	−33.84
	(24.52)	(23.35)
Government deficit	0.98*	0.87
	(0.56)	(0.54)
Share service sector employment	171.11*	174.47*
	(96.98)	(96.76)
Unemployment rate	2.00***	1.71***
	(0.70)	(0.63)
Gini	−0.33	−0.38
	(0.88)	(0.88)
Government outlays	2.39***	2.10***
	(0.72)	(0.69)
Real house prices	0.26***	0.24***
	(0.08)	(0.08)
Banking crisis dummy	−3.41**	
	(1.38)	
Systemic crisis dummy		−3.34
		(2.16)
Credit permissiveness × UI generosity	−22.46***	−23.40***
	(6.00)	(6.60)
Mean DV	67.74	67.97
State FE	✓	✓
Year FE	✓	✓
Observations	191	188
R^2	0.98	0.98
Adjusted R^2	0.98	0.98

Notes: *$p<0.1$; **$p<0.05$; ***$p<0.01$.

Appendix for Chapter 5

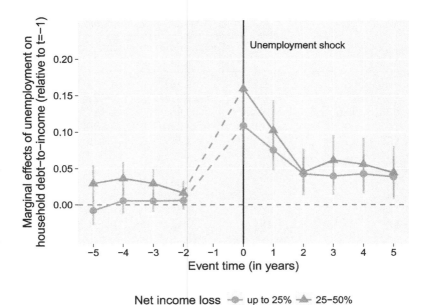

FIGURE A.5.1 Marginal effect of unemployment on debt-to-income ratio by size of financial gaps, debt normalized by prior income in Denmark

Notes: The plot shows event-year marginal effect coefficients for debt-income ratios relative to the year prior to unemployment estimated based on Equation 5.1, estimated separately for both income loss groups. The shaded areas are 95% confidence intervals based on robust standard errors clustered at the household level. The financial gap is measured as the size of the income loss and calculated as the change in household disposable income from $t=-1$ to $t=0$. The model is based on a balanced sample of households whose household head has his or her first unemployment between 1992 and 2007 such that individuals are observed during the entire period between five years before and after unemployment.

TABLE A.5.1 *Effect of unemployment insurance generosity on unsecured debt among unemployment benefit recipients in the United States*

	Dependent variable			
	Total unsecured household debt (log)			
	(1)	(2)	(3)	(4)
UI recipient	4.517**	4.501**	4.484**	4.927***
	(2.003)	(2.016)	(2.022)	(1.833)
Maximum UI benefits (log)	0.100	0.003	−0.184	
	(0.198)	(0.240)	(0.490)	
Income Q2	0.108*	0.106*	0.106*	0.110*
	(0.059)	(0.060)	(0.060)	(0.060)
Income Q3	0.310***	0.306***	0.308***	0.310***
	(0.060)	(0.061)	(0.061)	(0.061)
Income Q4	0.484***	0.480***	0.480***	0.479***
	(0.068)	(0.068)	(0.069)	(0.069)
Income Q5	0.525***	0.522***	0.521***	0.524***
	(0.108)	(0.108)	(0.110)	(0.109)
Education: some college	0.248	0.230	0.226	0.246
	(0.249)	(0.251)	(0.250)	(0.248)
Education: college	0.721***	0.702***	0.691***	0.735***
	(0.260)	(0.265)	(0.266)	(0.266)
Education: BA	0.732**	0.689**	0.705**	0.726**
	(0.319)	(0.324)	(0.324)	(0.329)
Education: MA	0.782*	0.751	0.763	0.823*
	(0.470)	(0.477)	(0.473)	(0.475)
Age	0.160**	0.159**	0.163**	0.164**
	(0.072)	(0.071)	(0.072)	(0.073)
Age square	−0.001**	−0.001**	−0.001**	−0.001**
	(0.001)	(0.001)	(0.001)	(0.001)
Number of children	0.034	0.037	0.037	0.036
	(0.043)	(0.044)	(0.043)	(0.041)
Married	1.055***	1.069***	1.067***	1.061***
	(0.112)	(0.112)	(0.112)	(0.111)
Single	−0.492***	−0.481***	−0.485***	−0.494***
	(0.070)	(0.070)	(0.071)	(0.070)
Renter	−0.002	−0.001	0.003	−0.004
	(0.078)	(0.079)	(0.079)	(0.079)
White	−0.236	−0.232	−0.246	−0.040
	(0.605)	(0.585)	(0.572)	(0.599)
Asian	1.197	1.230	1.234	1.434
	(1.011)	(1.050)	(1.059)	(0.954)

(*continued*)

TABLE A.5.1 *(continued)*

	Dependent variable			
	Total unsecured household debt (log)			
	(1)	(2)	(3)	(4)
Black	1.346	1.369	1.335*	1.624**
	(0.825)	(0.841)	(0.811)	(0.812)
Savings (log)	0.102***	0.102***	0.102***	0.100***
	(0.007)	(0.007)	(0.007)	(0.007)
Mortgage interest rate	0.007***	0.007***	0.007***	0.007***
	(0.001)	(0.001)	(0.001)	(0.001)
GSP (per-capita, log)		0.687	−0.090	
		(0.701)	(2.008)	
Change GSP		0.007	0.010	
		(0.010)	(0.010)	
Unemployment rate		0.001	0.013	
		(0.068)	(0.077)	
Expenditures (per capita, log)		0.181	0.021	
		(0.489)	(0.830)	
Revenues (per capita, log)		−0.136	−0.131	
		(0.159)	(0.169)	
UI recipient ×	−0.434**	−0.433**	−0.431**	−0.475***
Maximum UI benefits (log)	(0.197)	(0.198)	(0.199)	(0.180)
Mean DV	5.371	5.37	5.37	5.371
Household and year FE	✓	✓	✓	✓
State-quadratic time trends	−	−	✓	−
State-by-year FE	−	−	−	✓
Observations	242,612	241,661	241,661	242,612
R^2	0.721	0.721	0.721	0.723
Adjusted R^2	0.477	0.476	0.477	0.479

Notes: The models are based on Equation 5.4. The state-by-year fixed effects in column 4 absorb the estimate of the maximum UI benefit measure main effect. Robust standard errors are clustered at the state level and reported in parentheses. *$p<0.1$; **$p<0.05$; ***$p<0.01$.

TABLE A.5.2 *Effects of part-time work on unsecured debt in the United States*

	Dependent variable		
	Total household unsecured debt (log)		
	(1)	(2)	(3)
Work less than 35h	0.30***	0.31***	0.32***
	(0.05)	(0.05)	(0.05)
Total household income (log)			0.11***
			(0.03)
Total liquid savings (log)		0.05***	0.05***
		(0.01)	(0.01)
Education: BA		0.99*	0.98*
		(0.58)	(0.58)
Education: college		0.82	0.81
		(0.57)	(0.57)
Education: high school		0.33	0.33
		(0.40)	(0.40)
Education: MA		0.82	0.74
		(0.71)	(0.70)
Education: some college		0.36	0.36
		(0.53)	(0.53)
Age		0.14	0.13
		(0.10)	(0.10)
Age square		−0.00	−0.00
		(0.00)	(0.00)
Number of children		−0.02	−0.02
		(0.06)	(0.06)
Family: male head		0.08	0.05
		(0.35)	(0.35)
Married couple		1.19***	1.16***
		(0.20)	(0.20)
Non-family: female head		−0.50***	−0.48**
		(0.19)	(0.19)
Non-family: male head		−0.63**	−0.63**
		(0.31)	(0.31)
Renter		−0.12	−0.11
		(0.10)	(0.10)
Race: Asian		1.74	1.78
		(1.43)	(1.40)
Race: Black		0.89	0.88
		(1.12)	(1.12)
Race: Native American		−0.45	−0.45
		(1.35)	(1.34)
Limited set of controls	–	✓	–
Full set of controls	–	–	✓
Unit fixed effects	✓	✓	✓
Year fixed effects	✓	✓	✓
Observations	185,978	185,494	185,468
R^2	0.72	0.72	0.72
Adjusted R^2	0.45	0.46	0.46

Notes: Robust standard errors are clustered at the state level and reported in parentheses. Column 1 is the baseline model without controls, column 2 adds a set of unit-level controls, and column 3 additionally adds income as a control. *p<0.1; **p<0.05; ***p<0.01.

TABLE A.5.3 *Marginal effects of degrees of labor market attachment on unsecured debt in Germany*

	Dependent variable	
	Unsecured debt (log)	
	(1)	(2)
Unemployed	0.26	0.32
	(0.21)	(0.21)
Employed part-time (15-35h/week)	0.17	0.21
	(0.26)	(0.26)
Employed part-time (<15h/week)	0.06	0.12
	(0.26)	(0.26)
Employed: sometimes	−0.13	−0.03
	(0.34)	(0.34)
Total household income (log)		0.12***
		(0.04)
Total household savings (log)		0.00
		(0.00)
Education: other		0.08
		(0.34)
Education: public servant		0.55
		(0.43)
Education: university		0.41
		(0.36)
Education: vocational training		−0.11
		(0.28)
Number of people in household		0.10
		(0.06)
Homeowner		−0.11
		(0.25)
Dummy former East Germany		0.27
		(0.58)
Controls	–	✓
Unit fixed effects	✓	✓
Year fixed effects	✓	✓
Observations	11,466	11,466
R^2	0.57	0.57
Adjusted R^2	0.48	0.48

Notes: Results from a fixed effects model based on Equation 5.5. Robust standard errors clustered at the household level. The results are based on five multiple-imputed data sets. *$p<0.1$; **$p<0.05$; ***$p<0.01$.

TABLE A.5.4 *Marginal effects of unemployment on unsecured debt in Germany*

	Dependent variable		
	Unsecured debt (log)		
	(1)	(2)	(3)
Unemployed	0.36	0.39	0.36
	(0.26)	(0.26)	(1.85)
Household savings (log)		−0.00	−0.00
		(0.00)	(0.00)
Education: other		0.40	0.28
		(0.52)	(0.53)
Education: public servant		1.23*	1.12
		(0.68)	(0.69)
Education: university		0.54	0.45
		(0.61)	(0.60)
Education: vocational training		−0.02	−0.09
		(0.42)	(0.42)
Number of household members		0.09	0.07
		(0.10)	(0.10)
Dummy former East Germany		0.08	0.07
		(0.39)	(0.39)
Homeowner		0.60	0.59
		(0.72)	(0.73)
Household income (log)			0.25
			(0.16)
Unemployed × Household income (log)			0.01
			(0.18)
Controls	–	✓	✓
Unit fixed effects	✓	✓	✓
Year fixed effects	✓	✓	✓
Observations	6,102	6,102	6,102
R^2	0.61	0.61	0.61
Adjusted R^2	0.51	0.51	0.51

Notes: Results from a fixed effects model based on Equation 5.6. Robust standard errors clustered at the household level. The omitted baseline are households where the household head is full-time employed. *$p<0.1$; **$p<0.05$; ***$p<0.01$.

TABLE A.5.5 *Predicted probabilities of using overdraft lending facilities by employment status and income in Germany*

	Dependent variable
	Use of overdraft facilities
Unemployed	−1.31
	(1.05)
Income Q1	−0.69
	(0.67)
Income Q2	−0.12
	(0.39)
Income Q4	−0.60**
	(0.25)
Income Q5	−0.72***
	(0.27)
Education: other	0.48**
	(0.21)
Education: public servant	−0.76
	(0.68)
Education: university	−0.10
	(0.72)
Education: vocational training	−1.41**
	(0.57)
Total household savings (log)	−0.56
	(0.47)
Total household income (log)	−0.08
	(0.37)
Number of children	−0.23
	(0.36)
Dummy former East Germany	−0.29
	(0.32)
Married	0.59
	(0.36)
Number of people in household	−0.58**
	(0.27)
Homeowner	15.59
	(849.94)
Unemployed × Income Q1	0.11
	(1.76)
Unemployed × Income Q2	−0.77
	(1.25)
Unemployed × Income Q4	−2.22
	(2.04)

(continued)

268

Appendix

TABLE A.5.5 *(continued)*

	Dependent variable
	Use of overdraft facilities
Unemployed × Income Q5	−1.38
	(1.01)
Observations	2,004
Log Likelihood	−700.05
Akaike Inf. Crit.	1,444.10
Bayesian Inf. Crit.	1,567.37

Notes: Results from a mixed effects logistic regression. The dependent variable is a dummy which takes the value of one if respondents say they use their overdraft facility "often or always" and zero otherwise. The omitted baseline are households in the third income quintile. *p<0.1; **p<0.05; ***p<0.01.

TABLE A.5.6 *Predicted probabilities of using overdraft lending facilities by employment status and savings in Germany*

	Dependent variable
	Use of overdraft facilities
Unemployed	0.95
	(1.13)
Income Q1	−0.19
	(0.78)
Income Q2	−1.36
	(1.07)
Income Q4	−2.30*
	(1.29)
Income Q5	−0.25
	(2.02)
Education: other	0.36
	(2.07)
Education: public servant	−0.75
	(1.71)
Education: university	−0.02
	(1.46)
Education: vocational training	−0.42
	(0.47)
Total household savings (log)	0.72
	(0.58)
Number of children	0.76
	(1.13)

(continued)

TABLE A.5.6 *(continued)*

	Dependent variable
	Use of overdraft facilities
Dummy former East Germany	0.12
	(0.97)
Married	−0.21
	(0.50)
Number of people in household	−1.41*
	(0.73)
Homeowner	0.44
	(1.47)
Unemployed × Savings bottom tertile	−1.36
	(2.29)
Unemployed × Savings 2nd tertile	−1.23
	(2.76)
Unemployed × Savings top tertile	0.06
	(5.82)
Observations	2,004
Log Likelihood	−726.33
Akaike Inf. Crit.	1,492.67
Bayesian Inf. Crit.	1,604.73

Notes: Results from a mixed effects logistic regression. The dependent variable is a dummy which takes the value of one if respondents say they use their overdraft facility "often or always" and zero otherwise. The omitted baseline are households with no savings. $^{*}p<0.1$; $^{**}p<0.05$; $^{***}p<0.01$.

TABLE A.5.7 *Effect of the German Hartz IV labor market reform on unsecured debt*

	Dependent variable		
	Unsecured debt (log)		
	(1)	(2)	(3)
Unemployed	1.71***	1.89***	1.84***
	(0.62)	(0.66)	(0.66)
Total household income (log)	0.21*	0.21**	
	(0.11)	(0.11)	
Total household savings (log)	−0.00	−0.00	
	(0.00)	(0.00)	
Education: other	0.01	−0.11	−0.06
	(0.58)	(0.59)	(0.58)
Education: public servant	0.72	0.67	0.76
	(0.69)	(1.05)	(1.06)
Education: university	0.02	0.13	0.19
	(0.54)	(0.72)	(0.72)
Education: vocational training	−0.24	−0.19	−0.16
	(0.42)	(0.49)	(0.49)
Age squared	−0.00	−0.00	−0.00
	(0.00)	(0.00)	(0.00)
Number of children	0.18	0.03	0.00
	(0.25)	(0.28)	(0.28)
Dummy former East Germany	0.21	0.43	0.43
	(0.64)	(0.63)	(0.64)
Number of people in household	−0.16	−0.02	0.02
	(0.15)	(0.20)	(0.20)
Homeowner	0.14	0.54	0.54
	(0.43)	(0.50)	(0.50)
Unemployed × Period$_{post}$	−1.19**	−1.26**	−1.26**
	(0.58)	(0.61)	(0.62)
Full set of controls	✓	✓	–
Restricted set of controls	–	–	✓
Unit fixed effects	✓	✓	✓
Year fixed effects	✓	✓	✓
Observations	5,342	5,342	5,342
R^2	0.64	0.64	0.64
Adjusted R^2	0.53	0.54	0.54

Notes: Results from a fixed effects model based on Equation 5.7. Robust standard errors are clustered at the household level. In columns 2 and 3, the data are adjusted for imbalances between employed and unemployed respondents using entropy balance based on age, education, number of children living in household, number of people in household, and marital status. Column (3) excludes income and savings as covariates because they may introduce post-treatment bias. The results remain virtually unchanged. The lower-order term *Period$_{post}$* is a time-invariant indicator of reform status and is not identified in the presence of year fixed effects. *p<0.1; **p<0.05; ***p<0.01.

TABLE A.5.8 *Effect of home equity reform on household debt among savings-constrained households by employment status in Denmark*

			Dependent variable			
			Total household debt (log)			
	(1)	(2)	(3)	(4)	(5)	(6)
Unemployed	-0.45***	-0.33***	-0.41***	0.05**	-0.08***	-0.20***
	(0.02)	(0.02)	(0.02)	(0.02)	(0.02)	(0.02)
Savings constrained × Period$_{post}$	0.84***	0.80***	0.84***	1.07***	1.03***	1.05***
	(0.01)	(0.01)	(0.01)	(0.01)	(0.01)	(0.01)
Savings constrained × Unemployed	-0.42***	-0.43***	-0.41***	-0.37***	-0.38***	-0.34***
	(0.02)	(0.02)	(0.02)	(0.02)	(0.02)	(0.02)
Period$_{post}$ × Unemployed	0.09***	0.19***	0.21***	-0.14***	-0.04*	0.01
	(0.02)	(0.02)	(0.02)	(0.02)	(0.02)	(0.02)
Savings constrained × Period$_{post}$ × Unemployed	0.78***	0.73***	0.74***	0.62***	0.58***	0.58***
	(0.02)	(0.02)	(0.02)	(0.02)	(0.02)	(0.02)
Controls	–	✓	✓	–	✓	✓
Unit and year fixed effects	✓	✓	✓	✓	✓	✓
ZIP code fixed effects	–	–	✓	–	–	✓
Birth year fixed effects	–	–	✓	–	–	✓
Education fixed effects	–	–	✓	–	–	✓
Observations	16,762,242	16,762,242	16,762,242	16,762,242	16,762,242	16,762,242
R^2	0.67	0.71	0.71	0.71	0.74	0.74
Adjusted R^2	0.61	0.65	0.65	0.66	0.69	0.69

Notes: Results from a fixed effects model based on Equation 5.8. Robust standard errors clustered at the household level. The lower-order terms $S_{t,91}$ and Period$_{post}$ are time-invariant and not identified due to the presence of year fixed effects. Column 1 is the baseline unit and year fixed effects model without covariates, column 2 adds a set of control variables, and column 3 adds a set of additional fixed effects. The models in columns 4 through 6 replicate the same pattern, but the data are adjusted for imbalances between employed and unemployed respondents using entropy balancing based on birth year, education (five categories), ZIP code, family type, number of children, and the gender of the household head. The lower-order terms Period$_{post}$ and *Savings constrained* are time-invariant and not identified in the presence of year fixed effects. *p<0.1; **p<0.05; ***p<0.01.

Appendix for Chapter 6

TABLE A.6.1 *Effect of life course stages on unsecured debt by income in Denmark*

	Dependent variable		
	Unsecured debt (log)		
	(1)	(2)	(3)
Leave of absence	−0.31***		
	(0.03)		
Maternity leave		0.43***	
		(0.05)	
Student			−0.11***
			(0.01)
Income Q2	−0.23***	−0.23***	−0.26***
	(0.00)	(0.00)	(0.00)
Income Q3	−0.42***	−0.42***	−0.48***
	(0.01)	(0.01)	(0.00)
Income Q4	−0.77***	−0.77***	−0.85***
	(0.01)	(0.01)	(0.01)
Income Q5	−1.06***	−1.06***	−1.13***
	(0.01)	(0.01)	(0.01)
Leave × Income Q2	0.26***		
	(0.04)		
Leave × Income Q3	0.38***		
	(0.03)		
Leave × Income Q4	0.59***		
	(0.04)		
Leave × Income Q5	0.55***		
	(0.04)		
Maternity × Income Q2		0.32***	
		(0.06)	
Maternity × Income Q3		0.18***	
		(0.06)	
Maternity × Income Q4		0.10	
		(0.07)	
Maternity × Income Q5		−0.45***	
		(0.10)	
Student × Income Q2			−0.44***
			(0.01)
Student × Income Q3			−0.62***
			(0.01)
Student × Income Q4			−0.56***
			(0.01)
Student × Income Q5			0.13***
			(0.01)

(continued)

TABLE A.6.1 *(continued)*

	(1)	(2)	(3)
		Dependent variable	
		Unsecured debt (log)	
Controls	✓	✓	✓
Unit FE	✓	✓	✓
Year FE	✓	✓	✓
Birth-year FE	✓	✓	✓
Observations	26,585,895	26,486,508	28,627,432
R^2	0.65	0.65	0.66
Adjusted R^2	0.60	0.60	0.61

Notes: Marginal effects of layoff on unsecured debt (log) relative to individuals who are full-time employed. The results are based on Equation 6.1. Robust standard errors clustered at the household level. *$p<0.1$; **$p<0.05$; ***$p<0.01$.

TABLE A.6.2 *Unpaid maternity leave and unsecured debt in the United States*

	Dependent variable	
	Unsecured debt (log)	
	Single-mother households (1)	Married couples (2)
Birth period	−1.24***	−0.19
	(0.44)	(0.16)
Unpaid absence	0.26**	0.25***
	(0.12)	(0.07)
HH income Q1	−0.59***	−0.18
	(0.13)	(0.11)
HH income Q2	−0.35***	−0.14**
	(0.11)	(0.07)
HH income Q4	0.32***	0.17***
	(0.12)	(0.06)
HH income Q5	0.38**	0.25***
	(0.17)	(0.07)
Liquid savings (log)	0.06***	0.03***
	(0.01)	(0.01)
Education: BA	0.50	1.28***
	(0.56)	(0.35)
Education: college	0.32	0.88***
	(0.46)	(0.32)
Education: high school	0.35	0.49***
	(0.25)	(0.19)

(continued)

TABLE A.6.2 *(continued)*

	Dependent variable	
	Unsecured debt (log)	
	Single-mother households (1)	Married couples (2)
Education: MA	−0.04	1.41***
	(0.85)	(0.47)
Education: some college	0.49	0.77***
	(0.34)	(0.23)
Age	0.05	0.01
	(0.13)	(0.09)
Age square	−0.00*	−0.00
	(0.00)	(0.00)
Number of children	−0.09	−0.00
	(0.08)	(0.05)
Renter	−0.05	−0.43***
	(0.18)	(0.12)
Race: Asian	3.10	1.90
	(2.32)	(1.33)
Race: Black	1.35	1.80
	(0.92)	(1.39)
Race: Native American	4.45*	0.02
	(2.45)	(0.48)
Birth period	2.26***	0.26
× unpaid absence	(0.80)	(0.37)
Unit FE	✓	✓
Year FE	✓	✓
Observations	51,802	110,971
R^2	0.77	0.72
Adjusted R^2	0.45	0.42

Notes: Results from three separate regression models estimating the marginal effects of paying for childcare on unsecured debt (log); sample split by household type. Robust standard errors clustered at the household level. Model (2) is estimated for women only. *$p<0.1$; **$p<0.05$; ***$p<0.01$.

TABLE A.6.3 *Job switches, income changes, and unsecured debt in the United States*

	(1)	(2)	(3)	(4)
	Dependent variable			
	Total unsecured debt (log)			
Post-period	−0.47***	−0.40**	−0.43***	−0.40**
	(0.15)	(0.16)	(0.16)	(0.16)
Less income (dummy)	−0.17	−0.20	−0.23	−0.20
	(0.24)	(0.25)	(0.25)	(0.25)
Post-period × Less income	0.34*	0.40**	0.45**	0.40**
	(0.18)	(0.18)	(0.18)	(0.18)
Education: BA		1.32**	1.57**	1.34**
		(0.67)	(0.67)	(0.67)
Education: college		1.84***	2.00***	1.83***
		(0.64)	(0.64)	(0.64)
Education: high school		0.01	0.11	0.01
		(0.36)	(0.36)	(0.36)
Education: MA		0.44	0.64	0.45
		(0.92)	(0.97)	(0.92)
Education: some college		1.04**	1.19**	1.04**
		(0.48)	(0.48)	(0.48)
Age		−0.28*	−0.30*	−0.28*
		(0.15)	(0.16)	(0.15)
Age square		0.00	0.00	0.00
		(0.00)	(0.00)	(0.00)
Number of children		0.21**	0.24**	0.21**
		(0.10)	(0.11)	(0.10)
Male householder		−0.78*	−0.78*	−0.78*
		(0.45)	(0.46)	(0.45)
Married couple		1.16***	1.20***	1.17***
		(0.31)	(0.32)	(0.31)
Female householder		−0.24	−0.25	−0.23
		(0.37)	(0.37)	(0.37)
Non-family male householder		−0.64*	−0.54	−0.63*
		(0.38)	(0.38)	(0.38)
Renter		−0.58***	−0.56***	−0.58***
		(0.18)	(0.18)	(0.18)
Asian		−5.95**	−6.00**	−5.95**
		(3.01)	(2.97)	(3.01)
Black		0.80	0.79	0.80
		(0.51)	(0.48)	(0.51)
Native American		5.32	5.32	5.32
		(4.38)	(4.40)	(4.38)

(*continued*)

TABLE A.6.3 *(continued)*

	(1)	(2)	(3)	(4)
	Dependent variable			
	Total unsecured debt (log)			
Total income Q1		−0.00	0.00	−0.00
		(0.51)	(0.52)	(0.51)
Total income Q2		−0.00	−0.00	−0.00
		(0.40)	(0.40)	(0.40)
Total income Q4		−0.01	−0.01	−0.01
		(0.36)	(0.36)	(0.36)
Total income Q5		−0.03	−0.03	−0.03
		(0.48)	(0.48)	(0.48)
Savings-constrained			−0.12	
			(0.11)	
Savings as share				0.00
of pre-treatment income				(0.00)
Baseline controls	–	✓	✓	✓
Observations	16,779	16,752	16,428	16,727
R^2	0.70	0.70	0.70	0.70
Adjusted R^2	0.45	0.46	0.46	0.46

Notes: Regression models with unit and panel-year fixed effects. The sample consists of all households where all members of the household are full-time employed and one switches jobs without a period of unemployment. *Post-period* is a dummy indicating the period after the job switch. *Less income* is a dummy indicating that the job switch led to a decline in income. Robust standard errors in parentheses. *p<0.1; **p<0.05; ***p<0.01.

TABLE A.6.4 *Effect of labor market status on debt repayment in Germany*

	Dependent variable				
	Household has debt to pay off (dummy variable)				
	full-time employed (1)	part-time employed (2)	maternity leave (3)	school/ university (4)	vocational training (5)
Months in employment status	1.01	1.00	1.00	1.00	0.99
	(1.00)	(1.00)	(1.00)	(1.00)	(1.00)
Household income (log)	1.45	1.47	1.46	1.46	1.47
	(1.03)	(1.03)	(1.03)	(1.03)	(1.03)
Savings (log)	0.84	0.84	0.84	0.84	0.84
	(1.01)	(1.01)	(1.01)	(1.01)	(1.01)
Age	1.02	1.02	1.02	1.02	1.02
	(1.01)	(1.01)	(1.01)	(1.01)	(1.01)
Age squared	1.00	1.00	1.00	1.00	1.00
	(1.00)	(1.00)	(1.00)	(1.00)	(1.00)
Number of children in household	1.03	1.02	1.03	1.02	1.02
	(1.01)	(1.01)	(1.01)	(1.01)	(1.01)
Education: basic vocational	1.08	1.09	1.09	1.09	1.08
	(1.08)	(1.08)	(1.08)	(1.08)	(1.08)
Education: higher tertiary	1.05	1.08	1.09	1.07	1.07
	(1.14)	(1.14)	(1.14)	(1.14)	(1.14)
Education: intermed. vocational	1.10	1.12	1.12	1.11	1.10
	(1.10)	(1.10)	(1.10)	(1.10)	(1.10)

(*continued*)

TABLE A.6.4 (*continued*)

	Dependent variable				
	Household has debt to pay off (dummy variable)				
	full-time employed (1)	part-time employed (2)	maternity leave (3)	school/ university (4)	vocational training (5)
Education: lower tertiary	1.08	1.11	1.11	1.10	1.10
	(1.14)	(1.14)	(1.14)	(1.14)	(1.14)
Education: high school	0.97	0.97	0.97	0.97	0.96
	(1.12)	(1.12)	(1.12)	(1.12)	(1.12)
Single-household	0.94	0.94	0.94	0.94	0.95
	(1.03)	(1.03)	(1.03)	(1.03)	(1.03)
Homeowner	0.88	0.87	0.87	0.87	0.87
	(1.03)	(1.03)	(1.03)	(1.03)	(1.03)
Dummy former East Germany	1.27	1.27	1.26	1.27	1.27
	(1.08)	(1.08)	(1.08)	(1.08)	(1.08)
Observations	141,102	141,102	141,102	141,102	141,102
R^2	0.00	0.00	0.00	0.00	0.00
Max. possible R^2	0.59	0.59	0.59	0.59	0.59
Log Likelihood	−61,907.75	−61,917.11	−61,917.33	−61,917.36	−61,916.41
Wald Test (df = 14)	616.28***	597.96***	597.62***	597.50***	599.34***

Notes: Each column displays the main coefficients from a fixed effect regression model that estimates the effect of the number of months in each life course status in the previous year on unsecured debt relative to those who have zero months in that status (omitted baseline). Models with months in each status as continuous variables show the similar results. Robust standard errors clustered at the household level. *p<0.1; **p<0.05; ***p<0.01.

TABLE A.6.5 Odds ratios of childcare cost on the probability of debt repayment in Germany

	Dependent variable							
	Repay loans				Repay new loans			
	full sample		renters	homeowners	full sample		renters	homeowners
	(1)	(2)	(3)	(4)	(5)	(6)	(7)	(8)
Pay fee for daycare	0.92				0.66			
	(1.18)				(1.35)			
Amount paid for daycare		1.00	1.00	1.00		1.00	1.00	1.00
		(1.00)	(1.00)	(1.00)		(1.00)	(1.01)	(1.01)
Household net income (log)	1.70	3.99	2.68	8.38	2.40	4.04	15.09	1.59
	(1.34)	(2.67)	(3.91)	(8.44)	(1.71)	(8.98)	(16.00)	(91.30)
Savings (log)	0.78	0.67	0.52	0.80	0.84	0.62	0.39	0.89
	(1.11)	(1.35)	(1.72)	(1.48)	(1.20)	(1.60)	(2.43)	(2.27)
Age	1.00	0.83	0.95	0.40	0.58	1.70	7.70	0.12
	(1.20)	(1.76)	(2.12)	(3.33)	(1.45)	(4.71)	(9.66)	(12.31)
Age squared	1.00	1.00	1.00	1.01	1.01	0.99	0.97	1.02
	(1.00)	(1.01)	(1.01)	(1.02)	(1.00)	(1.02)	(1.03)	(1.03)
Number of children in household	1.00	0.57	0.55	1.15	0.82	0.34	0.04	2.21
	(1.17)	(1.69)	(2.47)	(2.23)	(1.37)	(3.41)	(12.74)	(5.76)
Single-household	1.00	0.67	0.46	2.22	0.83	0.20	0.23	0.00
	(1.37)	(2.14)	(2.94)	(6.74)	(1.76)	(5.42)	(12.70)	(0.00)
Homeowner	0.84	1.09			0.50	0.00		
	(1.29)	(1.95)			(1.71)	(0.00)		
Observations	3,926	1,130	531	599	3,866	1,117	528	589
R^2	0.00	0.01	0.01	0.01	0.00	0.01	0.01	0.01
Max. possible R^2	0.25	0.13	0.12	0.11	0.08	0.04	0.04	0.04
Log Likelihood	−545.95	−74.40	−32.19	−33.00	−147.50	−19.62	−9.63	−7.88

Notes: Odds ratios based on conditional maximum likelihood estimates from conditional logistic regressions with unit strata. Models (1) through (4) use the indicator whether household repay loans and interest, models (5) through (8) whether household repay new loans and interest. $^*p<0.1$; $^{**}p<0.05$; $^{***}p<0.01$.

TABLE A.6.6 *Absence from work to take care of sick children and household debt in Germany*

	Dependent variable		
	Household has debt to pay off (dummy variable)		
	All debt		New debt
	(1)	(2)	(3)
Absent from work because	0.99	0.92	0.85
of child's sickness	(1.06)	(1.09)	(1.18)
Household income Q2		1.25	1.26
		(1.10)	(1.18)
Household income Q3		1.37	1.21
		(1.11)	(1.20)
Household income Q4		1.42	1.21
		(1.12)	(1.21)
Household income Q5		1.42	1.34
		(1.13)	(1.24)
Savings (log)		0.89	0.85
		(1.03)	(1.05)
Age		1.10	1.20
		(1.06)	(1.10)
Age squared		1.00	1.00
		(1.00)	(1.00)
Number of children in household		0.95	0.71
		(1.07)	(1.11)
Education: basic vocational		1.75	1.52
		(1.66)	(2.03)
Education: higher tertiary		0.00	2.29
		(6.53)	(1.71)
Education: intermed. vocational		0.00	0.57
		(6.53)	(2.48)
Education: lower tertiary		0.00	0.21
		(6.53)	(2.08)
Education: high school		0.00	
		(6.53)	(1.00)
Single-household		0.86	0.63
		(1.11)	(1.21)
Homeowner		0.89	0.81
		(1.11)	(1.17)
Dummy former East Germany		0.76	0.64
		(1.35)	(1.68)

(continued)

TABLE A.6.6 *(continued)*

	Dependent variable		
	Household has debt to pay off (dummy variable)		
	All debt		New debt
	(1)	(2)	(3)
Observations	59,917	32,893	31,806
R^2	0.00	0.00	0.00
Max. possible R^2	0.41	0.35	0.14
Log Likelihood	−15,863	−7,136	−2,344
Wald Test	0.01	37.93***	40.05***

Notes: Odds ratios based on conditional maximum likelihood estimates from conditional logistic regressions with unit strata. Models (1) and (2) use the indicator whether households repay loans and interest, model (3) whether households repay *new* loans and interest. *p<0.1; **p<0.05; ***p<0.01.

TABLE A.6.7 *Job switches, income changes, and indebtedness in Germany*

	Dependent variable			
	Household has debt to pay off (dummy variable)			
	All debt			New debt
	(1)	(2)	(3)	(4)
Switch job	1.00	0.99	0.98	1.12
	(1.03)	(1.03)	(1.03)	(1.06)
Less income	0.97	0.97	1.00	1.02
	(1.01)	(1.01)	(1.02)	(1.04)
Months full-time employed		1.01	1.01	1.00
		(1.00)	(1.00)	(1.01)
Age		1.03	1.03	1.02
		(1.01)	(1.01)	(1.02)
Age squared		1.00	1.00	1.00
		(1.00)	(1.00)	(1.00)
Number of children in household		1.00	1.01	0.90
		(1.01)	(1.02)	(1.03)
Education: basic vocational		1.18	1.35	2.06
		(1.09)	(1.14)	(1.25)
Education: higher tertiary		1.18	1.40	1.72
		(1.16)	(1.23)	(1.41)
Education: intermed. vocational		1.13	1.35	1.75
		(1.11)	(1.17)	(1.30)

(continued)

TABLE A.6.7 *(continued)*

	Dependent variable			
	Household has debt to pay off (dummy variable) All debt			New debt
	(1)	(2)	(3)	(4)
Education: lower tertiary		1.16	1.43	1.57
		(1.15)	(1.23)	(1.40)
Education: high school		1.04	1.24	1.50
		(1.14)	(1.21)	(1.37)
Single-household		0.95	0.94	0.92
		(1.03)	(1.04)	(1.07)
Savings (log)		0.92	0.86	1.03
		(1.03)	(1.04)	(1.06)
Homeowner		1.05	1.08	0.89
		(1.09)	(1.12)	(1.24)
Dummy former East Germany			0.83	0.81
			(1.01)	(1.02)
Household income Q2			1.15	1.23
			(1.05)	(1.09)
Household income Q3			1.24	1.38
			(1.05)	(1.09)
Household income Q4			1.32	1.35
			(1.05)	(1.10)
Household income Q5			1.44	1.49
			(1.06)	(1.11)
Switch job × Less income	1.00	1.00	0.98	0.88
	(1.05)	(1.05)	(1.07)	(1.12)
Observations	127,438	121,514	83,249	82,327
R^2	0.00	0.00	0.00	0.00
Max. possible R^2	0.70	0.70	0.61	0.26
Log Likelihood	−77,005	−73,204	−38,594	−12,469
Wald Test	6.96*	119.40***	296.88***	141.89***

Notes: Odds ratios based on conditional maximum likelihood estimates from conditional logistic regressions with unit strata. Models (1) through (3) use the indicator whether households repay loans and interest, model (4) whether households repay *new* loans and interest. *p<0.1; **p<0.05; ***p<0.01.

Appendix for Chapter 7

TABLE A.7.1 *Detailed survey information*

Country	Completed interviews	Response rate (%)
Canada	2,198	58
Denmark	2,099	53
England	2,001	53
France	2,269	73
Germany	2,019	78
Netherlands	2,003	58
Spain	2,276	82
Sweden	2,288	65
United States	5,012	80

TABLE A.7.2 *Factor loadings for economic insecurity index*

Variable	PC1	PC1.1	PC1.2	com
Worried: job situation	0.84	0.70	0.30	1
Worried: maintaining income	0.89	0.79	0.21	1
Worried: health insurance coverage	0.81	0.66	0.34	1
Worried: enough money for retirement	0.83	0.68	0.32	1
Worried: getting out of debt	0.79	0.63	0.37	1
SS loadings	3.47			
Cronbach's alpha	0.89			

Notes: Question wording: "Please indicate your answer on a scale from 0 to 10, where 0 means that you are not worried at all and 10 means that you are very worried. If your views fall somewhere in between, you can choose any number between 0 and 10."

TABLE A.7.3 *Marginal effects of debt leverage and economic insecurity across countries*

	Dependent variable			
	Economic insecurity index			
	Full sample (1)	Denmark (2)	USA (3)	Germany (4)
Unsecured debt leverage	0.026***	0.018***	0.031***	0.033***
	(0.002)	(0.004)	(0.004)	(0.004)
Student debt leverage	0.013***	0.019**	0.012***	0.020**
	(0.002)	(0.008)	(0.004)	(0.009)

(continued)

TABLE A.7.3 *(continued)*

	Dependent variable			
	Economic insecurity index			
	Full sample (1)	Denmark (2)	USA (3)	Germany (4)
Mortgage debt leverage	0.010***	0.004	0.009**	0.012*
	(0.002)	(0.005)	(0.004)	(0.007)
Liquid assets (log)	−0.014***	−0.008***	−0.021***	−0.014***
	(0.001)	(0.003)	(0.003)	(0.003)
Homeowner	−0.071***	−0.089***	−0.072***	−0.099***
	(0.011)	(0.033)	(0.026)	(0.032)
Retired	−0.258***	−0.220***	−0.268***	−0.163***
	(0.014)	(0.036)	(0.035)	(0.040)
Unemployed	−0.001*	0.000	−0.000	0.000
	(0.000)	(0.001)	(0.001)	(0.001)
Age	−0.058***	−0.035	0.007	−0.098***
	(0.009)	(0.025)	(0.021)	(0.026)
Male	−0.039	−0.033	−0.002	−0.038
	(0.025)	(0.055)	(0.083)	(0.071)
Education: college	−0.025	−0.187***	0.049	−0.096
	(0.025)	(0.064)	(0.082)	(0.070)
Education: high school	−0.021	−0.097	0.061	−0.067
	(0.027)	(0.103)	(0.085)	(0.080)
Education: postgraduate	−0.017	−0.019	0.009	−0.071
	(0.025)	(0.051)	(0.083)	(0.065)
Education: vocational training	0.246***	0.465***	0.205***	0.352***
	(0.020)	(0.069)	(0.052)	(0.066)
Unemployed	−0.024	−0.136	−0.007	−0.016
	(0.022)	(0.095)	(0.055)	(0.063)
Couple without children	0.040	−0.056	0.070	−0.072
	(0.025)	(0.110)	(0.059)	(0.077)
Couple with children	0.002	−0.123	0.038	−0.019
	(0.022)	(0.096)	(0.054)	(0.063)
Single with children	0.024***	−0.010	0.009	0.075***
	(0.007)	(0.030)	(0.014)	(0.026)
Risk preferences	0.012***	−0.006	0.015***	0.007
	(0.002)	(0.006)	(0.004)	(0.005)
Income tertile: middle	−0.062***	−0.036	−0.066**	−0.077**
	(0.011)	(0.033)	(0.027)	(0.034)
Income tertile: top	−0.133***	−0.071**	−0.069**	−0.191***
	(0.013)	(0.036)	(0.031)	(0.039)
Observations	12,381	1,173	2,838	1,233
R^2	0.332	0.212	0.169	0.219
Adjusted R^2	0.330	0.198	0.163	0.206

Notes: The model in column 1 uses country-fixed effects. The full sample includes nine countries.
*$p<0.1$; **$p<0.05$; ***$p<0.01$.

TABLE A.7.4 *Question wording and scores*

Question wording	Coding scale
The government should do more to reduce differences in income levels	Five-point scale: strongly agree (-2) / disagree (2)
The government should do more to help people who become unemployed	Five-point scale: strongly agree (-2) / disagree (2)
There should be laws to limit how much an individual can borrow	Five-point scale: strongly agree (-2) / disagree (2)
Some people say that households should save money for purchases instead of borrowing money. Do you agree with this statement?	Five-point scale: strongly agree (-2) / disagree (2)
If your household were to experience (a period of) financial hardship tomorrow, how easy would it be for you to borrow money from a financial institution?	Five-point scale: very difficult (-2) / very easy (2)
What is the probability that you will experience a period of unemployment next year? Please pick a number between 0 and 100, where 0 means that the event certainly does not occur and 100 means that it occurs for sure.	100-point probability scale

TABLE A.7.5 *Factor loadings for political values score*

Social issues dimension

Variable	PC1	PC1.1	PC1.2	com
• Gvt. should do more to reduce differences in income levels	0.82	0.67	0.33	1
• Gvt. should do more to help people who become unemployed	0.85	0.72	0.28	1
• Gvt. should do more to help people who become sick or disabled or in other ways lose the ability to work	0.83	0.69	0.31	1
• Gvt. should do more to alleviate the consequences for people hurt by globalization	0.83	0.69	0.31	1
SS loadings	2.77			
Cronbach's Alpha	0.85			

Post-materialism and nationalism dimension

Variable	PC1	PC1.1	PC1.2	com
• Same-sex marriage should not be legal in this country	0.78	0.60	0.40	1
• Family life suffers when the woman has a full-time job	0.77	0.59	0.41	1
• It is better for a country if almost everyone shares the same customs and traditions	0.73	0.53	0.47	1
SS loadings	1.73			
Cronbach's Alpha	0.63			

Economic nationalism dimension

Variable	PC1	PC1.1	PC1.2	com
• When jobs are scarce, employers should give jobs to [COUNTRY's] people over immigrants	0.86	0.75	0.25	1
• Would you say that people who come to live here generally take jobs away from workers in [COUNTRY]	0.89	0.78	0.22	1
• We worry too much about future environmental problems and not enough about prices and jobs	0.70	0.49	0.51	1
SS loadings	2.02			
Cronbach's Alpha	0.75			

TABLE A.7.6 *Marginal effects of debt leverage and economic insecurity across countries*

	Dependent variable				
	Unemployment insurance				Redistribution
	(1)	(2)	(3)	(4)	(5)
Ease of credit access	−0.072***	−0.072***	−0.077***	−0.096***	−0.093***
	(0.012)	(0.012)	(0.009)	(0.008)	(0.014)
Probability of unemployment	0.207***	0.221***			0.145***
	(0.035)	(0.035)			(0.040)
Months unemployed			0.003*		
			(0.002)		
Months out of labor force				0.008***	
				(0.002)	
Ease of credit access × Probability of unemployment	−0.063***	−0.066***			0.000
	(0.024)	(0.024)			(0.027)
Ease of credit access × Months unemployed			−0.005***		
			(0.001)		
Ease of credit access × Months out of labor force				−0.002	
				(0.001)	
Age	0.001	0.001	0.002***	0.001**	−0.000
	(0.001)	(0.001)	(0.001)	(0.001)	(0.001)
Male	0.015	0.015	−0.027	−0.020	−0.052*
	(0.023)	(0.024)	(0.017)	(0.018)	(0.027)
Education: college	−0.127*	−0.117	−0.073	−0.071	−0.100
	(0.072)	(0.072)	(0.052)	(0.053)	(0.082)
Education: high school	−0.114	−0.104	−0.056	−0.055	−0.063
	(0.073)	(0.074)	(0.052)	(0.054)	(0.083)
Education: postgraduate	−0.149**	−0.146*	−0.096*	−0.080	−0.127
	(0.075)	(0.076)	(0.054)	(0.056)	(0.086)
Education: vocational training	−0.058	−0.047	−0.005	−0.011	0.026
	(0.071)	(0.072)	(0.051)	(0.052)	(0.081)
Couple without children	−0.011	−0.004	−0.081*	−0.065	0.031
	(0.052)	(0.053)	(0.042)	(0.042)	(0.060)
Couple with children	0.063	0.073	−0.004	0.010	0.107*
	(0.049)	(0.049)	(0.039)	(0.040)	(0.056)
Single with children	0.007	0.014	−0.055	−0.036	0.104*
	(0.051)	(0.052)	(0.041)	(0.042)	(0.059)
Homeowner	−0.080***	−0.082***	−0.113***	−0.114***	−0.128***
	(0.027)	(0.028)	(0.020)	(0.021)	(0.031)
Total income (log)	−0.028***	−0.027***	−0.023***	−0.020***	−0.043***
	(0.008)	(0.008)	(0.006)	(0.006)	(0.009)
Total debt (log)	−0.003	−0.004	0.001	0.000	−0.000
	(0.002)	(0.002)	(0.002)	(0.002)	(0.003)

(*continued*)

TABLE A.7.6 *(continued)*

	Dependent variable				
	Unemployment insurance				Redistribution
	(1)	(2)	(3)	(4)	(5)
Liquid assets (log)	−0.007**	−0.008***	−0.002	−0.002	−0.006*
	(0.003)	(0.003)	(0.002)	(0.002)	(0.003)
Risk tolerance	0.017***	0.018***	0.009**	0.009**	0.017***
	(0.005)	(0.005)	(0.004)	(0.004)	(0.006)
Income expectations		0.022			
		(0.014)			
Mean DV	0.889	0.886	0.835	0.839	0.795
Country FE	✓	✓	✓	✓	✓
Observations	7,188	7,107	13,330	13,063	7,181
R^2	0.087	0.088	0.059	0.061	0.115
Adjusted R^2	0.084	0.085	0.057	0.059	0.112

Notes: The full sample includes nine countries. *p<0.1; **p<0.05; ***p<0.01.

TABLE A.7.7 *Marginal effects of debt leverage on support for social insurance across countries*

	Dependent variable			
	Unemployment insurance			
	Full sample (1)	Denmark (2)	USA (3)	Germany (4)
Unsecured debt leverage	0.014***	0.018*	0.025***	0.011
	(0.003)	(0.010)	(0.007)	(0.009)
Student debt leverage	0.002	0.023	0.003	−0.002
	(0.005)	(0.018)	(0.009)	(0.020)
Mortgage debt leverage	−0.014***	−0.012	−0.030***	−0.020
	(0.004)	(0.011)	(0.008)	(0.014)
Liquid assets (log)	−0.010***	−0.013*	−0.014**	−0.005
	(0.002)	(0.007)	(0.006)	(0.006)
Homeowner	−0.103***	−0.084	−0.033	−0.127*
	(0.022)	(0.078)	(0.052)	(0.065)
Retired	−0.094***	−0.075	−0.040	−0.171**
	(0.029)	(0.083)	(0.070)	(0.081)
Unemployed	0.002***	0.006**	−0.008***	0.014***
	(0.001)	(0.003)	(0.002)	(0.002)
Age	−0.029	−0.133**	0.020	−0.001
	(0.018)	(0.058)	(0.042)	(0.054)

(continued)

TABLE A.7.7 *(continued)*

	Full sample (1)	Denmark (2)	USA (3)	Germany (4)
		Unemployment insurance		
Male	−0.094*	−0.219*	0.028	−0.178
	(0.051)	(0.130)	(0.163)	(0.148)
Education: college	−0.068	−0.279*	0.061	−0.183
	(0.051)	(0.152)	(0.161)	(0.146)
Education: high school	−0.094*	−0.625**	0.058	−0.304*
	(0.055)	(0.246)	(0.168)	(0.165)
Education: postgraduate	−0.041	−0.143	0.044	−0.143
	(0.050)	(0.121)	(0.163)	(0.135)
Education: vocational training	0.280***	0.264	0.225**	0.470***
	(0.041)	(0.161)	(0.102)	(0.137)
Unemployed	−0.040	−0.225	0.056	−0.170
	(0.045)	(0.222)	(0.110)	(0.131)
Couple without children	−0.070	−0.304	0.065	0.040
	(0.051)	(0.258)	(0.117)	(0.160)
Couple with children	−0.074	−0.037	0.009	−0.243*
	(0.045)	(0.223)	(0.107)	(0.131)
Single with children	0.073***	0.037	0.043	−0.014
	(0.015)	(0.070)	(0.028)	(0.055)
Risk preferences	0.005	−0.043***	0.033***	−0.014
	(0.004)	(0.013)	(0.009)	(0.011)
Income tertile: middle	−0.109***	0.006	−0.146***	−0.215***
	(0.023)	(0.076)	(0.053)	(0.070)
Income tertile: top	−0.214***	0.008	−0.207***	−0.231***
	(0.026)	(0.084)	(0.062)	(0.080)
Mean DV	0.849	0.704	0.731	0.805
Country FE	✓	✓	✓	✓
Observations	12,218	1,151	2,800	1,223
R^2	0.063	0.065	0.064	0.079
Adjusted R^2	0.061	0.048	0.057	0.064

Notes: The full sample includes nine countries. *p<0.1; **p<0.05; ***p<0.01.

Bibliography

Aalbers, Manuel B. 2007. "Place-Based and Race-Based Exclusion from Mortgage Loans: Evidence from Three Cities in the Netherlands." *Journal of Urban Affairs* 29(1):1–29.

Abildgren, Kim. 2007. Financial Liberalisation and Credit Dynamics in Denmark in the Post–World War II Period. Working Paper 47 Danmarks Nationalbank Working Papers.

Abildgren, Kim, Bodil Nyboe Andersen and Jens Thomsen. 2010. *Monetary History of Denmark, 1990-2005.* Copenhagen: Danmarks Nationalbank.

Abrahamson, Peter. 2015. Denmark from an International Perspective. In *The Danish Welfare State. A Sociological Investigation,* ed. Tea Torbenfeldt Bengtsson, Morten Frederiksen and Jørgen Elm Larsen. New York: Palgrave Macmillan pp. 25–40.

Abramowitz, Alan I. and Kyle L. Saunders. 1998. "Ideological Realignment in the U.S. Electorate." *The Journal of Politics* 60(3):634–652.

Achen, Christopher H. 1992. "Social Psychology, Demographic Variables, and Linear Regression: Breaking the Iron Triangle in Voting Research." *Political Behavior* 14(3):195–211.

Adda, Jérôme, Christian Dustmann, and Katrien Stevens. 2017. "The Career Costs of Children." *Journal of Political Economy* 125(2):293–337.

Addo, Fenaba R., Jason N. Houle, and Sharon Sassler. 2019. "The Changing Nature of the Association Between Student Loan Debt and Marital Behavior in Young Adulthood." *Journal of Family and Economic Issues* 40(1):86–101.

Adler, Barry, Ben Polak, and Alan Schwartz. 2000. "Regulating Consumer Bankruptcy: A Theoretical Inquiry." *The Journal of Legal Studies* 29(2):585–613.

Ahlquist, John S. 2017. "Labor Unions, Political Representation, and Economic Inequality." *Annual Review of Political Science* 20(1):409–432.

Ahlquist, John S. and Ben W. Ansell. 2017. "Taking Credit: Redistribution and Borrowing in an Age of Economic Polarization." *World Politics* 69(4):640–675.

Albæk, Erik. 2008. *Crisis, Miracles, and Beyond Negotiated Adaptation of the Danish Welfare System.* Aarhus: Aarhus University Press.

Albertini, Marco and Martin Kohli. 2013. "The Generational Contract in the Family: An Analysis of Transfer Regimes in Europe." *European Sociological Review* 29(4):828–840.

Alesina, Alberto and Edward Glaeser. 2004. *Fighting Poverty in the US and Europe.* Oxford: Oxford University Press.

Alesina, Alberto and George-Marios Angeletos. 2005. "Fairness and Redistribution." *American Economic Review* 95(4):960–980.

Allen, Christopher S. 1989. The Underdevelopment of Keynesianism in the Federal Republic of Germany. In *The Political Power of Economic Ideas: Keynesianism Across Nations*, ed. Peter A. Hall. Princeton, NJ: Princeton University Press pp. 263–289.

Allen, Franklin and Douglas Gale. 2000. *Comparing Financial Systems*. Cambridge, MA: MIT Press.

Almenberg, Johan, Annamaria Lusardi, Jenny Säve-Söderbergh, and Roine Vestman. 2018. Attitudes Toward Debt and Debt Behavior. Working Paper 24935 National Bureau of Economic Research. www.nber.org/papers/w24935

Ameriks, John, Andrew Caplin, and John Leahy. 2003. "Wealth Accumulation and the Propensity to Plan." *The Quarterly Journal of Economics* 118(3):1007–1047.

Andersen, Steffen, John Y. Campbell, Kasper Meisner Nielsen, and Tarun Ramadorai. 2015. Sources of Inaction in Household Finance: Evidence from the Danish Mortgage Market.Working Paper 21386 National Bureau of Economic Research. www.nber.org/papers/w21386

Andrews, Dan, Aida Caldera Sánchez, and Åsa Johansson. 2011. *Housing Markets and Structural Policies in OECD Countries*. OECD Economics Department Working Papers Paris: OECD.

Ansell, Ben. 2014. "The Political Economy of Ownership: Housing Markets and the Welfare State." *American Political Science Review* 108(2):383–402.

Ansell, Ben and Jane Gingrich. 2015. The Dynamics of Social Investment: Human Capital, Activation, and Care. In *The Politics of Advanced Capitalism*, ed. Pablo Beramendi, Silja Häusermann, Herbert Kitschelt, and Hanspeter Kriesi. New York: Cambridge University Press pp. 282–304.

Ansell, Ben W. 2010. *From the Ballot to the Blackboard: The Redistributive Political Economy of Education*. New York: Cambridge University Press.

Ansell, Ben W., J. Lawrence Broz, and Thomas Flaherty. 2018. "Global Capital Markets, Housing Prices, and Partisan Fiscal Policies." *Economics & Politics* 30(3):307–339.

Armingeon, K. and Giuliano Bonoli. 2006. *The Politics of Post-Industrial Welfare States: Adapting Post-War Social Policies to New Social Risks*. London; New York: Routledge.

Arrow, Kenneth J. 1963. "Uncertainty and the Welfare Economics of Medical Care." *The American Economic Review* 53(5):941–973.

Auspurg, Katrin, Thomas Hinz, and Laura Schmid. 2017. "Contexts and Conditions of Ethnic Discrimination: Evidence from a Field Experiment in a German Housing Market." *Journal of Housing Economics* 35:26–36.

Autor, David H and David Dorn. 2013. "The Growth of Low-Skill Service Jobs and the Polarization of the US Labor Market." *American Economic Review* 103(5):1553–1597.

Autor, David H., David Dorn, and Gordon H. Hanson. 2013. "The China Syndrome: Local Labor Market Effects of Import Competition in the United States." *American Economic Review* 103(6):2121–2168.

Autor, David H., Frank Levy, and Richard J. Murnane. 2003. "The Skill Content of Recent Technological Change: An Empirical Exploration." *The Quarterly Journal of Economics* 118(4):1279–1333.

Baccaro, Lucio and Jonas Pontusson. 2016. "Rethinking Comparative Political Economy: The Growth Model Perspective." *Politics & Society* 44(2):175–207.

Baker, Michael and Kevin Milligan. 2008. "How Does Job-Protected Maternity Leave Affect Mothers' Employment?" *Journal of Labor Economics* 26(4):655–691.

Baldwin, Peter. 1990. *The Politics of Social Solidarity: Class Bases of the European Welfare State, 1875-1975.* Cambridge: Cambridge University Press.

Banerjee, Mahasweta M., Terri Friedline, and Barbara J. Phipps. 2017. "Financial Capability of Parents of Kindergarteners." *Children and Youth Services Review* 81:178–187.

Bannier, Christina and Michael Grote. 2008. "Equity Gap? – Which Equity Gap? On the Financing Structure of Germany's Mittelstand." *Frankfurt School of Finance & Management Working Paper No 106* .

Baradaran, Mehrsa. 2012. "How the Poor Got Cut out of Banking." *Emory Law Journal* 62(3):483–548.

Baradaran, Mehrsa. 2015. *How the Other Half Banks: Exclusion, Exploitation, and the Threat to Democracy.* Cambridge, MA: Harvard University Press.

Baradaran, Mehrsa. 2017. *The Color of Money: Black Banks and the Racial Wealth Gap.* Cambridge, MA: Harvard University Press.

Barr, Nicholas. 2001. *The Welfare State as Piggy Bank: Information, Risk, Uncertainty, and the Role of the State.* Oxford: Oxford University Press.

Bartels, Larry M. 2010. *Unequal Democracy: The Political Economy of the New Gilded Age.* Princeton, NJ: Princeton University Press.

Baumberg, Ben. 2016. "The Stigma of Claiming Benefits: A Quantitative Study." *Journal of Social Policy* 45(2):181–199.

Bean, Clive and Elim Papadakis. 1998. "A Comparison of Mass Attitudes Towards the Welfare State in Different Institutional Regimes, 1985–1990." *International Journal of Public Opinion Research* 10(3):211–236.

Beck, Thorsten, Berrak Büyükkarabacak, Felix K. Rioja, and Neven T. Valev. 2012. "Who Gets the Credit? And Does It Matter? Household vs. Firm Lending Across Countries." *The B.E. Journal of Macroeconomics* 12(1):1–44.

Becker, Gary S. 1976. *The Economic Approach to Human Behavior.* Chicago: University of Chicago Press.

Belfrage, Claes and Markus Kallifatides. 2018. "Financialisation and the New Swedish Model." *Cambridge Journal of Economics* 42(4):875–900.

Bénabou, Roland and Jean Tirole. 2006. "Belief in a Just World and Redistributive Politics." *The Quarterly Journal of Economics* 121(2):699–746.

Benartzi, Shlomo and Richard H. Thaler. 1995. "Myopic Loss Aversion and the Equity Premium Puzzle." *The Quarterly Journal of Economics* 110(1):73–92.

Beramendi, Pablo, Silja Häusermann, Herbert Kitschelt, and Hanspeter Kriesi. 2015. *The Politics of Advanced Capitalism.* Cambridge: Cambridge University Press.

Berg, Jesper, Morten Bækmand Nielsen, and James Vickery. 2018. Peas in a Pod? Comparing the U.S. and Danish Mortgage Finance Systems. FRBNY Staff Reports 848 Federal Reserve Bank of New York.

Bergemann, Annette and Regina T. Riphahn. 2010. "Female Labour Supply and Parental Leave Benefits – the Causal Effect of Paying Higher Transfers for a Shorter Period of Time." *Applied Economics Letters* 18(1):17–20.

Bertrand, Marianne, Sendhil Mullainathan, and Eldar Shafir. 2006. "Behavioral Economics and Marketing in Aid of Decision Making Among the Poor." *Journal of Public Policy & Marketing* 25(1):8–23.

Bhargava, Saurabh and Dayanand Manoli. 2015. "Psychological Frictions and the Incomplete Take-Up of Social Benefits: Evidence from an IRS Field Experiment." *American Economic Review* 105(11):3489–3529.

BIS. 2019. *Credit Statistic: Credit to the Non-Financial Sector.* Basel: Bank for International Settlements.

Blackwell, Timothy and Sebastian Kohl. 2018. "The Origins of National Housing Finance Systems: A Comparative Investigation into Historical Variations in Mortgage Finance Regimes." *Review of International Political Economy* 25(1):49–74.

Blau, Francine D. and Lawrence M. Kahn. 2017. "The Gender Wage Gap: Extent, Trends, and Explanations." *Journal of Economic Literature* 55(3):789–865.

Blossfeld, Hans-Peter and Sonja Drobniéc. 2001. *Careers of Couples in Contemporary Societies: From Male Breadwinner to Dual Earner Families.* Oxford: Oxford University Press.

Blundell, Richard and Luigi Pistaferri. 2003. "Income Volatility and Household Consumption: The Impact of Food Assistance Programs." *The Journal of Human Resources* 38:1032.

Boarini, Romina and Lars Osberg. 2014. "Economic Insecurity: Editors' Introduction." *Review of Income and Wealth* 60:S1–S4.

Boersch-Supan, Axel H. and Lothar Essig. 2005. "Household Saving in Germany: Results of the First SAVE Study. Working Paper 9902 National Bureau of Economic Research. www.nber.org/papers/w9902

Boix, Carles. 2019. *Democratic Capitalism at the Crossroads: Technological Change and the Future of Politics.* Princeton, NJ: Princeton University Press.

Bonoli, Giuliano. 2013. *The Origins of Active Social Policy: Labour Market and Childcare Polices in a Comparative Perspective.* Oxford: Oxford University Press.

Bonoli, Giuliano and David Natali. 2012. *The Politics of the New Welfare State.* New York: Oxford University Press.

Bordo, Michael D. and Christopher M. Meissner. 2012. "Does Inequality Lead to a Financial Crisis?" *Journal of International Money and Finance* 31(8):2147–2161.

Bos, Marieke, Emily Breza, and Andres Liberman. 2018. "The Labor Market Effects of Credit Market Information." *The Review of Financial Studies* 31(6):2005–2037.

Bover, Olympia, Jose Maria Casado, Sonia Costa, Philip Du Caju, Yvonne McCarthy, Eva Sierminska, Panagiota Tzamourani, Ernesto Villanueva, and Tibor Zavadil. 2016. "The Distribution of Debt Across Euro-Area Countries: The Role of Individual Characteristics, Institutions, and Credit Conditions." *International Journal of Central Banking* 12(2):71–128.

Bowles, Samuel and Herbert Gintis. 2000. "Reciprocity, Self-Interest, and the Welfare State." *Nordic Journal of Political Economy* 26(1):33–53.

Bradley, David, Evelyne Huber, Stephanie Moller, François Nielsen, and John D. Stephens. 2003. "Distribution and Redistribution in Postindustrial Democracies." *World Politics* 55(2):193–228.

Braun, Benjamin. 2020. "Central Banking and the Infrastructural Power of Finance: The Case of ECB Support for Repo and Securitization Markets." *Socio-Economic Review.* 18(2): 395–418.

Braun, Benjamin and Richard Deeg. 2019. "Strong Firms, Weak Banks: The Financial Consequences of Germany's Export-Led Growth Model." *German Politics* 29(3): 358–381

Brewer, Mark D. and Jeffrey M. Stonecash. 2015. *Polarization and the Politics of Personal Responsibility*. Oxford: Oxford University Press.

Browning, Martin and Thomas F. Crossley. 2001. "The Life-Cycle Model of Consumption and Saving." *The Journal of Economic Perspectives* 15(3):3–22.

Brückner, Hannah and Karl Ulrich Mayer. 2005. "De-Standardization of the Life Course: What It Might Mean? And if It Means Anything, Whether It Actually Took Place?" *Advances in Life Course Research* 9:27–53.

Bundesagentur für Arbeit. 2017. Der Arbeitsmarkt 2016. Amtliche Nachrichten der Bundesagentur für Arbeit. Nürnberg: Bundesagentur für Arbeit.

Busemeyer, Marius R. and Torben Iversen. 2014. "The Politics of Opting Out: Explaining Educational Financing and Popular Support for Public Spending." *Socio-Economic Review* 12(2):299–328.

Busemeyer, Marius R. and Torben Iversen. 2020. "The Welfare State with Private Alternatives: The Transformation of Popular Support for Social Insurance." *The Journal of Politics* 82(2):671–686.

Calomiris, Charles W. and Stephen H. Haber. 2014. *Fragile by Design: The Political Origins of Banking Crises and Scarce Credit*. Princeton, NJ: Princeton University Press.

Campbell, Andrea Louise. 2003. *How Policies Make Citizens: Senior Political Activism and the American Welfare State*. Princeton, NJ: Princeton University Press.

Campbell, Andrea Louise. 2012. "Policy Makes Mass Politics." *Annual Review of Political Science* 15(1):333–351.

Campbell, Angus, Philip Converse, Warren Miller, and Donald E. Stokes. 1960. *The American Voter*. New York: Wiley.

Campbell, John L. and Ove K. Pedersen. 2007. "The Varieties of Capitalism and Hybrid Success: Denmark in the Global Economy." *Comparative Political Studies* 40(3):307–332.

Cappelli, Peter. 2020. "The Return on a College Degree: The US Experience." *Oxford Review of Education* 46(1):30–43.

Carruthers, Bruce G. and Arthur L. Stinchcombe. 1999. "The Social Structure of Liquidity: Flexibility, Markets, and States." *Theory and Society* 28(3):353–382.

Carruthers, Bruce G. and Jeong-Chul Kim. 2011. "The Sociology of Finance." *Annual Review of Sociology* 37(1):239–259.

Catte, Pietro, Nathalie Girouard, Robert Price, and Christophe André. 2005. "The Contribution of Housing Markets to Cyclical Resilience." *OECD Economic Studies* 2004(1):125–156.

Caughey, Devin and Christopher Warshaw. 2018. "Policy Preferences and Policy Change: Dynamic Responsiveness in the American States, 1936–2014." *The American Political Science Review; Washington* 112(2):249–266.

Caughey, Devin, Tom O'Grady, and Christopher Warshaw. 2019. "Policy Ideology in European Mass Publics, 1981–2016." *American Political Science Review* 113(3): 674–693.

Cavaillé, Charlotte and Kris-Stella Trump. 2015. "The Two Facets of Social Policy Preferences." *The Journal of Politics* 77(1): 146–60.

CEIC. 2019. *Global Databases*. New York: CEIC Data.

Cerutti, Eugenio, Jihad Dagher, and Giovanni Dell'Ariccia. 2017. "Housing Finance and Real-Estate Booms: A Cross-Country Perspective." *Journal of Housing Economics* 38:1–13.

Chetty, Raj and Nathaniel Hendren. 2018. "The Impacts of Neighborhoods on Intergenerational Mobility I: Childhood Exposure Effects." *The Quarterly Journal of Economics* 133(3):1107–1162.

Chinn, Menzie David and Jeffry A. Frieden. 2011. *Lost Decades: The Making of America's Debt Crisis and the Long Recovery.* New York: W. W. Norton & Co.

Chiteji, N. S. 2010. "The Racial Wealth Gap and the Borrower's Dilemma." *Journal of Black Studies* 41(2):351–366.

Christen, Markus and Ruskin M. Morgan. 2005. "Keeping Up With the Joneses: Analyzing the Effect of Income Inequality on Consumer Borrowing." *Quantitative Marketing and Economics* 3(2):145–173.

Chwieroth, Jeffrey M. and Andrew Walter. 2019. *The Wealth Effect: How the Great Expectations of the Middle Class Have Changed the Politics of Banking Crises.* Cambridge: Cambridge University Press.

Cioffi, John W. 2006. Building Finance Capitalism: The Regulatory Politics of Corporate Governance Reform in the United States and Germany. In *The State After Statism,* ed. Jonah D Levy. Cambridge, MA: Harvard University Press pp. 185–229.

Clark, Gordon L. 2000. *Pension Fund Capitalism.* New York: Oxford University Press.

Clasen, Jochen. 2005. *Reforming European Welfare States: Germany and the United Kingdom Compared.* Oxford: Oxford University Press.

Cohen-Cole, Ethan. 2011. "Credit Card Redlining." *The Review of Economics and Statistics* 93(2):700–713.

Coibion, Olivier, Yuriy Gorodnichenko, Marianna Kudlyak, and John Mondragon. 2020. "Greater Inequality and Household Borrowing: New Evidence from Household Data." *Journal of the European Economic Association* 18(6):2922–2971.

Conley, Dalton and Brian Gifford. 2006. "Home Ownership, Social Insurance, and the Welfare State." *Sociological Forum* 21(1):55–82.

Converse, Philip E. 1962. *The Nature of Belief Systems in Mass Publics.* Ann Arbor: Survey Research Center, University of Michigan.

Cooper, Melinda. 2017. *Family Values: Between Neoliberalism and the New Social Conservatism.* New York: Zone Books; MIT Press.

Copelovitch, Mark S. and David A. Singer. 2020. *Banks on the Brink: Global Capital, Securities Markets, and the Political Roots of Financial Crises.* New York: Cambridge University Press.

Crouch, Colin. 2009. "Privatised Keynesianism: An Unacknowledged Policy Regime." *The British Journal of Politics & International Relations* 11(3):382–399.

Culpepper, Pepper D. 2005. "Institutional Change in Contemporary Capitalism: Coordinated Financial Systems since 1990." *World Politics* 57(2):173–199.

Culpepper, Pepper D. 2011. *Quiet Politics and Business Power: Corporate Control in Europe and Japan.* Cambridge, MA: Cambridge University Press.

Culpepper, Pepper D. and Raphael Reinke. 2014. "Structural Power and Bank Bailouts in the United Kingdom and the United States." *Politics & Society* 42(4):427–454.

Currie, Janet. 2006. The Take-up of Social Benefits. In *Public Policy and the Income Distribution,* ed. Alan J. Auerbach, David Card, and John M. Quigley. New York: Russell Sage Foundation pp. 80–148.

Cusack, Thomas R., Torben Iversen, and David Soskice. 2007. "Economic Interests and the Origins of Electoral Systems." *American Political Science Review* 101(3):373–391.

Dahl, Molly, Thomas DeLeire, and Jonathan A. Schwabish. 2011. "Estimates of Year-to-Year Volatility in Earnings and in Household Incomes from Administrative, Survey, and Matched Data." *Journal of Human Resources* 46(4):750–774.

Davidsson, Simon. 2018. "Left-Right Orientation, Homeownership and Class Position in Sweden." *Scandinavian Political Studies* 41(4):309–331.

Davis, Gerald F. 2009. *Managed by the Markets: How Finance Reshaped America.* Oxford; New York: Oxford University Press.

Davis, Gerald F. and Suntae Kim. 2015. "Financialization of the Economy." *Annual Review of Sociology* 41(1):203–221.

Dawson, Michael C. and Megan Ming Francis. 2016. "Black Politics and the Neoliberal Racial Order." *Public Culture* 28(1 (78)):23–62.

Deeg, Richard. 2009. "The Rise of Internal Capitalist Diversity? Changing Patterns of Finance and Corporate Governance in Europe." *Economy and Society* 38(4):552–579.

Deeg, Richard. 2014. "Financialization and Institutional Change in Capitalisms: A Comparison of the US and Germany." *The Journal of Comparative Economic Studies* 9:47–68.

Department of Labor. 2014. *Family and Medical Leave in 2012.* Washington, DC: Department of Labor: Office of the Assistant Secretary for Policy.

DeSante, Christopher D. 2013. "Working Twice as Hard to Get Half as Far: Race, Work Ethic, and America's Deserving Poor." *American Journal of Political Science* 57(2):342–356.

Detzer, Daniel, Nina Dodig, Trevor Evans, Eckhard Hein, Hansjörg Herr, and Franz Josef Prante. 2017. *The German Financial System and the Financial and Economic Crisis.* New York: Springer.

Deutsche Bundesbank. 2015. *Zahlungsverhalten in Deutschland 2014. Dritte Studie Über Die Verwendung von Bargeld Und Unbaren Zahlungsinstrumenten.* Frankfurt a. M.: Deutsche Bundesbank.

Dietl, Helmut Max. 1998. *Capital Markets and Corporate Governance in Japan, Germany, and the United States: Organizational Response to Market Inefficiencies.* London; New York: Routledge.

DiPrete, Thomas A. 2002. "Life Course Risks, Mobility Regimes, and Mobility Consequences: A Comparison of Sweden, Germany, and the United States." *American Journal of Sociology* 108(2):267–309.

DiPrete, Thomas A., Dominique Goux, Eric Maurin, and Amelie Quesnel-Vallee. 2006. "Work and Pay in Flexible and Regulated Labor Markets: A Generalized Perspective on Institutional Evolution and Inequality Trends in Europe and the U.S." *Research in Social Stratification and Mobility* 24(3):311–332.

DIW. 2009. "Real Wages in Germany: Numerous Years of Decline." *DIW Weekly Report* 5(28):193–202.

Dobbie, Will, Paul Goldsmith-Pinkham, Neale Mahoney, and Jae Song. 2020. "Bad Credit, No Problem? Credit and Labor Market Consequences of Bad Credit Reports." *The Journal of Finance* 75:2377–2419.

Donovan, Sarah A. 2020. Paid Family and Medical Leave in the United States. Technical Report R44835 Congressional Research Service. https://crsreports.congress.gov/product/pdf/R/R44835

Downs, Anthony. 1957. *An Economic Theory of Democracy*. New York: Harper.

Dunsky, Robert M. and James R. Follain. 2000. "Tax-Induced Portfolio Reshuffling: The Case of the Mortgage Interest Deduction." *Real Estate Economics* 28(4): 683–718.

Dustmann, Christian, Bernd Fitzenberger, Uta Schönberg, and Alexandra Spitz-Oener. 2014. "From Sick Man of Europe to Economic Superstar: Germany's Resurgent Economy." *Journal of Economic Perspectives* 28(1):167–188.

Dwyer, Peter. 2004. "Creeping Conditionality in the UK: From Welfare Rights to Conditional Entitlements?" *The Canadian Journal of Sociology / Cahiers canadiens de sociologie* 29(2):265–287.

Dwyer, Rachel E. 2018. "Credit, Debt, and Inequality." *Annual Review of Sociology* 44(1):237–261.

Dynan, Karen, Douglas Elmendorf, and Daniel Sichel. 2012. "The Evolution of Household Income Volatility." *The B.E. Journal of Economic Analysis & Policy* 12(2): 1–40.

Eaton, Charlie, Jacob Habinek, Adam Goldstein, Cyrus Dioun, Daniela García Santibáñez Godoy, and Robert Osley-Thomas. 2016. "The Financialization of Us Higher Education." *Socio-Economic Review* 14(3):507–535.

Eggleston, Jonathan S. and Mark A. Klee. 2015. Reassessing Wealth Data Quality in the Survey of Income and Program Participation. In *Proceedings of the 2015 Federal Committee on Statistical Methodology (FCSM) Research Conference*.

Eichhorst, Werner, Othon Kaufmann, and Regina Konle-Seidl. 2008. *Bringing the Jobless into Work? Experiences with Activation Schemes in Europe and the US*. Berlin; London: Springer.

Eichhorst, Werner and Paul Marx. 2016. *Non-Standard Employment in Post-Industrial Labour Markets: An Occupational Perspective*. Cheltenham: Edward Elgar Publishing.

Eichhorst, Werner and Verena Tobsch. 2015. "Not so Standard Anymore? Employment Duality in Germany." *Journal for Labour Market Research* 48(2):81–95.

Elkjær, Mads Andreas and Torben Iversen. 2020. "The Political Representation of Economic Interests: Subversion of Democracy or Middle-Class Supremacy?" *World Politics* 72(2):254–290.

Ellis, Christopher and James A Stimson. 2012. *Ideology in America*. New York: Cambridge University Press.

Elsässer, Lea, Svenja Hense, and Armin Schäfer. 2018. "Government of the People, by the Elite, for the Rich: Unequal Responsiveness in an Unlikely Case." *MPIfG Discussion Paper* 18(5).

Emmenegger, Patrick, Jon Kvist, Paul Marx, and Klaus Petersen. 2015. "Three Worlds of Welfare Capitalism: The Making of a Classic." *Journal of European Social Policy* 25(1):3–13.

Emmenegger, Patrick, Silja Häusermann, Bruno Palier, and Martin Seeleib-Kaiser. 2012. *The Age of Dualization: The Changing Face of Inequality in Deindustrializing Societies*. Oxford: Oxford University Press.

Engelen, Ewald and Martijn Konings. 2010. Financial Capitalism Resurgent: Comparative Institutionalism and the Challenges of Financialization. In *The Oxford Handbook of Comparative Institutional Analysis*, ed. Glenn Morgan, John L. Campbell, Colin Crouch, Ove Kaj Pedersen, and Richard Whitley. Oxford: Oxford University Press pp. 601–624.

Engelen, Ewald, Martijn Konings, and Rodrigo Fernandez. 2010. "Geographies of Financialization in Disarray: The Dutch Case in Comparative Perspective." *Economic Geography* 86(1):53–73.

EPI. 2020. The Cost of Childcare in the US. Report Washington, DC: Economic Policy Institute.

ESRB. 2019. *National Measures of Macroprudential Interest in the EU/EEA.* Frankfurt am Main: European System Risk Board.

Esping-Andersen, Gøsta. 1990. *The Three Worlds of Welfare Capitalism.* Princeton, NJ: Princeton University Press.

Esping-Andersen, Gøsta. 1999. *Social Foundations of Postindustrial Economies.* Oxford: Oxford University Press.

Esping-Andersen, Gøsta. 2009. *The Incomplete Revolution: Adapting to Women's New Roles.* Cambridge, UK; Malden, MA: Polity.

Esping-Andersen, Gosta, Irwin Garfinkel, Wen-Jui Han, Katherine Magnuson, Sander Wagner, and Jane Waldfogel. 2012. "Child Care and School Performance in Denmark and the United States." *Children and Youth Services Review* 34(3):576–589.

Estevez-Abe, Margarita, Torben Iversen, and David W. Soskice. 2001. Social Protection and the Formation of Skills: A Reinterpretation of the Welfare State. In *Varieties of Capitalism: The Institutional Foundations of Comparative Advantage*, ed. Peter Hall and David W. Soskice. New York: Oxford University Press pp. 145–183.

European Commission. 2002. *Proposal for a Directive of the European Parliament and of the Council on the Harmonisation of the Laws, Regulations and Administrative Provisions of the Member States Concerning Credit for Consumers (Com(2002) 443).* Brussels: European Commission.

Fagereng, Andreas, Martin Blomhoff Holm, Benjamin Moll, and Gisle Natvik. 2019. Saving Behavior Across the Wealth Distribution: The Importance of Capital Gains. Working Paper 26588 National Bureau of Economic Research. www.nber.org/papers/w26588

Fahmy, Eldin. 2018. Poverty, Social Exclusion and Civic Engagement. In *Poverty and Social Exclusion in the UK: Vol. 2*, ed. Glen Bramley and Nick Bailey. First ed. Volume 2 - The Dimensions of Disadvantage Bristol University Press pp. 179–200, Bristol: Bristol University Press.

Farrell, Diana and Fiona E. Greig. 2015. *Weathering Volatility: Big Data on the Financial Ups and Downs of U.S. Individuals.* New York: JPMorgan Chase & Co. Institute.

Farrell, Diana and Fiona E. Greig. 2016. *Paychecks, Paydays, and the Online Platform Economy: Big Data on Income Volatility.* New York: JPMorgan Chase & Co. Institute.

Federal Reserve. 2016. *Report on the Economic Well-Being of U.S. Households in 2015.* Washington, DC: Federal Reserve.

Federal Reserve Bank of New York. 2020. *Household Debt and Credit Report, Q1 2020.* New York: Federal Reserve Bank of New York.

Feenstra, Robert C. 2010. *Offshoring in the Global Economy: Microeconomic Structure and Macroeconomic Implications.* Cambridge, MA: MIT Press.

Fergus, Devin. 2018. *Land of the Fee: Hidden Costs and the Decline of the American Middle Class*. Oxford: Oxford University Press.

Fisher, Jonathan D. 2019. "Who Files for Personal Bankruptcy in the United States?" *Journal of Consumer Affairs* 53(4):2003–2026.

Fligstein, Neil and Adam Goldstein. 2015. "The Emergence of a Finance Culture in American Households, 1989–2007." *Socio-Economic Review* 13(3):575–601.

Flynn, Lindsay. 2017. "Childcare Markets and Maternal Employment: A Typology." *Journal of European Social Policy* 27(3):260–275.

Fohlin, Caroline. 2007. *Finance Capitalism and Germany's Rise to Industrial Power*. New York: Cambridge University Press.

Fong, Christina. 2001. "Social Preferences, Self-Interest, and the Demand for Redistribution." *Journal of Public Economics* 82(2):225–246.

Foster, Chase and Jeffry Frieden. 2017. "Crisis of Trust: Socio-Economic Determinants of Europeans' Confidence in Government." *European Union Politics* 18(4):511–535.

Fourcade, Marion and Kieran Healy. 2013. "Classification Situations: Life-Chances in the Neoliberal Era." *Accounting Organizations and Society* 38(8): 559–572.

Frank, Robert H. 2010. *Luxury Fever: Weighing the Cost of Excess*. Princeton, NJ: Princeton University Press.

Frank, Robert H., Adam Seth Levine, and Oege Dijk. 2014. "Expenditure Cascades." *Review of Behavioral Economics* 1(1–2):55–73.

Freund, David M. P. 2007. *Colored Property: State Policy and White Racial Politics in Suburban America*. Chicago: University of Chicago Press.

Frick, Joachim R., Markus M. Grabka, and Jan Marcus. 2010. Editing Und Multiple Imputation Der Vermögensinformation 2002 Und 2007 Im SOEP. Technical Report 51 DIW Berlin, German Institute for Economic Research.

Fuller, Gregory W. 2015. "Who's Borrowing? Credit Encouragement vs. Credit Mitigation in National Financial Systems." *Politics & Society* 43(2):241–268.

Garon, Sheldon M. 2012. *Beyond Our Means: Why America Spends While the World Saves*. Princeton, NJ: Princeton University Press.

Garrett, Geoffrey. 1998. "Global Markets and National Politics: Collision Course or Virtuous Circle?" *International Organization* 52(4):787–824.

Gathergood, John. 2012. "Self-Control, Financial Literacy and Consumer Over-Indebtedness." *Journal of Economic Psychology* 33(3):590–602.

Geiger, Felix, John Muellbauer, and Manuel Rupprecht. 2016. *The Housing Market, Household Portfolios and the German Consumer*. ECB Working Paper No. 1904 Frankfurt a. M.: European Central Bank. www.ecb.europa.eu/pub/pdf/scpwps/ecbwp1904.en.pdf?ec382c464329adb515db3fb41aa2f981

Gerber, Alan and Donald Green. 1999. "Misperceptions About Perceptual Bias." *Annual Review of Political Science* 2(1):189–210.

Gerschenkron, Alexander. 1962. *Economic Backwardness in Historical Perspective: A Book of Essays*. Cambridge, MA: Harvard University Press.

Gershman, John and Jonathan Morduch. 2015. Credit Is Not a Right. In *Microfinance, Rights, and Global Justice*, ed. Tom Sorell and Luis Cabrera. Cambridge, MA: Cambridge University Press pp. 14–26.

Gilderbloom, John I. and John P. Markham. 1995. "The Impact of Homeownership on Political Beliefs." *Social Forces* 73(4):1589–1607.

Gilens, Martin. 1999. *Why Americans Hate Welfare: Race, Media, and the Politics of Antipoverty Policy*. Chicago: University of Chicago Press.

Gilens, Martin. 2012. *Affluence and Influence: Economic Inequality and Political Power in America*. Princeton, NJ: Princeton University Press.

Gingrich, Jane and Ben Ansell. 2014. "Sorting for Schools: Housing, Education and Inequality." *Socio-Economic Review* 12(2):329–351.

Gingrich, Jane R. 2011. *Making Markets in the Welfare State: The Politics of Varying Market Reforms*. Cambridge, MA: Cambridge University Press.

Golden, Lonnie. 2015. *Irregular Work Scheduling and Its Consequences*. Briefing Paper #394 Washington, DC: Economic Policy Institute.

Golden, Lonnie. 2016. *Still Falling Short on Hours and Pay: Part-Time Work Becoming New Normal*. Washington, DC: Economic Policy Institute.

Goldin, Claudia. 2006. "The Quiet Revolution That Transformed Women's Employment, Education, and Family." *American Economic Review* 96(2):1–21.

Goldin, Claudia. 2014. "A Grand Gender Convergence: Its Last Chapter." *American Economic Review* 104(4):1091–1119.

Goldrick-Rab, Sara. 2017. *Paying the Price: College Costs, Financial Aid, and the Betrayal of the American Dream*. Chicago: University of Chicago Press.

Gorbachev, Olga. 2011. "Did Household Consumption Become More Volatile?" *American Economic Review* 101(5):2248–2270.

Gospel, Howard F. and Andrew Pendleton. 2005. *Corporate Governance and Labour Management: An International Comparison*. Oxford: Oxford University Press.

Gottschalk, Peter and Robert Moffitt. 2009. "The Rising Instability of U.S. Earnings." *Journal of Economic Perspectives* 23(4):3–24.

Gottschalk, Peter, Robert Moffitt, Lawrence F. Katz, and William T. Dickens. 1994. "The Growth of Earnings Instability in the U.S. Labor Market." *Brookings Papers on Economic Activity* 1994(2):217–272.

Gould, Elise and Jessica Schieder. 2017. *Work Sick or Lose Pay? The High Cost of Being Sick When You Don't Get Paid Sick Days*. Washington, DC: Economic Policy Institute.

Gourevitch, Peter Alexis and James Shinn. 2005. *Political Power and Corporate Control: The New Global Politics of Corporate Governance*. Princeton, NJ: Princeton University Press.

Green, Donald P, Bradley Palmquist, and Eric Schickler. 2002. *Partisan Hearts and Minds: Political Parties and the Social Identities of Voters*. New Haven: Yale University Press.

Green, Richard K. and Susan M. Wachter. 2005. "The American Mortgage in Historical and International Context." *Journal of Economic Perspectives* 19(4):93–114.

Grusky, David B., Peter A. Hall, and Hazel Rose Markus. 2019. "The Rise of Opportunity Markets: How Did It Happen & What Can We Do?" *Daedalus* 148(3):19–45.

Hacker, Jacob S. 2002. *The Divided Welfare State: The Battle Over Public and Private Social Benefits in the United States*. New York: Cambridge University Press.

Hacker, Jacob S. 2004. "Privatizing Risk without Privatizing the Welfare State: The Hidden Politics of Social Policy Retrenchment in the United States." *American Political Science Review* 98(2):243–260.

Hacker, Jacob S. 2019. *The Great Risk Shift: The New Economic Insecurity and the Decline of the American Dream*. Second ed. New York, NY: Oxford University Press.

Hacker, Jacob S., Gregory A. Huber, Austin Nichols, Philipp Rehm, Mark Schlesinger, Rob Valletta, and Stuart Craig. 2014. "The Economic Security Index: A New Measure for Research and Policy Analysis." *Review of Income and Wealth* 60: S5–S32.

Hacker, Jacob S. and Paul Pierson. 2010. *Winner-Take-All Politics: How Washington Made the Rich Richer-and Turned Its Back on the Middle Class*. New York: Simon & Schuster.

Hacker, Jacob S. and Philipp Rehm. 2021. "Reducing Risk as Well as Inequality: Assessing the Welfare State's Insurance Effects." *British Journal of Political Science* pp. 1–11 www.cambridge.org/core/journals/british-journal-of-political-science/article/reducing-risk-as-well-as-inequality-assessing-the-welfare-states-insurance-effects/18456DDC5 D08441F5891317A36D410CB

Hacker, Jacob S., Philipp Rehm, and Mark Schlesinger. 2013. "The Insecure American: Economic Experiences, Financial Worries, and Policy Attitudes." *Perspectives on Politics* 11(1):23–49.

Hackethal, Andreas. 2004. German Banks and Banking Structure. In *The German Financial System*, ed. Jan Pieter Krahnen and Reinhard H Schmidt. Oxford: Oxford University Press pp. 71–105.

Hainmueller, Jens. 2012. "Entropy Balancing for Causal Effects: A Multivariate Reweighting Method to Produce Balanced Samples in Observational Studies." *Political Analysis* 20(1):25–46.

Hall, Peter A. and David W. Soskice. 2001. *Varieties of Capitalism: The Institutional Foundations of Comparative Advantage*. Oxford: Oxford University Press.

Haney-López, Ian. 2014. *Dog Whistle Politics: How Coded Racial Appeals Have Reinvented Racism and Wrecked the Middle Class*. Oxford: Oxford University Press.

Hardie, Iain, David Howarth, Sylvia Maxfield, and Amy Verdun. 2013. "Banks and the False Dichotomy in the Comparative Political Economy of Finance." *World Politics* 65(4):691–728.

Hariri, Jacob Gerner, Amalie Sofie Jensen, and David Dreyer Lassen. 2020. "Middle Class Without a Net: Savings, Financial Fragility, and Preferences Over Social Insurance." *Comparative Political Studies* 53(6):892–922.

Hassel, Anke, Marek Naczyk, and Tobias Wiß. 2019. "The Political Economy of Pension Financialisation: Public Policy Responses to the Crisis." *Journal of European Public Policy* 26(4):483–500.

Häusermann, Silja. 2010. *The Politics of Welfare State Reform in Continental Europe: Modernization in Hard Times*. New York: Cambridge University Press.

Hay, Colin. 2009. "Good Inflation, Bad Inflation: The Housing Boom, Economic Growth and the Disaggregation of Inflationary Preferences in the UK and Ireland." *The British Journal of Politics and International Relations* 11(3):461–478.

Hay, Colin. 2013. *The Failure of Anglo-Liberal Capitalism*. London: Palgrave Macmillan.

Heckman, James J. and Stefano Mosso. 2014. "The Economics of Human Development and Social Mobility." *Annual Review of Economics* 6(1):689–733.

Heidhues, Paul and Botond Kőszegi. 2010. "Exploiting Naïvete about Self-Control in the Credit Market." *American Economic Review* 100(5):2279–2303.

Helleiner, Eric. 1995. "Explaining the Globalization of Financial Markets: Bringing States Back In." *Review of International Political Economy* 2(2):315–341.

Hemerijck, Anton. 2013. *Changing Welfare States*. Oxford: Oxford University Press.

Henning, C. Randall. 1994. *Currencies and Politics in the United States, Germany, and Japan*. Washington, DC: Institute for International Economics.

Herbst, Chris M. 2018. "The Rising Cost of Child Care in the United States: A Reassessment of the Evidence." *Economics of Education Review* 64:13–30.

Hockett, Robert C. and Saule T. Omarova. 2016. "The Finance Franchise." *Cornell Law Review* 102(5):1143–1218.

Hohnen, Pernille, Malene Gram, and Turf Böcker Jakobsen. 2020. "Debt as the New Credit or Credit as the New Debt? A Cultural Analysis of Credit Consumption Among Danish Young Adults." *Journal of Youth Studies* 23(3):356–370.

Hopkin, Jonathan and Julia Lynch. 2016. "Winner-Take-All Politics in Europe? European Inequality in Comparative Perspective." *Politics & Society* 44(3):335–343.

Höpner, Martin and Lothar Krempel. 2004. The Politics of the German Company Network. Competition & Change. 8(4):339–356.

Hout, Michael. 2012. "Social and Economic Returns to College Education in the United States." *Annual Review of Sociology* 38(1):379–400.

Howard, Christopher. 1997. *The Hidden Welfare State: Tax Expenditures and Social Policy in the United States*. Princeton, NJ: Princeton University Press.

Hsu, Joanne W., David A. Matsa, and Brian T. Melzer. 2018. "Unemployment Insurance as a Housing Market Stabilizer." *American Economic Review* 108(1):49–81.

Hudon, Marek. 2009. "Should Access to Credit Be a Right?" *Journal of Business Ethics* 84(1):17–28.

Hyman, Louis. 2011. *Debtor Nation: The History of America in Red Ink*. Princeton, NJ: Princeton University Press.

Hyman, Louis. 2012. *Borrow: The American Way of Debt: [How Personal Credit Created the American Middle Class and Almost Bankrupted the Nation]*. New York, NY: Vintage Books.

Hynes, Richard M. 2004. "Non-Procrustean Bankruptcy." *University of Illinois Law Review* 2004(2):301–362.

IMF. 2007. *Denmark: Financial Sector Assessment Program: Technical Note: The Danish Mortgage Market: A Comparative Analysis*. Country Report No. 07/123 Washington, DC: International Monetary Fund.

IMF. 2011. *Global Financial Stability Report: Durable Financial Stability: Getting There from Here*. Washington, DC: International Monetary Fund.

IMF. 2020. *Integrated Macroprudential Policy (iMaPP) Database*. Washington, D.C.: International Monetary Fund.

Immergluck, Daniel. 1999. *Two Steps Back: The Dual Mortgage Market, Predatory Lending, and the Undoing of Community Development*. Chicago, IL: Woodstock Institute.

Iversen, Torben and David Soskice. 2001. "An Asset Theory of Social Policy Preferences." *American Political Science Review* 95(4):875–893.

Iversen, Torben and David W. Soskice. 2019. *Democracy and Prosperity: Reinventing Capitalism Through a Turbulent Century*. Princeton, NJ: Princeton University Press.

Iversen, Torben and Frances McCall Rosenbluth. 2010. *Women, Work, and Politics: The Political Economy of Gender Inequality*. New Haven: Yale University Press.

Jacobi, Lena, and Jochen Kluve. 2007. "Before and After the Hartz Reforms: The Performance of Active Labour Market Policy in Germany." *Zeitschrift Für Arbeitsmarktforschung – Journal for Labour Market Research* 40(1):45–64.

Jacobs, Lawrence R. and Desmond S. King. 2016. *Fed Power: How Finance Wins.* Oxford: Oxford University Press.

Jacobs, Lawrence R. and Suzanne Mettler. 2018. "When and How New Policy Creates New Politics: Examining the Feedback Effects of the Affordable Care Act on Public Opinion." *Perspectives on Politics* 16(2):345–363.

Jappelli, Tullio and Marco Pagano. 1994. "Saving, Growth, and Liquidity Constraints." *The Quarterly Journal of Economics* 109(1):83–109.

Jensen, Nathan M. and Scott Schmith. 2005. "Market Responses to Politics The Rise of Lula and the Decline of the Brazilian Stock Market." *Comparative Political Studies* 38(10):1245–1270.

Jensen, Thais Lærkholm, Søren Leth-Petersen, and Ramana Nanda. 2014. Housing Collateral, Credit Constraints and Entrepreneurship - Evidence from a Mortgage Reform. Working Paper 20583 National Bureau of Economic Research. www.nber.org/papers/w20583

Johnson, David S., Jonathan A. Parker, and Nicholas S. Souleles. 2006. "Household Expenditure and the Income Tax Rebates of 2001." *The American Economic Review* 96(5):1589–1610.

Johnson, Simon and James Kwak. 2010. *13 Bankers: The Wall Street Takeover and the Next Financial Meltdown.* New York: Pantheon Books.

Johnston, Alison and Aidan Regan. 2016. "European Monetary Integration and the Incompatibility of National Varieties of Capitalism." *JCMS: Journal of Common Market Studies* 54(2):318–336.

Johnston, Alison, Gregory W. Fuller, and Aidan Regan. 2020. "It Takes Two to Tango: Mortgage Markets, Labor Markets and Rising Household Debt in Europe." *Review of International Political Economy* 0(0):1–31. www.tandfonline.com/doi/full/10.10 80/09692290.2020.1745868

Jordà, Òscar, Moritz Schularick, and Alan M. Taylor. 2015. "Leveraged Bubbles." *Journal of Monetary Economics* 76:S1–S20.

Jorgensen, Helene and Eileen Appelbaum. 2014. Expanding Federal Family and Medical Leave Coverage: Who Benefits from Changes in Eligibility Requirements? Technical report Center for Economic and Policy Research. https://cepr.net/documents/fmla-eligibility-2014-01.pdf

Jørgensen, Tanja. 2014. "The Way to Over-Indebtedness—Intensive Marketing, Easy Access to Loans, and Insufficient Legislation." *Juridica International* 22: 71–95.

Kaiser Family Foundation. 2020. *Employer Health Benefits 2019 Annual Survey.* San Francisco: Henry J. Kaiser Family Foundation.

Kalckreuth, Ulf Von, Tobias Schmidt, and Helmut Stix. 2014. "Using Cash to Monitor Liquidity: Implications for Payments, Currency Demand, and Withdrawal Behavior." *Journal of Money, Credit and Banking* 46(8):1753–1786.

Kalleberg, Arne L. 2009. "Precarious Work, Insecure Workers: Employment Relations in Transition." *American Sociological Review* 74(1):1–22.

Kaplan, Greg, Giovanni L. Violante, and Justin Weidner. 2014. "The Wealthy Hand-to-Mouth." *Brookings Papers on Economic Activity* 2014(1):77–138.

Katzenstein, Peter J. 1985. *Small States in World Markets: Industrial Policy in Europe.* Ithaca, NY: Cornell University Press.

Kemeny, Jim. 1981. *The Myth of Home-Ownership: Private Versus Public Choices in Housing Tenure.* Boston, MA: Routledge & K. Paul.

Kilborn, Jason J. 2009. "Twenty-Five Years of Consumer Bankruptcy in Continental Europe: Internalizing Negative Externalities and Humanizing Justice in Denmark." *International Insolvency Review* 18(3):155–185.

Kiviat, Barbara. 2019. "The Art of Deciding with Data: Evidence from How Employers Translate Credit Reports into Hiring Decisions." *Socio-Economic Review* 17(2):283–309.

Kjær, Peter and Ove K. Pedersen. 2001. Translating Liberalization: Neoliberalism in the Danish Negotiated Economy. In *The Rise of Neoliberalism and Institutional Analysis*, ed. John L. Campbell and Ove K. Pedersen. Princeton, NJ: Princeton University Press pp. 219–248.

Kluve, Jochen and Marcus Tamm. 2013. "Parental Leave Regulations, Mothers' Labor Force Attachment and Fathers' Childcare Involvement: Evidence from a Natural Experiment." *Journal of Population Economics* 26(3):983–1005.

Klyuev, Vladimir and Paul Mills. 2007. "Is Housing Wealth an 'ATM'? The Relationship Between Household Wealth, Home Equity Withdrawal, and Saving Rates." *IMF Staff Papers* 54(3):539–561.

Kohl, Sebastian. 2018. "The Political Economy of Homeownership: A Comparative Analysis of Homeownership Ideology Through Party Manifestos." *Socio-Economic Review*, https://academic.oup.co /ser/advance article/doi/10.1093/ser/m y030/5051712?login=true

Krahnen, Jan Pieter. and Reinhard H. Schmidt. 2004. *The German Financial System*. Oxford: Oxford University Press.

Krebs, Tom and Martin Scheffel. 2013. "Macroeconomic Evaluation of Labor Market Reform in Germany." *IMF Economic Review* 61(4):664–701.

Krippner, Greta R. 2011. *Capitalizing on Crisis: The Political Origins of the Rise of Finance*. Cambridge, MA: Harvard University Press.

Krippner, Greta R. 2017. "Democracy of Credit: Ownership and the Politics of Credit Access in Late Twentieth-Century America." *American Journal of Sociology* 123(1):1–47.

Kuhn, Moritz, Moritz Schularick, and Ulrike Isabel Steins. 2020. "Income and Wealth Inequality in America, 1949-2016." *Journal of Political Economy* 128(9):3469–3519.

Kumhof, Michael, Romain Rancière, and Pablo Winant. 2015. "Inequality, Leverage, and Crises." *American Economic Review* 105(3):1217–1245.

Kvist, Jon. 2015. Social Investment as Risk Management. In *The Danish Welfare State. A Sociological Investigation*, ed. Morten Frederiksen, Jørgen Elm Larsen, and Tea Torbenfeldt Bengtsson. New York: Palgrave Macmillan pp. 41–55.

La Porta, Rafael, Florencio Lopez-De-Silanes, and Andrei Shleifer. 1999. "Corporate Ownership Around the World." *The Journal of Finance* 54(2):471–517.

La Porta, Rafael, Florencio Lopez-De-Silanes, Andrei Shleifer, and Robert W. Vishny. 1997. "Legal Determinants of External Finance." *The Journal of Finance* 52(3):1131–1150.

LaLonde, Robert J. 2007. *The Case for Wage Insurance*. New York: Council on Foreign Relations Press.

Langley, Paul. 2008. *The Everyday Life of Global Finance: Saving and Borrowing in Anglo-America*. Oxford; New York: Oxford University Press.

Lasswell, Harold D. 1950. *Politics: Who Gets What, When, How*. New York: P. Smith.

Laughlin, Lynda. 2013. *Who's Minding the Kids? Child Care Arrangements: Spring 2011*. Current Population Reports: P70-135 Washington, DC: US Census Bureau.

Lax, Jeffrey R. and Justin H. Phillips. 2012. "The Democratic Deficit in the States." *American Journal of Political Science* 56(1):148–166.

Le Galès, Patrick and Paul Pierson. 2019. "'Superstar Cities' & the Generation of Durable Inequality." *Daedalus* 148(3):46–72.

Leth-Petersen, Søren. 2010. "Intertemporal Consumption and Credit Constraints: Does Total Expenditure Respond to an Exogenous Shock to Credit?" *The American Economic Review* 100(3):1080–1103.

Levine, Adam Seth. 2015. *American Insecurity: Why Our Economic Fears Lead to Political Inaction.* Princeton, NJ: Princeton University Press.

Lewis, Jane. 2001. "The Decline of the Male Breadwinner Model: Implications for Work and Care." *Social Politics: International Studies in Gender, State & Society* 8(2):152–169.

Logemann, Jan L. 2012. *The Development of Consumer Credit in Global Perspective: Business, Regulation, and Culture.* New York: Palgrave Macmillan.

Lunde, Jens. 1997. "Fifteen Years with Index-Linked Mortgages: Successes and Failures." *Netherlands Journal of Housing and the Built Environment* 12(4):401–422.

Lusardi, Annamaria. 2008. *Overcoming the Saving Slump: How to Increase the Effectiveness of Financial Education and Saving Programs.* Chicago: University of Chicago Press.

Lusardi, Annamaria, Daniel J. Schneider, and Peter Tufano. 2011. "Financially Fragile Households: Evidence and Implications." *Brookings Papers on Economic Activity* Spring:83–134.

Lusardi, Annamaria and Olivia S. Mitchell. 2007. "Baby Boomer Retirement Security: The Roles of Planning, Financial Literacy, and Housing Wealth." *Journal of Monetary Economics* 54(1):205–224.

Lütz, Susanne. 2005. "The Finance Sector in Transition: A Motor for Economic Reform?" *German Politics* 14(2):140–156.

Marcussen, Martin. 1997. The Role of "Ideas" in Dutch, Danish and Swedish Economic Policy in the 1980s and the Beginning of the 1990s. In *The Politics of Economic and Monetary Union*, ed. Petri Minkkinen and Heikki Patomäki. Boston, MA: Springer pp. 76–104.

Mares, Isabela. 2003. *The Politics of Social Risk: Business and Welfare State Development.* Cambridge, UK; New York: Cambridge University Press.

Margalit, Yotam M. 2013. "Explaining Social Policy Preferences: Evidence from the Great Recession." *The American Political Science Review* 107(1):80–103.

Margalit, Yotam and Moses Shayo. 2020. "How Markets Shape Values and Political Preferences: A Field Experiment." *American Journal of Political Science*, https://onlinelibrary.wiley.com/doi/full/10.1111/ajps.12517

Markwardt, Kristoffer, Alessandro Martinello, and László Sándor. 2014. "Does Liquidity Substitute for Unemployment Insurance? Evidence from the Introduction of Home Equity Loans in Denmark." *Working paper.* https://ideas.repec.org/p/qsh/wpaper/197781.html

Marshall, T. H. 1964. *Class, Citizenship, and Social Development.* Garden City, NY: Doubleday.

Massey, Douglas S. and Nancy A. Denton. 1993. *American Apartheid: Segregation and the Making of the Underclass.* Cambridge, MA: Harvard University Press.

Mau, Steffen and Patrick Sachweh. 2014. "The Middle-Class in the German Welfare State: Beneficial Involvement at Stake?" *Social Policy & Administration* 48(5): 537–555.

Mayer, Karl Ulrich. 2009. "New Directions in Life Course Research." *Annual Review of Sociology* 35(1):413–433.

Mazzucato, Mariana and L. Randall Wray. 2015. Financing the Capital Development of the Economy: A Keynes-Schumpeter-Minsky Synthesis. Levy Economics Institute of Bard College Working Paper No. 837 Levy Economics Institute Bard College.

McCarty, Nolan, Keith T. Poole, Thomas Romer, and Howard Rosenthal. 2010. "Political Fortunes: On Finance & Its Regulation." *Daedalus* 139(4):61–73.

McCarty, Nolan M., Keith T. Poole, and Howard Rosenthal. 2013. *Political Bubbles: Financial Crises and the Failure of American Democracy.* Princeton, NJ: Princeton University Press.

McHugh, Rick and Will Kimball. 2015. *How Low Can We Go? State Unemployment Insurance Programs Exclude Record Numbers of Jobless Workers.* Briefing Paper #392 Washington, DC: Economic Policy Institute.

McIntosh, Kriston, Emily Moss, Ryan Nunn, and Jay Shambaugh. 2020. *Examining the Black-White Wealth Gap.* Washington, DC: The Brookings Institution.

Meltzer, Allen and Scott Richard. 1981. "A Rational Theory of the Size of Government." *The Journal of Political Economy* 89(5):914–927.

Mertens, Daniel. 2015. *Erst sparen, dann kaufen? Privatverschuldung in Deutschland.* Frankfurt a. M.: Campus-Verlag.

Mettler, Suzanne. 2011. *The Submerged State. How Invisible Government Policies Undermine American Democracy.* Chicago: University Of Chicago Press.

Mettler, Suzanne. 2018. *The Government-Citizen Disconnect.* New York: Russell Sage Foundation.

Meyer, Marco. 2018. "The Right to Credit." *Journal of Political Philosophy* 26(3):304–326.

Mezza, Alvaro, Daniel Ringo, Shane Sherlund, and Kamila Sommer. 2020. "Student Loans and Homeownership." *Journal of Labor Economics* 38(1):215–260.

Mian, Atif and Amir Sufi. 2009. "The Consequences of Mortgage Credit Expansion: Evidence from the U.S. Mortgage Default Crisis." *The Quarterly Journal of Economics* 124(4):1449–1496.

Mian, Atif and Amir Sufi. 2014. *House of Debt: How They (and You) Caused the Great Recession, and How We Can Prevent It from Happening Again.* Chicago: University of Chicago Press.

Mian, Atif, Amir Sufi, and Francesco Trebbi. 2013. "The Political Economy of the Subprime Mortgage Credit Expansion." *Quarterly Journal of Political Science* 8(4):373–408.

Mian, Atif R., Ludwig Straub, and Amir Sufi. 2020. The Saving Glut of the Rich and the Rise in Household Debt. Working Paper 26941 National Bureau of Economic Research. www.nber.org/papers/w26941

Minow, Martha. 2012. Seeing, Bearing, and Sharing Risk: Social Policy Challenges for Our Time. In *Shared Responsibility, Shared Risk*, ed. Jacob S Hacker and Ann O'Leary. Oxford; New York: Oxford University Press pp. 253–259.

Minton, Sarah and Christin Durham. 2013. *Low-Income Families and the Cost of Child Care State Child Care Subsidies, Out-of-Pocket Expenses, and the Cliff Effect.* Washington, DC: Urban Institute.

Moene, Karl Ove and Michael Wallerstein. 2001. "Inequality, Social Insurance, and Redistribution." *American Political Science Review* 95(4):859–874.

Moffitt, Robert, David Ribar, and Mark Wilhelm. 1998. "The Decline of Welfare Benefits in the U.S.: The Role of Wage Inequality." *Journal of Public Economics* 68(3):421–452.

Montgomerie, Johnna. 2013. "America's Debt Safety-Net." *Public Administration* 91(4):871–888.

Morduch, Jonathan and Rachel Schneider. 2017. *The Financial Diaries: How American Families Cope in a World of Uncertainty.* Princeton, NJ: Princeton University Press.

Morel, Nathalie, Bruno Palier, and Joakim Palme. 2012. *Towards a Social Investment Welfare State? Ideas, Policies and Challenges.* Bristol: Policy Press.

Morgan, Kimberly J. and Andrea Louise Campbell. 2011. *The Delegated Welfare State: Medicare, Markets, and the Governance of Social Policy.* New York: Oxford University Press.

Mortensen, Jens Ladefoged and Leonard Seabrooke. 2008. "Housing as Social Right or Means to Wealth? The Politics of Property Booms in Australia and Denmark." *Comparative European Politics* 6(3):305–324.

Mosley, Layna. 2003. *Global Capital and National Governments.* Cambridge, MA: Cambridge University Press.

Mounk, Yascha. 2017. *The Age of Responsibility: Luck, Choice, and the Welfare State.* Cambridge, MA: Harvard University Press.

Mughan, A., C. Bean, and I. McAllister. 2003. "Economic Globalization, Job Insecurity and the Populist Reaction." *Electoral Studies* 22(4):617–633.

Naczyk, Marek and Palier, Bruno. 2014. Feed the Beast: Finance Capitalism and the Spread of Pension Privatisation in Europe. Available at SSRN: https://ssrn.com/abstract 2551521

Nichols, Austin and Philipp Rehm. 2014. "Income Risk in 30 Countries." *Review of Income and Wealth* 60:S98–S116.

OECD. 2007. *Modernising Social Policy for the New Life Course.* Paris: Organisation for Economic Co-operation and Development.

OECD. 2010. *OECD Economic Surveys: Germany 2010.* Paris: Organisation for Economic Co-operation and Development.

OECD. 2013. *OECD Science, Technology and Industry Scoreboard 2013: Innovation for Growth.* Paris: Organisation for Economic Co-operation and Development.

OECD. 2016. *Society at a Glance 2016. OECD Social Indicators.* Paris: Organisation for Economic Co-operation and Development.

OECD. 2017. *Employment and Labour Market Statistics.* Paris: Organisation for Economic Co-operation and Development.

OECD. 2018a. *Affordable Housing Database.* Paris: Organisation for Economic Co-operation and Development.

OECD. 2018b. *Pensions Statistics: Pension Funds' Assets.* Paris: Organisation for Economic Co-operation and Development.

OECD. 2019. *Under Pressure: The Squeezed Middle Class.* Paris: Organisation for Economic Co-operation and Development.

OECD. 2020a. *Family Database.* Paris: Organisation for Economic Co-operation and Development.

OECD. 2020b. *National Accounts Statistics.* Paris: Organisation for Economic Co-operation and Development.

Olivetti, Claudia and Barbara Petrongolo. 2016. "The Evolution of Gender Gaps in Industrialized Countries." *Annual Review of Economics* 8(1):405–434.

Olivetti, Claudia and Barbara Petrongolo. 2017. "The Economic Consequences of Family Policies: Lessons from a Century of Legislation in High-Income Countries." *Journal of Economic Perspectives* 31(1):205–230.

ONS. 2019. *Household Debt in Great Britain: April 2016 to March 2018*. Newport: Office of National Statistics.

Oreopoulos, Philip and Uros Petronijevic. 2013. "Making College Worth It: A Review of the Returns to Higher Education." *The Future of Children* 23(1):41–65.

Ornston, Jr, Darius. 2018. *Good Governance Gone Bad. How Nordic Adaptability Leads to Excess*. Ithaca, NY: Cornell University Press.

O'Sullivan, Mary. 2000. *Contests for Corporate Control: Corporate Governance and Economic Performance in the United States and Germany*. Oxford: Oxford University Press.

Pagano, Marco and Paolo F. Volpin. 2005. "The Political Economy of Corporate Governance." *American Economic Review* 95(4):1005–1030.

Page, Benjamin I. and Robert Y. Shapiro. 1992. *The Rational Public Fifty Years of Trends in Americans' Policy Preferences*. Chicago: University of Chicago Press.

Pager, Devah and Hana Shepherd. 2008. "The Sociology of Discrimination: Racial Discrimination in Employment, Housing, Credit, and Consumer Markets." *Annual Review of Sociology* 34(1):181–209.

Palier, Bruno. 2010. *A Long Goodbye to Bismarck? The Politics of Welfare Reforms in Continental Europe*. Amsterdam: Amsterdam University Press.

Palier, Bruno and Kathleen Thelen. 2010. "Institutionalizing Dualism: Complementarities and Change in France and Germany." *Politics & Society* 38(1):119–148.

Passari, Evgenia and Hélène Rey. 2015. "Financial Flows and the International Monetary System." *The Economic Journal* 125(584):675–698.

Peacock, Alan T. and Hans Willgerodt. 1989. *Germany's Social Market Economy: Origins and Evolution*. New York: St. Martin's Press.

Pence, Karen M. 2006. "The Role of Wealth Transformations: An Application to Estimating the Effect of Tax Incentives on Saving." *The B.E. Journal of Economic Analysis & Policy* 5(1):1–26.

Petersson, Flemming, Mikkel Baadsgaard, and Lau Caspar Thygesen. 2011. "Danish Registers on Personal Labour Market Affiliation." *Scandinavian Journal of Public Health* 39(7 Suppl):95–98.

Pierson, Paul. 2001. *The New Politics of the Welfare State*. Oxford: Oxford University Press.

Piketty, Thomas. 2014. *Capital in the Twenty-First Century*. Cambridge, MA: The Belknap Press of Harvard University Press.

Piketty, Thomas and Gabriel Zucman. 2014. "Capital Is Back: Wealth-Income Ratios in Rich Countries 1700–2010." *The Quarterly Journal of Economics* 129(3):1255–1310.

Pistor, Katharina. 2019. *The Code of Capital: How the Law Creates Wealth and Inequality*. Princeton, NJ: Princeton University Press.

Polanyi, Karl. 1944. *The Great Transformation: The Political and Economic Origins of Our Time*. Boston, MA: Beacon Press.

Poole, Keith T. 2007. "Changing Minds? Not in Congress!" *Public Choice* 131(3):435–451.

Porter, Katherine. 2012a. *Broke: How Debt Bankrupts the Middle Class*. Stanford, CA: Stanford University Press.

Porter, Katherine. 2012*b*. "The Damage of Debt." *Washington and Lee Law Review; Lexington* 69(2):979–1022.

Prasad, Monica. 2012. *The Land of Too Much: American Abundance and the Paradox of Poverty*. Cambridge, MA: Harvard University Press.

Quinn, Sarah L. 2019. *American Bonds: How Credit Markets Shaped a Nation*. Princeton Studies in American Politics. Princeton, NJ: Princeton University Press.

Rajan, Raghuram G. 2010. *Fault Lines: How Hidden Fractures Still Threaten the World Economy*. Princeton, NJ: Princeton University Press.

Rajan, Raghuram G. and Luigi Zingales. 2003. "The Great Reversals: The Politics of Financial Development in the Twentieth Century." *Journal of Financial Economics* 69(1):5–50.

Rannenberg, Ansgar. 2019. Inequality, the Risk of Secular Stagnation and the Increase in Household Debt Working Paper Research 375 National Bank of Belgium. www.nbb.be/en/articles/inequality-risk-secular-stagnation-and-increase-household-debt

Reeves, Richard V. 2017. *Dream Hoarders: How the American Upper Middle Class Is Leaving Everyone Else in the Dust, Why That Is a Problem, and What to Do About It*. Washington, DC: Brookings Institution Press.

Rehm, Philipp. 2009. "Risks and Redistribution An Individual-Level Analysis." *Comparative Political Studies* 42(7):855–881.

Rehm, Philipp. 2016. *Risk Inequality and Welfare States: Social Policy Preferences, Development, and Dynamics*. Cambridge, MA: Cambridge University Press.

Rehm, Philipp, Jacob S. Hacker, and Mark Schlesinger. 2012. "Insecure Alliances: Risk, Inequality, and Support for the Welfare State." *American Political Science Review* 106(2):386–406.

Reisenbichler, Alexander. 2020. "The Politics of Quantitative Easing and Housing Stimulus by the Federal Reserve and European Central Bank, 2008–2018." *West European Politics* 43(2): 464–84.

Reisenbichler, Alexander. 2021. Housing Finance Markets Between Social Welfare and Growth Strategies. In *Growth and Welfare Reforms in Global Capitalism: How Growth Regimes Evolve*, ed. Anke Hassel and Bruno Palier. Oxford: Oxford University Press.

Rhein, Thomas. 2010. *Comparing Employment Dynamics Internationally: Is Europe on the Way to Becoming a "High-Speed Labour Market"?* IAB-Brief Report 19/2010 Nuremberg: Institute for Employment Research.

Roe, Mark J. 2003. *Political Determinants of Corporate Governance: Political Context, Corporate Impact*. Oxford; Oxford University Press.

Romer, Thomas. 1975. "Individual Welfare, Majority Voting, and the Properties of a Linear Income Tax." *Journal of Public Economics* 4(2):163–185.

Rosas, Guillermo. 2009. Bagehot or Bailout?: Policy Responses to Banking Crises. In *Curbing Bailouts*. Bank Crises and Democratic Accountability in Comparative Perspective. Michigan: University of Michigan Press pp. 1–17.

Rose, Caspar and Carsten Mejer. 2003. "The Danish Corporate Governance System: From Stakeholder Orientation Towards Shareholder Value." *Corporate Governance: An International Review* 11(4):335–344.

Rosenbluth, Frances and Ross Schaap. 2003. "The Domestic Politics of Banking Regulation." *International Organization* 57(2):307–336.

Rosenfeld, Jake. 2014. *What Unions No Longer Do*. Cambridge, MA: Harvard University Press.

Ross, Stephen L. and John Yinger. 1999. Does Discrimination in Mortgage Lending Exist? The Boston Fed Study and Its Critics. In *Mortgage Lending Discrimination: A Review of Existing Evidence*, ed. Margery Austin Turner and Felicity Skidmore. Washington, DC: Urban Institute Press pp. 43–83.

Rossin-Slater, Maya. 2017. Maternity and Family Leave Policy. In *The Oxford Handbook of Women and the Economy*, ed. Susan Averett, Laura Argys, and Saul Hoffman. New York: Oxford University Press.

Rothstein, Richard. 2017. *The Color of Law: A Forgotten History of How Our Government Segregated America*. New York: Liveright Publishing Corporation.

Rueda, David. 2007. *Social Democracy Inside Out: Partisanship and Labor Market Policy in Industrialized Democracies*. Oxford: Oxford University Press.

Sanfey, Peter. 2013. People and Transition: Life in Transition Survey. In *Handbook of the Economics and Political Economy of Transition*, ed. Paul Hare and Gerard Turley. New York: Routledge pp. 313–320.

Schelkle, Waltraud. 2012. "A Crisis of What? Mortgage Credit Markets and the Social Policy of Promoting Homeownership in the United States and in Europe." *Politics & Society* 40(1):59–80.

Schicks, Jessica. 2014. "Over-Indebtedness in Microfinance – An Empirical Analysis of Related Factors on the Borrower Level." *World Development* 54: 301–324.

Schmid, Günther. 2002. Towards a Theory of Transitional Labour Markets. In *The Dynamics of Full Employment: Social Integration Through Transitional Labour Markets*, ed. Günther Schmid and Bernard Gazier. Cheltenham, UK: Edward Elgar pp. 151–195.

Schularick, Moritz and Alan M. Taylor. 2012. "Credit Booms Gone Bust: Monetary Policy, Leverage Cycles, and Financial Crises, 1870–2008." *American Economic Review* 102(2):1029–1061.

Schwartz, Herman. 2008. "Housing, Global Finance, and American Hegemony: Building Conservative Politics One Brick at a Time." *Comparative European Politics* 6(3):262–284.

Schwartz, Herman. 2012. "Housing, the Welfare State, and the Global Financial Crisis: What Is the Connection?" *Politics & Society* 40(1):35–58.

Schwartz, Herman and Leonard Seabrooke. 2008. "Varieties of Residential Capitalism in the International Political Economy: Old Welfare States and the New Politics of Housing." *Comparative European Politics* 6(3):237–261.

Schwartz, Herman M. and Leonard Seabrooke. 2009. *The Politics of Housing Booms and Busts*. New York: Palgrave Macmillan.

Scruggs, Lyle, Detlef Jahn, and Kati Kuitto. 2017. *Comparative Welfare Entitlements Dataset 2. Version 2017-09*. University of Connecticut and University of Greifswald.

Servon, Lisa J. 2017. *The Unbanking of America: How the New Middle Class Survives*. Boston, MA: Houghton Mifflin Harcourt.

Shaw, Greg M. and Robert Y. Shapiro. 2002. "The Polls-Trends: Poverty and Public Assistance." *Public Opinion Quarterly* 66(1):105–128.

Sherraden, Michael, ed. 2005. *Inclusion in the American Dream: Assets, Poverty, and Public Policy*. New York: Oxford University Press.

Shin, Donggyun and Gary Solon. 2011. "Trends in Men's Earnings Volatility: What Does the Panel Study of Income Dynamics Show?" *Journal of Public Economics* 95(7):973–982.

Shin, Hyun Song. 2009. "Securitisation and Financial Stability." *The Economic Journal* 119(536):309–332.

Simmons, Beth. 1999. The Internationalization of Capital. In *Continuity and Change in Contemporary Capitalism*, ed. Herbert Kitschelt. Cambridge, MA: Cambridge University Press.

Simmons, Beth A. and Zachary Elkins. 2004. "The Globalization of Liberalization: Policy Diffusion in the International Political Economy." *American Political Science Review* 98(1):171–189.

Simonsen, Marianne. 2010. "Price of High-Quality Daycare and Female Employment." *Scandinavian Journal of Economics* 112(3):570–594.

Squires, Gregory. 2003. "The New Redlining: Predatory Lending in an Age of Financial Service Modernization." *Sage Race Relations Abstracts* 28:5–18.

Statista. 2016. *Umfrage Zur Durchschnittlichen Höhe von Dispokrediten in Deutschland 2015*. Hamburg: Statista Research Department.

Stiglitz, Joseph E. 2015. "8. Inequality and Economic Growth." *The Political Quarterly* 86(S1):134–155.

Stimson, James A. 2004. *Tides of Consent: How Public Opinion Shapes American Politics*. New York: Cambridge University Press.

Stockhammer, Engelbert. 2016. "Neoliberal Growth Models, Monetary Union and the Euro Crisis. a Post-Keynesian Perspective." *New Political Economy* 21(4):365–379.

Story, Jonathan and Ingo Walter. 1997. *Political Economy of Financial Integration in Europe: The Battle of the Systems*. Cambridge, MA: MIT Press.

Streeck, Wolfgang. 2011. "The Crises of Democratic Capitalism." *New Left Review* (71):5–29.

Streeck, Wolfgang. 2014. *Buying Time: The Delayed Crisis of Democratic Capitalism*. London: Verso.

Streeck, Wolfgang and Armin Schäfer. 2013. *Politics in the Age of Austerity*. Cambridge, MA: Polity.

Streeck, Wolfgang and Kathleen Thelen, eds. 2005. *Beyond Continuity: Institutional Change in Advanced Political Economies*. New York: Oxford University Press.

Suárez, Sandra and Robin Kolodny. 2011. "Paving the Road to 'Too Big to Fail': Business Interests and the Politics of Financial Deregulation in the United States." *Politics & Society* 39(1):74–102.

Sullivan, Teresa A., Elizabeth Warren, and Jay Lawrence Westbrook. 2000. *The Fragile Middle Class: Americans in Debt*. New Haven: Yale University Press.

Sussman, Abigail B. and Rourke L. O'Brien. 2016. "Knowing When to Spend: Unintended Financial Consequences of Earmarking to Encourage Savings." *Journal of Marketing Research* 53(5):790–803.

Svallfors, Stefan. 2010. Public Attitudes. In *The Oxford Handbook of the Welfare State*, ed. Francis G. Castles, Stephan Leibfried, Jane Lewis, Herbert Obinger, and Paul Pierson. Oxford: Oxford University Press pp. 241–251.

Svallfors, Stefan. 2012. *Contested Welfare States: Welfare Attitudes in Europe and Beyond*. Stanford, CA: Stanford University Press.

Swank, Duane and Hans-Georg Betz. 2003. "Globalization, the Welfare State and Right-Wing Populism in Western Europe." *Socio-Economic Review* 1(2):215–245.

Sweet, Elizabeth, Arijit Nandi, Emma K. Adam, and Thomas W. McDade. 2013. "The High Price of Debt: Household Financial Debt and Its Impact on Mental and Physical Health." *Social Science & Medicine (1982)* 91:94–100.

Swidler, Ann. 1986. "Culture in Action: Symbols and Strategies." *American Sociological Review* 51(2):273–286.

Taylor, Keeanga-Yamahtta. 2019. *Race for Profit: How Banks and the Real Estate Industry Undermined Black Homeownership*. Chapel Hill: The University of North Carolina Press.

Taylor-Gooby, Peter. 2004. *New Risks, New Welfare: The Transformation of the European Welfare State*. New York: Oxford University Press.

Thelen, Kathleen. 2004. *How Institutions Evolve: The Political Economy of Skills in Germany, Britain, the United States, and Japan*. Cambridge, MA: Cambridge University Press.

Thelen, Kathleen. 2014. *Varieties of Liberalization and the New Politics of Social Solidarity*. Cambridge, MA: Cambridge University Press.

Thelen, Kathleen and Andreas Wiedemann. 2021. The Anxiety of Precarity: The United States in Comparative Perspective. In *Who Gets What? The New Politics of Insecurity*, ed. Frances Rosenbluth and Margaret Weir. Cambridge, MA: Cambridge University Press pp. 281–306.

Thewissen, Stefan and David Rueda. 2019. "Automation and the Welfare State: Technological Change as a Determinant of Redistribution Preferences." *Comparative Political Studies* 52(2):171–208.

Thurston, Chloe N. 2018. *At the Boundaries of Homeownership: Credit, Discrimination, and the American State*. Cambridge, MA: Cambridge University Press.

Tilly, Charles. 1998. *Durable Inequality*. Berkeley, CA: University of California Press.

Tooze, Adam. 2018. *Crashed: How a Decade of Financial Crises Changed the World*. New York: Viking.

Toporowski, Jan. 2000. *The End of Finance: The Theory of Capital Market Inflation, Financial Derivatives, and Pension Fund Capitalism*. London; Routledge.

Traub, Amy. 2013. "Credit Reports and Employment: Findings from the 2012 National Survey on Credit Card Debt of Low- and Middle-Income Households." *Suffolk University Law Review* 46(3):983.

Traub, Amy and Sean McElwee. 2016. *Bad Credit Shouldn't Block Employment: How to Make State Bans on Employment Credit Checks More Effective*. New York: Demos.

Trumbull, Gunnar. 2014. *Consumer Lending in France and America. Credit and Welfare*. Cambridge, MA: Cambridge University Press.

Turner, Adair. 2016. *Between Debt and the Devil: Money, Credit, and Fixing Global Finance*. Princeton, NJ: Princeton University Press.

Turunen, Elina and Heikki Hiilamo. 2014. "Health Effects of Indebtedness: A Systematic Review." *BMC Public Health* 14(1):489.

van der Zwan, Natascha. 2014. "Making Sense of Financialization." *Socio-Economic Review* 12(1):99–129.

Vastrup, Claus. 2009. How Did Denmark Avoid a Banking Crisis? In *The Great Financial Crisis in Finland and Sweden: The Nordic Experience of Financial Liberalization*, ed. Lars Jonung, Jaakko Kiander, and Pentti Vartia. Cheltenham, UK: Edward Elgar pp. 245–264.

Ventry, Dennis J. 2010. "The Accidental Deduction: A History and Critique of the Tax Subsidy for Mortgage Interest." *Law and Contemporary Problems* 73(1):233–284.

Verdier, Daniel. 2002. *Moving Money: Banking and Finance in the Industrialized World*. Cambridge, MA: Cambridge University Press.

Vitols, Sigurt. 2001. Varieties of Corporate Governance: Comparing Germany and the UK. In *Varieties of Capitalism: The Institutional Foundations of Comparative Advantage*, ed. Peter A. Hall and David W. Soskice. Oxford: Oxford University Press pp. 337–361.

Wagner, Gert G., Joachim R. Frick, and Jürgen Schupp. 2007. The German Socio-Economic Panel Study (SOEP): Scope, Evolution and Enhancements. Technical Report 1 DIW Berlin, The German Socio-Economic Panel (SOEP). www.diw.de/documents/dokumentenarchiv/17/60184/diw_sp0001.pdf

Warren, Elizabeth and Amelia Warren Tyagi. 2003. *The Two-Income Trap: Why Middle-Class Mothers and Fathers Are Going Broke*. New York: Basic Books.

Weil, David. 2014. *The Fissured Workplace: Why Work Became so Bad for so Many and What Can Be Done to Improve It*. Cambridge, MA: Harvard University Press.

Western, Bruce, Deirdre Bloome, Benjamin Sosnaud, and Laura Tach. 2012. "Economic Insecurity and Social Stratification." *Annual Review of Sociology* 38(1):341–359.

Wiedemann, Andreas. 2021. "How Credit Markets Substitute for Welfare States and Influence Social Policy Preferences: Evidence from US States." *British Journal of Political Science*. 1–21. https://doi.org/10.1017/S0007123420000708

Wise, Tess. 2020. Personal Bankruptcy and Race: When the Public-Private Welfare State is Predatory. Available at SSRN: https://ssrn.com/abstract=3630278

Wolff, Edward N. 2013. "The Asset Price Meltdown, Rising Leverage, and the Wealth of the Middle Class." *Journal of Economic Issues* 47(2):333–342.

Woll, Cornelia. 2014. *The Power of Inaction: Bank Bailouts in Comparison*. Ithaca, NY: Cornell University Press.

Woll, Cornelia. 2016. "Politics in the Interest of Capital: A Not-so-Organized Combat." *Politics & Society* 44(3):373–391.

Wood, James D. G. 2019. "Mortgage Credit: Denmark's Financial Capacity Building Regime." *New Political Economy* 24(6):833–850.

Woodbury, Stephen A. 2014. Unemployment Insurance. In *Oxford Handbook of U.S. Social Policy*, ed. Daniel Beránd, Kimberly J. Morgan and Christopher Howard. Oxford: Oxford University Press pp. 471–491.

World Bank. 2017. *Global Financial Development Database*. Washington, DC: World Bank.

World Bank. 2019. *Bank Regulation and Supervision Survey*. Washington, DC: World Bank.

Wren, Anne. 2013. *The Political Economy of the Service Transition*. Oxford: Oxford University Press.

Wroe, Andrew. 2016. "Economic Insecurity and Political Trust in the United States." *American Politics Research* 44(1):131–163.

Zaloom, Caitlin. 2019. *Indebted: How Families Make College Work at Any Cost*. Princeton, NJ: Princeton University Press.

Zeldes, Stephen P. 1989. "Consumption and Liquidity Constraints: An Empirical Investigation." *Journal of Political Economy* 97(2):305–346.

Zysman, John. 1983. *Governments, Markets, and Growth: Financial Systems and the Politics of Industrial Change*. Ithaca, NY: Cornell University Press.

Index

Prerna Singh, *How Solidarity Works for Welfare: Subnationalism and Social Development in India*

Theda Skocpol, *Social Revolutions in the Modern World*

Dan Slater, *Ordering Power: Contentious Politics and Authoritarian Leviathans in Southeast Asia*

Austin Smith et al, *Selected Works of Michael Wallerstein*

Regina Smyth, *Candidate Strategies and Electoral Competition in the Russian Federation: Democracy Without Foundation*

Richard Snyder, *Politics after Neoliberalism: Reregulation in Mexico*

David Stark and László Bruszt, *Postsocialist Pathways: Transforming Politics and Property in East Central Europe*

Sven Steinmo, *The Evolution of Modern States: Sweden, Japan, and the United States*

Sven Steinmo, Kathleen Thelen, and Frank Longstreth, eds., *Structuring Politics: Historical Institutionalism in Comparative Analysis*

Susan C. Stokes, *Mandates and Democracy: Neoliberalism by Surprise in Latin America*

Susan C. Stokes, ed., *Public Support for Market Reforms in New Democracies*

Susan C. Stokes, Thad Dunning, Marcelo Nazareno, and Valeria Brusco, *Brokers, Voters, and Clientelism: The Puzzle of Distributive Politics*

Milan W. Svolik, *The Politics of Authoritarian Rule*

Duane Swank, *Global Capital, Political Institutions, and Policy Change in Developed Welfare States*

David Szakonyi, *Politics for Profit: Business, Elections, and Policymaking in Russia*

Sidney Tarrow, *Power in Movement: Social Movements and Contentious Politics*

Sidney Tarrow, *Power in Movement: Social Movements and Contentious Politics, Revised and Updated Third Edition*

Tariq Thachil, *Elite Parties, Poor Voters: How Social Services Win Votes in India*

Kathleen Thelen, *How Institutions Evolve: The Political Economy of Skills in Germany, Britain, the United States, and Japan*

Kathleen Thelen, *Varieties of Liberalization and the New Politics of Social Solidarity*

Charles Tilly, *Trust and Rule*

Daniel Treisman, *The Architecture of Government: Rethinking Political Decentralization*

Guillermo Trejo, *Popular Movements in Autocracies: Religion, Repression, and Indigenous Collective Action in Mexico*

Guillermo Trejo and Sandra Ley, *Votes, Drugs, and Violence: The Political Logic of Criminal Wars in Mexico*

Rory Truex, *Making Autocracy Work: Representation and Responsiveness in Modern China*

Lily Lee Tsai, *Accountability without Democracy: How Solidary Groups Provide Public Goods in Rural China*

Joshua Tucker, *Regional Economic Voting: Russia, Poland, Hungary, Slovakia and the Czech Republic, 1990-1999*

Ashutosh Varshney, *Democracy, Development, and the Countryside*

Yuhua Wang, *Tying the Autocrat's Hand: The Rise of The Rule of Law in China*

Jeremy M. Weinstein, *Inside Rebellion: The Politics of Insurgent Violence*

CPSIA information can be obtained
at www.ICGtesting.com
Printed in the USA
LVHW092226060821
694731LV00013B/967

9 781108 971584